GW00762779

30126 01403361 4

The Essential Writings of
Netaji Subhas Chandra Bose

The Essential Writings of Netaji Subhas Chandra Bose

edited by

SISIR K. BOSE

SUGATA BOSE

Netaji Research Bureau, Calcutta

DELHI

OXFORD UNIVERSITY PRESS

CALCUTTA CHENNAI MUMBAI

1997

Oxford University Press, Walton Street, Oxford OX2 6DP
Oxford New York
Athens Auckland Bangkok Calcutta
Cape Town Chennai Dar es Salaam Delhi
Florence Hong Kong Istanbul Karachi
Kuala Lumpur Madrid Melbourne Mexico City
Mumbai Nairobi Paris Singapore
Taipei Tokyo Toronto
and associates in
Berlin Ibadan

ISBN 0 19 563982 0

Typeset by Guru Typograph Technology, New Delhi 110045
printed at Pauls Press, New Delhi 110020
and published by Manzar Khan, Oxford University Press
YMCA Library Building, Jai Singh Road, New Delhi 110001

Acknowledgements

We would like to thank Professor Krishna Bose and Professor Leonard A. Gordon for editorial advice, Mr Kartic Chakraborty for secretarial assistance, Mr Naga Sundaram for archival support and Manohar Mandal and Munshi for unstinted, practical help in running the Bureau's publication division. We wish also to record our gratitude to Oxford University Press for their speedy and efficient handling of the publication process.

We take this opportunity once again to express our deep appreciation to Netaji's wife Emilie Schenkl and their daughter Anita Pfaff for having generously assigned the copyright in Netaji's works to the Netaji Research Bureau.

SISIR K. BOSE
SUGATA BOSE

Contents

ILLUSTRATIONS

Editors' Introduction

'India,' Subhas Chandra Bose wrote to his mother in 1912, when he was only fifteen years old, 'is God's beloved land. He has been born in this great land in every age in the form of the Saviour for the enlightenment of the people, to rid this earth of sin and to establish righteousness and truth in every Indian heart. He has come into being in many countries in human form but not so many times in any other country—that is why I say, India, our motherland, is God's beloved land.'[1] Near the end of a life devoted to the service of the motherland Netaji wrote in his last message to Indians on 15 August 1945: '. . . never for a moment falter in your faith in India's destiny. There is no power on earth that can keep India enslaved. India shall be free and before long.'[2]

The popular perception of Netaji Subhas Chandra Bose is that of a warrior-hero and revolutionary leader who led a life of suffering and sacrifice, and, during the Second World War, waged a great armed struggle for the freedom of India. What is often forgotten is that the warrior paused between battles to reflect on and write about the fundamental political, economic and social issues facing India and the world during his lifetime. Despite being immersed in the tumult of the anti-colonial struggle, Subhas Chandra Bose delved back in his writings into India's long and complex history and looked forward to the socio-economic reconstruction of India once political independence was won. The ideas he put forward were not of either a wandering mystic oblivious of the earth or a doctrinaire revolutionist reared on imported copybook maxims. They were the products of a philosophical mind applied to careful analyses of specific historical situations and informed by direct and continuous revolutionary experience in different parts of the world of a kind unknown to any other leader of contemporary India. Distilled out of a twelve-volume set of his *Collected Works*, his *Essential Writings* is designed to provide a single-volume introduction to the thought of India's foremost militant nationalist.

[1] For the full text see no. 1 'Mother India' in this volume.

[2] For the full text see no. 32 'India Shall Be Free' in this volume.

Subhas's 'discovery of India', unlike Jawaharlal Nehru's, occurred very early in his life when he was barely in his teens. Born on 23 January 1897, he was deeply influenced by the cultural and intellectual milieu of Bengal at the turn of the century and grew up in harmony with the evolution of India's anti-colonial movement. In the course of his school and college career he was in turn a pure humanitarian, a *paribrajaka* and social reformer in the manner and spirit of Vivekananda, and eventually a political activist. As the letters to his mother in 1912–13 reveal, his love for the country was at this stage tinged with a religious sensibility and expressed as devotion to the Mother. Yet he was dismayed at the current state of both the country and of religion: '[n]ow, wherever religion is practised there is so much bigotry and sin.' He asked his own mother, 'Will the condition of our country continue to go from bad to worse—will not any son of Mother India in distress, in total disregard of his selfish interests, dedicate his whole life to the cause of the Mother?'[3]

By the time Subhas graduated from Calcutta University in 1919, set out to study philosophy in Cambridge, and qualify for the Indian Civil Service, he already had a formed personality and his sense of mission was not in doubt. That mission admitted of no compromise. The letters to his elder brother Sarat Chandra Bose during 1921, which he quoted extensively in his unfinished autobiography of 1937, reveal what went through his mind as he moved towards the decision to resign from the ICS. He chose to 'chuck this rotten service' and not to wear 'the emblem of servitude' as 'national and spiritual aspirations' were 'not compatible with obedience to Civil Service conditions'. He was inspired at that time by the ideal of sacrifice set by Aurobindo Ghosh. 'Only on the soil of sacrifice and suffering,' he was convinced, 'can we raise our national edifice.'[4]

Subhas's acceptance of Deshbandhu Chittaranjan Das as his political guru during the non-co-operation movement was a surrender to a man who was similarly dedicated to the cause of India's deliverance. But the aprenticeship was short as the mentor passed away before his time in 1925 and Subhas, then a prisoner in Mandalay, felt 'desolate with a sense of bereavement'. The exile in Burmese prisons from 1924 to 1927

[3] See no. 1 'Mother India' below.

[4] See no. 2 'At Cambridge' in this volume. All of the letters of 1921 to Sarat Chandra Bose have been published in full in Netaji, *Collected Works, Vol. 1: An Indian Pilgrim* (Calcutta: Netaji Research Bureau, and Delhi: Oxford University Press, centenary edition, 1997).

witnessed the transformation of a lieutenant to a leader. In his numerous prison letters to Sarat Chandra Bose, Bivabati Bose, Dilip Kumar Roy and Sarat Chandra Chattopadhyay among others, he commented on a wide range of topics—art, music, literature, nature, education, folk culture, civic affairs, criminology, spirituality and, of course, politics. He bore the rigours of prison life with a combination of stoicism and sense of humour. 'If I had not been here,' he wrote, 'I would never realize the depth of my love for golden Bengal. I sometimes feel as if Tagore expressed the emotions of a prisoner when he wrote: "Sonar Bangla, ami tomae bhalobashi!" ' Yet forced inactivity through incarceration also strengthened his belief that for most people 'action in a spirit of service' ought to be 'the main plank of their *sadhana*'. He had reverence for Sri Aurobindo who had become 'a *dhyani*', but he also warned of the dangers of the active side of a man getting atrophied through prolonged seclusion. 'For a variety of reasons,' he observed, 'our nation has been sliding pauselessly down to the zero line in the sphere of action; so what we badly need today is a double dose of the activist serum, *rajas*.'[5]

Subhas's lengthy prison essay on Deshbandhu written in February 1926 contains insights into the fundamentals of his own political beliefs. 'I do not think that among the Hindu leaders of India,' he wrote, 'Islam had a greater friend than in the Deshbandhu . . . Hinduism was extremely dear to his heart; he could even lay down his life for his religion, but at the same time he was absolutely free from dogmatism of any kind. That explains how it was possible for him to love Islam.' It was this spirit of broad-minded generosity in the matter of India's religious diversity that Subhas sought to emulate in his politics, a quality he found to be sorely lacking in most of the other nationalist leaders. 'That Swaraj in India meant primarily the uplift of the masses, and not necessarily the protection of the interest of the upper classes,' he emphasized, 'was a matter of conviction with the Deshbandhu.' This too was an ideal not shared by many of the other front-rank leaders, but to which Subhas Chandra Bose was deeply committed. To the large question whether 'culture' was one or diverse, his answer was that it was 'both one and many'. Deshbandhu, he pointed out, 'loved Bengal with all his life', but that did not make him forget about India as a whole. 'The fulfilment of the Deshbandhu's nationalism,' Subhas wrote with obvious admiration, 'was in international amity; but he did not try to develop a love of the world by

[5] See no. 3 'Prison Life in Burma' in this volume.

doing away with love for his own land. Yet his nationalism did not lead him to exclusive ego-centricity.'[6] Deshbandhu's unfulfillled dreams and hopes were in Subhas's view his 'best legacy'.[7]

In the late 1920s and early 1930s Subhas Chandra Bose emerged, along with Jawaharlal Nehru, as the leader of the left-leaning younger generation of anti-colonial nationalists. Between further spells in prison he toured the country, addressing innumerable students, youth and labour conferences. 'Democracy,' he told the Maharashtra Provincial Conference in May 1928, 'is by no means a Western institution; it is a human institution.' He also put forward a reasoned defence of nationalism against its critics. Refusing to believe that nationalism necessarily hindered the development of internationalism in the domain of culture, he espoused the variant of Indian nationalism that was not narrow, selfish or aggressive, but had instilled 'the spirit of service' and aroused 'creative faculties' in its people. He made a plea for 'a coalition between labour and nationalism', using the term labour 'in a wider sense to include the peasants as well'. India, he believed, should become 'an independent Federal Republic'. He warned Indian nationalists not to become 'a queer mixture of political democrats and social conservatives'. He declared in unequivocal terms:

> If we want to make India really great we must build up a political democracy on the pedestal of a democratic society. Privileges based on birth, caste or creed should go, and equal opportunities should be thrown open to all irrespective of caste, creed or religion. The status of women should also be raised and women should be trained to take larger and a more intelligent interest in public affairs.

While not being opposed to 'any patch-up work' needed for 'healing communal sores', he sought a 'deeper remedy' through 'cultural rapprochement'. He regretted that the different communities inhabiting India were 'too exclusive'. 'Fanaticism is the greatest thorn in the path of cultural intimacy,' he told his audience, 'and there is no better remedy for fanaticism than secular and scientific education.' This was probably the first occasion on which Bose used the term 'secular'. It should be noted that his secularism was not hostile to religiously informed cultural identities, but rather was adduced to foster 'cultural intimacy' among India's different communities. Calling for a total boycott of the Simon Commission, which was then visiting India, Bose outlined three cardinal

[6] See no. 4 'Deshbandhu Chittaranjan Das' in this volume.

[7] See no. 5 'Bengal's Spiritual Quest' in this volume.

principles for the framers of India's constitution: popular sovereignty, citizenship rights and a system of joint electorates.[8]

Bose's appearance at the Calcutta Congress in December 1928 in resplendent military uniform was not so much a spectacle as a vision of the future. His sponsoring of the amendment demanding 'complete independence' instead of 'dominion status' at that session in opposition to Mahatma Gandhi was a sign that, as always, he was a step ahead of his contemporaries. He simply did not believe there was any 'reasonable chance' of the British granting 'dominion status' within twelve months, as was demanded in the main resolution. The resolution on 'complete independence' would help gain a 'new mentality', overcoming the 'slave mentality' that was at the root of India's political degradation. While meaning no disrespect to the elders, Bose opted to give priority to 'respect for principle'.[9] His amendment was narrowly defeated.

During 1929 Subhas Chandra Bose preached the ideal of all-round freedom for the individual and the nation to enthusiastic audiences of students and youth. Speaking to the Hooghly District Students conference in July 1929, he argued that both individual and national fulfilment should be achieved through the innate diversity of human life and by striking a balance between 'the one' and 'the many'. He reminded the students that Deshbandhu had been a staunch believer in a 'federation of cultures' and 'in the realm of politics, he liked a federal state for India better than a centralized state'. He exhorted the young to call the disadvantaged and downtrodden social groups to their side:

> In our country three large communities are lying absolutely dormant; these are the women, the so-called depressed classes and the labouring masses. Let us go to them and say: 'You also are human beings and shall obtain the fullest rights of men. So arise, awake, shed your attitude of inactivity and snatch your legitimate rights.'[10]

Bose took his message of complete emancipation to students of the Punjab assembled in Lahore a couple of months before the Congress passed the landmark 'Purna Swaraj' resolution in the same city. He lauded the sacrifice of Jatin Das and the heroism of Bhagat Singh in the cause of freedom. He saw the students' movement as a school for 'the training of the future citizen' and felt that the Congress 'should depend, for its

[8] See no. 6 'Democracy in India' in this volume.

[9] See no. 7 'Complete Independence' in this volume.

[10] See no. 8 'The Individual, the Nation and the Ideal' in this volume.

strength, influence and power on such movements as the labour movement, youth movement, peasant movement, women's movement, students' movement etc.'. '[T]o be free or at least to die in the pursuit of freedom' was the motto he gave to the students.[11]

When the civil disobedience movement was launched in 1930, Subhas Chandra Bose was behind prison bars. He was elected Mayor of Calcutta while in jail. He briefly assumed this office on his release later in the year, but on 26 January 1931 he was brutally attacked by mounted police as he led an independence day procession and was thrown back into prison. There he received news of the Gandhi–Irwin truce of March 1931 with deep disappointment. The Karachi Congress of April 1931 met under the shadow of a great tragedy—the execution of Bhagat Singh and his comrades. At the same time as the Congress meeting, Bose was invited to preside over the second session in Karachi of the All India Naujawan Bharat Sabha, a militant youth organization which took inspiration from Bhagat Singh. Bose clearly felt more comfortable in such radical company than among the Congress stalwarts and enunciated his political philosophy in a forthright manner. He articulated the meanings of five principles—justice, equality, freedom, discipline and love—which ought to 'form the basis of our collective life'. Bolshevism, he felt, had 'many useful lessons for humanity' but he did 'not believe that abstract principles can be applied in the same manner, form or degree to different nations and countries'. He wanted the Indian variant to be 'a new form or type of socialism'. 'While seeking light and inspiration from abroad,' he told the radical youth, 'we cannot afford to forget that we should not blindly imitate any other people and that we should assimilate what we learn elsewhere with a view to finding out what will suit our national requirements as well as our national genius.'[12] In his presidential address to the All India Trade Union Congress in July 1931 he addressed the specific problems of unemployment, retrenchment and wages in the context of the Depression. He also tried to carve out a middle ground between 'a reformist programme' of the 'Right Wing' of the the Congress and 'Communist friends' who were 'adherents and followers of Moscow'. He reiterated his belief in 'full-blooded socialism' but wanted India to 'evolve her own form of socialism as well as her own methods'.[13]

Bose spent the entire year 1932 in various jails in Seoni, Jubbulpore, Madras, Bhowali and Lucknow. His health deteriorated rapidly during

[11] See no. 9 'Punjab and Bengal, Students and Politics' in this volume.

[12] See no. 10 'Socialism in India' in this volume.

[13] See no. 11 'Trade Union and the Problems of Unemploynent' in this volume.

detention. Eventually in February 1933 he was released after being put on a ship setting sail from Bombay for Europe, where he sought medical treatment. A greater part of his years of enforced exile in Europe from March 1933 to March 1936 were spent as an unofficial ambassador of India's freedom. This was the period which saw the transformation of a leader into a statesman. Despite being in poor health, Bose travelled tirelessly across the continent. He met European political and intellectual leaders and organized and addressed bilateral friendship associations in various countries as well as Indian student organizations in different cities. He visited Austria, Bulgaria, Czechoslovakia, Egypt, France, Germany, Hungary, Ireland, Italy, Poland, Rumania, Switzerland, Turkey and Yugoslavia. The British authorities led him to believe that he was barred from visiting Britain. So his presidential address at the Third Indian Political Conference in London in June 1933 had to be read out in absentia. The speech—often referred to as 'the London thesis'—provided the most detailed exposition of his political philosophy prior to his address as Congress President in 1938. It contained an appreciation and critique of Gandhian satyagraha and an enunciation of the ideal of *samyavada.* Attracted by European political experiments in socialism, Bose nevertheless preferred to use the old, Buddhist, Indian term to articulate his ideology of a socialism, one that invoked equality in an atmosphere of balance and harmony. He expressed a messianic faith in the mission that India would fulfil in world history:

We all know that in the seventeenth century England made a remarkable contribution to world-civilisation through her ideas of constitutional and democratic government. Similarly, in the eighteenth century, France made the most wonderful contribution to the culture of the world through her ideas of 'liberty, equality and fraternity.' During the nineteenth century Germany made the most remarkable gift through her Marxian Philosophy. During the twentieth century Russia has enriched the culture and civilisation of the world through her achievement in proletarian revolution, proletarian government and proletarian culture. The next remarkable contribution to the culture and civilisation of the world India will be called upon to make.[14]

Bose's major study of the Indian independence movement—*The Indian Struggle, 1920–34*[15]—was published in early 1935. Towards the

[14] See no. 12 'The Anti-Imperialist Struggle and *Samyavada*' in this volume.

[15] This book was originally published by Lawrence and Wishart in London on 17 January 1935. It was particularly well-reviewed by the British press and warmly welcomed in European political and literary circles but banned in India. Bose extended

end of his political narrative Bose added a chapter in which he tried to assess the phenomenon in Indian politics called Mahatma Gandhi. Bose had fulsome praise for the Mahatma's 'single-hearted devotion, his relentless will and his indefatigable labour'. But he was critical of Gandhi's inability to comprehend the character of his opponents or to make use of international diplomacy in his efforts to win Swaraj. In the ultimate analysis Mahatma Gandhi had failed, in his view, because 'the false unity of interests that are inherently opposed is not a source of strength but a source of weakness in political warfare'.[16]

Throughout his European sojourn Bose was a keen student of international politics. While he was somewhat impressed by the organizational prowess of fascist (and communist) parties, he developed what Kitty Kurti has described as 'deep contempt' for the Nazis in Germany. He made repeated public protests against racism in Germany, especially anti-Indian racism, and supported a call for a boycott of trade with Germany after an especially provocative speech by Hitler. 'Against Germany,' he wrote to Amiya Chakravarti, 'we [Indians] have many complaints . . . Against Italy there are complaints from other standpoints—not from the standpoint of India's interest or prestige. But against Germany, we have many accusations from India's standpoint.' On the eve of his departure from Europe in March 1936 he denounced the 'new nationalism' in Germany in a letter to Dr Thierfelder as not only 'narrow and selfish, but arrogant'. But he pointed out to Amiya Chakravarti there was 'no early possibility of the fall of Hitler's Govt.'. 'If war breaks out some day and the war weakens Germany,' he wrote, 'then such a fall is possible, otherwise not.'[17]

A high point of Bose's years of European exile was his visit to Ireland in February 1936 during which he held three meetings with Eamonn De Valera. He found all the Irish parties to be 'equally sympathetic towards India and her desire for freedom'. He had always been a close student of Irish anti-colonialism and regretted that more Indians who spent years in England did not take the trouble to go over to England's oldest colony.

---

the narrative to 1942 while he was in Europe again during the Second World War. Netaji Research Bureau issued a combined edition for the first time in 1964. For the latest edition, see Sisir K. Bose and Sugata Bose (eds.), *Netaji Collected Works, Vol. 2: The Indian Struggle, 1920–42* (Calcutta: Netaji Research Bureau, and Delhi: Oxford University Press, centenary edition, 1997).

[16] See no. 13 'The Role of Mahatma Gandhi in Indian History' in this volume.

[17] See no. 14 'India and Germany' in this volume.

'Ireland,' he recorded in his impressions, 'is quite a different world from England.'[18]

The most difficult part of ending the days of European exile for Subhas Chandra Bose was not the prospect of imprisonment in India but the pain of separation from the woman he loved. He had met Emilie Schenkl, an Austrian woman, for the first time in June 1934 and had developed a close relationship with her during the next two years. As he prepared to go home, he wrote her a letter which is the most frank confession of his feelings. 'Even the iceberg sometimes melts,' he began, 'and so it is with me now.' He had 'already sold' himself to his 'first love'—his country—to whom he had to return. As usual it was an adventure into the unknown:

I do not know what the future has in store for me. May be, I shall spend my life in prison, may be, I shall be shot or hanged. But whatever happens, I shall think of you and convey my gratitude to you in silence for your love for me. May be I shall never see you again—may be I shall not be able to write to you again when I am back—but believe me, you will always live in my heart, in my thoughts and in my dreams. If fate should thus separate us in this life—I shall long for you in my next life.

He had 'never thought before that a woman's love could ensnare [him]'. And he mused:

Is this love of any earthly use? We who belong to two different lands—have we anything in common? My country, my people, my traditions, my habits and customs, my climate—in fact everything is so different from yours . . . For the moment, I have forgotten all these differences that separate our countries. I have loved the woman in you—the soul in you.[19]

[18] See no. 15 'Impressions of Ireland' in this volume.

[19] See no. 16 'Love' in this volume. One hundred and sixty-two letters written by Subhas Chandra Bose to Emilie Schenkl between 1934 and 1942 along with eighteen of Emilie Schenkl's letters that have survived have been published in Sisir K. Bose and Sugata Bose (eds.), *Netaji Collected Works: Vol. 7: Letters to Emilie Schenkl* (Calcutta: Netaji Research Bureau, and Delhi: Oxford University Press, 1994). The letter appearing in this volume, however, is previously unpublished. It was made available to us (along with two more letters) on 24 June 1994 after we had celebrated the 60th anniversary of their first meeting at a family gathering in Augsburg. 'This is a love letter,' Emilie said as she handed over the letter to Krishna Bose. Although the letter itself is undated, the envelope in which it came bears the postmark 5 March 1936. On 4 March Subhas had written, 'Today or tomorrow I shall write another letter to you. Please call for it. It is beautiful here and quiet. Plenty of snow. How are you?' (*Netaji Collected Works, Vol. 7,*

On his arrival in Bombay on 8 April 1936 Bose was immediately arrested and sent to prison. He spent a year in detention and was permitted to return to active political life only after the provincial elections of April 1937 under the 1935 Government of India Act, of which he was a strong critic. He continued to take great interest in international affairs during 1937. In particular, he wrote two very substantial essays on developments in Europe and East Asia. His 'Europe: Today and Tomorrow' was an incisive, realist analysis of the shifting configuration of power in that continent. 'If war comes,' he wrote with great prescience in August 1937, 'it will come as a result of a German challenge to the status quo in Central and Eastern Europe. But will it come? The answer rests primarily with Britain. Germany will not repeat the errors of 1914 and will not go into a war, if she knows that Britain will be against her. She might be trapped into it as she was in 1914, thinking that Britain would keep out of it.' His final comment on the enigma of the 'Russian Colossus' also had an uncanny quality about it: 'It baffled Napoleon—the conqueror of Europe. Will it baffle Hitler?'[20]

The substance of Bose's analysis of power relations in East Asia written in September 1937 was equally dispassionate, but towards the end of the essay he did not hesitate to declare his sympathy for China in the face of Japanese aggression. He concluded by drawing certain ethical implications for the future direction of Indian nationalism:

> Let us learn the lessons of this Far Eastern Conflict. Standing at the threshold of a new era, let India resolve to aspire after national self-fulfillment in every direction—but not at the expense of other nations and not through the bloody path of self-aggrandizement and imperialism.[21]

Mahatma Gandhi's choice of Subhas Chandra Bose as Congress President became known at the time of the meeting of the All India Congress Committee in Calcutta in October 1937. The following month on his own volition and with Gandhi's blessings he left on a trip to Europe. He spent nearly a month and a half from 22 November 1937 to 7 January 1938 at his favourite Austrian resort, Badgastain, where Emilie Schenkl joined him. There in the course of ten days in December 1937

---

p. 28) That letter written from Badgastein to Vienna is the one being published here. Subhas had added at the bottom 'Please destroy after perusal'. We are glad that Emilie did not. Emilie joined Subhas at Kurhaus Hochland in Badgastein for a week between 17 and 26 March 1936. On 26 March Subhas commenced his journey back to India.

[20] See no. 17 'Europe—Today and Tomorrow' in this volume.

[21] See no. 18 'Japan's Role in the Far East' in this volume.

he wrote ten chapters of his autobiography.[22] Bose had intended to write three chapters on his fundamental beliefs: 'My Faith—Philosophical', 'My Faith—Political' and 'My Faith—Economic'. Of these he was able to complete only the first which formed the final chapter of his unfinished autobiography. 'Reality,' he concluded, '. . . is Spirit, the essence of which is Love, gradually unfolding itself in an eternal play of conflicting forces and their solutions.'[23]

'My personal view today,' Subhas Chandra Bose said in an interview to Rajani Palme Dutt in London in January 1938, 'is that the Indian National Congress should be organized on the broadest anti-imperialist front, and should have the two-fold objective of winning political freedom and the establishment of a socialist regime.'[24] After holding talks with De Valera and British political leaders he arrived back in India on 23 January 1938, his 41st birthday, and during his tenure as Congress President worked towards the two-fold objective he had set himself.

Written in a day at his Calcutta home on the eve of his departure for Haripura, his presidential address provided an incisive analysis of the strengths and weaknesses of the worldwide structure of British imperialism and an egalitarian vision of the socio-economic reconstruction of free India. It was marked by a remarkable lack of rancour towards the colonial masters whom he challenged to transform the empire into 'a federation of free nations'. Once India had 'real self-determination', he saw no reason why there should not be 'the most cordial relations with the British people'.[25]

While sounding a note of warning against accepting colonial constitutional devices designed to divide and deflect the anti-colonial movement, Bose could see that 'the policy of divide and rule' was 'by no means an unmixed blessing for the ruling power'. Bose saw the 'principle of partition' ingrained in the 'juxtaposition of autocratic princes and democratically elected representatives of British India', and called for uncompromising opposition to the federal part of the Government of India Act of 1935. If that scheme got rejected, he feared that the British

[22] See Sisir K. Bose and Sugata Bose (eds.), *Netaji Collected Works, Vol. 1: An Indian Pilgrim* (Calcutta: Netaji Research Bureau, and Delhi: Oxford University Press, centenary edition, 1997). Subhas secretly married Emilie that month.

[23] See no. 19 'My Faith—Philosophical' in this volume.

[24] Sisir K. Bose and Sugata Bose (eds.), *Netaji Collected Works, Vol. 9: Congress President, January 1938–May 1939* (Calcutta: Netaji Research Bureau, and Delhi: Oxford University Press, 1995), p. 3.

[25] See no. 20 'The Haripura Address' in this volume.

would 'seek some other constitutional device for partitioning India and thereby neutralising the transference of power to the Indian people'. But equally Bose could see Britain getting 'caught in the meshes of her own political dualism' resulting from divisive policies, whether in India, Palestine, Egypt, Iraq or Ireland. He, therefore, resolved to urgently address the minorities question in India, advocating a policy of 'live and let live in matters religious and an understanding in matters economic and political'. He did not, interestingly enough, use the term 'secularism' in his broad-minded approach to the problem of religious difference. He also wanted justice done to the so-called 'depressed classes'. While promoting 'cultural autonomy for the different linguistic areas', Bose urged the acceptance of Hindustani (a mixture of Hindi and Urdu) in the Roman script as lingua franca. The objective of unifying India through 'a strong central government' would have to be balanced by the imperative 'to put all the minority communities as well as the provinces at their ease, by allowing them a large measure of autonomy in cultural as well as governmental affairs'.[26] This vision was a stretch removed from the insistence on a monolithic nationalism by some of the other leaders of the Congress including Nehru and Patel who in their own ways increasingly displayed scant respect for cultural difference.

Convinced of the need to be prepared for independence, Bose also outlined his 'long-period programme for a Free India'. In order to eradicate poverty, he felt the free Indian state would have 'to adopt a comprehensive scheme for gradually socialising our entire agricultural and industrial system in the spheres of both production and appropriation'. Bose believed in 1938 that the Congress party could not be asked to wither away but, on the contrary, had a key role to play in the work of national reconstruction after independence. The 'existence of multiple parties and the democratic basis of the Congress Party,' he trusted, would 'prevent the future Indian state becoming a totalitarian one'. Inner-party democracy would also 'ensure that leaders are not thrust upon the people from above, but elected from below'.[27] Subsequent developments were soon to show that Bose's views regarding the Congress party's commitment to internal democracy were overly optimistic. His opinions in favour of the Congress's granting collective affiliation to peasants' and workers' organizations, and being poised to take advantage of the international situation, were not shared by several of his colleagues within the Congress.

[26] Ibid.
[27] Ibid.

During 1938 Subhas Chandra Bose sought to act on most of the items on his Haripura agenda. Perhaps his most important step was to announce the formation of the National Planning Committee in October 1938. Among the leading persons who responded with enthusiasm to the idea of rational and scientific planning for India was Rabindranath Tagore, who, unlike Gandhi, was much more intellectually open to the positive achievements of modern science and technology. Tagore could only see two 'modernists' among India's nationalist leadership—Jawaharlal Nehru and Subhas Chandra Bose—and since the former had been made Chairman of the Planning Committee he wanted the latter to have a second term as Congress President. On the eve of his re-election in January 1939 the poet welcomed Subhas to his abode of peace—Santiniketan. In reply to Rabindranath's address, Subhas Chandra said:

> Those of us who spend most of our time in the political life of the country feel very deeply about the poverty of the inner life. We want the inspiration of the treasure that enriches the mind without which no man or nation can rise to great heights. Because we know if we can get a taste of that inspiration and truth our *Sadhana* for the fulfilment and success of our working life and outer life can be achieved. We seek that inspiration from you.[28]

On 29 January 1939 Subhas Chandra Bose defeated Mahatma Gandhi's nominee Pattabhi Sitaramayya to be re-elected Congress President. In recent months his rift with the Gandhian right-wing of the Congress had grown wider over the issues of his uncompromising attitude to the Federal Scheme, planning for socialism and insistence on inner-party democracy. Gandhi now decided to adopt the tactic of non-cooperation against the democratically elected Congress President. The Congress crisis deepened as Bose fell seriously ill in mid-February and all the members of the Congress Working Committee excepting Jawaharlal Nehru and Sarat Chandra Bose resigned on 22 February 1939. At the Tripuri session of the Congress in early March 1939 Bose was too ill to deliver his own presidential address, and it was read by his elder brother Sarat. In an uncharacteristically short speech Bose called upon the Congress to submit its national demand in the form of an ultimatum to the British government and to resort to mass civil disobedience if no satisfactory reply was received. He wanted the Congress to guide the popular movements in the princely states 'on a comprehensive and systematic basis' instead of doing work in the area of 'a piecemeal nature'. He was unequivocal on the need for close co-operation with 'all anti-imperialist

[28] See no. 21 'Sadhana' in this volume.

organizations in the country particularly the Kisan movement and the Trade Union movement'.[29]

At the Tripuri Congress the right-wing was able to pass a resolution stating that the Congress executive should be formed 'in accordance with the wishes of Gandhiji' and command his 'implicit confidence'. Since Gandhi remained obdurate and refused to suggest names for the Working Committee, Subhas Chandra Bose resigned as Congress President on 29 April 1939. Throughout the crisis Nehru had sought to play a mediating role, keeping at least a slight distance from the joint actions of the Working Committee led by Vallabhbhai Patel. Bose, however, felt completely betrayed by Nehru's latest attempt at 'riding two horses'. He had regarded Nehru as his 'elder brother' who had abetted his political opponents in their 'vendetta'. 'The unity that we strive for or maintain,' he wrote to Nehru, 'must be the unity of action and not the unity of inaction'.[30]

By the time the next Congress session met in March of the following year at Ramgarh, Bose was holding his own, parallel Anti-Compromise Conference close to the site of the official meeting. 'The age of Imperialism,' he declared, 'is drawing to a close and the era of freedom. democracy and Socialism looms ahead of us. India, therefore, stands at one of the crossroads of history.' He launched a scathing attack on the vacillating nature of the existing leadership at that fateful moment. He issued a call for a political consolidation of all genuine Leftists. 'In the present phase of our movement,' he explained, 'Leftists will be all those who will wage an uncompromising fight with Imperialism . . . In the next phase of our movement, Leftism will be synonymous with socialism . . .'[31]

On 2 July 1940 Subhas Chandra Bose was arrested for the eleventh time for leading the movement for the removal of the Holwell Monument in Calcutta. In November he decided to go on a hunger strike in an attempt to force the government to release him. The letter he wrote to the Governor of Bengal on 26 November 1940 before commencing his fast is one of the most stirring documents of sacrificial patriotism. '. . . [N]obody can lose,' he wrote, 'through suffering and sacrifice. If he does lose anything of the earth earthy, he will gain much more in return by becoming the heir to a life immortal.'[32]

The government released Bose on 5 December, having decided to

[29] See no. 22 'The Tripuri Address' in this volume.

[30] See no. 23 'Riding Two Horses' in this volume.

[31] See no. 24 'The Ramgarh Address' in this volume.

[32] See no. 25 'My Political Testament' in this volume.

play 'a cat and mouse policy' of rearresting him as soon as he recovered his health. His home in Elgin Road was put under round-the-clock surveillance. On the night of 16–17 January 1941 Subhas Chandra Bose made a carefully planned escape. He was driven by his nephew Sisir to Gomoh in Bihar from where he took the train to Delhi and on to Peshawar. In the Frontier Province he was received by Mian Akbar Shah who made the arrangements for Bose to cross into Afghanistan. During the agonizing month and a half he spent in Kabul in February and March 1941, he wrote another lengthy political tract which is often referred to as his 'Kabul thesis'. In it he reiterated the two criteria for 'genuine Leftism' in Indian politics—uncompromising anti-imperialism in the current phase and socialist reconstruction in the next. Having abandoned his fledgling pressure group within the Congress—the Forward Bloc—in the pursuit of the larger armed struggle, he could merely hope that '[h]istory will separate the chaff from the grain—the pseudo-Leftists from the genuine Leftists'.[33] This hand-written thesis was delivered by his frontier guide Bhagat Ram Talwar to Sarat Chandra Bose in Calcutta in late March 1941.

Bose went to Europe in 1941 primarily in order to gain access to Indian soldiers in the British Indian Army who were prisoners-of-war in the hands of Germany and Italy. He had long believed that the subversion of the loyalty of Indian soldiers to the Raj had to be a crucial part of the anti-imperialist movement. His own allegiance was to India and India alone and, as he emphasized in his broadcasts, his socio-economic views remained exactly the same as the ones he had articulated at home. With the help of Indian exiles, including students, he set up a Free India Centre, and from among Indian soldiers he raised an Indian Legion. He continued to write political essays and memoranda, some of which were published in his journal *Azad Hind*. He thought in 1942 that it would be 'wrong to dogmatize from now about the form of the future Indian state'. He did say, however, that to begin with there will be 'a strong Central Government' and 'a well-organized, disciplined all-India party'. The state would 'guarantee complete religious and cultural freedom for individuals and groups'. 'When the new regime is stabilised and the state-machinery begins to function smoothly,' he wrote, 'power will be decentralized and the provincial governments will be given more responsibility'.[34]

Netaji had initially planned an armed thrust from the traditional

[33] See no. 26 'Forward Bloc—Its Justification' in this volume.

[34] See no. 27 'Free India and Her Problems' in this volume.

north-westerly direction into India in support of India's unarmed freedom-fighters at home. Germany's invasion of the Soviet Union in June 1941 upset all his calculations. The invasion, he told the German Government in categorical terms, would win them no friends in India. Eventually on 8 February 1943 he was able to leave Europe and after a 90-day submarine journey arrived in South East Asia. The presence of nearly two million Indian civilians in the region gave his movement in Asia a much larger social base of support. On 5 July 1943 Netaji announced in Singapore that India's Army of Liberation—the Azad Hind Fauj—had come into being. In the months that followed he electrified massive audiences of civilians and soldiers with his speeches in Hindustani and elicited an overwhelmingly positive response to his call for 'total mobilization'. On 21 October 1943 he proclaimed the Provisional Government of Free India which gave Indians a taste of independent statehood. He wrote the proclamation himself the night before the ceremony drawing on Indian history and elements of the Irish and American declarations of independence. 'Having goaded Indians to desperation by its hypocrisy,' he wrote, 'and having driven them to starvation and death by plunder and loot, British rule in India has forfeited the goodwill of the Indian people altogether and is now living a precarious existence. It needs but a flame to destroy the last vestige of that unhappy rule. To light that flame is the task of India's Army of Liberation.'. In the final paragraph came the exhortation to the Indian people:

> In the name of God, in the name of bygone generations who have welded the Indian people into one nation, and in the name of the dead heroes who have bequeathed to us a tradition of heroism and self-sacrifice—we call upon the Indian people to rally round our banner and strike for India's freedom.[35]

With 'Chalo Delhi' on their lips the Azad Hind Fauj crossed the Indo-Burma frontier on 18 March 1944 and carried the armed struggle on to Indian soil. The most detailed justification of his course of action during the Second World War II was given by Netaji in his radio address to the Mahatma on 6 July 1944. Since Gandhi's decision to launch the Quit India movement, the two leaders had drawn closer in their aims and ideology. Netaji sought 'the blessings and good wishes' of the 'Father of Our Nation' for the 'holy war' that was then raging in north-eastern India.[36]

Netaji found one last occasion to give his views on the fundamental

[35] See no. 28 'Azad Hind' in this volume.

[36] See no. 29 'Father of Our Nation' in this volume.

problems of India when he was invited to address the students at Tokyo University in November 1944. He argued in what is called his 'Tokyo thesis' that the creative faculty of its people and their determination to resist imperialist domination gave ample proof of India's vitality as a nation. The speech had some glaringly weak points, especially in its discussion of caste in India. But Netaji was able to delineate with clarity for a foreign audience what he thought would be the three most urgent tasks facing free India—national defence, eradication of poverty and provision of education for all.[37]

Netaji was to be denied the opportunity to implement his ideas on national reconstruction, which he had developed since the 1920s, in free India. In his Azad Hind movement he was able to demonstrate by example how to achieve Hindu-Muslim unity and amity and also give women their rightful role in public affairs, ideals he had been committed to all his life. But the promised march of his Fauj to Delhi was halted at Imphal. In the spring of 1945 Netaji made a historic retreat with the men and women of his army from Burma to Thailand and on to Malaya. 'The roads to Delhi are many,' he wrote in a Special Order of the Day on 15 August 1945, 'and Delhi still remains our goal.'[38] He assured Indians in East Asia in his last message on the same day: 'Posterity will bless your name, and will talk with pride about your offerings at the altar of India's Freedom and about your positive achievement as well.'[39]

At the end of the war in 1945, the independence movement in Delhi was at a low ebb. At that crucial moment Netaji's soldiers descended upon the Red Fort of Delhi as a God-send. The trial of some of their leading officers reached the saga of the INA and its Netaji to every Indian home. '[T]he whole country has been roused,' Gandhi observed, 'and even the regular forces have been stirred into a new political consciousness and have begun to think in terms of independence.' Netaji had succeeded in his strategy to knock out the keystone of British imperialist domination over its Asian colonies by supplanting the loyalty of the Indian soldiers to their enslavers with a new loyalty to their country's freedom. But his supreme self-sacrifice at the climactic moment of the war of independence also meant that his ideas found no place in the fashioning of post-colonial India.

On the fiftieth anniversary of the achievement of India's independence, the country is gripped by an acute sense of uncertainty and

[37] See no. 30 'The Fundamental Problems of India' in this volume.

[38] See no. 31 'The Roads to Delhi are Many' in this volume.

[39] See no. 32 'India Shall Be Free' in this volume.

anomie in national affairs. India seems once again to be at one of the crossroads of history. At this critical juncture it may be worth taking a leaf out of Netaji's book of life and recall his unshakeable faith in India's destiny. A rare personality in contemporary history, he was at once deeply involved in the spiritual heritage of India and actively concerned with the most modern scientific advances anywhere in the world. His nationalism emphasized its emancipatory and creative aspects under colonial conditions and rejected its narrow, aggressive and potentially imperialistic dimensions. By contrast with Gandhi's nihilism and atomism, he put forth his own conceptions of the free Indian state. He occasionally spoke of the need for a strong centre in the immediate aftermath of independence to be able to carry out radical social and economic reforms. His socialism was, however, not of the dogmatic kind but one that was suited to Indian needs and aspirations. His discussion of powers at the centre was almost always balanced by a call for substantial autonomy for both religious communities and regionally based linguistic groups in cultural and governmental spheres. Netaji's approach to the intertwined challenges to the construction of an all-India nationalism presented by affiliations of religious community and linguistic region was significantly different from and substantially more generous than that of most others among the Congress leadership, especially Patel and Nehru. In other words, he did not wish away or seek to suppress the fact of cultural difference but rather gave it due respect in his efforts to build unity. He was acutely aware from very early in his political life of the imperative to redress the subalternity that operated along lines of class, caste and, most importantly, gender. He believed in India's historic obligation to evolve a new social order based on careful study and synthesis of revolutionary experiments across the world. The *samyavada* Netaji was searching for meant for him a new alternative. 'India freed,' he was fond of saying, 'means humanity saved.' As a political leader, he fought for India's all-round liberation. As a thinker, he sought a new ethical conception in human affairs. Prepared in 1996 on the occasion of Netaji's birth centenary, this book of his essential writings is offered to a new generation of Indians who may wish through his vision to rediscover India.

1
Mother India[1]

Cuttack, Saturday

Revered mother,

Today is the final day of the Puja; so you must now be in our country home—engrossed in the worship of the Goddess.

I expect the Puja this year will be performed with great pomp and ceremony. But, mother, is there any need of pomp and ceremony? It is enough if we invoke the One we seek to attain with all our heart and in all sincerity; what more is needed? When devotion and love take the place of sandal wood and flowers, our worship becomes the most sublime thing in the world. Pomp and devotion are incompatible. This year I have a pang in my heart. It is a great sorrow—not an ordinary one. This year I have been denied the fulfilment that comes through the *Darshan* of the Goddess *Durga,* the Queen of the three realms, our Saviour from all misfortune and Protector from all evil, the Mother of the Universe—attired in elaborate and magnificent robes and revealed in all Her resplendent glory with myriad lights shining around her; this time I have missed the happiness that comes from listening to the melodious chanting of the sacred hymns by our revered priest to the sound of the conch-shell and the gong; the satisfaction of sensing the sacred aroma of flowers, sandalwood and incense and of sharing with others the holy food offered to the Goddess; on this occasion I have been deprived of the privilege of being blessed by the priest with the holy flowers and, above all, of the mental peace that comes from contact with the holy water of the *Puja*; I missed everything; all my five senses remain unsatisfied. If I could perceive the omnipresent and universal image of the Goddess, I would not be so mortified and I would not hanker after the wooden image; but how many are so blessed and fortunate as to have this perception! So, I remain unconsoled.

I shall be pining away at this place on the immersion day but at heart

[1] Excerpts of letters to his mother, 1912–13.

I shall be with you all. There will be no happiness for me on such a sacred day. There is no help for it now—tomorrow evening we shall send you our *pronams* from here.

. . . India is God's beloved land. He has been born in this great land in every age in the form of the Saviour for the enlightenment of the people, to rid this earth of sin and to establish righteousness and truth in every Indian heart. He has come into being in many countries in human form but not so many times in any other country—that is why I say, India, our motherland, is God's beloved land. Look, Mother, in India, you may have anything you want—the hottest Summer, the severest Winter, the heaviest rains and again, the most heart-warming Autumn and Spring— everything you want. In the Deccan, I see the *Godavari*; with her pure and sacred waters reaching up to its banks, wending its way eternally to sea, a holy river indeed! To see her or think of her at once brings to one's mind the story of *Panchabati* of the *Ramayana*—and I can see with my mind's eye the three of them, *Rama, Lakshmana* and *Sita*, spending their time in great happiness and in heavenly bliss on the banks of the *Godavari*, forsaking their kingdom and wealth; no worldly grief or anxiety affect the contented look on their faces; the three of them are spending their time in great joy in the worship of Nature and the Almighty. And, at the other end, we are all the time being consumed in the fire of worldly sorrows! Where is that happiness! Where is the peace! We are hankering after peace! There can be peace only through the contemplation and worship of God. If there is any way of having peace on this earth, every home must resound with the song of God. Again, when I look in the northerly direction, a more sublime scene comes before my mind's eye. I see the holy Ganges proceeding along her course—reviving in me another scene of the *Ramayana*. I see *Valmiki's* sacred abode of meditation in the wilderness—resounding all the while with the voice of the great sage, chanting *mantras* from the Holy *Vedas*—I can see the aged sage sitting on a deer-skin with his two disciples at his feet, *Kusha* and *Laba*, who are receiving instruction from him. Even the crooked serpent has lost its venom and is silently listening to the *mantras* with its head raised in attention; herds of cattle, come to the Ganges to quench their thirst, are also stopping to listen to the blessed sound of the *mantras*; nearby a deer is lying on the ground and gazing intently at the face of the great sage. Every little thing in the *Ramayana* is so noble—the description of even a single blade of grass is so nobly done; but, alas, having forsaken religion, we are now unable to appreciate this nobility. I am reminded of another scene. The Ganges is on its course, carrying away all the filth of this world; the *Yogis* have collected on its bank—some have half-closed eyes engrossed in their morning prayers, some have built images and are worshipping them with sweet-smelling flowers collected from the forest and with burning sandalwood and incense, *mantras* chanted by some of them are being echoed and re-echoed through the atmosphere—some are purifying themselves with the holy water of the Ganges—some again are humming to themselves as they collect flowers for the *Puja*. Everything is so noble—and so pleasing to the eye as well as to the mind. But, alas! Where are those high-souled seers today? Do we hear their prayers any more? There is no more of their *yoga*, their prayers, their worship, etc.! It is a heart-rending situation. We have lost our religion, and everything else—even our national life. We are now a weak, servile, irreligious and cursed nation! O Lord! the same India has fallen on such evil days! Will you not come and resurrect us? This is Your land—but, look, O Lord, in what state she is now! Where is the eternal religion that your chosen men established here? The religion and the nation that our forebears the Aryans built up and established are now in ruins. O Merciful God, take pity on us and save us!

Mother, when I sit down to write a letter I lose all sense of proportion. I hardly know what I am going to write and what I am able to write. . .

. . . Mother, I wonder if Mother India in this age has one single selfless son—is our motherland really so unfortunate? Alas! What happened to our hoary past? Where are those Aryan heroes who would freely sacrifice their precious lives in the service of Mother India?

Your are a mother, but do you belong only to us? No, you are the mother of all Indians—if every Indian is a son to you, do not the sorrows of your sons make you cry out in agony? Can a mother be heartless? No, that can never be—because a mother can never be heartless. Then, how is it that in the face of such a miserable state of her children, mother remains unmoved! Mother, you have travelled in all parts of India—does not your heart bleed at the sight of the present deplorable state of Indians? We are ignorant and so we may be selfish but a mother can never be selfish because a mother lives for her children. If that be so, how is it that mother is unmoved when her children are suffering! Then, is the mother also selfish?

Mother, it is not only the country that is in a pitiable condition! Look at the state of our religion! How holy and eternal the Hindu religion was and how degraded our religion is now! Think of the Aryans who hallowed this earth by their presence and look at us their fallen descendants! Is that holy eternal faith going to be extinct? Look, how atheism, lack of faith and bigotry have become rampant—leading to so much sin and so much misery for the people. Look, how the descendants of the deeply religious Aryan race have now become irreligious and atheistic! Worship, prayer and contemplation were then man's only duty; how many today invoke His name once in their lifetime? Mother, does not the sight of all this and the thought of all this move you too deeply and to tears? Do you not really feel this way? That can never be. A mother can never be heartless!

Mother, please take a good look at the miserable condition of your children. Sin, all manner of suffering, hunger, lack of love, jealousy, selfishness and above all, lack of religion, have made their existence a veritable Hell. And, look at the state of the holy eternal religion! And look, it is on the way to oblivion! Lack of faith, atheism and superstition have brought our religion down and vulgarised it. What is more, nowadays so many sins are being committed in the name of religion—so much sacrilege in the holy places! Look at the terrible state in which the *pandas* of Puri find themselves! What a shame indeed! Look at the holy *Brahmin* of our olden days and the hypocritical *Brahmin* of the present time. Now, wherever religion is practised there is so much bigotry and sin.

Alas! What have we come to! What has our religion come to! Mother, when you think of such things, do you not become restless? Does not your heart cry out in pain?

Will the condition of our country continue to go from bad to worse—will not any son of Mother India in distress, in total disregard of his selfish interests, dedicate his whole life to the cause of the Mother?

Mother, how much longer shall we sleep? How much longer shall we go on playing with non-essentials? Shall we continue to turn a deaf ear to the wailings of our nation? Our ancient religion is suffering the pangs of near death—does that not stir our hearts?

How long can one sit with folded arms and watch this state of our country and religion? One cannot wait any more—one cannot sleep any more—we must now shake off our stupor and lethargy and plunge into action. But, alas! How many selfless sons of the Mother are prepared, in this selfish age, to completely give up their personal interests and take the plunge for the Mother? Mother, is this son of yours yet ready?

Yours ever affectionately
SUBHAS

2

At Cambridge[1]

When I left India the Jallianwalla Bagh massacre at Amritsar had already taken place. But hardly any news of it had travelled outside the Punjab. Punjab was under martial law and there was a strict censorship on all news sent out from that province. As a consequence, we had heard only vague rumours of some terrible happenings at Lahore and Amritsar. One of my brothers who was then working at Simla brought us some news—or rather rumours—about the Punjab happenings and about the Anglo-Afghan war in which the Afghans had got the better of the British. But on the whole the public were ignorant of what had been going on in the north-west, and I sailed for Europe in a complacent mood.

On the boat we found quite a number of Indian passengers, mostly students. Accordingly we considered it advisable to take a separate table where we would feel more at home. Our table was presided over by an elderly and estimable lady, the wife of a deceased Indian Civil Servant. The majority of the passengers were Britishers of the sun-burnt snobbish type. Association with them was hardly possible—so we Indians kept mostly to ourselves. Occasionally there would be friction between an Indian passenger and a Britisher over some thing or other, and though nothing very serious took place by the time we reached England, we all had a feeling of resentment at the supercilious attitude of the Britisher towards Indians. One interesting discovery I made during the voyage—Anglo-Indians develop a love for India and the Indian people when they are out of India. In the boat there were a few Anglo-Indian passengers. The nearer we came to Europe, the more home-sick—I mean 'India-sick'—they became. In England Anglo-Indians cannot pass themselves off as Englishmen. They have, moreover, no home there, no associations, no contacts. It is, therefore, inevitable that the farther they go from India, the closer they should feel drawn towards her.

[1] Chapter 9 of *An Indian Pilgrim.* Part of his unfinished autobiography, the chapter contains extensive quotations from letters to his brother Sarat Chandra Bose during 1921 on the decision to resign from the Indian Civil Service.

I do not think that we could have chosen a slower boat than the City of Calcutta. She was scheduled to reach Tilbury in 30 days but actually took a week more. That was because she was held up at Suez for want of coal, owing to the coal-strike in England. Our only consolation was that we called at a number of ports on our way. To make life on board for five weeks somewhat bearable, we had to fall back on that spice of life, humour. One fellow-passenger had been ordered by his wife not to touch beef. By another passenger he was tricked into taking 'copta curry' of beef—which he thoroughly enjoyed—under the impression that it was mutton 'copta curry'. Great was his remorse when he discovered his mistake after twelve hours. Another passenger had orders from his fiancee to write a letter every day. He spent his time reciting love-poems and talking about her. Whether we liked it or not, we had to listen. He was beside himself with joy when one day I remarked in reply to his importunity that his fiancee had Grecian features.

Even the longest day has its end; so we did reach Tilbury after all. It was wet and cloudy—typical London weather. But there was plenty of excitement to make us oblivious of outside nature. When I first went down into a tube-station, I enjoyed the experience, for it was something new.

The next morning I began exploring. I called at the office of the Adviser to Indian students at Cromwell Road. He was very nice to me, gave me plenty of advice, but added that so far as admission to Cambridge was concerned, there was nothing doing. There by chance I met some Indian students from Cambridge. One of them strongly advised me to proceed straight to Cambridge and try my luck there, instead of wasting my time at Cromwell Road. I agreed, and the next day I was at Cambridge. Some students from Orissa, whom I had known slightly before, lent me a helping hand. One[2] of them who belonged to Fitzwilliam Hall took me to Mr Reddaway, the Censor, and introduced me to him. Mr Reddaway was exceedingly kind and sympathetic, gave me a patient hearing, and at the end wound up by saying that he would admit me straightaway. The problem of admission settled, the next question was about the current term which had begun two weeks ago. If I lost that term then I would probably have to spend nearly a year more in order to qualify for a degree. Otherwise, I would take my degree by June 1921. On this point also Mr Reddaway was accommodating beyond my expectation. He made use of the coal-strike and of my military service in

[2] S.M.D.

order to persuade the University authorities to stretch a point in my favour. He succeeded, and the result was that I did not lose that term. Without Mr Reddaway I do not know what I would have done in England.

I reached London about the 25 October and it was the first week of November before I could settle down to work at Cambridge. I had an unusually large number of lectures to attend—part of them for the Mental and Moral Sciences Tripos and the rest for the Civil Service Examination. Outside my lecture hours I had to study as hard as I could. There was no question of any enjoyment for me, besides what I could get from hard work. I was to appear under the old Civil Service Regulations which necessitated my taking up eight or nine different subjects, some of which I had to study for the first time. My subjects were as follows: English Composition, Sanskrit, Philosophy, English Law, Political Science, Modern European History, English History, Economics, Geography. Over and above studying these subjects, I had to do surveying and map-making (Cartography) for the Geography paper and to learn something of French in connection with the Modern History paper.

The work for the Mental and Moral Sciences Tripos was more interesting but I could not devote much time to it, beyond attending the lectures. Among my lecturers were Prof. Sorley (Ethics), Prof. Myers (Psychology), and Prof. McTaggart (Metaphysics). During the first three terms I devoted practically my whole time to preparing for the Civil Service Examination. In the way of recreation, I attended the meetings of the Indian Majlis and the Union Society.

Cambridge after the war was conservative. Oxford was much the same but was beginning to go liberal. One could judge of the prevailing atmosphere from the fact that pacifists, socialists, conscientious objectors, and the like could not easily address a public meeting at Cambridge. The undergraduates would generally come and break up the meetings and 'rag' the lecturer by throwing bags of flour at him or giving him a ducking in the river. 'Ragging' was of course a legitimate recreation for the undergraduates there and I heartily approved of it. But breaking up meetings simply because the speaker represented a different ideology did not appeal to me.

What greatly impressed an outsider like myself was the measure of freedom allowed to the students, and the general esteem in which they were held by all and sundry. This undoubtedly had a very wholesome effect on their character. What a change, I thought, from a police-ridden city like Calcutta where every student was looked upon as a potential revolutionary and suspect! And living in the atmosphere of Cambridge, it was difficult to imagine the incidents in the Calcutta Presidency College—professors maltreating students—for there it was the professors who ran the risk of being maltreated by the undergraduates. In fact, unpopular dons were occasionally 'ragged' by the undergrads and their rooms raided by the latter though in a friendly way, for later on they were compensated for any damage done. Even when a ragging was going on in the streets of Cambridge, causing damage to public property the police would behave with remarkable restraint, a thing quite impossible in India.

Apart from the measure of freedom enjoyed by the students, which would naturally appeal more to me than to British students born and brought up in a free atmosphere, the consideration and esteem with which they were treated everywhere was very striking. Even a fresher coming up for the first time would at once get the impression that a high standard of character and behaviour was expected of him, and he would be bound to react favourably. This consideration shown towards the undergraduates was not confined to Cambridge but existed to some extent all over the country. In the trains when one was questioned and replied that he was at Cambridge (or Oxford), the attitude of the questioner would change at once. He would become friendly—or shall I say more respectful? This was my personal experience. If there is an element of snobbishness in those who go up to Cambridge or Oxford, I certainly do not hold a brief for it. But, having been brought up in a police-ridden atmosphere, it is my firm conviction that there is a lot to be said in favour of allowing students and young men more freedom and treating them with consideration as if they were responsible citizens.

I remember an incident when I was a College student in Calcutta. I was then awfully fond of buying new books. If I set my heart on a book in a shop-window, I would not rest till I possessed it. I would feel so restless till I got the book that I had to buy it before I returned home. One day I went to one of the biggest shops in College Street and asked for a book on philosophy, on which I was very keen at the time. The price was announced and I found that I was short by a few rupees. I requested the manager to let me have the book and promised to bring the balance the next day. He replied that that was not possible, I would have to pay the full price down first. I was not only disappointed at failing to get the book but was extremely hurt because I was distrusted in this way.[3] It was

[3] I know that things have changed now.

therefore such a relief to find that you could walk into any shop in Cambridge and order anything you liked without having to bother about payment on the spot.

There is another thing which drew my admiration—the debates at the Union Society's meetings. The whole atmosphere was so exhilarating. There was perfect freedom to talk what you liked or attack whomsoever you wished. Prominent members of Parliament and sometimes members of the Cabinet took part in these debates in a spirit of perfect equality and would, of course, come in for slashing criticism not unmixed with invective at times. Once Horatio Bottomley, M.P. was taking part in a debate. He was warned by an oppositionist speaker—'There are more things in heaven and earth, Horatio, than your John Bull dreams of.'

Sparkling bits of humour would enliven the proceedings. During the course of a debate on Ireland a pro-Irish speaker, while exposing the real character of the Government, referred to the 'forces of law and order on one side and of Bonar Law and disorder on the other'.

Among the guests at these debates, besides well-known parliamentary figures, there were also those who were on the threshold of a public career. I remember, for instance, that Dr Hugh Dalton was often present at these debates. He was a prospective M.P. nursing some constituency at the time. Sir Oswald Mosley, then a Left Wing Liberal (or Labourite), participated in a debate on India. He vehemently denounced[4] the policy of Dyer and O'dwyer and raised a storm in British circles by his remark that the events in Amritsar in 1919 were the expression of racial hatred. Sir John Simon and Mr Clynes once came to plead the miners' cause before the Cambridge public at Guildhall. The undergrads turned up with the object of giving them a hot time. Sir John Simon had to run the gauntlet, but when Mr Clynes got up (I think he had been a miner himself) he spoke with such sincerity and passion that those who had come to scoff remained to pray.

During the six terms that I was in Cambridge the relations between British and Indian students were on the whole quite cordial, but in few cases did they ripen into real friendship. I say this not from my personal experience alone but from general observation as well. Many factors were responsible for this. The war undoubtedly had its effect. One could detect in the average Britisher a feeling of superiority beneath a veneer of bon-homie which was not agreeable to others. On our side, after the post-war events in India and particularly the tragedy at Amritsar, we

[4] What a change now.

could not but be sensitive (perhaps ultra-sensitive) with regard to our self-respect and national honour. It also pained us to find that among middle-class Englishmen there was a great deal of sympathy for General Dyer. It is probable that speaking generally the basis for a friendship between Britishers and Indians did not exist. We were politically more conscious and more sensitive than we had been before. Consequently friendship with an Indian presupposed sympathy, or at least toleration, for his political ideas. That was not always easy to find. Among the political parties only Labour expressed sympathy for Indian aspirations. It followed that there was greater possibility of friendship with Labourites or people having pro-Labour views and sentiments.

The above remarks are of a general nature, and must provide for exceptions. I myself made friends with people, students and non-students, holding conservative views regarding British politics, which continues till the present day in spite of all that I have been through. That was possible because they had sufficient toleration for my ideas. The intelligentsia of Great Britain has been passing through something like an intellectual revolution during the last decade, and specially during the last five years, and I daresay that that is reflected in the atmosphere of Cambridge, Oxford, London, and other places. The experience of today may not therefore tally with that of 1919 and 1920.

That I have not misjudged British mentality as I found it soon after the war can be demonstrated from one or two incidents. It is generally claimed that the average Briton has a sense of fairplay, a sportsmanlike spirit. During my time at Cambridge we Indians wanted more proof of it. The tennis champion for the year was an Indian student, Sunder Dass, who naturally got the blue. We expected that he would be called upon to captain the team in the intervarsity matches. But in order to frustrate that, an old blue who had already gone down was sent for and made to stay on for another year. On paper it was all right. The senior blue had the priority in the matter of captaining the team, but everybody knew what had passed behind the scenes and there was silent resentment in the ranks of the Indian students.

Another instance. One day we saw a notice inviting applications from undergraduates for enlistment in the University Officers' Training Corps. Some of us went up and applied. We were told that the question would have to be referred to the higher authorities. After some time came the reply that the India Office objected to our enlisting in the O.T.C The matter was brought before the Indian Majlis and it was decided to take the matter up with the Secretary of State for India, and Mr K.L. Gauba and I were authorised to interview him if necessary. The then Secretary, Mr E.S. Montague, referred us to the Under-Secretary of State for India, the Earl of Lytton, who received us cordially and gave us a patient hearing. He assured us that the India Office had no objection at all and that the opposition came from the War Office. The War Office was informed that the enlistment of Indians in the O.T.C. would be resented by British students. Further, the War Office was afraid that since members of the O.T.C., when fully qualified, were entitled to commissions in the British Army, a difficult situation would arise if Indian students after qualifying in the O.T.C. demanded commissions in the British Army. Lord Lytton added that personally he thought it was inevitable that in future Indian officers should be in charge of mixed regiments, but the prejudice against Indians unfortunately persisted in certain circles and could not be ignored. We replied that in order to obviate the difficulty we were prepared to give an assurance that we would not ask for commissions in the British Army. We added that we were more interested in getting the training than in joining the army as a profession. On returning to Cambridge we again tackled the O.T.C. staff, and we were again told that the War Office was not objecting to the proposal but the India Office. Whatever the truth, no doubt there was prejudice against Indians in certain British circles. As long as I was there, our demands were not met by the authorities and I daresay the position is the same today as it was seventeen years ago.

Indian students at Cambridge at that time had, on the whole, a satisfactory record, especially in the matter of studies. In sports, too, they did not do badly at all. We would only have liked to see them doing well in boating. Now that boating is becoming popular in India, it is to be hoped that in future they will figure conspicuously in boating also.

The question is often raised as to whether it is desirable to send Indian students abroad and if so at what age. In 1920 an official committee was appointed, presided over by Lord Lytton, to consider the affairs of Indian students in Great Britain, and this point was also discussed in connection therewith. My considered opinion was and still is that Indian students should go abroad only when they have attained a certain level of maturity. In other words, as a rule, they should go after graduation. In that case they can make the most of their stay abroad. This was the view that I put forward when I represented the Cambridge Indian Majlis before the above Indian Students' Committee. Much is made of public school training in Britain. I do not desire to express any opinion as to how it affects British people and British students. But so far as Indian students are concerned, I do not have a kind word for it. At Cambridge I came across some Indian products of English public schools and I did not think highly of them.[5] Those who had their parents living with them in England and had home influence to supplement their school-education fared better than those who were quite alone. Education in the lower stages must be 'national', it must have its roots in the soil. We must draw our mental pabulum from the culture of our own country. How can that be possible if one is transplanted at too early an age? No, we should not, as a rule, countenance the idea of sending boys and girls to schools abroad quite alone at an immature age. Education becomes international at the higher stages. It is then that students can, with profit, go abroad, and it is then that the East and the West can commingle to the benefit of both.

In India members of the Civil Service used to be known formerly as 'subjunta', or one who knows everything. There was some justification for that because they used to be put up to all kinds of jobs. The education that they received did give them a certain amount of elasticity and a smattering of a large number of subjects which was helpful to them in actual administration. I realised this when I sat for the Civil Service Examination, with nine subjects on my shoulders. Not all of them have been useful to me in later life, but I must say that the study of Political Science, Economics, English History, and Modern European History proved to be beneficial. This was specially the case with Modern European History. Before I studied this subject, I did not have a clear idea of the politics of Continental Europe. We Indians are taught to regard Europe as a magnified edition of Great Britain. Consequently we have a tendency to look at the Continent through the eyes of England. This is, of course, a gross mistake, but not having been to the Continent, I did not realise it till I studied Modern European History and some of its original sources like Bismarck's Autobiography, Metternich's Memoirs, Cavour's Letters, etc. These original sources, more than anything else I studied at Cambridge, helped to rouse my political sense and to foster my understanding of the inner currents of international politics.

Early in July 1920, the Civil Service open competitive examination began in London. It dragged on for a month and the agony was a prolonged one. I had worked hard, on the whole, but my preparation was far below my expectation. So I could not feel hopeful. So many brilliant students had come down in spite of years of preparation that it would require some conceit to feel anything but diffident. My diffidence was

[5] Every rule has its exceptions, of course.

heightened when I foolishly threw away about 150 sure marks in my Sanskrit paper. It was the translation paper, English to Sanskrit, and I had done it well. I prepared a rough copy of the translation first with the intention of making a fair copy in the answer-book. But so oblivious was I of the time that when the bell went, I had transcribed only a portion of the text I had prepared in rough. But there was no help—the answer-book had to be surrendered and I could only bite my fingers.

I informed my people that I had not done well and could not hope to find a place among the selected candidates. I now planned to continue my work for the Tripos. Imagine my surprise, therefore, when I got a telegram one night when I was in London from a friend of mine which ran thus—'CONGRATULATIONS SEE MORNING POST'. I wondered what it meant. Next morning when I got a copy of the Morning Post, I found that I had come out fourth. I was glad. A cable went off to India at once.

I had now another problem to face. What should I do with the job? Was I going to give the go-by to all my dreams and aspirations, and settle down to a comfortable life? There was nothing new in that. So many had done it before—so many had talked big when they were young and had acted differently when grown up. I knew of a young man from Calcutta who had Ramakrishna and Vivekananda at the tip of his tongue in his college days, but later on married into a rich family and was now safely landed in the Indian Civil Service. Then there was the case of a friend from Bombay who had promised in the presence of the late Lokamanya Tilak that, if he happened to pass the I.C.S. Examination, he would resign and devote himself to national work.[6] But I had resolved early in

[6] When Lokamanya B.G. Tilak visited Cambridge in 1919 he appealed to the Indian students not to go in for Government service but to devote themselves to national service. He regretted that so many bright and promising students were hankering after Government jobs. This friend in a fit of inspiration stood up and announced that, though he was trying to qualify for the Indian Civil Service, if he manages to pass the examination, he would resign and then serve the national cause. He did not pass the first time but the next year he was successful and he is now in the service.

When Lokamanya Tilak was to visit Cambridge, the India Office and the Foreign Secretary, wrote to the Vice-Chancellor requesting him to stop his visit if possible. The Vice-Chancellor sent for the Indian students in that connection, but they declared that since Lokamanya Tilak had already been invited, it was quite impossible to cancel his visit. Thereafter, there was no interference on the part of the University, Lord Curzon's letter notwithstanding.

The burden of Lokmanya Tilak's speech at Cambridge was that he demanded 'Home Rule within fifteen years'. Some English undergrads who had heard that Lokmanya Tilak was a firebrand came to the lecture expecting some hot stuff. After the lecture they remarked: 'If these are your extremists, we don't want to hear your moderates.'

life not to follow the beaten track and, further, I had certain ideals which I wanted to live up to. It was therefore quite impossible for me to go into the Service unless I could make a clean sweep of my past life.

There were two important considerations which I had to weigh before I could think of resigning. Firstly, what would my people think? Secondly, if I resigned now in a fit of excitement, would I have any occasion in future to regret my action? Was I absolutely sure that I was doing the right thing?

It took me seven long months to make up my mind. In the meantime, I started a correspondence with my second brother, Sarat. Fortunately the letters I wrote have been preserved by him. The ones I received have all been lost in the storm and stress of a hectic political life. My letters are interesting inasmuch as they show the working of my mind in 1920.

The I.C.S. Examination result was declared about the middle of September 1920. A few days later when I was taking a holiday at Leigh-on-Sea in Essex I wrote to him on the 22 September as follows:

'I was so glad to receive the telegram conveying congratulations. I don't know whether I have gained anything really substantial by passing the I.C.S. Examination—but it is a great pleasure to think that the news has pleased so many and especially that it has delighted father and mother in these dark days.

'I am here as a paying guest of Mr B.'s family. Mr B. represents English character at its very best. He is cultured and liberal in his views and cosmopolitan in his sentiments. . . . Mr B. counts among his friends Russians, Poles, Lithuanians, Irishmen, and members of other nationalities. He takes a great interest in Russian, Irish and Indian literature, and admires the writings of Ramesh Dutt and Tagore. . . . I have been getting heaps of congratulations on my standing fourth in the competitive examination. But I cannot say that I am delighted at the prospect of entering the ranks of the I.C.S. If I have to join this service I shall do so with as much reluctance as I started my study for the I.C.S. Examination with. A nice fat income with a good pension in after-life—I shall surely get. Perhaps I may become a Commissioner if I stood to make myself servile enough. Given talents, with a servile spirit one may even aspire to be the Chief Secretary to a provincial Government. But after all is Service to be the be-all and end-all of my life? The Civil Service can bring one all kinds of worldly comfort, but are not these acquisitions made at the expense of one's soul? I think it is hypocrisy to maintain that the highest ideals of one's life are compatible with subordination to the conditions of service which an I.C.S. man has got to accept.

'You will readily understand my mental condition as I stand on the threshold of what the man-in-the-street would call a promising career. There is much to be said in favour of such a service. It solves once for all what is the paramount problem for each of us—the problem of bread and butter. One has not to go to face life with risk or any uncertainty as to success or failure. But for a man of my temperament who has been feeding on ideas which might be called eccentric—the line of least resistance is not the best line to follow. Life loses half its interest if there is no struggle—if there are no risks to be taken. The uncertainties of life are not appalling to one who has not, at heart, worldly ambitions. Moreover, it is not possible to serve one's country in the best and fullest manner if one is chained to the Civil Service. In short, national and spiritual aspirations are not compatible with obedience to Civil Service conditions.

'I realise that it is needless to talk in this fashion as my will is not my own . Though I am sure that the C. Service has no glamour for you, father is sure to be hostile to the idea of my not joining. He would like to see me settled down in life as soon as possible. . . . Hence I find that owing to sentimental and economic reasons, my will can hardly be called my own. But I may say without hesitation that if I were given the option—I would be the last man to join the Indian Civil Service.

'You may rightly say that, instead of avoiding the service, one should enter its ranks and fight its evils. But even if I do so, my position any day may become so intolerable as to compel me to resign. If such a crisis takes place 5 or 10 years hence, I shall not be in a favourable position to chalk out a new line for myself—whereas today there is yet time for me to qualify for another career.

'If one is cynical enough one may say that all this "spirit" will evaporate as soon as I am safe in the arms of the service. But I am determined not to submit to that sickening influence. I am not going to marry—hence considerations of worldly prudence will not deter me from taking a particular line of action if I believe that to be intrinsically right.

'Constituted as I am, I have sincere doubts as to whether I should be a fit man for the Civil Service and I rather think that what little capacity I possess can be better utilised in other directions for my own welfare as well as for the welfare of my country.

'I should like to know your opinion about this. I have not written to father on this point—I really don't know why. I wish I could get his opinion too.'

The above letter shows that the conflict had begun but was still far from being resolved. On the 26 January 1921, I reverted to the subject and wrote:

'. . . You may say that instead of shunning this wicked system we should enter it and fight with it till the last. But such a fight one has got to carry on single-handed in spite of censure from above, transfer to unhealthy places, and stoppage of promotion. The amount of good that one can do while in the service is infinitesimal when compared with what one can do when outside it. Mr R.C. Dutt no doubt did a lot of work in spite of his service but I am sure he could have done much more work if he had not been a member of the bureaucracy. Besides the question here involved is one of principle. On principle I cannot accept the idea of being a part of the machinery which has outlived the days of its usefulness, and stands at present for all that is connected with conservatism, selfish power, heartlessness, and red-tapism.

'I am now at the cross-ways and no compromise is possible. I must either chuck this rotten service and dedicate myself whole-heartedly to the country's cause—or I must bid adieu to all my ideals and aspirations and enter the service. . . . I am sure many of our relatives will howl when they hear of such a rash and dangerous proposal. . . . But I do not care for their opinions, their cheers or their taunts. But I have faith in your idealism and that is why I am appealing to you. About this time 5 years ago I had your moral support in an endeavour which was fraught with disastrous consequences to myself. For a year my future was dark and blank, but I bore the consequences bravely, I never complained to myself, and today I am proud that I had the strength to make that sacrifice. The memory of that event strengthens my belief that if any demands for sacrifice are made upon me in the future I shall respond with equal fortitude, courage and calmness. And in this new endeavour can I not expect the same moral support which you so willingly and so nobly lent me, five years ago? . . .

'I am writing to father separately this time and am appealing to him to give his consent. I hope that if you agree with my point of view you will try to persuade father to that effect. I am sure your opinion in this matter will carry great weight.'

This letter of the 26 January 1921, shows that I had moved towards a decision but was still awaiting approval from home.

The next letter in which there was reference to the same topic was dated the 16 February 1921. I wrote therein:

'. . . You have received my "explosive" letter by this time. Further thought confirms me in my support of the plans I have sketched for myself in that letter. . . . If C.R. Das at his age can give up everything and face the uncertainties of life—I am sure a young man like myself, who has no worldly cares to trouble him, is much more capable of doing so. If I give up the service, I shall not be in want of work to keep my hands full. Teaching, social service, cooperative credit work, journalism, village organisation work, these are so many things to keep thousands of energetic young men busy. Personally, I should like to take up teaching and journalism at present. The National College and the new paper Swaraj will afford plenty of scope for my activity. . . . A life of sacrifice to start with, plain living and high thinking, whole-hearted devotion to the country's cause—all these are highly enchanting to my imagination and inclination. Further, the very principle of serving under an alien bureaucracy is intensely repugnant to me. The path of Arabindo Ghosh is to me more noble, more inspiring, more lofty, more unselfish, though more thorny than the path of Ramesh Dutt.

'I have written to father and to mother to permit me to take the vow of poverty and service. They may be frightened at the thought that that path might lead to suffering in the future. Personally I am not afraid of suffering—in fact, I would rather welcome it than shrink from it.'

The letter of the 23 February 1921, is also interesting. Therein I say: 'Ever since the result of the I.C.S. was declared. I have been asking myself whether I shall be more useful to my country if I am in the service than if I am not. I am fully convinced now that I shall be able to serve my country better if I am one of the people than if I am a member of the bureaucracy. I do not deny that one can do some amount of good when he is in the service but it can't be compared with the amount of good that one can do when his hands are not tied by bureaucratic chains. Besides, as I have already mentioned in one of my letters, the question involved is mainly one of principle. The principle of serving an alien bureaucracy is one to which I cannot reconcile myself. Besides the first step towards equipping oneself for public service is to sacrifice all worldly interests—to burn one's boats as it were—and devote oneself whole-heartedly to the national cause. . . . The illustrious example of Arabindo Ghosh looms large before my vision. I feel that I am ready to make the sacrifice which that example demands of me. My circumstances are also favourable.'

It is clear from the above that I was still under the influence of Arabindo Ghosh. As a matter of fact it was widely believed about this time that he would soon return to active political life.

The next letter was written on the 6 April from Oxford where I was spending my holidays. By then I had received my father's letter disapproving of my plans, but I had definitely made up my mind to resign. The following extracts are interesting:

'Father thinks that the life of a self-respecting Indian Civil Servant will not be intolerable under the new regime and that home rule will come to us within ten years. But to me the question is not whether my life will be tolerable under the new regime. In fact, I believe that, even if I am in the service, I can do some useful work. The main question involved is one of principle. Should we under the present circumstances own allegiance to a foreign bureaucracy and sell ourselves for a mess of pottage? Those who are already in the service or who cannot help accepting service may do so. But should I, being favourably situated in many respects, own allegiance so readily? The day I sign the covenant I shall cease to be a free man.

'I believe we shall get Home Rule within ten years and certainly earlier if we are ready to pay the price. The price consists of sacrifice and suffering. Only on the soil of sacrifice and suffering can we raise our national edifice. If we all stick to our jobs and look after our own interests, I don't think we shall get Home Rule even in 50 years. Each family—if not each individual—should now bring forward its offering to the feet of the mother. Father wants to save me from this sacrifice. I am not so callous as not to appreciate the love and affection which impels him to save me from this sacrifice, in my own interests. He is naturally apprehensive that I am perhaps hasty in my judgement or overzealous in my youthful enthusiasm. But I am perfectly convinced that the sacrifice has got to be made—by somebody at least.

'If anybody else had come forward, I might have had cause to withdraw or wait. Unfortunately nobody is coming yet and the precious moments are flying away. In spite of all the agitation going on there, it still remains true that not a single Civil Servant has had the courage to throw away his job and join the people's movement. This challenge has been thrown at India and has not been answered yet. I may go further and say that in the whole history of British India, not one Indian has voluntarily given up the Civil Service with a patriotic motive. It is time that members of the highest service in India should set an example to members of the other services. If the members of the services withdraw their allegiance or even show a desire to do so—then only will the bureaucratic machine collapse.

'I therefore do not see how I can save myself from this sacrifice. I know what this sacrifice means. It means poverty, suffering, hard work, and possibly other hardships to which I need not expressly refer, but which you can very well understand. But the sacrifice has got to be made—consciously and deliberately. . . . Your proposal that I should resign after returning is eminently reasonable but there are one or two points to be urged against it. In the first place it will be a galling thing for me to sign the covenant which is an emblem of servitude. In the second place if I accept service for the present I shall not be able to return home before December or January, as the usual custom stands. If I resign now, I may return by July. In six months' time much water will have flowed through the Ganges. In the absence of adequate response at the right moment, the whole movement might tend to flag, and if response comes too late it may not have any effect. I believe it will take years to initiate another such movement and hence I think that the tide in the present movement must be availed of. If I have to resign, it does not make any difference to me or to any one of us whether I resign tomorrow or after a year, but delay in resigning may on the other hand have some untoward effect on the movement. I know full well that I can do but little to help the movement— but it will be a great thing if I have the satisfaction of having done my bit. . . . If for any reason I happen to change my decision regarding resignation, I shall send a cable to father as that will relieve his anxiety.'

In the letter written from Cambridge on the 20 April, I said that I would send in my resignation on the 22 April.

In my letter dated the 23 April from Cambridge I wrote as follows:

'I had a talk with the Censor of Fitzwilliam Hall, Mr Reddaway, about my resignation. Contrary to my expectations, he heartily approved of my ideas. He said he was surprised, almost shocked, to hear that I had changed my mind, since no Indian within his knowledge had ever done that before. I told him that I would make journalism my profession later on, and he said that he preferred a journalistic career to a monotonous one like the Civil Service.

'I was at Oxford for three weeks before I came up here and there the final stage of my deliberation took place. The only point which had been taxing me for the last few months was whether I should be justified morally in following a course which would cause intense sorrow and displeasure in many minds and especially in the minds of father and mother. . . . My position therefore is that, in entering a new career, I am acting against the express wishes of father and mother and against your advice though you have sent me your 'warmest felicitations in whatever course I choose.' My greatest objection to joining the service was based on the fact that I would have to sign the covenant and thereby own the allegiance of a foreign bureaucracy which I feel rightly or wrongly has no moral right to be there. Once I signed the covenant, it would not matter from the point of view of principle whether I served for three days or three years. I have come to believe that compromise is a bad thing—it degrades the man and injures his cause. . . . The reason why Surendra Nath Banerji is going to end his life with a knighthood and a ministership is that he is a worshipper of the philosophy of expediency which Edmund Burke preached. We have not come to that stage where we can accept a philosophy of expediency. We have got to make a nation and a nation can be made only by the uncompromising idealism of Hampden and Cromwell. . . . I have come to believe that it is time for us to wash our hands clean of any connection with the British Government. Every Government servant whether he be a petty chaprasi or a provincial Governor only helps to contribute to the stability of the British Government in India. The best way to end a Government is to withdraw from it. I say this not because that was Tolstoy's doctrine nor because Gandhi preaches it—but because I have come to believe in it. . . . I sent in my resignation a few days ago. I have not yet been informed that it has been accepted.

'C.R. Das has written, in reply to a letter of mine, about the work that is already being done. He complains that there is dearth of sincere workers at present. There will consequently be plenty of congenial work for me when I return home. . . . I have nothing more to say. The die is cast and I earnestly hope that nothing but good will come out of it.'

On the 18 May, I wrote from Cambridge as follows:

'Sir William Duke is trying to persuade me to withdraw my resignation. He wrote to *Bardada* about it. The Secretary of the Civil Service Board at Cambridge. Mr Roberts, also asked me to reconsider my decision and he said he was acting under instruction from the India Office. I have sent word to Sir William saying that I have acted after mature deliberation.'

This letter requires an annotation. Soon after I sent in my resignation, there was a flutter in the India Office dovecotes. The late Sir William Duke, then Permanent Under-Secretary of State for India, who knew my father when he was Commissioner of Orissa, got into touch with my eldest brother, Sjt. Satish Chandra Bose, who was then qualifying himself for the Bar in London. Sir William advised me through my brother not to resign the service. I was also approached by lecturers in Cambridge and asked to reconsider my decision. Then there was a request from the Secretary of the Civil Service Board in Cambridge, the late Mr Roberts. All these moves taken from different directions intrigued me, but most interesting of all was the last move.

Some months earlier I had a passage-at-arms with Mr Roberts over some printed instructions issued to Civil Service Probationers by the India Office. These instructions were under the caption 'Care of Horses in India' and contained remarks to the effect that the Indian syce (groom) eats the same food as his horse—that Indian Bunnias (traders) are proverbially dishonest, etc. I naturally felt indignant when I received them and had a talk with other fellow-probationers who had also got them. We all agreed that the instructions were incorrect and offensive and that we should make a joint protest. When the time came for us to write, everybody tried to back out. Ultimately I grew desperate and decided to act on my own.

I went straight to Mr Roberts and drew his attention to the incorrect statements in the printed instructions. He flared up and said, 'Look here, Mr Bose, if you do not take up the official point of view, I am afraid you will have to clear out.' I was not to be browbeaten so easily and I had gone prepared for a scrap. So I calmly replied, 'Yes, but what do you mean by the official point of view?' Mr Roberts realised at once that browbeating would not do, so he changed his tone and voice and remarked gently, 'What I mean is that you should not look out for offences.' I replied that I had not looked out for offences, but that the instructions were there in front of me. At the end he came round and said that he would draw the attention of the India Office to what I had told him. I thanked him and left.

A fortnight later Mr Roberts sent for me. This time he was very cordial. He read out a letter from the India Office in which they thanked me for drawing their attention to the printed instructions and assured me that when the instructions would be reprinted, the necessary corrections would be made.

After my resignation it was quite a different Mr Roberts that I met. He was so sweet. He argued long with me and tried to persuade me that under the new Constitution, I should try the service for a couple of years. It was possible under the new Constitution to serve the country while remaining in the service and if at the end of two years I found that I could not carry on, then I would be perfectly justified in resigning. I thanked him but told him that I had made up my mind because I felt that I could not serve two masters.

3
Prison Life in Burma[1]

To Dilip Kumar Roy[2]

Mandalay Central Jail,
2 May 1925

My dear Dilip,

I was delighted to receive your letter dated 24 March 1925. It didn't have to reach me this time through a process of 'double distillation'—to use you locution, which makes me feel happier still.

Your letter has touched such a tender chord in my heart that it is not easy for me to give an adequate reply by way of reciprocation. Besides, all I write has to pass through the Censor's hands which, too, acts as a damper. For none cares to see the deepest articulation of his heart published in the light of day open to the scrutiny of all and sundry. So, much of what I have been thinking and feeling today behind the stone-walls and prison-bars must remain unspoken for ever.

It is quite natural for a man of your susceptibilities to feel outraged that so many should be detained in jail on an unknown charge. But since accept it we must as a fact, we might as well look into the matter from a spiritual standpoint.

I cannot say that I would like to stay in a jail, for that would be unadulterated humbug . . . The whole atmosphere inside a jail tends, if anything, to pervert and dehumanise a human being; and I believe this must be true of all jails, more or less. I think the majority of convicts undergo a moral deterioration while in prison. After having been the guest of so many jails I must confess my eyes have been opened to the urgent need of a radical reform of prison-life and in future I will feel obligated to help bring about such a reform. Indian jail regulations are

[1] Excerpts of letters to his brother Sarat Chandra Bose, sister-in-law Bivabati Bose, friend Dilip Kumar Roy and novelist Sarat Chandra Chattopadhyay, 1924–27.

[2] Translated from the original Bengali.

a bad imitation of a bad model—the British, even as the University of Calcutta is a bad imitation of London.

What is most urgently called for is a new outlook based on sympathy for the convict. His wrong impulses must be regarded as symptomatic of a psychological derangement and remedies should be devised accordingly. The penalising mood which may well be assumed to be the inspiration of jail prescriptions has to give place to a new orientation guided by a flair for true reform.

I do not think I could have looked upon a convict with the authentic eye of sympathy had I not lived personally as a prisoner. And I have not the least doubt that the production of our artists and litterateurs, generally, would stand to gain in ever so many ways if they had some new experience of prison-life. We do not perhaps realise the magnitude of the debt owed by Kazi Nazrul Islam's verse to the living experience he had of jails.

When I pause to reflect calmly, I feel the stirring of a certitude within that some Vast Purpose is at work in the core of our fevers and frustrations. If only this faith could preside over every moment of our conscious life our suffering would lose its poignancy and bring us face to face with the ideal bliss even in a dungeon? But that is not possible yet, generally speaking. Which is why this duel must go on unremittingly between the soul and the body.

Usually a kind of philosophic mood instills strength into our hearts in prison surroundings. In any event, I have taken my station here and what little I have read of philosophy in addition to my conception of life in general has stood me rather in good stead here. If a man can find sufficient food for contemplation then his incarceration need hardly hurt him much unless of course his health deserts him. But our suffering is not merely spiritual—there is the rub—the body too has a say in the business, so that even when the spirit is willing the flesh might be weak.

Lokamanya Tilak wrote out his commentary on the Gita while in prison. I can say with certainty that he spent his days in mental happiness. But, alas, his premature death was as certainly attributable to his six year's detention in Mandalay Jail.

But the enforced solitude in which a detenu passes his days gives him an opportunity to delve into the ultimate problems of life. In any event, I claim this for myself that many of the most tangled questions which whirl like eddies in our individual and collective life are edging gradually to the estuary of a solution. The things I could only puzzle out feebly, or the views I could only offer tentatively in days gone by, are taking clearer shape from day to day. It is for this reason, if for no other, that I feel I will be spiritually a gainer through my imprisonment.

You have given my detention the name of martyrdom. This only testifies to the sympathy native to you character as also to your nobility of heart. But since I have some sense of humour and proportion—I hope so, anyway—I can hardly arrogate to myself the martyr's high title. Against hauteur and conceit I want to be sleeplessly vigilant. How far I have achieved this it is for my friends to judge. At all events, martyrdom can only be an ideal so far as I am concerned.

I have felt that the greatest tragedy for a convict who has to spend long years in prison is that old age creeps upon him unawares. He should therefore be specially on his guard. You cannot imagine how a fellow gets prematurely worn-out in body and in mind while serving a long sentence. Doubtless a variety of causes are responsible for this: lack of good food, exercise and life's amenities; segregation; a sense of cramped subordination; dearth of friends; and last, though by no means least, absence of music. There are some gaps which a man may fill from within, but there are others which can be only filled from without. To be denied these is not a little responsible for ageing before one's time. In the Alipore Jail musical entertainments are provided every week for the European prisoners; not so here, for the likes of us. . . .

I should not omit to mention that to a detenu the goodwill and sympathy of his friends and relations and the general public can, indeed, be a source of sustenance. Although the influence of such imponderables is a subtle and subterranean one, yet when I look at myself I realise how it is not a whit the less real for all that. There is here a difference between the hardness of lot of a political prisoner and a common convict. The former is sure of his welcome back into the fold of society. Not so the latter . . . To me such a state of affairs seems anything but satisfactory. Why shouldn't a civilised community feel for these unhappy men?

I could go on filling pages registering my thoughts and experiences of prison-life. But after all a letter must come to a terminus sometime. If I had a surplus of initiative left I might have written a whole book on Indian jails. But just at present I lack the strength adequate to such a task.

I am inclined to think that the suffering in jail-life is less physical than mental. When the blows dealt, of insult and humiliation, are not too brutal, the torments of prison-life do not become so hard to bear. . . But lest we forget too readily our outer material existence and conjure up an ideal world of bliss within, they will deal us these blows to awaken us to our bleak and joyless surroundings.

You write you are getting daily a sadder if not a wiser man to contemplate how our earth is soaked by tears of humanity from crust to centre. But then these tears are not all of pain and anguish: there are drops of compassion and love as well. Would you really decline to traverse the shoals of pain and suffering if you knew there were richer tides of bliss waiting? So far as I am concerned I see little warrant for pessimism or despondency. On the contrary, I feel, sorrow and suffering should give us courage for a higher fulfilment. Do you think that what you win without pain and struggle has any lasting value?

I received the books you had sent. I won' be able to return these as there is a considerable circle of readers here. It is hardly necessary to add that more such books will be welcome—yours being a beautiful choice, always.

Affectionately yours
SUBHAS

Mandalay Central Jail
25 June 1925

My dear Dilip,

After my last letter I have received in all three letters from you so far, dated 6 May, 15 May, 15 June.

I am in receipt also of the parcel of books you sent, with the sole exception of Turgenev's Smoke. The parcel was opened in the office, so I have asked our Superintendent to look into the matter.

I left behind Bertrand Russell's Prospects of Industrial Civilisation in Berhampore whence I was transferred here. Quite a group of my fellow prisoners were eager about keeping the book. But Russell's Free Thought and Official Propaganda isn't with me. You never sent it, did you?

I thank you, Dilip, for selecting books for me. We all hope the work you have started will fare famously, God willing. I need hardly tell you that your own writing I will read with the respect it deserves. But do see to the get-up of your books, for they should leave nothing to be desired.

You can imagine what dominates my thought today. I believe there is but one thought in all minds now: the death of our great Deshbandhu. When I first read the news in print I could hardly believe my eyes. But alas, the report is cruelly true. Ours is indeed an ill-starred nation.

The thoughts that are running riot in my mind today must remain unvoiced although sometimes I feel like publishing them if only to get some reprieve. But they are too sacred and precious to be shared with strangers—and the Censor is worse than a stranger. So I will only say that if for the country the loss is irreparable, for the youth of Bengal it is cataclysmic, appalling.

I am desolate with a sense of bereavement. For I feel so vividly near to the great departed in the world of memory that it is impossible for me just now to write something about him analysing his great qualities. I hope when the time comes I will be able to give the world some idea of the glimpses I had of him in his unguarded moments as I watched him at close range. There must be a good many like me who, though they know a great deal about him, yet do not feel equal to writing about it all lest through vocal praise they diminish the stature of his outstanding nobility.

When you say, categorically, that the last residue of pain and sorrow is not suffering, I am at one with you. There are certain tragedies in life—like the one mentioned just now—which I cannot acclaim. Being neither a sage nor a humbug, I cannot declare that all kinds of affliction are acceptable to me. At the same time, it has often made me pause to think that there are a few unfortunates (they may indeed be fortunate for all we know!) who seem to be born as targets for flings of Fate of every description. But leaving aside this question of degree I may say that if some must drain to the dregs the cup of sorrow, it were better if they drank the potion in a spirit of self-surrender. For even if we admit that such a spirit may not withstand, like a Chinese wall, the assaults of destiny, it must, for all that, greatly heighten our natural powers of fortitude. When Russell says there are tragedies which men would be spared if they could, he only speaks for the typical worldling. For I believe that a stainless saint—or his polar opposite, the mountebank—will disown such a statement.

But I wonder if you are right in holding that those who are neither philosophic nor thoughtful meet in pain nothing but pain. For even the unphilosophic (I call them so from the abstract point of view) may have an idealism of their own which they will cherish and love as a thing to be worshipped. When they are up against pain and sorrow they derive their courage and hope from their source of adoration. Among those who are with me bearing up against the suffering of jail-life, there are some who are neither thoughtful nor philosophic, and yet they face pain calmly, even like heroes. These may not be philosophic in the common use of the term, but you can hardly class them as aliens to the world of ideas. Probably this applies more or less to all who are activists by temperament, the world over.

My eyes have opened not a little through a study of criminal psychology. When I was jailed, in 1922, a convict used to work in our yard as a servant. At that time I used to live in the same room with Deshbandhu. His heart of tenderness went all out to the fellow although he was an old hand, having had already eight previous convictions to his credit. Nonetheless, he felt unconsciously drawn towards Deshbandhu till he became exceedingly attached to his master. When Deshbandhu was released he asked his devotee to go straight to his house at the expiry of his term, shunning even the shadow of his old comrades in crime. The poor wretch acquiesced and, subsequently, was as good as his word. You will be surprised to learn that the man who had been a felon all his life has been living in our great leader's house ever since and through he does sometimes revert to his tantrums still, yet overall, he is today a different man altogether, living a harmless enough life with the rest. I have no doubt that he is among those on whom the blow of this bereavement has fallen at its heaviest. Some say the greatness of a man may best be judged through his little acts, little things. On this criterion too Deshbandhu must be adjudged a great soul even if you reckoned without his great service to the country. . . .

Ever affectionately yours,
SUBHAS

Mandalay Jail
11 September 1925

My dear Dilip,

My last letter to you was unfinished and I intended to follow it up with another one the next week. But a terrible calamity intervened—which swept us off our feet. Even today I do not know where I stand and I am sure the feelings of all are much the same—though in my case there is an irrecoverable personal loss to deepen my misery, as well as a double dose of bondage to heighten my suffering. The sense of personal loss may wane with the passage of time, but I am sure that the magnitude of the loss to the public will become more and more manifest as the days roll by. So versatile was his talent and so many-sided his activities—that people in different and widely separate spheres—will be hard hit by the loss. I used to criticise him by saying that he had too many irons in the fire—but creative spirits do not submit to pragmatic or logical limitations and I have no doubt that it was only the fullness of life and realisation that impelled him to attempt reconstruction in so many different spheres of our national life.

You all had at least the opportunity of paying your last homage and even now you can find some solace in trying to perpetuate his memory. But it has pleased God to drive home into our minds a feeling of utter destitution as a result of confinement in remote Mandalay during such a crisis as this. It is only because I am exceedingly optimistic by temperament that I can still maintain my equilibrium. It is difficult to find adequate expression when one's feelings are stirred to their depths and I shall therefore pass on to something else.

How far have you proceeded with your books? Are they in the press? When do you expect them to be out? Why don't you write a treatise in English (for the benefit of other provinces as well) on the need for the revival and popularising of Indian music? . . .

. . . Could you send us a complete set of the books of your great father? We want to read them over again. If you can, you may send them direct to the Superintendent of this jail along with a letter (containing the names of the books) intimating him about the despatch of the books. All our letters have to pass the Calcutta office but the Supdt. of the jail is empowered to censor books. So you may save time by sending literature direct to him. By-the-way, have you been able to trace Turgenev's 'Smoke'? I have been informed by the Calcutta C.I.D. that no such book was sent to them. I shall be sorry if the book is really missing.

Though the climate of the place does not agree with me, I am feeling happier from day to day. Problems which to me were unsolved seem to be nearing solution. And I must thank solitude and distance from home—for giving me that detached viewpoint which is necessary for the solution of many of our problems. If I had been more fit physically, I would have profited more by my enforced exile but as things stand I still hope to make the most of my stay here. Burma is in many respects a wonderful country and my study of Burmese life and civilisation is furnishing me with many new ideas. Their various shortcomings notwithstanding, I consider the Burmese—like the Chinese—to be considerably advanced from a social point of view. What they do lack most of all is initiative—what Bergson would call 'elan vital'—the vital impulse to overcome all obstacles and march along the road to progress. They have developed a perfect social democracy—women, by the way, are more powerful here than in any European country—but alas! the enervating climate seems to have robbed them of all initiative. Abundance of crops in a sparsely populated country has for centuries past made living easy in Burma—with the inevitable result that slackness of mind and body seems to have taken possession of the Burmese. But I feel sure that once they are able to develop sufficient initiative, there will be no limit to their progress.

You probably know that the percentage of literate people in Burma, both among males and females, is more than in any other part of India. This is due to the indigenous and wonderfully cheap system of primary education through the agency of the priests. In Burma, even today, every boy is supposed to don the yellow robe for a few months. This system has not only an educative and moral value but has a levelling effect as well—since rich and poor are thus brought together. There is thus an extensive system of primary education which hardly costs anything.

In your last letter you seem to assume that the unphilosophic are doomed to suffer in their confinement. This is not wholly true. There are people who are inspired by idealism of some kind but who are unphilosophic. During the last war innumerable people went through suffering and pain of every kind, who were inspired by love of country but were altogether unphilosophic. As long as that idealism is present, I believe a man can brave suffering with equanimity—and even joy. Of course one who is philosophically inclined can turn his suffering to a higher purpose, enriching himself thereby. But then is it not true that we are all philosophers in embryo and it only requires a touch of suffering to awaken the philosophic impulse? . . .

I am,

Ever yours affectionately
SUBHAS

To Sarat Chandra Chattopadhaya[1]

Mandalay Jail
12 August 1925

Revered Sir,

I read your 'Reminiscences' in the monthly *Basumati* three times over and liked it immensely. Your insight into human character is indeed deep; the power to bring out what is beautiful and true out of your friendship and intimacy with Deshbandhu and through a wonderful analysis of the many small episodes—it is this faculty that has made it possible for you to produce something so delightful.

Those who were intimate with him are left with a hidden pain in their

[1] Translated from the original Bengali.

hearts. By mentioning some of our unspoken tender feelings, you have not only helped in revealing the truth but also lightened the burden in our minds. Verily, 'the greatest curse in a subject country is that in the struggle for liberty one has to fight his own countrymen more than the aliens.' The cruel truth of this statement and what follows in its wake was felt and is being felt keenly by the workers.

The following words in your article appealed to me most—'The gnawing in one's heart that man feels for the most beloved and the most intimate—this is it.' We, who were around him, have today no words to express our bitter sorrow; nor do we feel like expressing it to others. 'Verily, can one express his innermost thoughts to strangers? If they taunt us, it may well be bearable. But if they fail to appreciate their inner meaning, it becomes intolerable, and one feels, as the saying goes, '. . . *Arasikeshu rasanibedanam shirashi ma likha*'.

There is something else that you have written I liked very much. 'We were doing Deshbandhu's work.' I actually know many such people who did not share his views, but who on account of the magnetic pull of his leonine heart, could not help working for him. And he also could love all people regardless of difference of opinion. I have not seen him judge human character with the usual yardstick of our society. He used to believe in the concept that one should accept man as mixture of good and evil and love him—and this belief was the basis of his life.

Many people think that we followed him blindly. But he used to fight most of all with his principal lieutenants. As for myself I can say that I fought with him on innumerable questions. But I knew that however much I might fight, my devotion and loyalty would remain unshaken and that I would never be deprived of his love. He also believed that come what may in the shape of trials and tribulations, he would have me at his feet. Our quarrels were settled by mother's (Basanti Devi) mediation. But, alas, 'the refuge for lodging our grievances and recording our discontent has now ceased to exist'.

You have said somewhere—'Not a man, no funds, not a newspaper in his favour, even the nonentities heaping abuse on him—what a predicament for the Deshbandhu!' Memories of those days are still quite fresh in my mind. When we returned to Calcutta after the Gaya Congress—all the newspapers of Bengal were overflowing with untruths and half-truths. Not to speak of saying anything in our favour—they would not even publish our point of view. Swaraj Fund was by then almost completely depleted. When money was sorely needed, funds were not available. The house that used once to overflow with people—was deserted by one and all, friend or foe. So, we a handful of beings kept the show going. Later, when the house regained its pristine glory—when outsiders and careerists came back to reoccupy the arena—we were not getting the chance even to talk business. Outsiders do not know and will probably never know what labour, what gruelling labour led to the building up of the Fund, how we had a newspaper of our own and how public opinion was won back in our favour. But he who was the initiator, leader and high-priest of the great movement has disappeared before the final fulfilment of the mission. His mortal frame could no longer bear the two-fold stress of his inner fire and the burden of work outside.

Many are of the view that the goal of his mission of service to the nation was to sacrifice his whole being at the altar of the motherland. But I know that his aim was even higher. He wanted to sacrifice his entire family in the service of his motherland. And he succeeded in this considerably. During the arrests of 1921 he firmly made up his mind to send every member of his family to prison one by one and also join them himself. That he could not send others' sons to prison before sending his own—was to my mind an extremely narrow view in the context of his ideal. We knew that he would be arrested soon. So we said that it was quite unnecessary to send his son to prison before his own arrest and that we would not allow a woman to court arrest till a single man was left outside. No decision could be taken even after prolonged argument—we were not by any means prepared to accept his contention. Ultimately he said 'This is my order—it has to be carried out.' We thereupon accepted his orders under protest.

His elder daughter was married—he had no authority or claim on her—so he could not send her to jail. The younger daughter was then betrothed—there was heated argument as to whether it was right to send her; he wanted to do it and the daughter was also very eager, but all the rest were of the opinion that she should not be. Because, on the one hand, she was ill and, on the other, was already betrothed and was to be married soon. In this case Deshbandhu was compelled to abide by the general opinion. Finally it was decided that Bhombal would be the first to go—followed by Besanti Devi and Urmila Devi and he himself would remain prepared to go whenever the call came.

What happened outside is public knowledge. But how many have any idea of the feeling, the ideal and the inspiration that lay behind these actions—and which were closed to public view. His mission did not merely concern his own self—it involved his entire family. I am of opinion that the greatness of a great man is manifested more through small incidents rather than big events. I read with care the articles written by Deshbandhu's fellow-workers and close followers in the *Ashar* and *Shraban* issues of the *Basumati*. Most of the writings are rather superficial and full of set phrases; only you have tried to delineate Deshbandhu's character through an analysis of small incidents. So I can hardly tell you how pleased I was to read your article—I had expected more than this from Deshbandhu's disciples and colleagues. They had better not written at all.

Sometimes I cannot help feeling that Deshbandhu's countrymen and followers are partly responsible for his premature demise. If they had shared his burden to some extent, it would perhaps not have been necessary for him to overwork himself to death. But our ways are such that once we accept somebody as the leader, we burden him so much and expect so much from him that it becomes humanly impossible for him to carry all that burden or fulfil all the expectations. We are content to sit back leaving all political responsibilities in the leader's hands.

Well—I have digressed so far from where I began. It is not only my wish but the wish and request of all of us here that you should write a number of other articles or stories about Deshbandhu like your 'Reminiscences'. Your resources cannot be exhausted so quickly and so I do not fear that there will be any dearth of material. And, if you write, there cannot be any doubt that the handful of Bengali State prisoners in far-off Mandalay Jail will read your writings with great interest and appreciation.

I shall probably not be here for very long. But, then, I have no more that desire to be free. My heart recoils from the prospect of facing the emptiness of the graveyard that will surround me when I go out. I am passing my days here somehow—partly in joy, partly in sorrow, and with memories and dreams. I am not sure that there is no happiness in the pain you get by banging against the iron bars of this cage. The realisation that my love for my country—the love that has brought me here—is real comes through this pain. That is why, I think, even if the heart bleeds, one finds in this some happiness, peace and a sense of fulfilment. I am mentally not inclined at the moment to face the frustration, emptiness and the responsibility awaiting me outside.

If I had not been here, I would never realise the depth of my love for golden Bengal. I sometimes feel as if Tagore expressed the emotions of a prisoner when he wrote:

'Sonar Bangla, ami tomae bhalabasi!
Chiradin tomar akash tomar batas
Amar prane bajae banshi'
(O my golden Bengal, I love you so,
Your sky and the air ever play
the music in my heart.)

When, even for a moment, the vision of Bengal's variegated beauty rises before my mind's eye—I have the realisation that going through all this trouble and coming to Mandalay have been worth the while. Who knew before that there was so much of charm hidden in the soil of Bengal, in her waters, in her skies and air!

I do not know why I wrote this letter. It never occurred to me before that I should write to you. But after reading your articles, certain thoughts came up in my mind and I wrote them down. Having written after all, I should send it on. Please accept *pronams* from all of us. Please reply to this letter if you feel like it. I do not feel confident enough to demand a reply. In case you do and in the hope that you will, I am giving my address below:

C/o. D.I.G., I.B., C.I.D.
13 Elysium Row
Calcutta

To Bivabati Bose[1]

The Great Durga be with us!

Mandalay Jail
11 September 1925

My dear Mejobowdidi,

I was delighted beyond measure to receive your letter. That you found my letter entertaining made me happy—because I feel concerned from time to time lest I should lose all sense of humour as a result of prolonged imprisonment. The *Shastras say: 'Raso bai sah'*, that is to say, God is but all-pervading delight. So, one who has lost his sense of humour, he has undoubtedly lost the cream of life—*Ananda*, or bliss; his life has then become worthless, devoid of happiness and full of misery. If my letters make you happy, I shall take it that I have not yet lost the power to bring

[1] Translated from the original Bengali.

happiness to others. The greatest in this world—for instance, Deshbandhu, Rabindra Nath Tagore and others—till very late in life or even till the last day of their lives—never lost their sense of humour and enjoyment. This is the ideal that we should emulate.

Never mind—let me now stop sermonising and start with my stories. We have had such an event here that when you hear about it you will perhaps think that I am narrating a novel or a drama. Our Malay was suddenly released and has left for home. He was sentenced to seven years and served about three and half years. According to the new government regulations, the long-term convicts may be released after serving half their sentence. According to this rule, news was received suddenly one day that Malay would be set free the next day. You may probably imagine the state of mind of a person who is yet to serve half his term but is suddenly informed that he will be released tomorrow. When all of a sudden the memories and images of such people come rushing into one's mind as one has not seen or heard of for ages and whom one did not expect to see for a long time—the person will probably become ecstatic with joy. We expected Malay would dance around in joy on receiving news suddenly of his release. But when he did not do so we could realise that he was completely overwhelmed. When asked how he felt he only said 'kaunde, kaunde', this is, 'good, good'.

The day prior to his release I called him to my side and asked to know all about his family. He told me that he had two wives, two daughters and three sons. One wife was childless. For a very long time, that is about four years, he has had no news of them. So, at the time of release he was so worried lest all was not well with them. Whether they were all alive or were all well—such thoughts remained dormant all this time. But as he was about to be set free, while on the one hand he was feeling happy to think of it, on the other hand all sorts of anxious thoughts were entering his mind. That is why he could not be over-enthusiastic even after being informed of his release.

Then, I made enquiries about the state of his properties and was told that he was a landowner in the countryside or a Raja. Formerly they were entirely independent and fought with the Rajas of Burma for independence. Subsequently they were subjugated by the British. Meanwhile, about seven years ago, they had a fight with the British for non-payment of taxes. In that fight, many lost their lives on both sides. Ultimately he accepted defeat and ran away. After being in hiding for nearly three years, he and his brother were captured with the connivance of a step-brother.

His brother was sentenced to transportation for life and he, Malay, got a prison term of seven years.

Thereafter Malay showed me quite a few scars on his body which were the result of injuries sustained in the battle. Thereupon we checked up on the history of Burma and found that what he said was indeed true. After his release I found out on enquiry from other prisoners of this country that not a word of what Malay told me was untrue.

When we knew that we made a sweeper of a village Raja, we felt ashamed. Eventually we asked him why he agreed to serve as a sweeper. He answered in great sorrow—'What could I do—such were the jail orders! Am I a human being here? I have been reduced to a dog. When I go out, I shall be a man again.'

After hearing his pitiful tale we asked him what he proposed to do in future. After considerable thought he said, 'I have not yet been able to decide anything. I do not know if my step-brother will again take a hostile attitude, because in my absence he was enjoying the estate. God forbid—there may still be lots of trouble in store for me.'

As he was leaving we asked him if he would forget us on reaching home. He replied in a choked voice—'I shall not forget your love as long as I live—and I shall talk about you to my children and grand-children.'

Now, will you tell me if the story sounds true or reads like a novel? There is a saying in English that truth is often stranger than fiction. This is it.

I have not been able to learn the Burmese language well—I have picked up enough to carry on ordinary conversation. Some among the Burmese know either English or Hindustani and we take their help in following Burmese. In spite of some difficulty we manage somehow on the whole.

Thanks to the tennis court we can have some physical exercise. Otherwise I would perhaps return home with arthritis. As it is, it appears as if there are signs of arthritis. Formerly we could play badminton. I had always taken badminton to be a ladies game and so never played it. But everything gets topsy-turvy in prison—so we went back to our boyhood days and started playing badminton. I cannot but admit that initially I felt somewhat embarrassed. But as the *Shastras* say—when honey is scarce, one should use molasses instead. So, in the absence of facilities for other games, we have to be content with playing badminton. All the time we have to be in a small jail inside the jail—there is no way of our mixing with anybody outside our ward. In most of the jails, the wards allotted to us have been just spacious enough to play badminton. There is a little more here so as to make tennis possible. Even so the trouble is that balls often fly over the walls and land outside. And the ones which do not go out hit against the walls and return to the court. Nevertheless, something is better than nothing.

There is no way of adding to the water in the pool. Because a little addition causes the water to overflow into the drain. And, from time to time we have to empty the pool and fill it with fresh water. In fact, there is no real reason for calling this a pool rather than a reservoir. But then, one can at least console himself that he is bathing in a pool.

Arrangements are being made here for Durga Puja. We hope we shall be able to worship the Mother here. But a quarrel is going on with the authorities regarding the expenses; let us see what happens. Please do not forget to send Puja clothing here—we have to spend *Bijoya Dashami* here after all.

Anything is available in our hotel. The other day the Manager fed us with hot *jilebis*—and we blessed him wholeheartedly praying he may ever remain in prison. Some time ago he entertained us with *rosogollas*; although the balls were floating in the syrup all right, they had no syrup inside and if you threw them at anybody, there was the risk of his head getting fractured. Nevertheless, we swallowed the hard-as-iron *rosogollas* without a tear and in gratitude prayed for the Manager's long life.

We being Bengalis, we have of course been cooking in Bengali style. The Manager has come to the conclusion that in this world, papaya is the queen of vegetables—and therefore papaya is everywhere, in the stew, in the curry, in pickles or anything else. And as our Manager is a half-doctor, he has given the verdict that the more you eat papaya, the better will be your digestion. To put it simply, it is a case of permutation and combination of the same common items. We cannot get the common items of Bengali cookery here. So, in case of vegetarian dishes here, it is papaya, egg-plant, spinach—egg-plant and papaya again. Thank God, I am used to eating mutton and chicken; I cannot but therefore praise the Manager's efforts—what would have happened otherwise is anybody's guess.

I shall be guilty of ingratitude if I did not mention that at our persistent request the Manager has given us *Dhonkar dalna, Chhanar kalya and Chhanar pulao.*[2] So, let us sing his praise. Let not even the scandal-mongers defame him!

[2] Bengali delicacies made with lentil paste and casine or cottage cheese.

You have asked about the garden. The garden here is in a miserable state. We planted some flowering seeds but thanks to ants and insects not much has grown. The few that survived, the chickens have finished them. As a result, what has remained of them are sunflower plants and one or two others of the same category. There are a few *Rajanigandhas*[3] but with hardly any scent. From time to time I miss scent and music. But what can one do?

Good tea is not available in this part of the world—so we have asked the dealer to order some from Calcutta. Lipton's and Brookebond's tea that is available here is undrinkable and imported from England. I wrote about mortar and pestle in my last letter. I need a good mortar and pestle for taking Kaviraji medicines. And, please ask Uncle Sailen to let me know the address of a good tea dealer. We drink the Orange Pekoe brand Darjeeling. We shall ask the local supplier to order tea from that particular dealer in Calcutta.

'Hilsa' fish of this place is most wonderful. It looks exactly like 'hilsa' from the Ganges. But in taste it has no resemblance whatever with 'hilsa' from Bengal or the Ganges. You cannot tell what fish you are eating. Apart from 'rohu' you cannot get any other good fish here. One can get prawns but the price is prohibitive.

I hope all is well at home. Where is Kanchi *Mama* now? How is he getting on in practice? Please ask *Mejdada* to remit the money I wanted. Will you be visiting our country home during the Pujas? What about my Financial Secretary? He is probably in Cuttack now. Have the marriages of Aruna and Gora been fixed up? How are *Bardidi* and her family? How is your health?

You have asked about my clothing. Do you not know that we are guests of the Emperor? How can we be in want of anything? If there be any, the prestige of the Emperor will be at stake! Is that at all possible?

You have asked about my health. Days pass somehow. There was a lot of discomfort during the summer and health deteriorated. I applied for a transfer but it was refused. The authorities may be thinking that I am pretending to be ill. Else, they may be taking me to be most ungrateful; the government is taking all the trouble of providing me with food and clothing free of charge and I, instead of being grateful, am pining for a transfer! Anyway, I do not wish for a transfer any more. The heat is less and so I am feeling better. If digestive troubles do not get worse, I expect to keep well during the Winter. We can see the palace of the King of

[3] White scented flower.

Burma from here—and we are confined in the prison that forms part of his fort. Often I am reminded of our past glory; and when I think of our present state, I can hardly restrain my tears. What India was—where is she today!

I have learnt a lot here and in that sense have gained a lot. Whatever God wills is all to the good. I have come to realise after coming here how deeply I love my country.

Please accept my *pronams*.

Yours
SUBHAS

To Dilip Kumar Roy[1]

Mandalay Central Jail
9 October 1925

My Dear Dilip,

Never think that my vision is narrow or parochial. I do, indeed, believe in the 'greatest good of the greatest number'. But that good I do not equate to the purely material. Economists say that all work is either productive or unproductive. But the question which of these are really productive gives rise to furious controversy. I for one cannot look upon art and its kindred activities as unproductive, nor despise philosophic contemplation or spiritual quest as futile and pointless. I may not be an artist myself—to tell you the truth, I know I am not—but for that it isn't I who am responsible, it is nature or God if you will. Of course if you say that I am reaping in this birth what I sowed in my last, then I go to the wall. Leaving it at that, the real reason, in a nutshell, why I did not shape into an artist is: I couldn't. But this does not mean, mind you, that a layman is debarred even from enjoying art. And the amount of training necessary to a proper appreciation of an art isn't, I think, hard to acquire for a cultivated person.

Do not sigh regretfully that you have been wasting your days on music when, to put it in Shakespeare's language, 'the time is out of joint'. Flood our whole countryside, my friend, with songs and recapture for life the spontaneous joy we have forfeited. He who has no music in his composition, whose heart is dead to music is unlikely to achieve anything big or great in life. Carlyle used to say that he who had no throb of music in his blood was capable of any misdeed. Whether this be true or no, I am

[1] Translated from the original Bengali.

persuaded that he who cannot respond to music can never scale heights of thought or action. We want that the experience of *ananda*—sheer causeless delight—should quicken every drop of our blood, because we only create in the fullness of *ananda*. And what is there that can elicit *ananda* like music?

But we must make the artistic and its kindred joys amenable to the poorest of the poor. High research in music will, of necessity, continue in small expert coteries, but simultaneously, music must be dispensed as a spiritual pabulum of the masses. Just as the high ideals of art are stultified through lack of adequate research, even so art must wilt when, sundered from the life-soul of the masses, it is made inaccessible to all and sundry. I think art joins up with life through folk-music and folk-dance. The Western civilisation has hewed away this isthmus between the two continents, of art and life, without substituting anything in its place. Our *jatra, kathakata, kirtan,*[2] etc., survive today almost as relics of the past. One shudders to think of the poverty of life that must ensue if our artists and musicians fail to restore the connection between art and life. You may remember I told you once how fascinated I had been by the beauty of the gambhira music of Maldah. In it music is happily blended with dance. I do not know of any other district in Bengal where such a happy union has been effected. But in Maldah it is sure to die away soon unless, first, new vitality be injected into it and, in the second place, people in other parts of Bengal come forward to take it up. You ought to visit the place once if only to give a fillip to the folk-music of Bengal. I warn you though that gambhira has little or no element of complexity or grandeur about it. Its salient features are spontaneity and simplicity. Our indigenous music and dance of the people still survive, I think, in Maldah alone. So those who would revive such folk-art may as well start work from there.

From the point of view of folk-music and folk-dance Burma is a marvellous country. Pure native dance and music are in full swing here and they cater for tens of thousands, zigzagging deep into the heart of remote villages. After having mastered the different idioms of our Indian music you may as well study the Burmese. It may not be an evolved art, but its capacity of delighting the illiterate poor has, somehow, appealed to me. I am told that their dance, too, is very beautiful. Furthermore, its art is not confined to select coteries, because, I imagine, there is no caste system in Burma (as a result art here has infiltrated everywhere). And probably also because folk-music and folk-dance have always had a

[2] Folk drama and devotional songs.

tremendous vogue in this country. So the common folk have warmed to a deeper understanding of beauty than the Indian.

I echo all you write about Deshbandhu as also your remark that the innate nobility of a man is revealed more through little private incidents of his life than through his public activities or political achievements caught in the lime-light. In fact I gave him my heart's deep devotion and reverent love not so much because I happened to be his follower in the arena of politics, as because I had come to know him rather intimately in his private life. He had no family, properly speaking, outside that of his colleagues and adherents. Once we lived together in jail for eight months: for two months in the same cell, for six in adjacent ones. I took refuge at his feet because I came to know him thus through a very close relationship.

I subscribe to most of what you write about Sri Aurobindo, if not to all. He is a *dhyani* (a contemplative) and, I feel, goes even deeper than Vivekananda, though I have a profound reverence for the latter. So I agree with you when you say that one may from time to time—and, on occasion, for a long spell—remain withdrawn in silent contemplation in perfect seclusion. But here there is a danger; the active side of a man might get atrophied if he remained cut off for too long from the tides of life and society. This need not, indeed, apply to a handful of authentic seekers of uncommon genius, but the common run, the majority, ought, I think, to take to action in a spirit of service as the main plank of their *sadhana*.[3] For a variety of reasons our nation has been sliding pauselessly down to the zero line in the sphere of action; so what we badly need today is a double dose of the activist serum, *rajas*.

I say ditto to you again when you say that each of us must strive to develop his powers to their fullness. Real service is only achieved when we dedicate what is the best in our composition. Not till our inner being, our *swadharma*, has fulfilled itself, shall we have won through to our inalienable right, *adhikar*, to what I call real service. To put it in the language of Emerson, we must be moulded from within. This does not mean that we all have to tread the same path, though it is possible that the same ideal may inspire us all. The artist's *sadhana* is not the same as the activist's, no more than the contemplative's *sadhana* is the same as the public servant's, though I think, in the last analysis, the ideals of all are one. But in the practical field of self-realisation I wouldn't put a round peg in a square hole. One who was true to oneself could hardly be false

[3] Sadhana originally, spiritual discipline, askesis: nowadays it has come to mean any disciplined endeavour for a high ideal.

to humanity. The nature of each must indicate the clue to the path that is his, the path that leads to his self-amelioration and self-expansion. If each of us could fulfil himself following his native capacity and temperament, then a new sunrise would occur over the entire life of the nation. It is, indeed, possible that a man may have to lead, during a particular phase of his *sadhana*, a life which looks on the surface like selfishness or egocentricism. But while he is passing through that phase he must follow the dictates of his own conscience—not those of public opinion. The public shall not judge till the results of the *sadhana* are published. Consequently, once you choose to tread the true path of self-expression you may well ignore public opinion. So you see we are much less at variance with each other than you seem to think.

Yours ever affectionately
SUBHAS

To Sarat Chandra Bose
Censored and Passed
Illegible
26.3.26
for D.I.G., I.B., C.I.D., Bengal

Mandalay
17 March 1926

. . . We had a very interesting though by no means a novel experience, a couple of days ago. The sun fell and the shades of evening descended upon us. But darker even than the evening tints, there rose skyward in the dim distant a dust storm so frequent in Mandalay in summer. Before the screens could be lowered, the dust like a moving canopy completely shrouded us. Not without difficulty, the screens were lowered but so high was the wind that they began to float in the air and served only to add to the music of the scene. The dust lay thick all over the room and not even the remotest corner was free from its touch. The wind persisted and tiles began to blow off the roof. The wooden structure began to croak much like a ship tossed about in a storm, sundry articles began to take wings. But the wrath of Heaven did not last long and the 'twice blest' drops of mercy soon began to fall from above. Philosophers say that God's mercy shines even in darkness. It was therefore meet that the merciful drops should fall in the dark. So, to complete the harmony of the situation the electric current conveniently failed and we were enveloped in what Milton would describe as 'Cimmerian darkness.' The lurid flashes of lighting served only to make the 'darkness visible' I am again using a Miltonic expression for is not saintly Milton as effective in his description of darkness as Shakespeare is sweet in his descriptions of fairy moonlight?) and to reveal to the more devoted the terrible beauty of the smile of Kali—the Queen of the Dark. (Chimmaya mukhamandale shobhe attaheshi)

Dust was soon overpowered but we and our slender belongings were rendered the sport of the wind and the rain. I remember to have read a description of rain at school as follows:

> Pitter, patter, pit, pat,
> Down the window-pane etc.

But there were no window-panes and, altogether ignoring the existence of palisades, the rains began to fall pit pat on us and drown our clothes. The wind suddenly turned and began to blow from the north—the side on which no screens at all had been provided. Bathed by the rain and chilled by the wind to our very bones, we nevertheless dared not move from our places lest we should stumble against tables and cots or strike other heads—and we could only keep up our spirits and add to the humour of the fray by exercising our throats and lungs. Darkness and confusion reigned supreme till light returned and the wind abated. And then what did we behold? Books drenched, clothes dripping and bedding moistened and, on the top of it all, a miniature rivulet flowing down the room. Heaven, to relieve our monotony, had planned to give us some novel work to do and for full two hours we were kept busy scrubbing the floor, drying up the water and wiping the books and furniture. The books and the clothing had no doubt a good night's rest after a refreshing bath but what about ourselves? There was the Chief Jailor whom we could hold responsible for the vagaries of the weather—and in fact for everything happening under the sun. And out went a peremptory order at ten o'clock at night for a supply of dry blankets and bed-sheets. That august person already unnerved by the inclement weather was well-nigh staggered—but he did not consider it wise to send a supply of 'brand new' jail-made blankets and from his own surplus store there came a number of decent sheets and blankets. Sympathy and warmth could not be too welcome at that hour of the night and praying for the blessings of the Lord we surrendered to the lock-up man as the clock struck eleven.

I am afraid I must stop here as I may be getting a touch of poetic affectation.

Yours very affectionately
SUBHAS

4

Deshbandhu Chittaranjan Das[1]

Mandalay Jail
20 February 1926

I do not feel confident enough to write anything publicly about the late Deshbandhu Chittaranjan Das. I do not think I shall ever be able to do so. My personal relations with him were of such a deep nature that I do not feel like talking about those things except with those who are most intimate with me. Moreover, he was so great and I consider myself so small in comparison that I have not yet been able to fully realise how versatile was his genius, how large was his heart, and how noble was his character. With my limited powers of head and heart and my poor language it would be impudent on my part to attempt to say anything about that great soul. But one has to do ever so many things at the request of friends although one might have neither the desire nor the ability to do so. In fact, I am making this humble attempt only at the request of my friend Srijut Hemendranath Das Gupta. It would make a volume if I were to write all that I have known about him from personal association, or if I were to attempt an analysis of his life and work as for as I could understand them. I have neither the capacity nor am I in a mood to write at any considerable length. I shall only say a few things in response to a friend's request.

I am not aware of a good many things regarding the Deshbandhu's chequered career. Perhaps I do not know even all the facts that have appeared in the biographies so far published. Only for the last three years of his life did I associate with him and worked as one of his followers. During this brief period I might have learnt a world of things from him; but one does not know how to value a thing so long as the thing is there. Particularly in the case of the Deshbandhu I had persuaded myself that

[1] A letter to Hemendra Nath Dasgupta. Translated from the original in Bengali—ed.

he would be living for a few more years and that he was not going to die till his earthly mission had been fulfilled. The Deshbandhu was a great believer in horoscopes. Although I was no believer in those things, still it would not be wholly correct if I were to say that I was not partially infected with his faith in his own horoscope. So far as I remember he had told me several times that he was destined to undergo two years' exile in a foreign land. On the termination of the period of exile he would return in fully glory. Government would come to an understanding with him and he would be installed a power; not till then would he die. I had told him at that time that I would be always willing to go into exile with him. To tell the truth, after my own exile I very often remembered the reading of his horoscope and was afraid lest he should have to come here too. But who knew then that far greater misfortune would befall Bengal, and, for that matter, the whole of India.

* * *

I had my last meeting with him in Alipore Central Jail. The Deshbandhu was not keeping well; he had gone to Simla for a few days' rest but came down to Calcutta immediately on receipt of the news of our arrest. He came twice to Alipore Central Jail to see me, and we met for the last time on the eve of my transfer to Berhampore Jail. At the end of the talk, I touched his feet and said, 'Perhaps it will be long before we meet again.' 'Oh, no,' he said in his characteristic cheerful voice, 'I am going to have you released very soon.' Alas, who knew then, I would not meet him again on this earth! Every little detail of that last meeting, every word that he had spoken made a deep impression on me and it will remain with me throughout my life. The memory of that last meeting is practically my only treasure in life.

Many have tried to find out the secret behind his tremendous hold on our masses. As one of the Deshbandhu's followers I would like to point out one thing which accounts for his great influence. I have seen how he could love people irrespective of their failings and shortcomings. His love came as a spontaneous flow from within his heart without ever taking into account the qualities or faults of the person concerned. He would easily draw towards him people whom we usually shun and hate. People of all kinds used to be attracted to him so that his influence extended to all spheres of life, like a whirlpool in the sea he could draw into his fold numerous people from all around. I know of numerous instances where people literally slaved for him. Even those who did not yield to his great learning, people who remained unimpressed by his eloquence, or even unmoved by his tremendous sacrifices, would yet feel the irresistible attraction of his great heart. His followers and co-workers had become like members of his own family. He could have staked everything for their good and welfare. Give your own life for others, and others will lay down their lives for you. This was exemplified in the life of the Deshbandhu. There was nothing his followers would not do for him. They would ungrudgingly go through any suffering and hardship for his sake. Of course, there was actually no occasion for sacrifice of life,[2] but barring that, it could be said of his followers that they gladly went through all kinds of sufferings for him and even felt proud to have done so. The Deshbandhu knew it very well that on his non-violent soldiers he could depend under all conditions. I feel proud to say that till the last day of his life these non-violent soldiers of his carried out his commands unflinchingly in the face of all risks and dangers.

This disciplined and fearless band of followers made some of our so-called leaders feel jealous of the Deshbandhu, although, I think, they themselves yearned to have a similar band of workers under them. But I do not think they were ready to pay the price for it. Unless you know how to love your followers how can you expect them to make sacrifices for you? The Deshbandhu never made any distinction, like ordinary men, between what was his own and what belonged to others. His house had become almost a public property. Everybody had free access everywhere—even to his bedroom, and all people had equal claims to his worldly possessions as well as on his generous heart. He not only loved his followers but was even prepared to court insults on their account. One day a near relation of his found fault with one of our workers on account of certain lapses on his part and said, 'I hate him.' The Deshbandhu was evidently hurt. 'Well, you may; but I don't hate him. That's my difficulty.' On many an occasion he quarrelled with outsiders on behalf of his co-workers. Several times this happened in my presence, and I saw how great was his love for his followers and how he courted insults for their sake.

Those who did not know the inside story used to be astonished at his tremendous power of organisation, and astonishing certainly it was, for what the Deshbandhu did was absolutely new in the field of Indian politics. The organisation that he had built up was solid as a rock, and I can say very definitely that at the root of it all was the bond of love that

[2] Satta workers actually died while engaged in Congress work in connection with Tarakeswar Satyagraha.

existed between the leader and his followers. With his immense capacity for loving people, irrespective of their merits or demerits, and by virtue of his extraordinary tact he succeeded in bringing together people of different tastes and different ways of thinking. Numerous people used to help him in private although they neither belonged to his party nor subscribed to his views.

Many of our so-called leaders have openly characterised the Deshbandhu's followers as being servile to him. I do not think anybody who was ever present at our discussion at the Deshbandhu's residence would corroborate this charge against us. How could I call those people servile in temperament when I found them expressing their views in a most fearless and outspoken manner during these discussions? Fierce differences of opinion arose between the leaders and the followers and not unoften wordy battles were fought. At times the Deshbandhu used to lose his temper; but he never really got displeased with an outspoken member of the party. On the contrary, we often felt he paid much too close an attention to a dissentient voice. Of course it was true that in spite of difference of opinion his followers never behaved in an indisciplined manner, nor did they ever in revenge launch an attack on the leader and subsequently join the enemy's camp. Difference of opinion there might be, but once the issue was decided by vote, the course adopted was to be followed by everybody. Loyalty to a party or to a community is no new thing in India. Indians first received this teaching from Lord Buddha two thousand five hundred years ago. Even to-day the following Buddhist prayer rings throughout the world:

> I dedicate myself to the Buddha;
> I dedicate myself to the Dharma;
> I dedicate myself to the Sangha.

In fact, no great undertaking, whether religious or political, is possible in this world without party organisation and party discipline.

I know of another charge brought against him. It has been said that moving as he did in the vortex of politics the Deshbandhu had to associate with people without education and culture. From 1921 till his death the Deshbandhu had come into contact with numerous workers. I do not know that he considered these people to be uneducated and uncultured. At least, he never gave any indication of it in his ordinary dealings with them. Free from vanity as he was, and exceedingly modest by nature, he might have successfully concealed his real feelings towards them. I have definite recollection of at least one incident. After his release from jail he was given a great ovation at a meeting organised by the students of Calcutta. In the address that was presented to him mention was made of his great qualities of head and heart and of his tremendous sacrifice for the cause of the country. The Deshbandhu was deeply touched by this spontaneous expression of love and affection by the youths of the nation. His was a spirit ever fresh and young. So the message of the youths easily touched the chords of his heart. When he rose for a reply to the address he was overwhelmed by his own feelings. Completely ignoring his own sacrifices and sufferings, he began to speak about the sacrifices of the youths of the country; but he could hardly proceed with the speech. Overpowered by emotion his voice was choked. He stood silent and motionless, and tears ran down his cheeks. The idol of the youths wept and the youths wept too.

I cannot imagine how he could consider those people unworthy of association for whom his love was so great and sympathies even greater.

Of course those who worked with the Deshbandhu and are still serving the cause he held dear, have no inflated notion of their own learning, or culture, or social status. I hope they will continue to be as humble and modest as they used to be.

The last letter I received from the Deshbandhu was written from Patna. That letter is my most treasured possession today. It gives a clear indication of his mental agonies caused by the wholesale arest of his trusted followers. How intense was his pain could be realised only by those who came into contact with this great-hearted man.

I had the privilege to be in the same jail with him for eight months in 1921–22. For a couple of months, we were in the Presidency Jail occupying two adjacent cells, and the remaining six months we were in one big hall along with several other friends in the Alipore Central Jail. During those few months I used to look after his personal comforts. We did the cooking too for him in Alipore Jail. I consider it a rare privilege to have had the opportunity of serving him for those eight months. Prior to my arrest in December 1921, I had worked under him only for three or four months. During that brief period, I had not had the opportunity of knowing him very intimately. But during the eight months I spent with him in jail I came to know him really well. There is a saying in English, 'familiarity breeds contempt,' but of the Deshbandhu, at least, I can safely say that having known him most intimately my love and admiration for him increased a hundredfold. I think many will bear me out what I say.

The Deshbandhu had an endless fund of humour and fun in him.

This came as a revelation to me during those jail-days. He used to keep us in excellent spirits by his incessant sallies of humour. In the Presidency Jail, a Gurkha soldier kept guard on us, bayonet in hand. One morning it was found that the Gurkha soldier was replaced by a Hindusthani sepoy with a baton in his hand. 'Well, Subhas', he called out, 'so, at last a flute replaces a sword. Do they really think, we are quite as harmless as that?' There was never any conscious effort in his humour. It flowed out as spontaneously as a mountain torrent. I want to refer specifically to this particular trait in his character, because I think that Bengalees as a race have not a very high sense of humour, in comparison with the other races of the world.

With a little sense of humour a man can keep up his spirits even under most adverse circumstances. You will fully realise the truth of this if you ever happen to be in the stifling atmosphere of a jail. The Deshbandhu's humour was of such simple and innocent type that it never made us feel ill at ease in spite of our difference in age and status.

He was vastly read in English and Bengali literature. Of the English poets, he was a great admirer of Browning, many of whose poems he knew by heart. In jail, we very often found him reading the works of Browning. His ordinary talk and even his jokes were interspersed with literary quotations so that sometimes I missed the point unless he explained things for me. He was forgetful about many things, but in matters literary his memory was prodigious. By introducing a literary flavour in his daily life he made literature an object of perennial interest—a thing to be enjoyed and appreciated by all.

Once the Deshbandhu borrowed a sum of Rs 10,000 at an interest of 9 p.c. from a certain relation of his. He could not repay the amount within the specified time, so the creditor's attorney came to see him to get the hand-note renewed. The Deshbandhu was then in Alipore Jail, and we were with him. His son Chitranjan too was there. He told us that nobody in the family was aware of that particular debt. The relative for whom he had borrowed the money was now worth several lacs; but the Deshbandhu readily put his signature to a new bond. There had been numerous cases in which he incurred debts for others without the knowledge of his wife and children.

I have seen people who never lost an opportunity of speaking ill of the Deshbandhu, though running to him for help in times of difficulty. One of those people once came for a loan of Rs 200. The Deshbandhu said, 'I have got only Rs 600 with me, how can I give you Rs 200?' But the gentleman insisted, and our Deshbandhu at once gave him the money without further argument. This happened after his release from jail.

During the eight months I spent with him, I had the occasion to know him thoroughly well, but never did I notice either in his speech or action one single thing that smacked of pettiness. He had numerous opponents in the field of politics; but he never had any grievance against them; on the contrary, he was always ready to help them if his help were needed.

His time in jail was mostly spent in studies. With the intention of writing a book on the national problems of India he had ordered a large number of books on politics and economics. Sufficient materials were collected and he had started writing the book but could not finish it while in jail. Once he was out, he found himself in the midst of ceaseless activities and never could finish the work he had set his hands to. During those days, I used to have long discussions with him about our political and national problems. In no sphere of life—whether it were politics, economics or religion—was he ever in favour of following set doctrines. It was his belief that our society, our politics, and our philosophy would in the natural course be evolved out of our cultural heritage and our pressing national problems. Hence he could never countenance any struggle or conflict between classes and communities. In this respect he was opposed to the doctrines of Karl Marx. Till the last day of his life it was his hope that all our differences could be resolved by concluding pacts between different religious communities, so that all Indians, irrespective of race, caste and creed, would come forward to join the fight for Swaraj. Many used to ridicule his idea of bringing about unity through pacts. Unity, they said, depended on real sympathy for each other; it could not possibly come through bargaining. The Deshbandhu used to argue that human society itself was based on pacts and compromises, and that man could not last a day on this earth without mutual understanding. Whether it be in family life, in friendly circles, in community life, or in the political field, men could not possibly live as social beings unless they came together in a spirit of compromise though possessing different tastes and views. All over the world trade and commerce are carried on through pacts and contracts. The question of love and affection does not come in there.

I do not think that among the Hindu leaders of India, Islam had a greater friend than in the Deshbandhu. Still it was this Deshbandhu who came forward to lead the Satyagraha movement at Tarakeswar. Hinduism was extremely dear to his heart; he could even lay down his life for his religion, but at the same time he was absolutely free from dogmatism of any kind. That explains how it was possible for him to love Islam. Let me ask, how many of our Hindu leaders can declare on oath that they do not hate the Muslims? On the other hand, how many of the Muslim leaders can likewise say that they do not hate the Hindus? In religious belief, the Deshbandhu was a Vaishanavite; but people of all faiths had a place in his large heart. We might settle our disputes through pacts but he did not believe that that was the only means of securing cordial relations between the Hindus and Muslims. It was his intention, therefore, to bring about a lasting Hindu-Muslim entente through a kind of cultural synthesis. While in jail, he used to have frequent discussions with Maulana Akram Khan regarding the points of affinity between the two cultures. If I remember aright, Maulana Sahib had agreed to write a treatise on the cultural unity between the two great communities.

That Swaraj in India meant primarily the uplift of the masses, and not necessarily the protection of the interest of the upper classes, was a matter of conviction with the Deshbandhu. I cannot think of any other front-rank leader of our country preaching that doctrine with as much emphasis as he did. Swaraj for the masses is not a new thing in the world. Europe preached this doctrine long ago; but it is comparatively new in the field of Indian politics. Of course, thirty years ago Swami Vivekananda spoke in that vein in his book entitled 'Bartaman Bharat', but that message of the Swamiji was never echoed from our political platforms.

The things which the Deshbandhu went on preaching ever since his release till the last day of his life had been deeply pondered over by him while he was in prison. Sometimes he used to discuss those things with us. The question of entering the Councils was decided upon there, and only after prolonged discussions could he win us over to his point of view. There was a good deal of party wrangling inside the jail over this controversial issue. The idea of bringing out a daily paper in English was also mooted there. Unfortunately, some of his most cherished wishes are yet to be fulfilled.

I cannot help mentioning another thing in connection with his jail life—his love for the convicts. When we were in Alipore Jail, a convict named Mathur used to work in our ward. Mathur was what in jail language is called a Purano Chor (old thief). Perhaps it would be wrong to call him a mere thief, he was a dacoit. He had eight or nine previous convictions. But like many more of his class he was otherwise a very simple-hearted person. After working for a few days Mathur grew very attached to the Deshbandhu, and he started calling him 'father'. The Deshbandhu, too, grew very fond of him. Gradually this man was drawn towards us all. As he sat massaging his feet, Mathur used to tell him the story of his life. Before his release the Deshbandhu asked Mathur to come to his house after he was set free, and never again take to dacoity. Mathur was really glad to hear this and promised not to revert to his old ways of life.

On the day Mathur was released the Deshbandhu sent a man to the jail gate to bring him home. Mathur was with him for three years. As his personal servant, he travelled from one end of India to the other. Being an old convict he was for sometime shadowed by the police. But they left watching him when they found he had actually taken sanctuary with the Deshbandhu. The policemen used to say, 'Ah, the Deshbandhu has made a man of this wretch.' I had expected that Mathur would never again go astray; but when after the Deshbandhu's death I made enquiries in one of my letters about Mathur I was informed that during the Deshbandhu's stay in Darjeeling he ran away with a large number of silver plates and dishes from the Russa Road residence. This strange story reminded me of Les Miserables. I still believe, if Mathur were all the time with the Deshbandhu, he would have by no means fallen a prey to temptation. He must have committed the theft under a momentary impulse of weakness but, I am sure, if the great man were living to-day Mathur would again return to him in tears, and throw himself at his feet. God alone knows what will now happen to Mathur.

Everyone will wonder how a man can at once be a big lawyer, a great lover of men, a devout Vaishnava, a shrewd politician, and a conquering hero. I have tried to get a solution of this problem through anthropological studies. I do not know if I have succeeded in my attempt. The present-day Bengalee race is an admixture of Aryan, Dravidian and Mongolian blood. Each race has some peculiar characteristics of its own. Hence, when there is an admixture of blood, there must be an admixture of racial characteristics too. Due to this admixture of blood the genius of the Bengalee is so versatile and Bengal's life so colourful. The religiosity and idealism of the Aryans, love of art and devotionalism of the Dravidians, intellectuality and realism of the Mongolians have all very happily blended together in the Bengalee character. That the Bengalees are intellectual and emotional at the same time, at once realistic and idealistic, imitative and creative is due to this admixture of blood. If the blood of a particular race runs through your veins you must have imbibed from birth some characteristics, something from the culture of that race.

Those acquainted with Bengal's history and literature will admit that in spite of its belonging to Aryan culture, the culture of Bengal has assumed a distinct form of its own. Swami Dayanand's Arya Samaj movement swept the whole of Northern India, but how was it that he could not get any footing on the soil of Bengal? And why do thousands of educated Bengalees adore and draw inspiration from Ramkrishna Paramhansadeva, the devotee of the goddess Kali? Why does the system of Dayabhaga prevail in Bengal? Why did Buddhism, driven out from everywhere, find its last refuge in Bengal? Why did Navanyaya, or New-logic, originate in Bengal? Why did not Bengal accept Shankara's Mayavada? Why, after Buddhism was ousted from Bengal, did Achintya-Bhedabhedavada rise up as a protest against Shankara's theory? No sooner do we raise these questions than it begins to be clear that Bengal's culture has something uncommon and unique about it. On its cultural side three strains are visible: (1) Tantra, (2) Vaishnavism and (3) Navanyaya and Raghunandan's Smriti. On the side of Nyaya and Smriti, Bengal has a close kinship with Aryavarta; through Vaishnavism she maintains a life-line with the south, while through the tantras she has a relationship with the races living in the Tibetan, Burmese and Himalayan regions.

The pursuit of Nyaya has helped the Bengalee to be logical and argumentative. It was this racial characteristic in the Deshbandhu which had made him a formidable barrister. The logician and the advocate both are dealers in logomachy. I do not know if he had ever studied the ancient Nyaya systems of India, but he was well grounded in Western logic. He could argue like some great Nyaik Pundit and had also the gift of devastating his opponents by torrents of eloquence. I have no doubt that he would have been a famous logician had he been born a few centuries earlier in Nabadwipa.

It was Bengal's Vaishnavism and Dvaitadvaitavada (a form of qualified Monism) that saved him from agnosticism, and through dry Vedanta led him finally to the path of Love. As a philosophical doctrine he accepted Achintya-Bhedabhedavada as the most genuine one. Though in many ways an ascetic, asceticism was not a part of his religion. God and His Lila (Creation, Doings) are equally true; the world is not false because God is true. So in order to attain God there is no need of annulling the world of the senses. God's Lila is eternal and its stage is not only in the world outside but also in the heart of man. Man's soul is an eternal Vrindaban[3] and there the Lila of God with His Jiva (created being), of Krishna with Radha, is for ever and ever. He is the Lord of

[3] The name of the place of Krishna's Lila in the traditional story.

Delight and He is enjoyed and approached through all that is delightful. It is obvious that a man who holds such views cannot be a negativist. Indeed the Deshbandhu had accepted the world and the human life in its fullest. He believed that with the help of Dvaitadvaitavada all the contradictions of life could be resolved and harmony attained. That is why Vaishnavism became the last refuge of his life. In his conversations and lectures he would often point out that he should not view politics, economics, philosophy and religion in isolation. They are intimately related to one another and our life would miss its completeness if we left out any of these.

The philosophy which had thus resolved the conflicts of his religious strivings, had also succeeded, in its practical aspect, in establishing a relationship of love and friendliness with all and sundry. As he had achieved a synthesis in life, in the sphere of action also he could unite men of various tastes and temperaments. Since there was nothing false, nor a sham, in his own make-up, he could never stand such a thing in others.

If, in the course of our discussions in jail, we ever referred to his indiscriminate generosity, he would at once retort by saying, 'You think I am an utter fool and that people cheat me. Well, I know everything; it is my duty to give, and I do that. It will be for Him to judge, not me.'

It was the influence of the Tantras which have taught the Bengalees to worship Shakti, or Power, and that must have made the Deshbandhu a hero of extraordinary prowess. Of course, he had never done any Sadhana (religious practices) of the Tantric school—at least I know of none. But I do not accept that one cannot be strong unless one does such Sadhana as Kulachar, Virachar, Chakranusthan, etc. The essence of the Tantras is the worship of power. According to them, the ultimate reality is Adya Shakti (Basic Power), that which creates, upholds, and destroys, that is Brahma, Vishnu, Maheswar. The devotee worships that Basic Power in the image of the Mother. It is because of the deep influence of the Tantras that the Bengalees as a race are devoted to mother, and this is also the reason why they love to worship the Supreme Being in the image of the Mother. People of other races and religions (such as the Jews, the Arabs, the Christians) worship God as father. Sister Nivedita thinks that in those communities, in which men occupy a more important position than women, people naturally contemplate God as father. On the other hand, in societies where women have precedence over men, people learn to worship God as Mother. Anyway, it is well known that the Bengalees love to think of God—and why God alone, even Bengal and India—as Mother. We think of our country as Motherland, but the correct English expression is Fatherland, and our use of 'Motherland' is rather faulty from the point of view of English usage.

Most of our great writers afford illustrations of this mother-cult in their writings.

Bankim wrote:

> Hail O Mother;
> Well-watered, fruitful, cooled by the western breeze
> Green with crops, O Mother;

Dwijendralal sang:

> When Mother India emerged out of the blue waters of the Sea.

And Rabindranath sang:

> Oh my mother-land let me lay my head at your feet.

The above instances reveal the influence of the Tantric conception of the Mother. The Deshbandhu was a votary of the mother-cult. In family-life his devotion to his mother is quite well known. In Alipore Jail he used often to give us readings from Bankim Chandra. He was extremely fond of the three different images of the mother as painted by Bankim. He used to go into ecstasies over these descriptions. One could easily feel the depth of his emotions to see him in that state of ecstasy. His journal 'Narayana' contained discussions on both Vaishnavism and Saktism. The few articles on Durga Puja published in that journal are fuil of profound thoughts.

The influence of the Tantras is apparent even in his daily life. Everyone knows of his great reverence for his mother and his belief in women's education and their emancipation. He did not at all accept the view of the Sankarites that women are the gateway to hell. Both in his thoughts and practical life we see the influence of the Tantras in the most pronounced form. In the Deshbandhu were embodied the finest elements of Bengal's culture and tradition.

Both his virtues and failings were peculiar to the race he belonged to. The greatest pride in his life was that he was a Bengalee. That was why he was so much loved and adored by the Bengalees.

He often used to say that what makes the Bengalee is a compound of his good and bad points. He felt wounded if any one made fun of or satirized the Bengalees as being emotional. It was, he thought, a matter of pride, and not of shame, that we are susceptible to emotions.

That Bengal has a certain distinction, which has expressed itself in her landscape, her literature, her folk-songs and her character. I do not think that any one before the Deshbandhu had expressed with such emphasis. True, these ideas were not his own. Thinkers like Bankim, Bhudev and others had initiated them in the fields of culture and literature and the Deshbandhu followed their lead. All the same, I am bound to admit it was through his deep realisation of these tendencies, and for his attempt in the pages of the 'Narayana,' and through other means to spread these ideas, as well as for the money and labour he spent on original research in these subjects, that the Bengalees must always remain grateful to him. I for myself can say that it was from him and his writings that I have learnt about this uniqueness of Bengal.

The question has been raised if culture is one or diverse. There are those who say that they are one and without difference—these are the Monists. There are others who think that culture includes racial characteristics, hence there will be difference of cultures—these are the Dualists. But the Deshbandhu was Dualist-cum-Monist. Culture is both one and many. Even if it is basically one, it is through the utmost variety and multiplicity that unity expresses itself. As there are many trees in a garden and various flowers bloom on the different trees, in the same manner does human society develop different cultures. And as the garden is complete with its many trees and flowers, so does a number of cultures make the Culture of Man. Thus every race developing its own culture also develops the culture of mankind. It is not possible to serve humanity at large by leaving aside or by neglecting one's own national culture. The fulfilment of the Deshbandhu's nationalism was in international amity; but he did not try to develop a love of the world by doing away with love for his own land. Yet his nationalism did not lead him to exclusive egocentricity.

In his love for the nation the Deshbandhu would not forget Bengal, nor in loving Bengal would be forget the nation. He loved Bengal with all his life, but the love was not confined to the four corners of the province. I have it from his non-Bengalee colleagues that within a few days of their coming to know him, they were attracted by his great heart. The Maharashtrians loved and respected him with the same ardour as they did Tilak Maharaj, for the people of Maharashtra too received from him equal sympathy and affection.

The Deshbandhu used to say that Bengal should be the vanguard of the Swaraj movement. In 1920, Bengal had lost her lead of the movement. But thanks to his untiring efforts and labour, in 1923 she won it back. With the death of the Deshbandhu that lead has again been lost for Bengal. God alone knows when she will recover that position.

Another frequent statement of his was that if any Indian movement has to be worked in Bengal it must have the stamp of Bengal on it. If satyagraha has to be launched in Bengal it must first be made suitable for the province. Those who have intimate experience of actual conditions as they prevail cannot but endorse this opinion.

Everyone has wondered at his strange influence over the masses and even with the so-called rich class. Some have tried to analyse it to get at its secret. Whenever he adopted a course of action he made it real. The mantra, 'Either I succeed in my resolve or I perish', was engraved on his heart. Whatever path he would choose he would pursue it with unabated vehemence and none could stop him. Like the mounting sea waves, he would rush after his ideals, driven by his own force, drowning all dangers and difficulties. The wails of the dear ones, or the words of caution of his followers, were powerless to call him back. From where did he receive this Divine Power? Is this 'Sakti' to be had by true efforts, or 'Sadhana'?

I have already said that in spite of being a devotee of 'Sakti', the Deshbandhu had never worshipped Power according to the Tantric rites. He was large-hearted and his aspirations were immense. 'In the Great alone is bliss, what is small cannot give happiness'—this was, so to speak, his soul's message. Whatever he desired, he desired with all his life, mind and utterance. He would go mad over it. The utmost impediments were unable to frighten him or force him to withdraw. Like Napoleon Bonaparte who, seeing the Alps standing before him, had said, 'There shall be no Alps,' the Deshbandhu also wholly ignored difficulties and obstructions. All those who know with what little capital he had launched on the publication of the 'Forward,' and of his attempts to capture the Council, will bear this out. If we ever spoke of difficulties he would scold us as incorrigible pessimists. It had also become my task to bring up before him the risks and dangers; so he would often refer to us as 'You young old men'. Those who think that the Deshbandhu was a moderate by conviction, but in the company of and under pressure from young people acted as an extremist, do not know his temperament and character. In fact he was ever new and youthful—he had an instinctive understanding of the hopes and aspirations of the youth. He could sympathise with them in their joys and sorrows. He liked the company of the young, and they too did not like to part company with him. It is for all this that I have elsewhere called him the King of the Youth.

His countrymen know of his sacrifices, his vast erudition, his tact, and like things—there is little to be said on these scores.

I will end this letter after I have mentioned another reason for the extraordinary influence which he wielded. I have hinted at it earlier. It was the Deshbandhu's constant experience that through all his actions he had succeeded in establishing Vaishnavism which was very much part of his religious life. Thanks to a fine synthesis between his ideal and his practical life, his entire being was getting progressively saturated with this synthesis. Thanks to this, he came to look upon himself as merely an instrument of God's world-play. As a result of inner purity, which follows the pursuit of action without caring for results, man loses the awareness of the ego. And when the ego is transcended he becomes an instrument for the expression of the Divine Will. Then ordinary human beings cannot withstand the energy and magnetism of a person so inspired. That is what had happened with the Deshbandhu; towards the end of his life, even his fiercest opponents, when they were face to face with him, seemed to collapse. The conviction was also growing on his countrymen that wherever Mr Das would be, victory also would be there as a matter of course.

People do not probably know how he had tried to get work done by people of so many different types. These will be known only when his inspiration will have borne fruit. The inspiration from ideals was ever his, and all those who came in contact with him were equally energized. Whatever the occasion, in life as in death, asleep or awake, the Deshbandhu had one thought, one dream—service to the nation, and that service was a step in his religious striving.

If in speaking of the Deshbandhu's life we forget to mention another person—his wife—then little will have been said. That goddess, embodying service and serenity, removed from public gaze, always stood by his side like a shadow, if we leave her out of account a good deal is then left out of the Deshbandhu's life. She who, in the height of luxury had never forgotten the Hindu ideals of feminine modesty, humility and service, who amidst the deep gloom of danger had never failed to render the support of a devoted wife, always holding up the ideal of faith and equanimity—in speaking of that goddess my language fails me. The Deshbandhu was King of the Youth. His devoted helpmate was their mother. After the Deshbandhu's death she is not merely Chiraranjan's mother. The highest offering of the Bengalee heart is laid at her sacred feet.

In the course of his defence of Sri Aurobindo in the Alipore case, the Deshbandhu had said in rich and powerful language:

'He will be looked upon as the poet of patriotism, the prophet of nationalism, and the lover of humanity. His words will be echoed and re-echoed. . . .'

Do not these words apply, to-day, to the Deshbandhu himself?

5
Bengal's Spiritual Quest*

Kelsall Lodge, Shillong
17 July 1927

Revered mother,

I received your letter of the 10 July on the 13th inst. I did not write to you as I had promised—the fault is therefore mine and I hope to be forgiven. If a man accepts certain relationships, certain responsibilities also come upon him automatically and it is wrong for him not to fulfil those responsibilities. So there is no doubt that I am at fault.

You often say and sometimes even write: 'my company cannot bring joy any more to anyone in this world'. This is not at all true. Don't you know with what reverence the youth of Bengal (not mentioning others for the sake of argument) look up to you even today? Is it not an injustice to them for you to consider them 'outsiders'? Have they not offered at your feet the best in themselves? How they had hoped that when Deshbandhu left this world, you would come forward and take up their leadership! When their hope was not fulfilled, where could they contain their immeasurable sorrow and disappointment? In his time Deshbandhu used to say that you might not openly participate in public work so long as he was alive, but in his absence you would fill the void left by him.

Perhaps you will say that a Hindu woman's duty lay within the limits of her family—behind the scenes and not on the public platform. I do not have the impudence to offer advice as to the duties of my mother. But I think this is not a normal phase in the life of our country and society. Mother, today our house is on fire. When the house is on fire, even a woman observing *purdah* has to take courage in both hands and come out on the street. She has to work as hard as a man to save her child, to protect valuable property from fire. Does that detract from her prestige or grace?

*Excerpts of letters to Basanti Devi. Translated from the original Bengali.

The spiritual quest of Bengal has always been voiced through the cult of the Mother. Be it God or be it motherland—whatever we have worshipped we have done so in the image of the Mother. But alas! Today the menfolk of Bengal have become so impotent and cowardly that they are incapable of preventing the molestation of women that is going on in the districts of Bengal. The other day (several months ago) *Sanjeebani* wrote—'O Mother, you must take up arms yourself to protect your honour'. I was touched by these words. Indeed, the condition of our country today is very much so; what is more, most probably the mother will have to come forward to protect the honour of her children as well—the nation has become so degenerate and cowardly.

Sometimes I have the feeling that if you could occupy yourself with various public welfare activities, that would perhaps at least partially lessen the agony of your mind. Is it proper that our life should be entirely controlled by domestic weal and woe? You were an Empress once; today you are a pauper in the material sense. Whoever thinks about it cannot but feel a pang in his heart. But we have this consolation that from time immemorial the people of India have considered the glory of renunciation to be greater and more covetable than the fortunes of a king. Perhaps you are not even aware how high you have risen in the estimation of your countrymen because of your background of glorious renunciation.

I do not know whether it is childish on my part to say all this to you; my only justification is that the deep sorrow that afflicts you also haunts me now and then—may be to a lesser degree; and it will be no exaggeration to say that so does it affect countless young men of Bengal.

You wrote in your previous letter—'everything in my cursed life has come to an end. Now there is nothing else for me but to wait patiently for the final end. I do not know how many ages must pass before I reach my fulfilment'.

I am afraid due to excessive brooding you sometimes forget where your place is in the hearts of your countrymen and in our hearts. Had you not forgotten this, you could never have described your life as 'cursed' despite these terrible domestic disasters? Those whom the God loves are victims again and again of sorrow and disaster. Is this absolutely untrue? And the bigger a man's heart the more he gets his share of sorrow—is this also entirely untrue? Please fulfil our hopes and desires—your place shall always remain secure in the hearts of your countrymen. The devotion, the respect, the affection that the people of your country have offered at your feet—and are still offering and will continue to offer—could any so-called fortunate man expect even a tenth of it. Deshbandhu has left us with many of his hopes and dreams unfulfilled. Those dreams of his are his best legacy. You have also inherited that legacy along with us. So, can you honestly declare that your work is done and the time has come for you to quit? It would be impudent of me to say so but still I wish to say that your God will never support your stand but rather support me.

You have written 'it is here that my soul has a perfect union with mute nature. I like this dense, impenetrable darkness'. Perhaps, nowadays you like darkness all he time—well, everyone likes darkness at least now and then. If you love darkness can't you also love the light that lies hidden in darkness? What is wrong with that? The light is meant to make everybody happy, by bringing the glow of happiness.

Perhaps you do not wish to have any bonds—be they of work or of human relationship. But we have no other way. The day we called you 'mother' we accepted the relationship. This bond is not to be severed—at least not in our lifetime. In this material world there are narrowness, obstacles, social obligations—but in spite of all this, kinship of the spirit can never be false.

Man hankers for a corner in his life where there will be no arguments, no critical judgment, no intelligent appraisal but only 'Blind Worship'. That explains the creation of 'mother'. I pray to God I may go on worshipping 'mother' in this spirit. . . .

Devotedly yours
SUBHAS

Kelsall Lodge, Shillong
30 July 1927

Revered mother,

In my previous letter out of impudence I had tried to enlighten you about your duties. You have affectionately forgiven my childishness. I have more than my share of impudence, otherwise how could I aspire to achieve the impossible? After all, we are a pack of vagabonds.

It is not because of our lack of self-confidence that we are still looking up to our mother. We have enough self-confidence, perhaps a little too much. Still why do we want our mother? The reason is that no worship is complete if we leave the mother out. In our social history, whenever we have faced danger and misfortune we have invoked the Mother. We have created the image of the Mother with all that was best in our being. Our national struggle began with the song 'Bande Mataram' (salutations to the Mother). That is why we are calling upon our mother in this manner. But will not the heartless image respond?

As I am proclaiming to myself that I am a son of the mother—bless me so that I may not do anything that will sully the name of my mother. I do not have the impertinence to declare that I shall be a worthy son of the mother. My path is full of thorns—bless me so that I may march on in the same way till the last. May my life not wither away in the desolation of *Sannyasa*; may my life blossom forth in beneficent fulfilment with the touch of the inspiration that is behind this desolation—I crave for this blessing. Need I say how I value your blessings?

Looked at from one point of view there is no limit to my impudence; on the other hand I am always troubled by the thought of my unworthiness. It is not an imaginary conflict—it is very real. I always pray to God—'Grant your chosen one the strength to carry your banner'. Still, sometimes I get apprehensive that I may not be able to give to the country what she expects of me. I am afraid that my boat may sink in midstream—that my attempt may turn out to be like that of a dwarf trying to reach up to the moon! Would you not give me a word of assurance?

There is something else I wish to say—I have been trying to say this for some time but I could not. Your son has a duty and a right. Shall I always be deprived of my right to serve you? Shall I forever remain an 'outsider' to you? In this vast world, is the narrow family circle created by man the greatest truth? You have much to give—your country is still waiting for that. It is not an idea manufactured in my brain—it is the voice of your country. But whether you'll give your due or not depends on you. If the country does not get what it expects to get, the country is unfortunate, what more can I say?

You have written—'The trends of thought and the line of action cannot be the same for the old and the young'. True, but many old people can be found among the so-called young and among the so-called old, a number of youthful people. If the youth consider you to be one of them, if they wish to bestow their leadership on you—what objection can you have to that?

The question I put to you in Calcutta has been solved. The answer is that if you do not accept our leadership there is no one else in Bengal whom we can accept from our heart as the leader. If someone is invited to be the chairman of a meeting he does not necessarily become the leader. There are many such leaders in Bengal. But a real leader—to whom one's heart bows down with reverence is rare in Bengal today. If we do not get you, then this pack of vagabonds will have to fend for themselves. Your blessings will undoubtedly be a priceless thing for us but we want a little more than that. . . .

Devotedly yours
SUBHAS

6

Democracy in India

Presidential Address at the
Maharashtra Provincial Conference, Poona, 3 May 1928

Friends, I thank you from the bottom of my heart for the high honour you have done me by requesting me to preside over the deliberations of the Sixth Session of the Maharashtra Provincial Conference. You are probably aware that I did not at first venture accept the kind invitation, but by referring to the old relations between Bengal and Maharashtra some of my friends touched a most tender chord in my heart. The appeal then proved to be irresistible and every other consideration had to stand aside.

Before I proceed to place before you my view with regard to our present policy and programme, I would like to raise some fundamental problems and attempt to answer them. It is sometimes urged by foreigners that the new awakening in India is entirely an exotic product inspired by alien ideals and methods. This is by no means true. I do not for one moment dispute the fact that the impact of the West has helped to rouse us from intellectual and moral torpor. But that impact has restored self-consciousness to our people, and the movement that has resulted therefrom and which we witness today is a genuine Swadeshi movement. India has long passed through the traditional period of blind imitation—of reflex action, if you put it in psychological language. She has now recovered her own soul and is busy reconstructing her national movement along national lines and in the light of national ideals.

I agree with Sir Flinders Petrie that civilisations, like individuals grow and die in a cyclical fashion and that each civilisation has a certain span of life vouchsafed to it. I also agree with him that, under certain conditions, it is possible for a particular civilisation to be reborn after it has spent itself. When this rebirth is to take place, the vital impetus, the elan vital, comes not from without but from within. In this manner has Indian civilisation been reborn over and over again at the end of each cycle, and that is why India in spite of her hoary antiquity is still young and fresh.

The charge has often been levelled against us that since democracy is an Occidental institution, India, by accepting democratic or semi-democratic institutions, is being Westernised. Some European writers—Lord Ronaldshay for instance—go so far as to say that democracy is unsuited to the oriental temperament and political advancement in India should not, therefore, be made in that direction. Ignorance and effrontery could not go further. Democracy is by no means a Western institution; it is human institution. Wherever man has attempted to evolve political institutions, he has hit upon this wonderful institution of democracy. The past history of India is replete with instances of democratic institutions. Mr K.P. Jayaswal in his wonderful book, 'Hindu Polity', has dealt with this matter at great length and has given a list of 81 republics in ancient India.

The Indian languages are also rich in terminology required in connection with political institutions of an advanced type. Democratic institutions still exist in certain parts of India. Among the Khasis of Assam, for instance, it is still the custom to elect the ruling chief by a vote of the whole clan; and this custom has been handed down from time immemorial. The principle of democracy was also applied in India in the government of villages and towns. The other day while visiting the Varendra Research Society Museum at Rajshahi in North Bengal, I was shown a very interesting copper-plate inscription in which it was stated that civic administration in the good old days was vested in a committee of five, including the Nagar Sreshthi (i.e. our modern Mayor). With regard to village self-government, it is not necessary to remind an Indian audience about the village Panchayats—democratic institutions handed down to us from days of yore. Not only democratic but other socio-political doctrines of an advanced character were not unknown to India in the past.

Communism, for instance, is not a Western institution. Among the Khasis of Assam, to whom I have referred, private property as an institution does not exist in theory even today. The clan as a whole owns the entire land. I am sure that similar instances can still be found in other parts of India and also in the past history of our country.

I think it necessary at this stage to warn my countrymen, and my young friends in particular, about the attack that is being made on nationalism from more than one quarter. From the point of view of cultural internationalism, nationalism is sometimes assailed as narrow, selfish and aggressive. It is also regarded as a hindrance to the promotion of internationalism in the domain of culture. My reply to the charge is that Indian nationalism is neither narrow, nor selfish, nor aggressive. It is inspired by the highest ideals of the human race, viz., Satyam (the true), Shivam (the good), Sundaram (the beautiful). Nationalism in India has instilled into us truthfulness, honesty, manliness and the spirit of service and sacrifice. What is more, it has roused the creative faculties which for centuries had been lying dormant in our people and, as a result, we are experiencing a renaissance in the domain of Indian art.

Another attack is being made on nationalism from the point of view of international labour or international Communism. This attack is not only ill-advised but unconsciously serves the interests of our alien rulers. It would be clear to the man in the street that before we can endeavor so reconstruct Indian society on a new basis, whether socialistic or otherwise, we should first secure the right to shape our own destiny. As long as India lies prostrate at the feet of Britain, that right will be denied to us. It is, therefore, the paramount duty not only of nationalists but anti-nationalistic Communists to bring about the political emancipation of India as early as possible.

I have already hinted that I plead for a coalition between labour and nationalism (I am using 'labour' here in a wider sense to include the peasants as well). It has to be admitted that though we have passed resolutions from the Congress platform time and again regarding the desirability of organising labour, much has not been achieved in that direction.

If we view the programme of the Congress during the last few years we shall find that only in our Khadi programme have we been able to offer to our masses something which means bread and butter to them. Khadi, I am glad to say, has brought food to thousands and thousands of hungry mouths all over India. Given money and organisation there is plenty of scope for pushing on Khadi. There are lakhs and lakhs of poor Indians living on the verge of starvation to whom Khadi can offer a means of subsistence, but the appeal of Khadi cannot be universal. We find from bitter experience in some parts of Bengal that as soon as the masses are a little better off, their Charkhas lie idle and that the peasant who gets a better return from paddy or jute cultivation refuses to cultivate cotton.

Except when Congressmen have joined the Kisan movement, as in the U.P. or have taken up the question of jute cultivation, as in Bengal, or have undertaken a campaign for nonpayment of taxes in order to resist illegal taxation or oppressive legislation, as in Gujarat, we have seldom been able to make a direct appeal to the economic interests of the masses. And until this is done—human nature being what it is—how can we expect the masses to join the freedom movement?

There is another reason why I consider it imperative that the Congress should be more alive to the interests of the masses. Mass consciousness has been roused in India, thanks to the extensive and intensive propaganda undertaken during the non-cooperation movement; and the mass movement cannot possibly be checked now. The only question is along what lines this mass consciousness should manifest itself. If the Congress neglects the masses it is inevitable that a sectional—and if I may say so, anti-national movement will come into existence and class war among our people will appear even before we have achieved our political emancipation. It would be disastrous in the highest degree if we were to launch class war while we are all bed-fellows in slavery, in order that we may afford amusement to the common enemy. I regret to say that there is at present a tendency among some Indian labourites to belittle the Congress and to condemn the Congress programme. This recrimination should cease and the organised forces of labour and of the Congress should join hands for furthering the economic interests of the masses and promoting the cause of India's political emancipation.

Friends, you will pardon me if for one moment I ask you to lift your eyes from the realities of the present and attempt to scan the future that looms before us. It is desirable that we should search our hearts in order to find out what it is that we are running after, so that we and our succeeding generations may grow up in the light of the ideal and shape our course of action accordingly.

Speaking for myself, I stand for an independent Federal Republic. That is the ultimate goal which I have before me. India must fulfil her own destiny and cannot be content with colonial self-government or Dominion Home Rule. Why must we remain within the British Empire? India is rich in resources, human and material. She has outgrown the infancy which foreigners have been thrusting upon her, and cannot only take care of herself but can function as an independent unit. India is not Canada or Australia or South Africa. Indians are an Oriental People, a coloured race, and there is nothing common between India and Great Britain from which we may be led to think that Dominion Home Rule within the British Empire is a desirable consummation for India. Rather, India stands to lose by remaining within the Empire. Having been under British domination so long, it may be difficult for Indians to get rid of the inferiority complex in their relations with England. It may also be difficult to resist British exploitation so long as we remain an integral part of the British Empire.

The usual argument that India without the help of Britain cannot defend herself is puerile. It is the Indian army—much more than the British army—which is defending India today. If India is strong enough to fight the battles of England outside her borders—in Tibet, China, Mesopotamia, Persia, Egypt and Flanders—she is certainly strong enough to defend herself from foreign aggression. Moreover, once India is able to free herself, the balance of power in the world will save India, as it has saved China. And if the League of Nations becomes a living organisation with some sanction behind it, invasion and aggression will be a thing of the past.

While striving to attain liberty we have to note all its implications. You cannot free one half of your soul and keep the other half in bondage. You cannot introduce a light into a room and expect at the same time that some portion of it will remain dark. You cannot establish political democracy and endeavour at the same time to resist the democratisation of the society. No, my friends, let us not become a queer mixture of political democrats and social conservatives. Political institutions grow out of the social life of the people and are shaped by their social ideas and ideals. If we want to make India really great we must build up a political democracy on the pedestal of a democratic society. Privileges based on birth, caste or creed should go, and equal opportunities should be thrown open to all irrespective of caste, creed or religion. The status of women should also be raised and women should be trained to take a larger and a more intelligent interest in public affairs.

While I do not condemn any patch-up work that may be necessary for healing communal sores, I would urge the necessity of discovering a deeper remedy for our communal troubles. It is necessary for the different religious groups to be acquainted with the traditions, ideals and history of one another because cultural intimacy will pave the way towards communal peace and harmony. I venture to think that the fundamental basis of political unity between different communities lies in cultural rapprochement. As things stand today, the different communities inhabiting India are too exclusive.

In order to facilitate cultural rapprochement a dose of secular and scientific training is necessary. Fanaticism is the greatest thorn in the path of cultural intimacy, and there is no better remedy for fanaticism than secular and scientific education. This sort of education is useful in another way, in that it helps to rouse our economic consciousness. The dawn of economic consciousness spells the death of fanaticism. There is much more in common between a Hindu peasant and a Muslim peasant than between a Muslim peasant and a Muslim Zamindar. The masses have only got to be educated wherein their economic interests be, and once they understand it, they will no longer consent to be pawns in communal feuds. By working from the cultural, educational and economic side, we can gradually undermine fanaticism and thereby render possible the growth of healthy nationalism in this country.

One of the most hopeful signs of the time is the awakening among the youth of this country. The movement has spread from one end of the country to the other end, as far as I am aware, and has attracted not only young men but young women as well. The youth of this age have become self-conscious; they have been inspired by an ideal and are anxious to follow the call of their inner nature and fulfil their destiny. The movement is the spontaneous self-expression of the national soul, and on the course of this movement depends the nation's future. Our duty, therefore, is not to attempt to crush this new-born spirit but to lend it our support and guidance.

Friends, I would implore you to assist in the awakening of youth and in the organisation of the youth movement. Self-conscious youth will not only act, but will also dream; will not only destroy, but will also build. It will succeed where even you may fail; it will create for you a new India—and a free India—out of the failures, trials and experience of the past. And, believe me, if we are to rid India once for all of the canker of communalism and fanaticism, we have to begin work among our youth.

There is another aspect of our movement which has been somewhat neglected in this country—the women's movement. It is impossible for one-half of the nation to win liberty without the active sympathy and support of the other half. In all countries—and even in the Labour Party in England—women's organisations have rendered invaluable service. There are various non-political organisations among women in different parts of the country, but I venture to think that there is room for a countrywide political organisation among them. It should be the primary object of this organisation, which will be run by women alone, to carry on political propaganda among their sex and to help the work of the Indian National Congress.

Our benign rulers and our self-appointed advisers are in the habit of lecturing day after day on our unfitness for Swaraj. Some say that we must have more education before we can hope to be free; others maintain that social reform should precede political reform; still others urge that without industrial development India cannot be fit for Swaraj. None of these statements is true. Indeed it would be far more true to say that without political freedom—i.e., without the power to shape our own destiny—we cannot have either compulsory free education or social reform or industrial advancement. If you demand education for your people as Shri Gokhale did long ago, the plea is put forward by Government that there is no money. If you introduce social legislation for the advancement of your countrymen, you find Miss Mayo's cousins on this side of the Atlantic arrayed against you and on the side of your social die-hards. When you are working yourself to death in order to bring about the economic and industrial regeneration of India you find to your infinite regret and surprise that your Imperial Banks, your Railways and your Stores Departments are least inclined to help your national enterprises. You pass resolutions in your Municipalities and in your Councils in favour of Prohibition and you find that the Government meets you with a stonewall of indifference or hostility. I have no doubt in my own mind that Swaraj and Swaraj alone is the sovereign remedy for all our ills. And the only criterion of our fitness for Swaraj is the will to be free.

How to rouse the national will within the shortest possible period is, then, the problem before us; our policies and programmes have to be drawn up with a view to this end. The Congress policy since 1921 has been a dual policy of destruction and obstruction; of opposition and consolidation. We feel that the bureaucracy has entrenched itself in this country by erecting a network of organisations and institutions and by appointing a hierarchy of officials to run them. These are the seats of bureaucratic power and through them the bureaucracy has a grip on the very heart of the people. We have to storm these citadels of power and for that purpose we have to set up parallel institutions. These parallel organisations are our Congress offices. As our power and influence increase through the organisation of Congress Committees, we shall be able to capture the bureaucratic seals of power. We know from personal experience that in districts where Congress Committees are well organised, the capture of local bodies has been possible without any difficulty. The Congress offices are, therefore, the forts where we have to entrench ourselves and whence we have to stir out every day in order to raid the bureaucratic citadels. Congress Committees are our army, and no plan of campaign however skilfully devised, can succeed unless we have a strong, efficient and disciplined army at our command.

Friends, you will remember that when, after the Gaya Congress of

1922, there was a tendency among a large section of our countrymen to concentrate wholly on the constructive programme to the exclusion of everything else Deshbandhu Das pointed out in the manifesto of the Swaraj Party that it was absolutely necessary to keep up a spirit of resistance to the bureaucracy. He firmly believed that without an atmosphere of opposition it was not possible to push on the constructive programme or to achieve success in any other direction. But this basic principle we often seem to forget. 'Non-cooperation is barren'—'opposition has failed'—'obstruction is fruitless'—these are catchwords which mislead the unwary public. The most tragic element in our character is that we do not look ahead; we are easily upset by failures. We lack the dogged tenacity of John Bull, and unlike him, we cannot therefore fight a longlasting game.

I have often been asked how the end will come, how the bureaucracy will ultimately be forced to accede to our terms. I have no misgivings in this matter for I have already had a foretaste of what will come. The movement will reach its climax in a sort of general strike or country-wide hartal coupled with a boycott of British goods. Along with the strike or hartal to bring about which labour and the National Congress will heartily cooperate, there will be some form of civil disobedience because the bureaucracy is not likely to sit idle while a strike is going on. It is also possible that there may be non-payment of taxes in some form or other, but this is not essential. When the crisis is reached the average Britisher at home will feel that to starve India politically means economic starvation for him. And the bureaucracy in India will find that it is impossible to carry on the administration in the face of a country-wide non-cooperative movement. The jails will be full as in 1921, and there will be general demoralisation within the ranks of the bureaucracy, who will no longer be able to count upon the loyalty and devotion of their servants and employees. There will be a paralysis of the administration and possibly of foreign trade and commerce. The bureaucracy will consider the situation as chaotic but, from the point of view of the people, the country will be organised, disciplined and determined. The bureaucracy will then be forced to yield to the demands of the people's representatives, for saving themselves from unnecessary trouble and anxiety and for restoring their trade with India.

Our immediate task is among other things to make the boycott of the Simon Commission complete and effective. We, Congressmen, have never accepted the pernicious preamble of the Government of India Act, 1919. This Act has been forced down our throats but we have never owed willing allegiance to it; in fact we have tried our level best to non-cooperate with it. We take our stand on the sacred and inviolable rights of men, and the principle of self-determination. We maintain that it is for India to frame her own constitution according to her needs, and it is for Britain to accept it in toto. This procedure has been followed not only in the case of the self-governing dominions within the British Empire including the Irish Free State.

The counterpart of this boycott, in fact its positive aspect, is the framing of a national constitution. The All Parties' Conference has taken this matter in hand and all lovers of India should wish the Conference complete success. The Secretary of State for India has in a fit of pompous pride challenged India to produce an agreed constitution. If there is a spark of honour and self-respect left in us, we should take up the gauntlet and give a fitting reply by producing a constitution.

I shall not tire you with any details of the constitution that should be drafted. I shall leave that task to our constitution framers and shall content myself by referring to three cardinal points. These three points are as follows:

(1) The constitution should guarantee national sovereignty, i.e., the sovereignty of the people. What we want is government of the people, by the people and for the people.
(2) The constitution should be prefaced by a 'declaration of rights' which will guarantee the elementary rights of citizenship. Without a 'declaration of rights' a constitution is not worth the paper it is written on. Repressive laws, ordinances and regulations should be unknown in a free India.
(3) There should be a system of joint electorate. As a temporary arrangement, there may be reservation of seats if that is found necessary. But we should by all means insist on a joint electorate. Nationalism and separate electorates are self-contradictory. Separate electorates are wrong in principle and it is futile to attempt to build up a nation on a bad principle. We have had a bitter experience of separate electorates, and the sooner we get rid of them the better for us and for our country.

In order to enforce our national demand, it is necessary to take such steps as lie in our power, because a mere appeal to the sweet reasonableness of Britishers will be of no avail. Weak and unarmed though we are, Providence has in His mercy given us a weapon which we can use with great effect. This weapon is economic boycott, i.e., boycott of British goods. It has been used with great effect in Ireland and in China. It was also used to great advantage during the Swadeshi movement nearly 20 years ago and partly during the non-cooperation movement. Boycott of British goods is necessary for the revival of Swadeshi and for effecting our political salvation.

It is also necessary that, while the political fight is going on, some of us should take up the work of village reorganisation. In a vast country like ours there is room for a variety of talent, and scope for diversity of temperament.

We must all be pained to notice that our masses, and particularly our labourers, are at present passing through a severe economic crisis. Drastic retrenchment is going on in the different Railways, and particularly in the railway workshops. I understand that several crores worth of railway materials are imported from Great Britain for our Railways whereas these could easily be manufactured in India if the workshops were extended. If an attempt were made to manufacture these goods in India, far from retrenching the existing labour staff, the administration would be able to provide employment for many more. But here again the interests of the Britishers and their industry have to be safeguarded at the cost of poor India.

It is the bounden duty of all Indians, and of Congressmen in particular, to come to the aid of labour in their hour of trial. Let us try and help them with all the means at our disposal.

Friends, we have reached a most critical stage in our nation's history and it behoves us to unite all our forces and make a bold stand against the powers that be. Let us all stand shoulder to shoulder and say with one heart and with one voice that our motto is, as Tennyson said through Ulysses, 'To strive, to seek, to find, and not to yield.'

7

Complete Independence

Speech at the Calcutta Session of the Congress, December 1928

I am sorry that I have to rise to move an amendment to a resolution moved by Mahatma Gandhi and which has the support of some, if not many, of our older leaders. The fact that I rise today to move the amendment is a clear indication of a cleavage, the fundamental cleavage between the elder school and the new school of thought in the Congress.

I have been asked by some friends why, being a signatory to the Nehru Report, I have stood up to speak for independence. I would only refer to the statement made in the report itself that the principles of the constitution which we submitted in the report can be applied in all their entirety to a constitution of independence. I do not think that in moving this amendment my action can be construed as in any way inconsistent.

There is another matter to which I shall refer by way of personal explanation. You are aware that in private conversations and elsewhere I have said that I do not desire to stand in the way of elder leaders. The reason why I did so was that at that time I did not feel prepared to accept the responsibility of the consequences of a division in this House in case our amendment was accepted. Today I feel prepared to accept the consequences and to face the issue till the end if my amendment is accepted.

There are certain incidents which have made me somewhat alter my previous views. You are aware that the Bengal delegates, or at least the majority of them, assembled and resolved to have this amendment moved on their behalf and that they were prepared to accept the vote of the House, whatever the consequence might be. Even if I did not stand here today to move the amendment. I can assure you that some other members would have stood up to do so on their behalf.

There is another fact. And that is the decision of the Independence for India League, by an overwhelming majority, to support the amendment and to accept the vote of the House, whatever it might be.

We who feel it our duty to move or support the amendment feel very sincerely that the time is so momentous that India should express herself in a clear and unambiguous manner as to what she feels on the issue of Dominion Status vs. Independence. I have told our leaders that after the death of Lala Lajpat Rai and the happenings at Lucknow and Kanpur and the speech of His Excellency the Viceroy, we would expect the Congress to take up a bold attitude, which would fit in with an attitude of self-respect. Instead of that, we find that the Madras Resolution is to be lowered in some measure.

We feel and we say that we are not prepared to lower the flag of Independence even for one single day. Whether we win or lose in this House does not concern us. It is not a matter of concern so far as the younger generation are concerned, for they have accepted the responsibility of making India free. We want our leaders, we love them, we revere them, but at the same time we want them to keep abreast of the times. I have also told them that I and Pandit Jawaharlal are regarded as moderates among the extremists, and if the elder leaders are not prepared to compromise even with these moderates, then the breach between the old and the new will be irreparable. A new consciousness has dawned upon the youth of the country. They are no longer prepared to follow blindly. They have realised that they are the heirs of the future, that it is for them to make India free, and with this new consciousness they are preparing themselves for the arduous task that awaits them.

There is one other argument which appeals to me strongly. And that is the international situation. You should remember that after the Madras Resolution India has got a new status in international politics. I am afraid if this resolution is passed, then we shall lose at least a part, if not much, of the prestige that we have acquired after the Madras Congress. You may be aware that after that we have received messages from far and distant parts of the world. The question now is: are we to go back upon the decision we took at Madras? Or are we to go ahead? Are we to respond in a befitting manner to the attitude of the Government? And what has been that attitude? We have the lamentable death of Lalaji, and the regrettable happenings at Lucknow and Kanpur. After all these, do we not feel called upon to take up a defiant and bold attitude?

I should like to put one straight question. In the main resolution you have given twelve months' time to the British Government. Can you lay your hands on your breasts and say that there is a reasonable chance of getting Dominion Status within the period? Pandit Motilal has made it clear in his speech that he does not believe so. Then why should we lower the flag for these twelve months? Why not say we have lost the last vestige of faith in the British Government and that we are going to take a bold stand?

You may ask what we shall gain by this resolution of Independence. I say, we develop a new mentality. After all, what is the fundamental cause of our political degradation? It is a question of mentality, and if you want to overcome the slave mentality you do so by encouraging our countrymen to stand for full and complete independence. I go further and say, assuming that we do not follow it up by action, that merely by preaching the gospel honestly and placing the goal of independence before our countrymen we shall bring up a new generation.

But I tell you we are not going to sit down with folded hands. I have already said that the younger generation realise their responsibility and they are prepared for their task. We shall devise our own programme and work it out according to the best of our ability so that there is no danger that our resolution will be thrown into the waste-paper basket.

There is another matter to which I shall refer before I sit down. All events show that another world war is imminent. I say this for many reasons. The first reason is that the causes which contribute to war are present in different parts of the world. The settlement brought about by the Treaty of Versailles has not satisfied the national aspirations of all people. It has not satisfied the people of Italy, the Balkans, Russia, Australia-Hungary and so on. Then there is the Asiatic situation. We have the combination of capitalistic countries against Soviet Russia. Again there is the race for armaments. These factors tend to a world war. I tell you that talk of disarmament is a huge farce. The fact is, all these countries which are free are working for another war. If India is to be on the alert, we must create a new mentality, a mentality that will say that we want complete independence. This can only be done by proclaiming the ideal in a clear and unequivocal manner.

I do not think we can afford to lose even a single moment. So far as Bengal is concerned, you are aware that since the dawn of the national movement in this country we have always interpreted freedom as complete and full independence. We have never interpreted it in terms of dominion status. After so many of our countrymen laid down their lives, after our poets preached the gospel, we have understood freedom as full and complete independence. The talk of dominion status does not make the slightest appeal to our countrymen, to the younger generation who are growing up, and we should remember that after all it is the younger generation who are the heirs of the future.

In conclusion, I wish to make a final appeal. I do not think it will mean the slightest disrespect to our leaders if we accept the amendment. Respect and love, admiration and adoration for leaders, is one thing; but respect for principle is another thing. Accept my resolution, and inspire the younger generation with a new consciousness.

8

The Individual, the Nation and the Ideal

Speech at the Hooghly District Student's Conference in Chinsurah on Sunday, 22 July 1929

Mr Chairman of the Reception Committee and students,

You know best why you have called me to this conference of students to-day. But so far as I am concerned, the reason why I have felt the inclination or rather the courage to come to this assembly today is that I still consider myself a student like yourselves. I study the 'Vedas of Life' carefully and am at the present moment engaged in gathering the knowledge that comes to a man through the hard knocks of experience for the real life.

Every single nation or individual has got a special trait or ideal of his own. He shapes his life in accordance with that ideal. It becomes the sole object of life to realise that ideal as fully as possible. And minus that ideal his life becomes absolutely meaningless and unnecessary. Just as in the case of the individual the pursuit of an ideal continues through long years, so also in the case of the nation it works from generation to generation. That is why the wise people say that an ideal is not a lifeless and motionless entity. It has got speed, locomotion and life-giving power.

We may not always succeed in catching a glimpse of the ideal that has been trying to unfold itself in our society for the last one hundred years; but he who is thoughtful and endowed with real insight can certainly detect the general trend of this ideal behind all visible phenomena, like the steady subterranean flow of the river Falgoo. And it is this ideal which constitutes the idea of the age. When a man attains a complete perception of the ideal, he can easily find out his destination and his guide on the way. But because this perception does not always come to us, we pretty often run after mistaken ideals and follow false prophets. Students, if you really want to shape your lives to some purpose, then protect yourself by all means from the influence of false guides and mistaken ideals and make your own settled choice of your own ideal in life.

The ideal that used to enthuse the student community of Bengal, say, fifteen years ago, was the ideal of Swami Vivekananda. Under the hypnotic spell of that glorious ideal, the Bengalee youth went in with grim determination for a life of purity and spiritual powers freed from all taint of selfishness and shabbiness. At the root of the construction of the society and the nation lies the unfoldment of individuality. That is why Swami Vivekananda was never tired of repeating that 'man-making' was his mission.

When a new era was ushered in our country before the age of Vivekananda, Raja Ram Mohan Roy was our guide. From the age of Ram Mohan onwards the desire for freedom in India has been manifesting itself through all sorts of movements, and when in the last decade of the nineteenth century and the first of the twentieth, the soul-stirring message of Swami Vivekananda—'Freedom, freedom is the song of the soul,'—burst the locked gates of the Swadeshi's heart and came forth in a flood of irresistible might, the whole country caught it up and nearly went mad.

It was Swami Vivekananda who had on the one hand, boldly asked his fellowmen to shed all sorts of fetters and be 'men' in the truest sense of the term; and, on the other hand, laid the foundation of true nationalism in India by preaching the essential unity of all religions and sects. But the image of freedom, whole and entire that we come across in Vivekananda, had not yet been reflected in the realm of politics in his age. It was in the voice of Aurobindo that we heard the message of political freedom for the first time. And when Aurobindo wrote in the columns of his 'Bandemataram'—'we want complete autonomy free from British control'—the freedom-loving Bengalee youth could feel that he had at last got the man of his heart.

Having thus received the impetus to complete independence, the Bengalee people have been forging ahead, making light of all obstacles and stumbling-blocks on the way. And when we come down to the year 1921, along with the message of non-cooperation we get another message from the lips of Mahatma Gandhi: 'There can be no Swaraj without the masses, and until we can rouse a hunger for freedom amongst them.' This potent message became clearer still in the life of Deshbandhu Chittaranjan. In the course of his Lahore Speech, he very clearly declared that the kind of Swaraj that he wanted was not for the few but for all, for the masses in general. The ideal of 'Swaraj for the masses' was put up by him before his countrymen at the All-India Labour Conference.

We get another message exemplified in the life of Deshbandhu. It is this, the life of man—that of a nation as well as of an individual—that is a piece of immutable truth. It is not possible to divide this life into two or more water-tight compartments. When the life of a man quickens into consciousness, we get ample proofs of this new awakening from all sides, and pulsation of a new life is felt all round. The world—and so the life of man—is full of diversity. If we kill this diversity, there will be no fulfilment of life; we shall rather bring ourselves nearer to death or destruction by so doing. That is why the unfoldment of both the individual and the nation has to be achieved through this diversity, through the 'many'.

The unity which Ramkrishna and Vivekananda established between 'the one' and 'the many' in the spiritual world, Deshbandhu achieved or at least tried to achieve in the life of the nation and in the political sphere. In one word, he firmly believed in a 'federation of cultures', and in the realm of politics, he liked a federal state for India better than a centralised state.

The all-round development and self-fulfilment in which Deshbandhu so firmly believed, is the ideal of the present age. If we want to make this 'Sadhana' fruitful, we shall first of all have to visualise an unbroken image of independence in our minds. Unless a man can realise his ideal wholly and completely; he can never hope to come out victorious in the battle of life. That is why it has become so necessary to tell all India, and specially the youth of the country, that in the free India of which we are dreaming, everybody is free—free from all kinds of shackles, social, political and economic.

Today I have come to tell this one thing to the student community here—that the 'idea' of the age in which you are born is the attainment of complete and all-round freedom. Our people want to live, grow and have their being in a free country and in the midst of a free atmosphere. We need not take fright at the idea of independence. our claim to independence is nothing but the right to make mistakes. So let us not get upset by a nightmare vision of chaos which may or may not follow the attainment of political salvation by us. Let us have an abiding faith in ourselves and go forward to snatch our birthright from unwilling hands.

In our country three large communities are lying absolutely dormant; these are the women, the so-called depressed classes and the labouring masses. Let us go to them and say: 'You also are human beings and shall obtain the fullest rights of men. So arise, awake, shed your attitude of inactivity and snatch your legitimate rights'.

You students and youngmen of Bengal, be you all the votaries of complete independence. You are the inheritors of the future India. It is therefore up to you to take upon yourselves the task of reawakening and galvanising the whole nation. Go out in your thousands into the remote villages and corners of Bengal and preach the life-giving message of equality and freedom to all and sundry. The picture of freedom which I have just held before your eyes must, in its turn, be held by you before the whole country. Go forward in the right spirit and your victory is absolutely certain. Let your 'sadhana' be fruitful in good results—let India be free again—and let your lives be crowned with glory and renown.

'Bandemataram'

9

Punjab and Bengal, Students and Politics

Speech at the Lahore Session of the
Punjabi Students' Conference, 19 October 1929

Sisters and Brothers of the Punjab,

I thank you from the very core of my heart for the warm and cordial welcome you have given me on the occasion of my first visit to the sacred 'Land of the Five Rivers'. I know how little I deserve the honour and the welcome which you have been pleased to accord me and my only wish today is that I may be a little more worthy of the kindness and hospitality with which I have been greeted here.

You have summoned me from distant Calcutta to come and speak to you. Here I am standing before you today ready to respond to your call. But why have you summoned me of all persons? Is it because the East and the West must meet to solve their common problems? Is it because Bengal, which was the first to come under foreign yoke, and Punjab, which was the last to be enslaved, have needed each other? Or is it because you and I have something in common—sharing the same thoughts and cherishing the same aspirations?

And what an irony of fate that you want me—once an expelled student of a sister University to address a gathering of students here in Lahore? Can you now object if our elders complain that the time is out of joint, for strange persons and novel ideas now find favour with the world? If you have invited me with full knowledge of my past record, you ought really to be able to anticipate what I am going to say.

Friends, you will pardon me if at the very outset I take this opportunity of giving public utterance—however feeble it may be—to the feelings of gratitude that surge within me as I think of what the Punjab and particularly the youths of the Punjab have done for Jatindranath Das and his fellow-sufferers from Bengal during their stay in the Punjab jails. The arrangements for their defence, the extreme anxiety and solicitude felt for them as long as they were on hunger strike and the sympathy, affection and honour bestowed on Jatin during his lifetime and after—have stirred the heart of Bengal to its depths.

Not content with what they had done at Lahore prominent members of the Defence committee travelled all the way to Calcutta to escort the mortal remains of the great martyr and hand them over to us there. We are an emotional people and the largeness of your heart has endeared you to us to an indescribable degree. Bengal will ever remember with thankfulness and gratitude what Punjab did for her in one of her darkest days.

One of your distinguished leaders, Dr Alam, was describing to us one day in Calcutta, while referring to the great martyr, how the sun rose in the East and set in the West and how after sun set the moon rose in the West and travelled back to the East. Thus did Jatin live and die. From Calcutta to Lahore he travelled in life, and after death, his mortal remains went back to Calcutta. They went back not as dead clay but as a symbol of something pure, noble and divine. Jatin today is not dead. He lives up in the heavens as a star 'Of purest ray serene' to serve as a beaconlight to posterity. He lives in his immortal sacrifice and in his celestial suffering. He lives as a vision, as an ideal—as an emblem of what is purest and noblest in humanity. And I believe that he has through his self-immolation not only roused the soul of India but has also forged an indissoluble tie between the two provinces where he was born and where he died. I therefore envy your great city which has been the 'tapasyakshetra'—the place of penance of this modern 'Dadhichi'.

As we are gradually approaching the dawn of freedom, our cup of suffering and sorrow is becoming full. It is but natural that our rulers, like despots elsewhere, should become more and more relentless as they find power gradually slipping out of their hands. And one should not be surprised if by and by they cast off all pretension to civilisation and rid themselves of the mask of decency in order that the nailed fist may be used freely and without hesitation. Punjab and Bengal are at the present moment enjoying the largest doses of repression. This is indeed a matter for congratulation for we are thereby qualifying for swaraj in an effective manner. The spirits of heroes like Bhagat Singh and Batukeswar Dutta cannot be cowed down by repression. On the contrary, it is through repression and suffering, through humiliation and sorrow, that heroes will be made. Let us therefore welcome repression with all our heart and make the fullest use of it when it comes.

Little do you know how much Bengali literature has drawn from the earlier history of the Punjab in order to enrich itself and edify its readers.

Tales of your heroes have been composed and sung by our great poets including Rabindranath Tagore and some of them are today familiar in every Bengali home. Aphorisms of your saints have been translated into elegant Bengali and they afford solace and inspiration to millions in Bengal. This cultural contact has its counterparts in the political sphere and we find your political pilgrims meeting ours not only in the jails in India but also in the jails of distant Burma and in the wilds of the Andaman across the Seas.

Friends, I shall make no apology if in this discourse I refer at length to political questions and endeavour to answer them. I know that there are people in this country—even eminent personages—who think that 'a subject race has no politics' and that students in particular should have nothing to do with politics. But my own view is that a subject-race has nothing but politics. In a dependent country every problem that you can think of, when analysed properly, will be found to be at bottom a political problem. Life is one whole—as the Late Deshbandhu C.R. Das used to say—and you cannot therefore separate politics from economics or from education. Human life cannot be split up into compartments. All the aspects or phases of national life are inter-related and all the problems are, as it were, interwoven. This being the case, it will be found that in a subject race all the evils and all the shortcomings can be traced to a political cause—viz., political servitude. Consequently students cannot afford to blind themselves to this all-important problem of how to achieve our political emancipation.

I do not understand why a special ban should be imposed on participation in politics if no such ban is imposed on national work in general. I can understand a ban on all national work but a ban merely on political work is meaningless. If in a dependent country, all problems are fundamentally political problems—then all national activity is in reality political in character. There is no ban on participation in politics in any free country—on the contrary, students are encouraged to take part in politics. This encouragement is deliberately given because out of the ranks of the students arise political thinkers and politicians. If in India, students do not take active part in politics, from where are we to recruit our political workers and where are we to train them? Further, it has to be admitted that participation in politics is necessary for the development of character and manhood. Thought, without action, cannot suffice to build character and for this reason, participation in healthy activity—political, social, artistic, etc.—is necessary for developing character. Bookworms, goldmedalists and office-clerks are not what universities should endeavour to produce—but men of character who will become great by achieving greatness for their country in different spheres of life.

One of the most encouraging signs of the time is the growth of a genuine students' movement all over India. This movement I consider to be a phase of the wider youth movement. There is a great deal of difference between the students' conference of to-day and those of the previous decade. The latter were generally held under official auspices and on the gateway appeared the motto—'thou shall not talk politics'. These conferences could in a manner be compared with those sessions of the Indian National Congress in the earlier stages of its history, where the first resolution passed was one affirming our loyalty to the King Emperor. We have fortunately outgrown that stage not only in the Indian National Congress but also in the students' movement. The students' conferences of today meet in a freer atmosphere and those who participate in these conferences think and talk as they like, subject to the restrictions imposed by the Indian Penal Code.

The youth movement of today is characterised by a feeling of restlessness, of impatience with the present order of things and by an intense desire to usher in a new and a better order. A sense of responsibility and a spirit of self-reliance pervades this movement. Youth of the present day no longer feel content by handing over all responsibility to their elders. They rather feel that the country and the country's future belong more to them than to the older generation and it is therefore their bounden duty to accept the fullest responsibility for the future of their country and to equip themselves for the proper discharge of that responsibility. The students' movement, being a phase of the larger youth movement, is inspired by the same outlook, psychology and purpose as the latter.

The students' movement of today is a movement of responsible, thoroughgoing men and women who are inspired with one ideal—viz., to develop their character and personality and thereby render the most effective and useful service to the cause of their country. This movement has, or should have, two lines of activity. In the first place it should deal with the problems which relate exclusively to the student population of the day and endeavour to bring about their physical, intellectual and moral regeneration. In the second place, looking upon the subject as the future citizen, it should endeavour to equip him for the battle of life and for this purpose, it should give him a foretaste of what problems and activities are likely to confront him when he enters the arena of life.

The first aspect of the students' movement, to which I have just referred, may not in the ordinary course of things be looked upon with disfavour by the powers that be—but the other aspect of the movement is likely to be discouraged, condemned and even thwarted at times. It is neither desirable nor necessary for me to attempt to give a detailed programme of what you should undertake under the first head. That will depend partly on your special needs and shortcomings and partly on the arrangements, if any, that are made by the educational authorities to fulfil those needs and remove those shortcomings. Every student requires a strong and healthy physique, a sound character and a brain full of useful information and healthy dynamic ideas. If the arrangements provided by the authorities do not conduce to the proper growth of physique, character and intellect, you will have to provide facilities which will ensure that growth. And if the authorities welcome your efforts in that direction all the better for you—but if they do not—leave them alone and go your own way. Your life is your own and the responsibility for developing it is after all yours, more than anybody else's.

In this connection there is one suggestion I have to offer to which I should like to draw your attention. I wish our students' associations could start cooperative Swadeshi stores within their respective jurisdiction for the exclusive benefit of the student population. If these stores are run efficiently by the students themselves, they will serve a dual purpose. On the one hand Swadeshi goods will be made available to the students at a cheap price and thereby home industries would be encouraged. On the other hand, students could acquire experience in running cooperative stores and could utilise the profits for advancing the welfare of the student community. For advancing the cause of student welfare, other items in your programme would be physical culture societies, gymnasium, study circles, debating societies, magazines, music clubs, libraries and reading rooms, social service leagues, etc.

The other, and probably more important aspect, of the students' movement is the training of the future citizen. This training will be both intellectual and practical. We shall have to hold out before the students a vision of the ideal society which he should try to realise in his own lifetime and at the same time chalk out for him a programme of action which he should try to follow to the best of his ability—so that while performing his duties as a student he may at the same time be preparing himself for his post-university career. It is in this sphere of activity that there is a likelihood of conflict with the authorities. But whether the conflict will actually rise or not, depends largely on the attitude of the educational authorities. If the conflict does unfortunately arise, there is no help for it and students should once for all make up their minds to be absolutely fearless and self-reliant in the matter of preparing themselves, through thought and action, for their post-university career.

Before I proceed to give you my conception of the ideal that we should all cherish, I shall with your permission indulge in a digression which will not be altogether irrelevant. There is hardly any Asiatic today to whom the spectacle of Asia lying strangled at the feet of Europe does not cause pain and humiliation. But I want you to get rid of the idea, once for all, that Asia has always been in this state. Europe today may be the top-dog but time was when Asia was the top-dog. History tells us how in the days of old Asia conquered and held away over a large portion of Europe and in those days Europe was mightily afraid of Asia. The table are turned now but the wheel of fortune is still moving and there is no cause for despair. Asia is at the present moment busy throwing off the yoke of thraldom and the time is not far off when rejuvenated Asia will rise resplendent in power and glory out of the darkness of the past and take her legitimate place in the comity of free nations.

The immortal East is sometimes stigmatised by the hustlers from the West as 'unchanging' just as Turkey was once upon a time called the sick man of Europe. But this abuse can no longer apply to Asia in general or to Turkey in particular. From Japan to Turkey and from Siberia to Ceylon, the entire orient is astir. Everywhere there is change, there is progress, there is conflict with custom, authority and tradition. The East is unchanging as long as she chooses to be so, but once she resolves to move, she can progress faster than even Western nations. This is what is happening in Asia at the present day.

We are sometimes asked if the activity and the agitation that we witness in Asia and particularly in India are signs of real life or whether they are simply reactions to external stimuli and one has to be sure that the movements we behold are not like the reflex actions of muscles that are dead. My conviction is that the test of life is creative activity and when we find that present day movements give evidence of originality and creative genius we feel sure that we are really alive as a Nation and the renaissance that we witness in different spheres of our national life is a genuine awakening from within.

In India today we are in the midst of a whirlpool of ideas. Numerous currents, cross currents and undercurrents are flowing from all directions. A strange intermingling is going on and in the midst of the confusion of ideas that has arisen, it is not possible for the ordinary man to distinguish between good and bad and right and wrong.

But if we are to rejuvenate our country and guide it along the right path, we must have a clear vision of the goal and of the path we shall have to travel in order to reach that goal.

Indian civilisation has just emerged out of the dark ages and is now entering on a new lease of life. At one time there was a genuine danger as to whether that civilisation would die a normal death like the civilisation of Phoenicia and Babylon. But it has once again survived the onslaught of time. If we want to continue the work of rejuvenation that has begun, we must bring about a revolution of ideas in the thought world and an intermingling of blood in the biological plane. Unless we refuse to accept the verdict of history and the considered opinion of thinkers like Sir Flinders Petrie—we have to admit that it is only by this means that old and worn out civilisations can be rejuvenated. If you do not accept this view of mine you will have to discover by your own investigation the law underlying the rise and fall of civilisations. Once we succeed in discovering this law, we shall be able to advise our countrymen as to what is necessary for us to do if we are to create a new, healthy and progressive nation in this ancient land of ours. If we are to bring about a revolution of ideas we have first to hold up before us an ideal which will galvanise our whole life. That ideal is Freedom. But freedom is a word which has a varied connotation and even in our country, the conception of freedom has undergone a process of evolution. By freedom I mean all-round freedom i.e., freedom for the individual as well as for society, freedom for man as well as for woman, freedom for the rich as well as for the poor, freedom for all individuals and for all classes. This freedom implies not only emancipation from political bondage but also equal distribution of wealth, abolition of caste barriers and social iniquities and destruction of communalism and religious intolerance. This is an ideal which may appear utopian to hard-headed men and women—but this ideal along can appease the hunger of the soul.

Freedom has as many facets as there are aspects in our national life. There are individuals who when they talk of freedom think only of some particular aspects of freedom. It has taken us several decades to outgrow this narrow conception of freedom and to arrive at a full and all-round conception of it. If we really love freedom and love it, not for some selfish end, but for its own sake the time has come for us to recognise that true freedom means freedom from bondage of every kind and freedom not only for the individual but also for the whole of society. This, to my mind, is the ideal of the age and the vision that has captivated my soul is the vision of a completely free and emancipated India.

The only method of achieving freedom is for us to think and feel as free men. Let there be a complete revolution within and let us be thoroughly intoxicated with the wine of freedom. It is only freedom-intoxicated men and women who will be able to free humanity. When the 'will to be free' is roused within us we shall then proceed to plunge headlong into an ocean of activity. The voice of caution will no longer deter us and the lure of truth and glory will lead us on to our cherished goal.

Fiends, I have tried to tell you something about what I feel, think and dream about my life's goal and what is at present the motive power behind all my activities. Whether this will attract you or not, I do not know. But one thing is to me perfectly clear—life has but one purpose, viz., freedom from bondage of every kind. Hunger after freedom is the song of the soul—and the very first cry of the newborn baby is a cry of revolt against the bondage in which it finds itself. Rouse this intense desire for freedom within yourselves and in your countrymen and I am sure India will be free in no time.

India is bound to be free—of that there is not the slightest doubt. It is to me as sure as day follows night. There is no power on earth which can keep India in bondage any longer. But let us dream of an India for which it would be worthwhile to give all that we have—even life itself—and for which we could sacrifice our dearest and nearest. I have given you my own conception of freedom and I have tried to portray before you India as I want her to be; let a completely emancipated India preach to the world her new gospel of freedom.

Even at the risk of being called a chauvinist, I would say to my countrymen that India has a mission to fulfil and it is because of this that India still lives. There is nothing mystic in this word 'mission'. India has something original to contribute to the culture and civilisation of the world in almost every department of human life. In the midst of her present degradation and slavery, the contribution she has been making is by no means a small one. Just imagine for a moment how great her contribution will be once she is free to develop along her own lines and in accordance with her own requirements.

There are people in this country and some of them eminent and respectable personages—who will not agree to an all-round application of the principle of freedom. We are sorry if we cannot please them, but in no circumstance can we give up an ideal which is based on truth, justice, and equality. We shall go our own way, whether others join us or not—but you can be rest assured that even if a few desert us, thousands and even millions will ultimately join our army of freedom. Let us have no compromise with bondage, injustice or inequality. Friends, it is time for all lovers of freedom to bind themselves into one happy fraternity and form the army of freedom.

Let this army send out not only soldiers to fight the battle of freedom but also missionaries to propagate the new cult of freedom. It is from amongst you that these missionaries and these soldiers will have to be created. In our programme of action we must have intensive and extensive propaganda on the one hand and a country-wide volunteer organisation on the other. Our missionaries will have to go amongst the peasants and factory workers and preach the new message. They will have to inspire the youths and organise youth leagues all over the country. And last but not least, they will have to rouse the entire womanhood of the country—for woman must now come forward to take her place in society and in the body politic as an equal partner of man.

Friends, many of you must be now training yourselves for joining the ranks of the Indian National Congress. The Indian National Congress is undoubtedly the supreme national organisation in this country and in it all our hopes are centered. But the Indian National Congress itself depends, or should depend, for its strength, influence and power on such movements as the labour movement, youth movement, peasant movement, women's movement, students' movement etc. If we succeed in emancipating our labour, peasantry, depressed classes, youths, students and womenfolk we shall be able to rouse such a force in the country as will make the Indian National Congress a potent instrument for achieving our political salvation. If therefore you want to serve the Indian National Congress most effectively you will at the same time have to promote the allied movements to which I have referred above.

Next door to us is China—let us therefore take a leaf out of recen Chinese history. See what the students in China have done for thei motherland. Can we not do the same in India? The renaissance i modern China is due almost wholly to the activities of Chinese stu dents—both men and women. They have on the one hand gone out int the villages and into the towns and factories to preach the new messag of freedom and on the other hand they have organised the whole countr from one end to the other. We shall have to do the same thing in India There is no royal road to freedom. The path to freedom is no doubt thorny one but it is a path which also leads to glory and immortality. Le us break with the past, destroy all the shackles which have bound us fo ages and like true pilgrims let us march shoulder to shoulder towards th destined goal of freedom. Freedom means life, and death in the pursuit of freedom means the highest glory imperishable. Let us therefore resolve to be free or at least to die in the pursuit of freedom—and let us show by our conduct and character that we are worthy of being the countrymen of the great martyr—Jatindra Nath Das.

'Bande Mataram'

10
Socialism in India

Speech at All-India Naujawan Bharat Sabha in Karachi, 5 April 1931

My Dear Friends,

You have called upon me to preside over the deliberations of the second session of All-India Naujawan Bharat Sabha at Karachi. I am grateful to you not only for the honour you have done me by your selection but also for the affection that has undoubtedly inspired your choice. You are holding this conference at a momentous period in our history and I only hope that I shall be able to throw some light on the problems that are ahead of us and the path that we shall have to travel.

Since the earliest ages humanity has been in search of a better order of things. This search has gone on alike in the East and in the West and not only sages and dreamers, but politicians and statesmen as well, have been after it. The vision of an ideal society or state has appeared in different forms in different climes, but the impulse behind them all has been the same. In the East people dreamt of an ideal republic. People have sometimes endeavoured to go back to the state of nature from whence they think they came—at other times, they have tried to demolish the agelong social, economic and political structure in order to rear up something great and noble on the ruin of the past.

The psychological impulse behind this universal human effort is a feeling of acute discontent with the present order and environment and a desire for a radical change. Urged by this impulse people have in utter helplessness looked beyond this earth and beyond this human existence to a kingdom of heaven where the human soul could live an ideal life amidst ideal surroundings. Others have followed a different course of action and believing that the kingdom of heaven is within us, have sought, through asceticism and worship, or through song and prayer, to attain the maximum peace and happiness here on earth.

We are not concerned with these two schools of thought and we need neither accept nor reject either of them. We are concerned more with the consideration of that socio-economic structure and body-politic which will bring us the maximum happiness, will help us to foster manhood and develop character and will translate into reality the highest ideals of collective humanity. We are also interested in investigating the methods that will bring about the earliest attainment of the above goal.

In the search for a better order humanity has throughout the ages been groping in the twilight of darkness and light. Religion, philosophy and literature have all tried to throw some light on that elusive will-o'-the-wisp—the Ideal. It would be interesting to trace and study these efforts made in almost every civilised country from age to age but that would take too much time and may divert us from the immediate problem before us. It will suffice to say that mankind has now accepted the theory of progress and has rejected the opposite theory viz., the theory of man's fall and his subsequent degradation. This theory of progress may be made the starting point of our discussion.

If we undertake a comparative analysis of the different socio-political ideals that have inspired human endeavour and activity we shall arrive at certain common principles. The same result may be attained by searching our heart and asking ourselves as to what principles and ideals would make our life worth living. By following either course I am led to the conclusion that the principles that should form the basis of our collective life are—justice, equality, freedom, discipline and love. There is hardly any necessity of arguing that all our affairs and relations should be guided by a sense of justice. In order to be just and impartial, we shall have to treat all men as equal. In order to make men equal we shall have to make them free. Bondage within the socio-economic or political system—robs men of their freedom and gives rise to inequalities of various kinds. Therefore, in order to ensure Equality, we must get rid of bondage of every kind—social, economic and political—and we must become fully and wholly free. But freedom does not mean indiscipline or license. Freedom does not imply the absence of law. It only means the substitution of our own law and our own discipline in a place of an externally imposed law and discipline. Discipline imposed on us by ourselves is necessary not only when we have attained freedom but is more necessary when we are struggling to achieve freedom. Therefore discipline, whether for the individual of for society, is necessary as a basis of life. Lastly all these fundamental principles viz., Justice, Equality. Freedom and Discipline—presuppose or imply another higher principle viz., Love. Unless we are inspired by a feeling of love for humanity we can neither be just towards all, nor treat men as Equal, nor feel called upon to suffer and sacrifice in the cause of freedom nor enforce discipline of the right sort. These five principles therefore, should in my opinion be the basis of our collective life. I shall go further and say that these principles constitute the essence of Socialism as I understand it, and the Socialism that I would like to see established in India.

I believe that in the future that is before us India will be able to evolve a socio-economic and political structure which will be in many respects an object lesson to the world just as Bolshevism today has many useful lessons for humanity. But I do not believe that abstract principles can be applied in the same manner, form and degree to different nations or countries. Marxian principles when applied to Russia and Russian conditions gave birth to Bolshevism. Similarly socialism when applied to India and Indian conditions will develop a new form or type of socialism which we may hail as Indian Socialism. Environment, racial temperament, socio-economic conditions all these cannot be ruled out by a stroke of the pen. They are therefore bound to influence or modify and principle that is sought to be translated into reality.

While seeking light and inspiration from abroad, we cannot afford to forget that we should not blindly imitate any other people and that we should assimilate what we learn elsewhere with a view to finding out what will suit our national requirements as well as our national genius. There is a great deal of truth in the proverb—'What is one man's meat is another's poison.' I should therefore like to strike a note of warning to those who may feel tempted to follow blindly the tenets and methods of Bolshevism. With regard to the tenets of Bolshevism I may say that Bolshevik theory is at present going through an experimental stage. There has been a departure not only from the original theory of Marx but also from the principle enunciated by Lenin and other Bolsheviks before they captured political power. This departure has been caused by the peculiar conditions or circumstances prevailing in Russia which have compelled a modification of original Marxian or Bolshevik theory. With regards to the methods and tactics employed by the Bolsheviks in Russia I may say that they will not necessarily suit Indian conditions. As a proof of this I may say that in spite of universal and human appeal of communism, communism has not been able to make much headway in India—chiefly because the methods and tactics generally employed by them are such as tend to alienate rather than win over possible friends and allies.

To summarise what I have said I want a Socialist republic in India.

The exact from the Socialist State will take—it is not possible to detail at this stage. We now only outline the main principles and features of the socialist state.

The message which I have to give is one of complete, all-round undiluted freedom. We want political freedom, whereby is meant the constitution of an independent Indian State, free from the control of British Imperialism. It should be quite clear to everybody that independence means severance from the British Empire and on this point there should be no vagueness or mental reservation. Secondly, we want complete economic emancipation. Every human being must have the right to work and the right to a living wage. There shall be no drones in our society. There must be equal opportunities for all. Above all there should be a fair, just and equitable distribution of wealth. For this purpose it may be necessary for the state to take over the control of the means of production and distribution of wealth. Thirdly, we want complete social equality. There shall be no caste, no depressed classes. Every man will have the same rights—the same status—in the society. Further there shall be no inequality between the sexes either in social status or in law—and woman will be in every way an equal partner with man.

We therefore have a new message for every group or class or individual in society who may be exploited or oppressed in any way. We have a message for the political workers, for the wage earner, for the landless and propertyless proletariat, for the so-called depressed classes in society and for the weaker sex. These exploited or oppressed classes represent the radical—or if I may say so—revolutionary elements in our society. If we can go out to greet them with a new message—the message of complete all-around freedom—I have no doubt that they can be inspired in no time. Until these radical or revolutionary elements are stirred up—we cannot get freedom and we cannot stir up the revolutionary elements among us except by inspiring them with a new message which comes from the heart and goes straight to the heart.

The fundamental weakness in the Congress policy and programme is that there is a great deal of vagueness and mental reservation in the mind of the leaders. Further the programme is based not on radicalism but on adjustment. Adjustment between the landlord and the tenant, between the capitalist and the wage earner, between the so-called upper classes and the so-called depressed classes, between man and woman—may be an ideal state of thing for one who would like to maintain the present equilibrium—but I am doubtful whether this adjustment can stir up the revolutionary elements in society which alone can win freedom. I doubt if the Indian National Congress with its present attitude of the adjustment in all controversial matters—can win independence for India; it will be a cheap price to pay for freedom. But whether this small price can bring us freedom—I seriously doubt.

We do not want to tinker with the gigantic problem we have to solve—therefore, we want a radical militant programme. I shall not in this introductory address go into details on this question, but shall content myself with outlining the main features of the programme. In consonance with 5 principles I have enunciated at the outset, and keeping in view the different aspects of freedom—we should direct our activities along the following lines:

(1) Organisation of peasants and workers on a socialist programme.
(2) Organisation of the youths into volunteer corps under strict discipline.
(3) Abolition of caste and the eradication of social and religious superstitions of all kinds.
(4) Organisation of women's associations for getting our women folk to accept the new gospel and work out the new programme.
(5) Intensive campaign for the boycott of British goods.
(6) Countrywide propaganda for explaining the new cult and for organising a new party.
(7) Creation of a new Literature for propagating the new cult and programme.

Workers and comrades to whom the new cult and programme appeal should seriously consider whether or not they should organise themselves as the Left-Wing of the Indian National Congress. There is much to be said in favour of doing so. The Indian National Congress in the first place has a tradition as well as an international reputation. Further, it is built on the gigantic sacrifices made by successive generations. And if the Left-Wing is properly organised, I have no doubt that the time will soon come when they will be called upon by the sheer logic of events to take charge of the Congress. Once this party comes into existence with its own programme it will be the only alternative to the present order and the present programme.

Friends, before I wind up, you will no doubt like me to express my views on the truce that has been arrived at, between the Government and the Working Committee of the Congress. But before I do so, I should like to unburden myself on a matter which has profoundly moved the whole of India. I mean the recent execution of Sardar Bhagat Singh and his comrades. This event is an historic one and is pregnant with lessons for the future and I shall crave your indulgence for dwelling on it at length.

Bhagat Singh is dead! Long live Bhagat Singh! For months and months have the people of India watched and waited with tense anxiety for the end of the tragic drama that was being enacted at Lahore. The end has at last come. The curtain has ultimately been rung down on a scene indescribable for its deep pathos and memorable for its selflessness. From start to finish the drama has been so rich in variety and so alive in its colouring that we have had to hold our breath in awe and anxious expectation. It ended with the self-sacrifice of Bhagat Singh and Jatin Das. With rapture and reverent admiration do we gaze at these two rare types of martyrdom which recent history has produced. Just as the funeral procession of Jatin Das was one long triumphal march—so also the execution of Bhagat Singh is an act of consecration which will inspire the whole nation. No wonder that the Lahore Conspiracy here have stirred the heart of India to its very depth. But do the Government realise it? Again I say 'Bhagat Singh is dead! Long Live Bhagat Singh!' Bhagat Singh is not a person. He symbolises the spirit of revolt which has taken possession of the country from one end to the other. The spirit is unconquerable, the flame that spirit has lit up will not die. Therefore we do not grieve that Bhagat Singh, Rajguru and Sukhdev are no more. India may have to lose many more sons before she can hope to be free. But if we grieve it is because they have had to die at a time when the premier nationalist organisation in the country—the Indian National Congress—has declared a truce with the British Government. What fate is in store for the other sons of India, like Harkishinalal, Dinesh Gupta and Ramkrishna Biswas cannot be easily visualised. The question may therefore be pertinently asked what is the value of this truce if these acts of hostility are to go on and if we cannot save the lives of our best heroes?

It may be argued logically that there was nothing in the truce terms to say that the capital sentences would not be given effect to. I admit this point. But may we not ask what the object of the truce is? It will be admitted on all hands that the object of the truce is to bring about an atmosphere of peace and goodwill, prior to the negotiations at the Round Table Conference, so that the discussions take place in a cool and dispassionate manner, and without bitterness or prejudice. Will that atmosphere be created if capital sentences are passed and executed and if a large number of political prisoners are still in imprisonment? If the Government today are so exacting about the letter of the truce terms—if they are so keen about having their pound of flesh—what hope is here that they will part with power when the time for negotiation or discussion arrives? It is not for nothing that Mahatma Gandhi has always insisted on a change of heart prior to a settlement or negotiations for a settlement. The Government that continues to have the same bureaucratic, and if I may say so vindictive, mentality is not the Government that will voluntarily hand over India to the people's representatives. It may be urged that we shall negotiate for transference of power not with the Indian Civil Service or the Government of India, but with the British Cabinet or with the British people altogether. But if in the matter of holding an enquiry into police excess or commuting death sentence the British Government has to surrender to the will of men on the spot, is it not to be expected that in much larger questions involving transference of power, the same Government will be guided to a very large extent by the will of the steel frame?

The recent executions are to me, therefore, a sure indication that there has been no change of heart on the side of the Government. The time for an honourable settlement is not yet ripe. We have yet to travel a long way along the path of suffering and sacrifice before we can hail the advent of Swaraj. A page from recent Irish history will substantiate my point. Alderman MacSweeney Lord Mayor of Cork went on hunger strike as a protest against his imprisonment. When he was on the point of death, passionate appeals were made to His Majesty the King on behalf of Britishers and Irishmen alike asking him to exercise his royal prerogative and save MacSweeney's life. The King was deeply moved but announced through his Secretary that he was unable to do anything because his ministers were opposed to clemency. The King therefore had to capitulate. The effect of this in Ireland was that the fight with Britain went on with increasing bitterness. After some time both parties felt it desirable to call a truce and settlement. The question of amnesty to political prisoners was then broached and the Sinn Fein leaders demanded the release of all prisoners, including those who had been sentenced to death. The British Cabinet agreed to release every body except Seon McKeon who had been condemned to death. The Sinn-Fein leaders thereupon threatened to break off the truce if Seon McKeon was not released within twenty-four hours. In reply to ultimatum, the same Cabinet which had declined to spare the life of Terence MacSweeny in spite of country-wide agitation released Seon McKeon within twenty-four hours. MacSweeney had to die because the time for settlement had not arrived. Seon McKeon was saved because there was going to be a lasting peace and a change of heart had taken place on the side of the British people. May we not apply the same moral to Indian history?

Bravẹ as Bhagat Singh and his comrades were, they did not ask for clemency. They had resolved to give their all, so that India could be free. But the whole country desired their lives to be spared. If truce had been declared, if peace was within sight then the lives of these brave and selfless men could be transformed and could be utilised in the task of national reconstruction. The whole country, including all parties and shades of opinion, had given unmistakable expression to the desire and demand for commutation. But if every possible effort had been made on the side of the people, there was one more effort which could have been made. When the negotiations for a truce were going on, the Congress as the one representative nationalist organisation in the country could have espoused the cause of the revolutionaries and of the Labour party of India. The Congress need not thereby have identified itself with the methods or tactics of the revolutionaries and of the Labour party. It could have simply pointed out that since these two parties existed and since they were also working for the salvation of India according to their own light, abiding peace could not possibly be established until they were somehow made parties to it.

A generous gesture on the part of Government at this juncture would have had a most wholesome effect on these two parties and on the country at large. If after a generous gesture coming from the official side—any group, party or individual did not reciprocate it, then that group or individual would stand condemned in the eyes of the whole world. The Government with all its strength and resources would in either case have lost nothing if by conciliation they could placate all the militant parties in the country, it would be a moral triumph for them. If conciliation failed, they could once again resort to repression and could then do so with greater justification.

If the Government have blundered, so also has the Congress. During the truce-talks the Congress could have spoken for the whole country, just as Sinn Fein had spoken for the whole of Ireland. Without identifying itself with the methods of the revolutionary and Labour parties, the Congress could very well have identified itself with their demands. But the Congress failed to do so and in failing it has only lowered itself in the estimation of the country and of the world. A similar attitude could have been adopted by the Congress after the petition for the commutation of the death sentences passed on Bhagat Singh and others was rejected by the Government.

If the Congress had officially demanded the commutation of the death sentences it would not have lost anything but have risen in the estimation of the whole country and might possibly have saved the life of Bhagat Singh. Even if the demand had been rejected by the Government, the Congress would have had this satisfaction that it had done its duty and no one could then have nursed any complaint or grievance against the Congress for not doing its best to save Bhagat Singh and his comrades.

With regard to the truce embodied in what is known as the Gandhi-Irwin Pact I may say that it is exceedingly unsatisfactory and highly disappointing. What pains me most is the consideration that at the time this pact was drawn up, we actually had more strength than would appear from the contents of the document. I shall here summarise some of the unsatisfactory features of the truce terms:

(1) Ordinances like the Bengal Ordinance (Bengal Criminal Amendment Act) and the Burma Ordinance whereby people are incarcerated without trial on mere suspicion have not been repealed.

(2) Provisions for the return of fines and of confiscated property are not satisfactory.

(3) The demand for the enquiry into the police excesses should not have been given up, particularly after it was made on behalf of the Congress. Further the Congress should have stood by Garhwalis who refused to fire on unarmed people and the policemen who were dismissed on political grounds. The Government refused to let down their own men in spite of the many excesses committed by them whereas the Congress did not stand by their own men.

(4) The Congress should not have given up the boycott of British goods—particularly when this does not form part of the Civil Disobedience movement. In normal times before the Civil Disobedience was started last year we could carry on the Boycott of British Goods, but unfortunately now we cannot. Therefore we are now in a worse position after the Civil Disobedience Movement than we were before it.

(5) The provisions for the manufacture of salt are not adequate—since salt could be manufactured only within a limited area.

(6) The restrictions that have been agreed to in connection with picketing places us in a more difficult position than before the Civil Disobedience Movement was started last year. If these restrictions are strictly adhered to it will be difficult, if not impossible, to have picketing at all.

(7) Above all, the provisions regarding amnesty are exceedingly unsatisfactory. In the first place all Civil Disobedience prisoners have not

so far been released. Further we cannot, under the truce terms claim amnesty for revolutionary and Labour party prisoners. The hanging orders will not be stopped—the different conspiracy cases like Chittagong Armoury Raid case and Meerut conspiracy case are to go on. Political prisoners who had been in prison for 10 or 12 years like the Martial law prisoners in the Punjab are to remain in jail. Last but not the least, the Bengal detenus imprisoned as detained without trial are not to be released. What then is the value of this amnesty. I should further point out that the distinction between violent and non-violent prisoners now made by the Congress is a new stunt. It was not made in the Delhi Manifesto in 1929 nor was it made in the celebrated eleven points of Mahatma Gandhi.

It does not require any further argument to expose the unsatisfactory character of the truce terms. On perusing the document one cannot help feeling that it was agreed to with a defeatist mentality on the side of the Congress and the language at several places militates against our sense of self respect and honour. If we really had been in a weak position when the truce was arrived at—I would not have made much protest—but were we really so weak at that time? I doubt it.

But the truce is now an accomplished fact and the question is that we should ponder very carefully before we take any aggressive step. Instead of wasting our energy in negative criticism, let us do something positive and beneficial. I do not for one moment question the patriotism of those who are responsible for the truce terms. Far from it. Consequently the best course for us would be to do some positive work which will further strengthen the nation and the nation's demands. For this purpose at the very outset I have indicated the outlines of a new programme which the more radical section among our country would do well to adopt and carry out. This will avoid unnecessary conflict with the Congress leaders at a time when such conflict may tend to weaken the people and strengthen the Government. Above all let us have restraint and self-control even when we have to criticise others. We shall lose nothing by being courteous and restrained and we may gain much. If we believe in our programme let us carry it out to the best of our ability. If our programme is based on truth it is bound to be accepted by our country men in the long run for truth will ultimately prevail in this world. Friends, I have taken up a lot of your valuable time but I have done. Let us address ourselves to our task in all seriousness, with unflinching courage but in all humility. The vision of free India, a completely free and emancipated India is what has captivated my soul. It is the dream of my life and the goal of all my activities. India has much to contribute to the culture and civilisation of the world. The whole world is anxiously awaiting that gift. And the last gift which India will make to the world is a new socio-economic order and a body politic which will have lessons for the whole of humanity. India is the keystone of the world edifice and free India spells the destruction of Imperialism throughout the world. Let us therefore rise to the occasion and make India free so that humanity may be saved.

11

Trade Union and the Problems of Unemployment

Presidential address at the
All-India Trade Union Congress Session in Calcutta,
4 July 1931

I doubt if we can claim that during the last eighteen months the trade union movement has gained in strength and in volume. I would rather be inclined to say that during this period, the movement received a setback. Many factors account for this setback but in my humble opinion the two most important factors are: firstly, the split which occurred in Nagpur, and, secondly the diversion caused by the launching of the civil disobedience movement. Some of our comrades may be disposed to think that the split did not weaken us; but I cannot share this view, for I have no doubt in my mind that, for the time being at least, we have been weakened by the split. I am therefore one of those who sincerely deplore the split, and if it be possible for us to close up our ranks I shall heartily welcome that event. So far as the second factor is concerned, I venture to think that the attention of the country as a whole was drawn away from the trade union movement owing to the superior attraction of the civil disobedience movement. Under different circumstances the trade union movement could have benefited by the civil disobedience movement and could have gained in strength as a result of it. But on this occasion the normal progress of the trade union movement has been impeded.

Attempts at unity within the ranks of the trade union movement have been made from time to time by various individuals and groups. I consider it desirable, therefore, to state clearly what the main problems are over which we quarrelled, and how unity could best be achieved at this stage. The main issues are: (1) The question of foreign affiliation; (2) Representation at Geneva; (3) Mandatory character of the Trade Union Congress resolutions.

With regard to the first issue, my personal view is that we need have no foreign affiliation now. The Indian trade union movement can well be expected to take care of itself. We should be prepared to learn from every quarter and even to accept any help that may come from any part of the world. But we should not surrender to the dictates of Amsterdam or Moscow. India will have to work out her own methods and adapt herself to her environment and her own special needs.

With regard to representation at Geneva, I am afraid that too much importance has been given to this question. The best course for us would be to have an open mind and come to a decision every year on this question. We need not decide before hand, once for all, as to whether we should send any representative to Geneva or not. Personally, I have no faith in Geneva. Nevertheless if any friend will be satisfied by our keeping the question open for decision every year, I have no objection to it.

With regard to the mandatory character of the Trade Union Congress resolutions, I am afraid there can hardly be any compromise if the Trade Union Congress is to exist and function. If it is to work for the attainment of working class solidarity in the country, the resolutions of the Trade Union Congress should be binding on all unions affiliated to the Congress. To reduce the Trade Union Congress to the position and status of a loose federation, or to something like an All-Parties Conference, would be suicidal.

With regard to the question of trade union unity, my position is quite clear. I want unity because thereby we can have a strong and powerful organisation. But if we are to quarrel again and part company, then we need not attempt a patch-up unity now. The Trade Union Congress is public property. All unions are welcome to join the Congress and make their presence felt. If thereby the office of the Congress passes into the hands of a particular party, then no one can legitimately complain. I would, therefore, earnestly invite all unions to join the Trade Union Congress and to capture the executive if they so desire.

Some of our workers feel very much concerned over the settlement arrived at between Mahatma Gandhi and Lord Irwin. I do not propose to launch into a criticism of the settlement because that would amount to something like a post-mortem examination. The truce is an accomplished fact and we may ignore it at this stage. We can use our time and energy more profitably if we look to the future and try to prepare for it. The Trade Union Congress as a body did not have much to do with the civil disobedience movement last year. But it is open to it to take a larger share in the movement that is to come. In order to do that, preparations must begin from today.

The Karachi session of the Indian National Congress passed a resolution, now popularly known as the Fundamental Rights resolution. Various opinions have been expressed with regard to that resolution. On the one hand, some have roundly condemned it as altogether inadequate and unsatisfactory, while others have waxed eloquent over it. Both these views appear to me to be one-sided. However unsatisfactory the resolution may be, there is no doubt that the resolution stands for a departure from the old tradition, for a recognition of the workers and peasants, for a definite move in the direction of socialism. The value of the resolution is not in what it contains in an explicit form but in what it contains in an implicit form. It is the potentiality of the resolution, rather than the actual contents of the resolution, which appeals to me. The contents of the resolution have to be amplified and improved before it can be altogether satisfactory. We are glad to note that a committee is already at work for the purpose.

People in this country are at the moment awaiting the result of the Round Table Conference. I cannot persuade myself to believe that anything substantial will come out of the conference in the present temper and mentality of the British Government. Further, the Round Table Conference is such as to make it exceedingly difficult to press home the popular point of view and the popular demand. When the result of the conference is announced, it will then be time for the people to take such action as they think fit. That psychological moment should not be lost by the people when it does arrive.

At the Nagpur session of the Congress, the boycott of the Whitley Commission had been decided upon. That Commission have just issued their report. If I were to act like a logician, I should ignore that Report altogether but I shall not do that. Whether it be good, bad or indifferent, we should not ignore a document of that character which is now before the public and which he public are bound to take serious notice of and criticise.

I should say at the very outset that the value of the report of a particular commission lies not in what it contains on paper but in what will ultimately come out of it. Will the expenditure over the commission be justified? For one thing, that is a question which even the man in the street will ask. We Indians have seen so much of reports that only if some tangible good actually comes out of a particular commission, apart from the mere issuing of a report, we are inclined to be highly sceptical and suspicious about the results. I may even say that in the past the reports of some commissions have met with wholesale condemnation owing to the failure of the Government to implement even the good points in those reports.

The present report has laid considerable emphasis on the problem of welfare works for labour, and though I voted for the boycott of the Whitley Commission I have no hesitation in saying that if recommendations on this point are given effect to, there will be an improvement on the present position. Nevertheless, I am constrained to say that some of the larger and more important questions have not been dealt with properly. Labour today wants the right to work. It is the duty of the state to provide employment to the citizens and where the State fails to perform this duty it should accept the responsibility of maintaining them. In other words, the worker citizen cannot be at the mercy of the employer to be thrown out on the streets at his sweet will and made to starve. The industry of the country is today faced with a crisis owing to the application of the axe. I am not unmindful of the difficulties of the employers. It is sometimes impossible for them to maintain their old staff and they are forced to resort to retrenchment. But even in such cases the State cannot absolve itself of all responsibility and the employer should be told that if in his brighter days he has made his pile with the help of his poor workers, he cannot leave them to their fate when adversity overtakes them. Until this problem of retrenchment is satisfactorily solved, there can be no industrial peace in the country.

Just as every worker can claim the right to work, he can also claim the right to a living wage. Does the factory worker in India get a living wage today? Look at the jute factories and the textile mills. What portion of their enormous profits did they spend for the welfare of the poor and oppressed workers? I know that they will say that of late they are in a bad way. But granting that proposition, may we not ask what reserves they have piled up during their past history? I should not in this connection forget the Indian Railways either. They are now busy applying the axe. But those who are resorting to drastic retrenchment have certainly some duty towards those who in the past enabled them to swell their profits and pile up their reserves. We can also refer to our tea planters. What are the profits that they have been making, and how have they been treating their labour? Is it not a fact that in some areas at least the poor workers are still subjected to conditions which have much in common with the old institution of slavery? What has, then, the Labour Commission recommended for securing to the Indian worker a living wage and decent treatment? They have referred to minimum wages in the jute and textile industry. But can we be rest assured that the minimum wages mean a living wage?

It is not necessary for me to enter into a detailed examination of the different recommendations made by the Whitley Commission. I shall refer, however, to one point which, though apparently insignificant, is of vital interest to the growth of the trade union movement in India. The report says that 'Section 22 of the Trade Unions Act should be amended so as to provide that ordinarily not less than two-thirds of the officers of a registered trade union shall be actually engaged or employed in an industry with which the union is concerned.' The Commission should have known that in India outsiders or non-workers are usually elected as office bearers of trade union because employees who agree to work as office-bearers are usually victimised by the employers on some flimsy pretext or other. Therefore if employees are to be forced to become office-bearers themselves, there should be some arrangement for preventing their victimisation at the hands of their employers. Otherwise, if the present policy of victimisation continues, it will be impossible for the employees to become office-bearers.

To sum up, the major problems of unemployment, retrenchment and living wage for the workers have not been handled properly. The ameliorative programme drawn up by the Commission is attractive in many places, but who is giving effect to that programme? Can anything be expected from the present Government which is definitely anti-labour? The labour problem is, therefore, ultimately a political problem. Until India wins her freedom and establishes a democratic—if not socialistic—Government, no ameliorative programme for the benefit of labour can be given effect to. It is clear from the report that everything is practically left to the Government. The report does not say anything as to how labour can capture or influence the governmental machinery. But till this is done, no amount of reports can actually benefit labour. The Commission should have recommended adult franchise in connection with the new constitution. In addition to this, or as an alternative, the commission could also have recommended a certain percentage of seats in the provincial and central legislatures to be reserved for the representatives of labour.

The trade union movement is destined to grow in strength and in volume in spite of the temporary setbacks that it may have received in the past. Various currents and cross-currents of thought sometimes make trade union workers feel bewildered as to the path or the modus operandi they should follow. There is, on the one hand, the Right Wing who stand for a reformist programme above everything else. On the other side there are our Communist friends who, if I have understood them alright, are adherents and followers of Moscow. Whether we agree with the views of either group or not, we cannot fail to understand them. Between these two groups is another group which stands for socialism—for full-blooded socialism—but which desires that India should evolve her own form of socialism as well as her own methods. To this group I humbly claim to belong.

I have no doubt in my own mind that the salvation of India, as of the world, depends on socialism. India should learn from and profit by the experience of other nations—but India should be able to evolve her own methods in keeping with her own needs and her own environment. In applying any theory to practice, you can never rule out geography or history. If you attempt it, you are bound to fail. India should, therefore, evolve her own form of socialism. When the whole world is engaged in socialistic experiments, why should we not do the same? It may be that the form of socialism which India will evolve will have something new and original about it which will be of benefit to the whole world.

12

The Anti-Imperialist Struggle and Samyavada[1]

We had been engaged in a non-violent war with the British Government—for the attainment of our political freedom. But today our condition is analogous to that of an army that has suddenly surrendered unconditionally to the enemy in the midst of a protracted and strenuous campaign.[2] And the surrender has taken place, not because the nation demanded it—not because the national army rose in revolt against its leaders and refused to fight—not because the supply of the sinews of war was cut off—but either because the Commander-in-Chief was exhausted as a result of repeated fasting or because his mind and judgement were clouded owing to subjective causes which it is impossible for an outsider to understand.

What would have happened—I ask—if a similar incident had taken place in any other country? What happened to all the Governments that surrendered to the enemy at the end of the Great War? But India is a strange land.

The surrender of 1933 reminds one of the Bardoli Retreat of 1922. But in 1922, some explanation, however unsatisfactory, could be offered to justify the retreat. The outbreak of violence at Chauri Chaura was suggested as the pretext for suspending the Civil Disobedience campaign in 1922. What explanation or pretext can one suggest to account for the surrender of 1933?

There can be no doubt that the non-cooperation movement that was launched in 1920 and has been in existence in some form or other since that date—was the movement best suited to India in the fateful year 1920. There can be no doubt that in 1920 when political India was look-

[1] Presidential address at the Third Indian Political Conference, London, 10 June 1933, delivered in absentia.

[2] Bose is referring here to the sudden suspension of the Civil Disobedience Campaign by Mahatma Gandhi—eds.

ing forward to a more militant plan of action—Mahatma Gandhi was the one man who could stand up as the undisputed spokesman of the people and lead them on from victory to victory. And there can also be no doubt that during the last decade India has completed the march of a century. But standing today at the crossroads of Indian History—it is meet and proper that we should try to discover the mistakes of the past—so that our future activity may be directed along the right lines and all possible pitfalls may be avoided.

For the attainment of freedom two paths are open to us. One is the path of uncompromising militancy. The other is the path of compromise. If we follow the first path, the fight for liberty will have to be pursued till we are able to wrest political power in its entirety. There can be no question of a compromise along the road to freedom. If, on the other hand, we follow the second path, periodical compromises may have to be made with our opponents for consolidating our position, before further attempts are made.

At the outset it should strike everybody that it is not at all clear if our movement during the last thirteen years has been following the path of uncompromising militancy or that of compromise. This ideological ambiguity has been responsible for a lot of mischief. If our policy had been one of uncompromising militancy, the Bardoli surrender of 1922 would never have taken place—nor would the Delhi Pact of March 1931, have been entered into. On the other hand, if we had been following the path of compromise, we should never have missed the opportunity of a bargain with the British Government in December 1921—when the situation was so opportune. In March 1931, the situation was not opportune for a compromise from our point of view—nevertheless a truce was established between the Indian National Congress and the British Government. And considering our strength in March 1931—the terms of the truce were altogether unsatisfactory. In short, as political fighters we have been neither sufficiently militant—nor sufficiently diplomatic.

In a fight between an unarmed subject people like the Indians and a first-class imperialist power like Great Britain—the supply of our necessary resources depends on our ability to keep up the enthusiasm of the people and maintain the spirit of opposition towards the Government. In the case of a war between two well-equipped and well-trained armies, the psychological factor is not so important as in our case. In 1922, when the whole nation had been roused to passionate activity and greater daring and sacrifice could be expected of the people the Commander-in-Chief suddenly hoisted the white flag. And this happened after he had thrown away, a couple of months earlier, a unique opportunity for what would have appeared in the existing circumstances as an honourable compromise with the Bureaucracy.

It is not easy to learn or to remember the lessons of past history and the latest developments in India go to show that we have not yet assimilated the lessons of 1921 and 1922. And unfortunately for us, with the death of Deshbandhu C.R. Das and Pandit Motilal Nehru of hallowed memory in 1925 and 1931 respectively—there disappeared from the Indian scene two political giants who might have saved India from the political mess in which she now finds herself.

In December 1927, when the Indian National Congress met at Madras, the unanimous acceptance of the resolution on Independence gave an indication of the rising temper of our people. And when early in 1928 the Simon Commission landed at Bombay, the demonstrations throughout India were reminiscent of the glorious days of 1921. From one point of view, the situation in 1928 was more favourable than in 1921—because while in 1921 the Indian Liberals were actively opposed to the British Government, in the campaign against the Simon Commission there was a united front of the Congress and the Liberal Party. The arrival of the Simon Commission should therefore have been the occasion for reviving the movement which had been suspended arbitrarily by Mahatma Gandhi in 1922. Nevertheless, for full two years, instead of marching ahead we began to retreat. In December 1928, a resolution was passed at the Calcutta Congress by approximately 1,300 votes to 900, which put back the clock by definitely committing the Congress to the acceptance of Dominion Status. Thus at Calcutta we retreated not only from the position at Madras in December 1927—but also from the position at Nagpur in December 1920—because the Nagpur resolution on Swaraj, in view of its vague terminology, could be interpreted to mean that the goal of the Indian people was to be 'Independence' and not 'Dominion Status'.

The resolution of the Calcutta Congress gave the British Government one year's time within which they could offer Dominion Status to India. But the Government had no intention of making any such offer to India. The situation therefore became rather critical for the Congress leaders when the year 1929 began to draw to a close without Dominion Status being in sight. Another gesture was made by the Congress leaders in November 1929, on the eve of the Lahore Congress, but to no avail. In a joint manifesto—now generally known as the Delhi Manifesto—the leaders agreed to participate in the Round Table Conference in London if some assurance would be given that Dominion Status would be granted to India.

I was one of those who had the temerity to oppose Mahatma Gandhi's resolution on Dominion Status at the Calcutta Congress in 1928 and who had the presumption to condemn the Delhi Manifesto of November 1929. We had to point out that the Round Table Conference was a misnomer because it was not a Conference of plenipotentiaries representing the belligerent parties. A large number of nondescript Indians nominated by the alien Government would be present at the Conference to do the bidding of the wily British politicians. Moreover, if the Conference by any chance arrived at any conclusions favourable to India—they would nor be binding on the British Government. We also pointed out that the primary object of the Government in convening this Conference was to bring the Indians to England and make them fight amongst themselves for the amusement of the British people. We therefore urged that as the Sinn Feiners had boycotted the Irish Convention, which was Mr Lloyd George's creation, so also the Indian National Congress should leave the Round Table Conference severely alone.

But ours was a cry in the wilderness. The leaders as a body were too anxious to find some honourable escape from the impending fight with the Government which was every day becoming unavoidable. But no such opportunity was given by the Government. Consequently when the Lahore Congress met in December 1929, the temper of the people had risen and there was no alternative for the leaders but to swallow the resolution on Independence.

But 'Independence' which implied severance of the British connection—was like a pill bitter to the taste and difficult to digest. When the Congress unanimously adopted the resolution on Independence and thereby once for all ended the shilly-shallying of the last nine years—the moderate elements in the country were alarmed. Our leaders lost no time in trying to reassure them and beautiful phrases and attractive slogans were evolved for the purpose. We were told that Independence meant 'Purna Swaraj' (an expression which one could interpret according to his convenience). Mahatma Gandhi issued early in 1930 his famous 'eleven points' which according to him represented the substance of Independence and could form the basis of a compromise with the British

Government. Thus the significance and the effect of the Lahore Congress resolution on Independence was nullified to a great extent through the action of the leaders themselves.

After the Lahore Congress it was impossible for the leaders not to do anything. The movement was therefore launched with the celebration of the Independence Day on the 26 January 1930. By April the whole of India was in the throes of a revolution (may be a non-violent revolution). So great was the response of the people to the call to action that even Mahatma Gandhi was taken by surprise and he stated that the movement could have been started two years earlier.

The movement of 1930—like the earlier movement of 1921—took the Government by surprise and for a long time they were at a loss to decide as to the most effective means for crushing the movement. The international situation—economic and political—also helped India. It was therefore a mistake to suspend operations on the basis of what is known as the Delhi Pact (the Gandhi-Irwin Pact) of March 1931. Even if the leaders wanted a compromise, they should have waited for a more opportune moment, and such a moment would certainly have arrived if the operations had continued for another six months or one year. But once again subjectivism prevailed—and objective factors and considerations were not taken into account when the Delhi Pact was entered into. I shall even go so far as to say that in the circumstances which prevailed in March 1931—better terms could have been extracted from the Government if our leaders had possessed greater statesmanship and diplomacy.

As matters stood, the Delhi Pact was an advantage to the Government and a disaster to the people. The Government got time to study the tactics adopted by the Congress organisations in 1930 and 1931, so that they could perfect their machinery for striking a crushing blow whenever the Congress launched the movement once again. It is now a matter of common knowledge that the ordinances promulgated by the Government in January 1932, and the detailed tactics adopted by them throughout the year, were carefully worked out before the year 1931 came to a close. But what did the Congress do? In spite of the fact that there was seething discontent in the Frontier province, in the United Provinces and Bengal, nothing was done by the leaders to prepare the country for the unavoidable resumption of the fight. In fact, I shall not be wrong if I say that till the last everything was done to avoid a possible resumption of hostilities.

The Delhi Pact had on the whole a soporific effect on the popular enthusiasm and passion—nevertheless, the temper of the people was too militant to be soothed by soft phrases. And if this had not been the case, I am sure that a resumption of hostilities would have been successfully avoided by the leaders. It is necessary for the workers of tomorrow to realise that the movement of 1932 was not planned and organised by the leaders, as it should have been, but that they were dragged into it. And if this statement be true, should it surprise anybody if the leaders today feel anxious to get out of the troubles into which they were forced in January 1932?

The Delhi Pact of March 1931, will appear to be a painful document the more we study it:

(1) In the first place there was not one word of commitment on the part of the British Government on the major issue of Swaraj.
(2) In the second place there was a tacit acceptance of the proposal of federation with the Indian Princes—a proposal which, in my humble opinion, is disastrous to the political progress of the country.
(3) Thirdly, there was no provision for the release of the incarcerated Garhwali soldiers—the finest apostles of non-violence—who refused to shoot down their unarmed countrymen.
(4) Fourthly, there was no provision for the release of the state-prisoners and detenus who were imprisoned without any trial, charge or justification.
(5) Fifthly, there was no provision for the withdrawal of the Meerut Conspiracy Case which had been dragging on for years.
(6) Sixthly, there was no provision for the release of other classes of political prisoners, not convicted for participation in the Civil Disobedience movement.

It will thus be seen that the Delhi Pact, by refusing to espouse the cause of the Garhwali soldiers, the state-prisoners, the Meerut Conspiracy prisoners and the revolutionary prisoners, deprived the Indian National Congress of the claim to be the central organ of the anti-imperialist struggle in India. By declining to be the spokesman of these militant anti-imperialist elements in India, the Indian National Congress stood out before the Indian public as the spokesman and representative of the 'Satyagrahies' (Civil resisters) alone.

If the Delhi Pact of March 1931 was a blunder, the surrender of May 1933, is a calamity of the first magnitude. According to the principles of political strategy, at a time when the new constitution for India is under discussion, the maximum pressure should have been brought to bear on the Government by a strengthening of the Civil disobedience movement in the country. By suspending the movement at this critical hour, the work, the suffering and the sacrifice of the nation for the last thirteen years have been virtually undone. And the tragedy of the situation is that the people who could have effectively protested against this gross betrayal are now safely lodged behind prison bars. As to those who are outside prison, a real protest has not probably been possible because of the 21 days fast of Mahatma Gandhi.

But the die has been cast. Suspension of the Civil disobedience campaign for one month means virtually a permanent suspension—because mass movements cannot be created overnight. So the problem now before us is what we should do to make the most of a bad situation and what policy and plan we should adopt for the future.

Before we can solve this problem, two other questions will have to be answered by us:

(1) With regard to our goal, is a compromise between England and India ultimately possible?
(2) With regard to our method, can India win political freedom by following the path of periodical compromise and without adopting an uncompromisingly militant plan of action?

To the first question I say that such a compromise is not possible. A political compromise is possible only when there is some community of interest. But in the case of England and India there are no common interests which can make a compromise between the two nations possible and desirable, as we shall see from the following:

(1) There is no social kinship between the two countries.
(2) There is hardly anything in common between the cultures of India and of Britain.
(3) From the economic standpoint, India is to Britain is a supplier of raw materials and a consumer of British manufactures. On the other hand, India aspires to be a manufacturing country, so that she could become self-contained in the matter of manufactured goods and could also export not only raw materials but manufactured goods as well.
(4) India is at present one of the biggest markets for Great Britain. The industrial progress of India therefore is against Britain's economic interests.

(5) India affords employment at present to young Britishers in the army and in the civil administration in India. But this is against India's interests and India wants her own children to occupy all these posts.

(6) India is sufficiently strong and has enough resources to be able to stand on her own legs without the help or patronage of Great Britain. In this respect the position of India is quite different from that of the dominions.

(7) India has so long been exploited and dominated by Britain that there is a genuine apprehension that in the event of a political compromise between the two countries, India will stand to lose and Britain will stand to gain. Moreover, India has developed an 'inferiority complex' as a result of her long servitude, and this 'inferiority complex' will remain as long as India is not completely independent of Britain.

(8) India wants the status of a free country, with her own flag, her own army, navy and defence force, and with her own ambassadors in the capitals of free countries. Without this invigorating and life-giving freedom, Indians will never be able to rise to the full stature of their manhood. Independence is to India a psychological, ethical, cultural, economic and political necessity. It is an essential condition of the new awakening in India. Independence, which India aspires after today, is not 'Dominion Home Rule', as we find in Canada or Australia, but full national sovereignty as obtains in the United States of America or in France.

(9) As long as India remains within the British Empire she will not be able to safeguard the interests of other Indians who have settled in other parts of the Empire. The weight of Great Britain has always been, and always will be thrown on the side of white races—as against the Indians. An independent India, on the other hand, will be able to secure better treatment for her children who have settled in different parts of the British Empire.

It will thus be seen that the basis of a compromise between India and Great Britain does not exist. Consequently, if the leaders of the Indian people disregard this fundamental fact and effect a compromise with the British Government, the arrangement will not last. Like the 'Gandhi-Irwin Pact' of March 1931, it will be short-lived. The social, economic and political forces working within India are such that no peace is possible between India and Britain till her legitimate aspirations are fulfilled.

The only solution of the present deadlock that is possible is through the attainment of India's freedom. This implies the defeat of the British Government in India. How India can win freedom for herself, we shall now have to consider.

With regard to the second question—namely, the question of the method we should adopt—I may say that the country has already rejected the path of periodical compromise. The support which the country gave to the Indian National Congress was due to the fact that the Congress promised to win Independence for India and promised to fight on and on till this was accomplished. Therefore, in determining our future policy and plan, we should rule out, once for all, the prospect of periodical compromises.

The Congress hoped to win political freedom for India by paralysing the Civil administration of the country through non-cooperation and Civil disobedience. It is necessary now to analyse the causes of our failure in doing so in order that we may by more successful in the future.

The position of the British Government in India today in relation to the Indian National Congress can be compared to a well-armed and well-equipped fortress standing in the midst of territory which has suddenly become hostile. Now, however well-equipped a fortress may be it requires for its safe existence for all time a friendly civil population living around and near it. But even if the surrounding population become hostile, the fortress has nothing to fear in the immediate future, so long as the people round about it do not make an active attempt to seize the fortress. The objective of the Indian National Congress is to get possession of the fortress now occupied by the British Government. Towards this end the Congress has succeeded in winning over the sympathy and support of the population living round about and near the fortress. This is the first stage of the campaign from the Indian side. For the next stage of the campaign, either or both of the following steps can be taken:

(1) A complete economic blockade of the fortress, which will starve into submission the army occupying the fortress.
(2) An attempt to capture the fortress by force of arms.

In the history of war both these methods have been tried with success. In the last great war Germany was the victor from a military point of view, but she was starved into submission through the economic blockade of the Allies. This blockade was possible because the Allies had control over the seas and over the lines of communication leading into Germany.

In India no attempt has been made to storm the enemy's citadel by force of arms, as the Congress policy has been pledged to non-violence. The economic blockade, though attempted in a general way by the Congress, has failed for three reasons:

(a) All the external communications leading to India are controlled by the Government.
(b) Owing to defective organisation inside India the lines of communication from the seaports to the interior and from one part of the country to another are not controlled by the Congress, but by the Government.
(c) The machinery for collecting revenue—on which depends the existence of the British Government in India—has not been seriously impaired. There have been deficits in most provinces, no doubt, but the Government have been able to make up either by increased taxation or by borrowing.

In should always be remembered that a nationalist movement can succeed in paralysing a foreign Government only when either or all of the following steps are taken:

(1) Prevention of tax and revenue collection.
(2) Adoption of measures whereby help from other quarters—whether financial or military—may not reach the Government in times of distress.
(3) Winning over the sympathy and support of the present supporters of the British Government in India—that is, of the Army, the Police and Civil Servants—so that orders given by the Government for crushing the movement will not be carried out.
(4) Actual attempt to seize power by force of arms.

The last step has to be ruled out, because the Congress is pledged to non-violence. But it is nevertheless possible to paralyse the present administration and compel it to submit to our demands if we can adopt the following measures:

(1) Prevent collection of tax and revenue.
(2) Through labour and peasant organisation prevent all kinds of help from reaching the Government when they are in difficulty.
(3) Win the sympathy and support of the Government's own supporters by means of our superior propaganda.

If these three measures are adopted, the Governmental machinery can be thrown out of gear. In the first place, they will have no money to meet the cost of administration. In the second place, the orders they may issue will not be carried our by their own officers. And, help sent to the Government from other quarters will not reach them.

There is no royal road to success in winning political freedom. The above three measures have to be adopted in part or in whole if victory is to be achieved. The Congress has failed, simply because it has not succeeded in giving effect satisfactorily to any of the above three measures. The peaceful meetings, processions and demonstrations that have been held during the last few years, in spite of the official ban, show a spirit of defiance no doubt and also cause some annoyance to the Government, but they do not yet menace the very existence of the Government. In spite of all our demonstrations and in spite of seventy thousand persons having gone to prison since January 1932, the Government can still claim:

(1) That their army is quite loyal.
(2) That their police forces are quite loyal.
(3) That the Civil administration (collection of revenue and taxes, administration of law courts and of prisons, etc.) is still unimpaired.
(4) That the life and property of Government officials and of their supporters are still quite safe.

And the Government can still boast that they do not care if the general population in India today are passively hostile. As long as the people do not actively menace the Government and their supporters, either with arms or through an effective economic blockade, the present Government can continue to exist for an indefinite period, in spite of our non-cooperation and Civil disobedience.

During the last decade there has been an unprecedented awakening all over India. The placid self-complacence of the people is gone. The whole country is throbbing with new life and is yearning for freedom. Fear of official frowns, of imprisonment and of baton charges has disappeared. The prestige of the British has reached its lowest ebb. There is no question of goodwill on the Indian side towards the British Government. The moral basis of British rule has been demolished, and it rests today on the naked sword and on nothing else. And India has managed to capture the imagination of the world.

But the fact has to be faced that 'free India' is still a thing of the future! The intentions of the British Government with regard to Indian aspirations as embodied in the recently published White Paper show clearly that they are not yet prepared to part with an iota of real power. Apparently the British Government think that they are strong enough to resist successfully the demand of the Indian people. And if they are strong enough to resist us, it clearly shows that the most strenuous efforts of the Indian people since 1920 have failed to bring us appreciably nearer our goal of 'Swaraj'.

India therefore must resolve to launch another fight on a bigger and more intensive scale. The intellectual and practical preparation for this must be scientific and must rest on objective foundations. The intellectual preparation for this task will entail the following measures:

(i) A scientific examination of the strong and weak points of British Rule in India in relation to the Indian people.
(ii) A scientific examination of the strong and weak points of the Indian people in relation to British rule in India.
(iii) A scientific examination of the rise and fall of empires in other parts of the world.
(iv) A scientific examination of the history of freedom movements in other lands and a study of the gradual evolution of freedom in all its aspects in this world.

When this study is completed—and not till then—shall we be able to form a conception of the magnitude of the task that awaits us.

Our next requirement will be a party of determined men and women who will take upon themselves the task of delivering India—no matter what the suffering and sacrifice involved may be. Whether India will be able to free herself and to live once again as a free nation will depend on whether she can produce the requisite leadership. Her ability to produce the requisite leadership will be the test of her vitality and of her fitness for 'Swaraj'.

Our next requirement will be a scientific plan of action and a scientific programme for the future. The method of action beginning from today and right up to the conquest of power will have to be visualised and planned out in detail as far as humanly possible. The movement of the future must therefore be made to rest on an objective and scientific foundation in keeping with the facts of history and of human nature. Hitherto, too much appeal has been made to 'inner light' and to subjective feeling in guiding a political campaign which is after all an objective movement.

Besides a plan of action which will lead up to the conquest of power, we shall require a programme for the new state when it comes into existence in India. Nothing can be left to chance. The group of men and women who will assume the leadership of the fight with Great Britain will also have to take up the task of controlling, guiding and developing the new state and, through the state, the entire Indian people. If our leaders are not trained for post-war leadership also there is the possibility that after the conquest of power a period of chaos will set in and incidents similar to those of the French Revolution of the eighteenth century may be repeated in India. It should therefore be clear that the generals of the war-time period in India will have to carry through the whole programme of post-war reform in order to justify to their countrymen the hopes and aspirations that they will have to rouse during the fight. The task of these leaders will not be over till a new generation of men and women are educated and trained after the establishment of the new state and this new generation are able to take complete charge of their country's affairs.

The party of the future will have to part company with the erstwhile leaders of the Indian people, because there is no possibility that the latter will be able to adopt the principles, programme, policy and tactics that will be required for the next phase of the grim fight with Great Britain. Rarely in history—if ever at all—do we find the leaders of one epoch figuring as the leaders of the next. The times always produce the required men, and this will happen in India also.

The new party will have to play the role of the fighters and leaders in the 'national' campaign against Great Britain and also the role of the architects of new India, who will be called upon to undertake the work of post-war social reconstruction. The Indian movement will have two phases. In the first phase the fight will be a 'national' fight against Great Britain—though the leadership will be in the hands of the 'party of the people' representing Indian labour and the second phase will be an inter-class fight under the leadership of the same party, and during this phase of the campaign—all privileges, distinctions and vested interests will have to be abolished, so that a reign of perfect equality (social, economic and political) may be established in our country. India will be called upon to play an important role in world-history in the near future. We all know that in the seventeenth-century England made a remarkable contribution to world-civilisation through her ideas of constitutional and democratic Government. Similarly, in the eighteenth century, France made the most wonderful contribution to the culture of the world through her ideas of 'liberty, equality and fraternity'. During the nineteenth-century Germany made the most remarkable gift through her Marxian Philosophy. During the twentieth-century Russia has enriched the culture and civilisation of the world through her achievement in proletarian revolution, proletarian Government and proletarian culture. The next remarkable contribution to the culture and civilisation of the world, India will be called upon to make.

It is sometimes urged by our British friends that the British public have an open mind on the Indian question and that we would gain much if we could win their sympathy by means of our propaganda. I do not, however, think that the British Public have an open mind on the Indian question—it is not humanly possible. In India, administration and exploitation go hand in hand, and it is not exploitation by a group of British capitalists and financiers, but the exploitation of India by Great Britain as a whole. The British capital that has been invested in India has not come from the upper classes alone, but also from the middle classes, and probably to some extent from the poorer classes as well. Further, even the working classes of Great Britain cannot afford to see the Indian textile industry thrive at the expense of Lancashire. That is why India has not been made a party question by the great political parties in Great Britain. That is why the policy of brutal repression and persecution was continued in India even when there was a Labour Government in power in London. I know that there are individual members in the Labour Party who rise above selfish consideration and who are sincere in their desire to do justice to India. But however much we may admire them and however cordial our personal relations with them may be, the fact remains that they are not in a position to influence party decisions. And, judging from our past experience, we may say that we cannot expect any improvement in the Indian situation through a change of Government in Downing Street.

Since politics and economics are inextricably bound up together in India—and since British Rule in India exists not only for political domination but also for economic exploitation—it follows that political freedom is primarily an economic necessity to us. The problem of giving bread to our starving millions—the problem of clothing and educating them—the problem of improving the health and physique of the nation—all these problems cannot be solved so long as India remains in bondage. To think of economic improvement and industrial development before India is free politically is to put the cart before the horse. We are frequently asked as to what will be the internal condition of India when British Rule disappears from our country. Thanks to British propaganda, India has been portrayed before the world as a country full of internal conflicts in which peace has been preserved by the might of England. India certainly had her internal conflicts in the past, as every other country has. But these conflicts were solved by the people themselves. That is why Indian history from the most ancient times abounds in instances of mighty empires like that of Asoka the Great, under the aegis of which peace and prosperity reigned throughout the land. But the conflicts of today are permanent in character and they are artificially engineered by the agents of the third party in our country. And I have no doubt in my mind that real unity among the Indian people can never be achieved as long as British Rule exists in India.

Though we cannot expect anything from any political party in England, it is exceedingly important and necessary for our purpose that we should organise international propaganda on behalf of India. This propaganda must be both positive and negative. On the negative side we must refute the lies that are told about India consciously or unconsciously by the agents of Great Britain throughout the world. On the positive side we must bring to the notice of the world the rich culture of India in all its aspects as well as India's manifold grievances. It goes without saying that London must be an important centre for this international propaganda. It is to be regretted that till quite recently the Indian National Congress did not realise the value and the necessity of international propaganda. But we now hope that our countrymen in the days to come will realise in an increasing degree the value of international propaganda.

There is probably nothing which I admire so much about the Britisher as his skill in propaganda. A Britisher is a born propagandist, and to him propaganda is more powerful than howitzers. There is one other country in Europe which has learnt this lesson from Britain, and that is Russia. And it is not surprising that Britain cordially dislikes Russia and is even afraid of her for having discovered the secret of her (Britain's) success.

There is so much of hostile propaganda carried on in this world against India by British agents that if only we could state the real condition of India and her grievances against Britain—we would at once get a large measure of international sympathy. I will now mention some of the points in connection with which active propaganda is necessary throughout the world:

(1) Ill-treatment of political prisoners in India and the transportation of long-term political prisoners to the unhealthy Andaman Islands, where recently two of them have died as a result of hunger-strike.

(2) Extreme vindictiveness displayed by the Government in the matter of issuing passports to Indians. (It is not known outside

India that innumerable Indians have been refused passports for going out of India, while Indians living abroad have been refused passports for returning to India.)

(3) The systematic practice of aeroplane bombing in India, particularly in the North-Western Frontier, for terrorising helpless villagers.

(4) The strangling of India's indigenous industries—including the shipbuilding industry—by Great Britain during her rule in India.

(5) The popular and widespread opposition in India to any scheme of Imperial Preference, including the Ottawa Pact. (The world should be informed that India never accepted the Ottawa Pact, but that it was forced down our unwilling throats.)

(6) The popular opposition in India to any proposal for a tariff truce, since India urgently wants protection for her infant industries.

(7) The fixing of the exchange rate arbitrarily by England in a manner that is prejudicial to India's interests. The world should know how Great Britain has robbed India of crores of rupees merely through the manipulation of the exchange rate.

(8) Further, the world should be told that Great Britain has saddled India with a heavy public debt for which Indian nationalists refuse to accept any responsibility. As early as in 1922 the Indian National Congress at its Gaya session gave notice to the Government that it would refuse to accept any responsibility for this public debt. It is a matter of common knowledge that the debt was incurred nor for India's benefit, but for the interests of British imperialists.

It is exceedingly important and necessary that some propaganda should be conducted on behalf of India for the World Economic Conference and the Disarmament Conference. A carefully prepared memorandum stating the economic grievances of India against Great Britain and giving expression to the real voice of India on economic questions should be placed before every member of the World Economic Conference.

With regard to the Disarmament question, India should tell the world that British sincerity should be put to the test by making India a test case. In a land where the people have been disarmed for nearly 80 years, where the entire population is altogether emasculated, what justification is there for spending more than 50 per cent of the central revenues on military expenditure?

I feel sure that if all the facts in this connection are brought to the notice of the world, there will be an unanswerable case against England.

Whenever the question of India is brought up before a World Congress or a World Conference the usual plea raised by the protagonists of Great Britain is that India is a domestic question so far as the British Empire is concerned. This is a position which Indians should refuse to accept any longer. If India is a member of the League of Nations, surely she is a nation and has all the rights and privileges of a nation. I know that we shall have to fight hard and fight strenuously before we can alter the present status of India in international affairs. Nevertheless it is imperative that the attempt should begin without delay.

It is not necessary for me to go into a detailed consideration of the contents of the White Paper, as they do not deserve such an examination. I shall only say that the proposal of Federation with the Princes is an impossible and unacceptable proposition. We shall certainly work for the unification of the whole of India—for a federation of the Indian people. But we cannot accept the present proposal of substituting the Princes for the present official bloc in the Legislatures, in order to satisfy the whims of Mr Ramsay MacDonald or of Lord Sankey. And it is futile to talk of 'freedom' and 'safeguards' in the same breath. If we are to have freedom there can be no safeguards, for freedom itself is the only safeguard that we can have. To talk of 'safeguards in the interest of India' is but a species of self-deception.

It is not possible to say today when we shall get a constitution which will give some substantial power to the people. But there can be no doubt that when we do get that power the people will insist on having the right to bear arms. They also will say to the world, and particularly to the British Government: 'Disarm, or we shall arm.' While voluntary disarming is a great blessing to this sorrow-stricken world, the forcible disarming of a conquered people for nearly 80 years, as we see in India, is one of the greatest of curses. And the much-vaunted Pax Britannica which we see in India is not the peace of a healthy life, but peace of the graveyard.

I have already referred to the dual role which the new party will be called upon to play if it is to justify its existence. In order to be able to seize political power and thereafter use it for the creation of a new social order it is necessary that our people should be trained for the task from today. I have no doubt in my own mind that in solving the problems of our national life, when India is free, original thought and fresh experiment will be necessary if we are to achieve success. The experience of the older generation and of the teachers of the past will not be of much avail. The socio-economic conditions of free India will be altogether different from what prevails now. In industry, agriculture, land-tenure, money, exchange, currency, education, prison administration, public health, etc., new theories and novel experiments will have to be devised. We know, for example, that in Soviet Russia a new scheme of national (or political) economy has been evolved in keeping with the facts and conditions of the land. The same thing will happen to India. In solving our economic problem, Pigou and Marshall will not be of much help.

Already in Europe and in England old theories in every department of life are being challenged and new theories are taking their places. As an instance, let me mention the new theory of Free Money, evolved by Silvio Gesell, which has been put into operation in a small community in Germany and proved thoroughly satisfactory. The same thing will happen in India. Free India will not be a land of capitalists, landlords and castes. Free India will be a social and a political democracy. The problems of Free India will be quite different from those of present-day India, and it will therefore be necessary to train men from today who will be able to visualise the future, to think in terms of Free India and solve those problems in anticipation. In short, it will be necessary to educate and train from today the future cabinet of Free India.

Every great movement starts from small beginnings, and so it will be in India. Our first task will be to gather together a group of men and women who are prepared to undergo the maximum sacrifice and suffering which will be necessary if we are to attain success in our mission. They must be whole-time workers—'Freedom-intoxicated' missionaries—who will not be discouraged by failure or deterred by difficulty of any kind and who will vow to work and strive in the service of the great cause till the last day of their lives.

When these 'morally prepared' men and women are available they must be given the requisite intellectual training so that they may be able to realise the magnitude of their task. They will have to make a scientific and critical study of the freedom movements in other lands, so that they may understand how similar problems have been solved in other countries, in spite of similar difficulties. Side by side with this they must also make a scientific and critical study of the rise and fall of empires in other ages and climes. Armed with this knowledge, they should proceed to make a scientific examination of the strong and weak points of the British Government in India in relation to the Indian people and a similar scientific examination of the strong and weak points of the Indian people in relation to the British Government.

When this intellectual training is completed we shall have a clear notion of the plan of action that will be necessary for the conquest of power and also of the programme that should be put into operation when the new state is brought into existence after the seizure of power. It is thus evident that we want a party of determined men and women who have consecrated their life to the great cause, who have had the necessary intellectual training and who have formed a clear conception of the work they will have to do before the conquest of power and thereafter.

It will be the task of this party to deliver India from foreign yoke. It will be the task of this party to create a new, Independent and sovereign state in India. It will be the task of this party to execute the entire programme of post-war socio-economic reconstruction. It will be the task of this party to create a new generation of men and women in India fully trained and equipped for the battle of life. Last, but not least, it will be the task of this party to lead India on to her honoured place among the free nations of the world.

Let this party be called the Samyavadi Sangh. It will be a centralised and well-disciplined All-India Party—working amongst every section of the community. This party will have its representatives working in the Indian National Congress, in the All-India Trade Union Congress, in the Peasants' organisations, in the women's organisations, in the youth organisations, in the student organisations, in the depressed classes' organisations, and, if necessary in the interests of a great cause, in the sectarian or communal organisations as well. The different branches of the party working in different spheres and in different places must be under the control and guidance of the central committee of the party.

This party will work in cooperation with any other party that may be working towards the same end, in whole or in part. It will not bear enmity towards any individual or party, but at the same time it will look upon itself as especially called upon to play the role in history that has been described above.

In addition to the activities of the Samyavadi Sangh that we have described above, branches of the Sangh should be started all over the country for carrying on a general propaganda about the ideals, aims and objects of the new party. The Samyavadi Sangh will stand for all round freedom for the Indian people—that is for social, economic and political freedom. It will wage a relentless war against bondage of every kind till the people can become really free. It will stand for political independence for India so that a new state can be created in Free India on the basis of the eternal principles of justice, equality and freedom. It will stand for the ultimate fulfilment of India's mission, so that India may be able to deliver to the world the message that has been her heritage through the past ages.

13

The Role of Mahatma Gandhi in Indian History[1]

The role which a man plays in history depends partly on his physical and mental equipment, and partly on the environment and the needs of times in which he is born. There is something in Mahatma Gandhi, which appeals to the mass of the Indian people. Born in another country he might have been a complete misfit. What, for instance, would he have done in a country like Russia or Germany or Italy? His doctrine of non-violence would have led him to the cross or to the mental hospital. In India it is different. His simple life, his vegetarian diet, his goat's milk, his day of silence every week, his habit of squatting on the floor instead of sitting on a chair, his loin-cloth—in fact everything connected with him—has marked him out as one of the eccentric Mahatmas of old and has brought him nearer to his people. Wherever he may go, even the poorest of the poor feels that he is a product of the Indian soil—bone of his bone, flesh of his flesh. When the Mahatma speaks, he does so in a language that they comprehend, not in the language of Herbert Spencer and Edmund Burke, as for instance Sir Surendra Nath Banerji would have done, but in that of the *Bhagavad-Gita* and the *Ramayana*. When he talks to them about Swaraj, he does not dilate on the virtues of provincial autonomy or federation, he reminds them of the glories of *Rama-rajya* (the kingdom of King Rama of old) and they understand. And when he talks of conquering through love and *ahimsa* (non-violence), they are reminded of Buddha and Mahavira and they accept him.

But the conformity of the Mahatma's physical and mental equipment to the traditions and temperament of the Indian people is but one factor accounting for the former's success. If he had been born in another epoch in Indian history, he might not have been able to distinguish himself so well. For instance, what would he have done at the time of the Revolution of 1857 when the people had arms, were able to fight and wanted

[1] Chapter 16 in *The Indian Struggle*, 1935.

a leader who could lead them in battle? The success of the Mahatma has been due to the failure of constitutionalism on the one side and armed revolution on the other. Since the eighties of the last century, the best political brains among the Indian people were engaged in a constitutional fight, in which the qualities most essential were skill in debate and eloquence in speech. In such an environment it is unlikely that the Mahatma would have attained much eminence. With the dawn of the present century people began to lose faith in constitutional methods. New weapons like Swadeshi (revival of national industry) and Boycott appeared, and simultaneously the revolutionary movement was born. As the years rolled by, the revolutionary movement began to gain ground (especially in Upper India) and during the Great War there was an attempt at a revolution. The failure of this attempt at a time when Britain had her hands full and the tragic events of 1919 convinced the Indian people that it was no use trying to resort to the method of physical force. The superior equipment of Britain would easily smash any such attempt and in its wake there would come indescribable misery and humiliation.

In 1920 India stood at the cross-roads. Constitutionalism was dead; armed revolution was sheer madness. But silent acquiescence was impossible. The country was groping for a new method and looking for a new leader. Then there sprang up India's man of destiny—Mahatma Gandhi—who had been biding his time all these years and quietly preparing himself for the great task ahead of him. He knew himself—he knew his country's needs and he knew also that during the next phase of India's struggle, the crown of leadership would be on his head. No false sense of modesty troubled him—he spoke with a firm voice and the people obeyed.

The Indian National Congress of today is largely his creation. The Congress Constitution is his handwork. From a talking body he has converted the Congress into a living and fighting organisation. It has its ramification in every town and village in India, and the entire nation has been trained to listen to one voice. Nobility of character and capacity to suffer have been made the essential tests of leadership, and the Congress is today the largest and the most representative political organisation in the country.

But how could he achieve so much within this short period? By his single-hearted devotion, his relentless will and his indefatigable labour. Moreover, the time was auspicious and his policy prudent. Though he appeared as a dynamic force, he was not too revolutionary for the majority of his countrymen. If he had been so, he would have frightened them, instead of inspiring them; repelled them, instead of drawing them. His policy was one of unification. He wanted to unite Hindu and Moslem; the high caste and the low caste; the capitalist and the labourer; the landlord and the peasant. By this humanitarian outlook and his freedom from hatred, he was able to rouse sympathy even in his enemy's camp.

But Swaraj is still a distant dream. Instead of one, the people have waited for fourteen long years. And they will have to wait many more. With such purity of character and with such an unprecedented following, why has the Mahatma failed to liberate India?

He has failed because the strength of a leader depends not on the largeness—but on the character—of one's following. With a much smaller following, other leaders have been able to liberate their country—while the Mahatma with a much larger following has not. He has failed, because while he has understood the character of his own people—he has not understood the character of his opponents. The logic of the Mahatma is not the logic which appeals to John Bull. He has failed, because his policy of putting all his cards on the table will not do. We have to render unto Caesar what is Caesar's—and in a political fight the art of diplomacy cannot be dispensed with. He has failed, because he has not made use of the international weapon. If we desire to win our freedom through non-violence, diplomacy and international propaganda are essential. He has failed, because the false unity of interests that are inherently opposed is not a source of strength but a source of weakness in political warfare. The future of India rests exclusively with those radical and militant forces that will be able to undergo the sacrifice and suffering necessary for winning freedom. Last but not least, the Mahatma has failed, because he had to play a dual role in one person—the role of the leader of an enslaved people and that of a world-teacher, who has a new doctrine to preach. It is this duality which has made him at once the irreconcilable foe of the Englishman, according to Mr Winston Churchill, and the best policeman of the Englishman according to Miss Ellen Wilkinson.

What of the future? What role will the Mahatma play in the days to come? Will he be able to emancipate his dear country? Several factors have to be considered. So far as his health and vitality are concerned, it is highly probable that he will be spared many years of active and useful public life and his determination to achieve something tangible in the direction of his country's freedom will keep up his spirits. So far as his popularity and reputation are concerned, they will endure till the end of his life—because unlike other political leaders, the Mahatma's popularity and reputation do not depend on his political leadership—but largely on his character. The question we have to consider, however, is whether the Mahatma will continue his political activities or whether he will voluntarily withdraw himself from active politics—of which there are indications at the present moment—and devote himself exclusively to social and humanitarian work. A prediction in the case of the Mahatma is a hazardous proposition. Nevertheless, one thing is certain. The Mahatma will not play second fiddle to anyone. As long as it will be possible for him to guide the political movement, he will be there—but if the composition or the mentality of the Congress changes, he may possibly retire from active politics. That retirement may be temporary or permanent. A temporary retirement is like a strategic retreat and is not of much significance because the hero will come back into the picture once again. We have had experience of the Mahatma's retirement from active politics once before—from 1924 to 1928. Whether there is a possibility of the Mahatma's permanent retirement depends to some extent at least, on the attitude of the British Government. If he is able to achieve something tangible for his country, then his position will be unassailable among his countrymen. Nothing succeeds like success, and the Mahatma's success will confirm public faith in his personality and in his weapon of non-violent non-cooperation. But if the British attitude continues to be as uncompromising as it is today, public faith in the Mahatma as a political leader and in the method of non-violent non-cooperation will be considerably shaken. In that event they will naturally turn to a more radical leadership and policy.

In spite of the unparalleled popularity and reputation which the Mahatma has among his countrymen and will continue to have regardless of his future political career, there is no doubt that the unique position of the Mahatma is due to his political leadership. The Mahatma himself distinguishes between his mass-popularity and his political following and he is never content with having merely the former. Whether he will be able to retain that political following in the years to come, in the event of the British attitude being as unbending as it is today, will depend on his ability to evolve a more radical policy. Will he be able to give up the attempt to unite all the elements in the country and boldly identify himself with the more radical forces? In that case nobody can possibly supplant him. The hero of the present phase of the Indian struggle will then he the hero of the next phase as well. But what does the balance of probability indicate?

The Patna meeting of the All-India Congress Committee in May 1934 affords an interesting study in this connection. The Mahatma averted the Swarajist revolt by advocating council-entry himself. But the Swarajists of 1934, are not the dynamic Swarajists of 1922–23. Therefore, while he was able to win them over, he could not avoid alienating the Left Wingers, many of whom have now combined to form the Congress Socialist Party. This is the first time that a Socialist Party has been started openly within the Indian National Congress, and it is extremely probable that economic issues will henceforth be brought to the fore. With the clarification of economic issues, parties will be more scientifically organised within the Congress and also among the people in general.

The Congress Socialists appear at the moment to be under the influence of Fabian Socialism and some of their ideas and shibboleths were the fashion several decades ago. Nevertheless, the Congress Socialists do represent a radical force within the Congress and in the country. Many of those who could have helped them actively are not available at present. When their assistance will be forthcoming, the Party will be able to make more headway.

At the present moment another challenge to the Mahatma's policy has crystallised within the Congress in the Congress Nationalist Party led by Pandit Malaviya. The dispute has arisen over the Communal Award of the Prime Minister, Mr Ramsay Macdonald. The issue is, however, a comparatively minor one, because the official Congress Party and the Congress Nationalist Party are agreed in the total rejection of the White Paper of which the Communal Award is an integral part. Only the official Congress Party is foolishly afraid of openly condemning the Communal Award. Since the Congress Nationalist Party does not represent a more radical force in the country, the ultimate challenge to the Mahatma's leadership cannot come from that direction.

One definite prediction can be made at this stage—namely, that the future parties within the Congress will be based on economic issues. It is not improbable that in the event of the Left Wingers capturing the Congress machinery, there will be a further secession from the Right and the setting up of a new organisation of the Right Wingers like the Indian Liberal Federation of today. It will of course take some years to clarify the economic issues in the public mind—so that parties may be organised on the basis of a clear programme and ideology. Till the issues are clarified, Mahatma Gandhi's political supremacy will remain unchallenged, even if there is a temporary retirement as in 1924. But once the clarification takes place, his political following will be greatly affected. As has been already indicated, the Mahatma has endeavoured in the past to hold together all the warring elements—landlord and peasant, capitalist and labour, rich and poor. That has been the secret of his success, as surely as it will be the ultimate cause of his failure. If all the warring elements resolve to carry on the struggle for political freedom, the internal social struggle will be postponed for a long time and men holding the position of the Mahatma will continue to dominate the public life of the country. But that will not be the case. The vested interests, the 'haves', will in future fight shy of the 'have-nots' in the political fight and will gradually incline towards the British Government. The logic of history will, therefore, follow its inevitable course. The political struggle and the social struggle will have to be conducted simultaneously. The Party that will win political freedom for India will be also the Party that will win social and economic freedom for the masses. Mahatma Gandhi has rendered and will continue to render phenomenal service to his country. But India's salvation will not be achieved under his leadership.

14
India and Germany

To Amiya Chakravarti*

Kurhaus Hochland
Badgastein, Austria
11 March 1936

. . . There are many things to tell; today I'll bring up one or two subjects. You must have noticed in the newspapers the excitement that Hitler's speech has created in India. It seems to me that there should be a sharp refutation on behalf of the federation. I am saying this after serious consideration. The result of such refutation will be favourable rather than unfavourable. I do not know what the Indians who are in Germany will do, perhaps it is a little difficult for them to do anything. But those of us who are abroad, our duty is clear. In this matter you should not feel hesitant. If it takes too much time or it is inconvenient to get the committee's approval before making such a refutation, then you, as the president, can make the reply of the federation. If some cowardly person in the future raises any question about this, then you can say that at home you have always worked with the backing of public support.. But when Indians at home are registering strong dissent, then, it becomes doubly necessary for Indians who are in Europe, to do the same. After a great deal of thought, I have sent a protest for the Indian newspapers (at home) and supported the proposal for halting trade with Germany. Very soon I will send a personal protest to the German leaders. But because behind me there is no organisation, perhaps it won't have too much effect. The protest that the federation made two years ago had some effect because a very mild reply came from 'The Foreign Office'. In your protest you might refer to the fact that the spirit of that letter has not been followed up. Instead a new insult has been inflicted on the Indian people. You have perhaps noted that in Japan there has been an 'official' protest against this.

*Translated from the original Bengali.

The Lucknow Congress will convene on the 8 April. I must arrive before that. Therefore my European tour is coming to an end, I must go. After considering what you have said and also what my friends have said in the same vein, I am telling you that is not possible to fully discus these things in a letter. Needless to say that as soon as I return, I stand the chance of being arrested. If they don't arrest me, then I agree with your views on how we should work. It is not possible to go anywhere else, because of the haste with which I have to return home. I have a great unfulfilled desired to travel in many countries, but for many reasons I cannot fulfil my desire.

. . . Something else should have been said about Hitler. It is not true that the very fact of protest would cause separation from the federation because two years ago a sharp protest was made and its result was not unfavourable. Against Germany, we (Indians) have many complaints. The other day (in January), I made known my protest, when I was in Berlin. They worship strength, not weakness. I am saying this even prepared for separation from the federation. Against Italy there are complaints from other standpoints—not from the standpoint of India's interest or prestige. But against Germany, we have many accusations from India's standpoint.

There is no early possibility of the fall of Hitler's Govt. If war breaks out some day and the war weakens Germany, then such a fall is possible, otherwise not. But if as a result of our boycott, Germany's trade suffers, then German businessmen will put pressure on Hitler. Now, in Germany there are two groups that are highly successful—army and businessmen . . .

As ever yours
SUBHAS CHANDRA BOSE

To Dr Thierfelder

Kurhaus Hochland
Badgastein
25 March 1936

Dear Dr Thierfelder,

It is time for me to return to India, but before I do so, I feel that I must say a few words in a frank but friendly manner.

When I first visited Germany in 1933, I had hopes that the new German nation which had risen to a consciousness of its national strength and self-respect, would instinctively feel a deep sympathy for other nations struggling in the same direction. Today I regret that I have to return to India with the conviction that the new nationalism of Germany is not only narrow and selfish but arrogant. The recent speech of Herr Hitler in Munich gives the essence of Nazi philosophy. I know that the Deutsche Nachrichtenburo has sent a dementi relating to this speech, to India and to Japan. But we do not accept this dementi, because it has not been published in the British or in the German press. The new racial philosophy which has a very weak scientific foundation stands for the glorification of the white races in general and the German race in particular. Herr Hitler has talked of the destiny of white races to rule over the rest of the world. But the historical fact is that up till now the Asiatics have dominated Europe more than have the Europeans dominated Asia. One has only to consider the repeated invasions of Europe by Mongols, the Turks, the Arabs (Moors), the Huns, and other Asiatic races to understand the strength of my argument. I am saying this not because I stand for the domination of one people by another, but simply because I want to point out that it is historically false to say that Europe and Asia should not be at peace with one another. It therefore pains us that the new nationalism in Germany is inspired by selfishness and racial arrogance. Herr Hitler in his *Mein Kampf* denounced Germany's old colonial policy. But Nazi Germany has begun to talk for her old colonies.

Apart from this new racial philosophy and selfish nationalism there is another factor which affects us even more. Germany in her desire to curry favour with Great Britain finds it convenient to attack India and the Indian people. We have had repeated examples of this in the history of the National Socialist Party. The attempt began nearly ten years ago when the party published a pamphlet in English for propaganda in England consisting of anti-Indian passages from the books of Herr Hitler and Dr Rosenberg.

I have great regard for the work that you and the Deutsche Academie have been doing for an understanding between our two countries. But I feel sorry, that owing to the reasons given above, much of this work is being undone. I can only hope that in the long run your efforts will prevail; but the present atmosphere in Germany is rather disappointing for us. The older generation who had been brought up under the influence of a different racial and political philosophy are quite different from the people who are trained under the influence of a new and different philosophy—racial and political. I know that we shall not lose our old friends, but I doubt if we shall gain new ones from among the new generation. According to our past experience, the Germans were a very warm-hearted people, particularly friendly to Indians. But do we know what will happen when the new education has had its full effect on the rising generation?

I am extremely thankful to you for the efforts you made in arranging the meeting in January last. I had two long meetings with Ministerialdirektor Dieckhoff and Gesandter Dr Prufer. Both of them were personally very cordial to me, as on former occasions. But the result of the interview was practically nil. I left them with the conviction that they attached very little importance to the Indian question. I also had the feeling that if an understanding with India is to be realised, some other Ministry or Ministries should be approached.

After the speech of Herr Hitler, I have issued a very strong statement to the Indian press which I hope will be published in due course. But I would like to say this before I leave Europe that I am still prepared to work for an understanding between Germany and India. This understanding must be consistent with our national self-respect. When we are fighting the greatest Empire in the world for our freedom and for our rights and when we are confident of our ultimate success, we cannot brook any insult from any other nation or any attack on our race or culture.

I am an optimist and I still hope that the present atmosphere will change and we shall ultimately arrive at an understanding. Meanwhile I assure you of my warmest esteem and of the great regard I have for the work of the Deutsche Akademie. You need not take the trouble of replying to this letter because within a few days I shall be on my way and on my arrival in India, I shall in all probability be imprisoned.

With warmest compliments, I am,

Yours sincerely
Subhas C. Bose

PS The above represents not only my personal views but also the views of Indian nationalists in general. I have no objection if you forward a copy of this letter to any friends or any state department in order to inform them about the Indian attitude towards Germany.

S.C. Bose

15
Impressions of Ireland*

30 March 1936

I am grateful to President De Valera for the permit to visit the Irish Free State and thereby fulfil a long-cherished desire of mine—and also for the warm and cordial reception I received at his hand in Dublin. It was the desire and command of the late Mr V.J. Patel that I should visit Dublin before returning home and attempt to revive the activities of the Indian Irish League which he had helped to found. I hope that my visit to Ireland has served some useful purpose in that direction.

While in Ireland I endeavoured to meet as many parties and personalities as I possibly could in order to get a correct picture of the social and political life of the country. I believe I have learned much that will be useful and interesting to us in India.

In the Parliament (Dail) the majority party is President De Valera's Fianna Fail which has also the support of the Labour Party led by Mr Norton. The opposition party is Mr Cosgrave's 'Fine Geel' Party. Mr Cosgrave's party has many fine speakers and able debaters but the country as a whole is behind 'Fianna Fail'—because Mr Cosgrave's party is looked upon as a Pro-British Party and practically all the old unionists support it. Mr Cosgrave's party has been weakened by the defection of General O'Duffy, the organiser of the Blue-Shirts, who has founded the National Corporate Party on Fascist lines. This has naturally strengthened the position of 'Fianna Fail' in the country.

The only unfortunate feature in Irish politics today is the breach between 'Fianna Fail' and the Republicans. The Republicans allege that President De Valera is not moving towards a Republic which he had promised and that his Government is persecuting the Republicans, 25 of whom have been put in prison. The feeling of the Government is that the

*Bose's statement on impressions about Ireland in Lausanne on Monday, 30 March 1936.

Republicans are too impatient and tactless and are blind to the realities of the situation—namely the existence of a Pro-British Party in the country and a partitioned Ireland in actual existence—which make it difficult if not impossible to declare a Republic at once. The members of the 'Fianna Fail' Party affirm it, but that the actual declaration of it must depend on several factors or conditions. On the whole, the existence of a Republican Party independent of the Government Party is in my opinion a blessing. It is a guarantee that 'Fianna Fail' will never forget its republican aims—for if it does, then the people will withdraw their support. I would only have liked to see a more cordial relationship between 'Fianna Fail' and the Republicans—such as existed when President De Valera first came to power in 1932. But people and difference of opinion soon led to estrangement of feeling among them.

Besides having prolonged discussions with Mr De Valera, I met individually most of the 'Fianna Fail' ministers. All of them are exceedingly sympathetic, accessible and humane. They had not yet become 'respectable'. Most of them had been on the run when they were fighting for their freedom and would be shot at sight if they had been spotted. They had not yet [become] hardened bureaucratic ministers and there was no official atmosphere about them. With the Minister for Lands I discussed how they were abolishing landlordism by buying up the big estates and dividing the land among the peasantry. With the Minister for Agriculture I discussed how they were trying to make the country self-sufficient in the matter of food supply. It was interesting to know that wheat and sugar-beet were now being cultivated in large areas and the development of agriculture was making the country less dependent on cattle-rearing and therefore less dependent on the English market. I also discussed with him the question of restriction of jute-cultivation in India and he gave me valuable suggestions as to how he would tackle the problem if he were put in charge. With the Minister for Industries I discussed the industrial policy of the Government. He explained to me that they wanted to make the country self-sufficient, not only in agriculture but also in industry. This would make for the economic prosperity of the country and at the same time make them less vulnerable, should they have to face economic reprisals in the future. A colossal amount of work had already been done within a few years to build up new industries. While appreciating all that the Government had done and were doing for industrial regeneration, I felt that possibly they could have gone in for more state-enterprise in the sphere of industrial revival. On the whole I found that the work of the 'Fianna Fail' ministers was of interest and value to us in India when we would have to tackle the problems of nation-building through the machinery of the state.

There was so much to learn in Ireland and my stay was so short—I was surprised that so few of our countrymen who spend years in England ever care to go over to Ireland which is next door. Ireland is quite a different world from England.

I was agreeably surprised to find that all the Irish parties were equally sympathetic towards India and her desire for freedom regardless of their own internal differences. I was glad to do some publicity on behalf of India while I was there. At several receptions and public meetings, I was asked to talk about present-day conditions in India and about our fight for freedom. Outside their own shores the two countries which interested them most were India and Egypt.

16
First Love

A letter to Emilie Schenkl

March 1936

My darling!

Even the iceberg sometimes melts and so it is with me now. I can no longer restrain myself from penning these few lines to convey my deep love for you—my darling—or as we would say in our own way—the queen of my heart. But do you love me—do you care for me—do you long for me? You called me 'pranadhik'—but did you mean it? Do you love me more than your own life? Is that possible? With us it may be possible—for a Hindu woman has, for centuries, given up her life for the sake of her love. But you Europeans have a different tradition, moreover, why should you love me more than your own life? I am like a wandering bird that comes from afar, remains for a while, and then flies away to its distant home. For such a person why should you cherish so much love?

My dearest!

In a few weeks I must fly to my distant home. My country calls me—my duty calls me—I must leave you and go back to my first love—my country. So often have I told you that I have already sold myself to my first love. I have very little left to give any one. What little I have—I have given you. It may not be worthy of you and of your great love for me—but that is all that I have to give—and you cannot expect anything more from me.

I do not know what the future has in store for me. May be, I shall spend my life in prison, may be, I shall be shot or hanged. But whatever happens, I shall think of you and convey my gratitude to you in silence for your love for me. May be I shall never see you again—may be I shall not be able to write to you again when I am back—but believe me, you will always live in my heart, in my thoughts and in my dreams. If fate should thus separate us in this life—I shall long for you in my next life. And if you believe in my religion—pray similarly.

My angel! I thank you for loving me and for teaching me to love you.

My sweetest! Be a good girl, be a pure girl—and above all, be unselfish. Care not for any sorrow or suffering that may come. Sorrow and suffering cannot make you unhappy if you are unselfish. If you are selfish, nothing can make you happy. This is the only advice I can give you—your 'guru' (I think you once called me as such). I hate selfishness and I dislike selfish people. You have an unselfish heart—that is why I could love you. Make that heart more and more unselfish and you will increase your happiness in this life and after.

My queen! Should we not meet again after I leave Europe, think kindly of me. Do not blame me for not loving you more. I have given what I had—how can I give more? With these lines, I send you the tears that are now flowing.

I never thought before that a woman's love could ensnare me. So many did love me before, but I never looked at them. But you, naughty woman, have caught me. And why?

Is this love of any earthly use? We who belong to two different lands—have we anything in common? My country, my people, my traditions, my habits and customs, my climate—in fact everything—is so different from yours. Then, why do you love? And what is it that you love? What is there in me that attracts you and compels you to love? Can you tell.

For the moment, I have forgotten all these differences that separate our countries. I have loved the woman in you—the soul in you. You are the first woman I have loved. God grant that you may also be the last. Adieu, my dearest!

17
Europe—Today and Tomorrow[1]

Dalhousie
21 August 1937

It is customary in modern Politics to classify the different nations as the 'Haves' and 'Have-nots.' The 'Haves' are those, like Great Britain and France, that have profited as a result of the Treaties of Versailles, Trianon and Neuilly, following the Great War. The 'Have-nots' are those that have lost territory under some of these Treaties or have specific grievances against their provisions. In Europe, Great Britain, France, as well as the succession states that have been carved out of the former Austro-Hungarian Empire are among the 'Haves'. On the other hand, Germany, Italy, Hungary, Austria and Bulgaria are among the 'Have-nots'. Though Russia lost much of her territory as a result of the last War, she is now interested in maintaining the status quo and is therefore classified among the 'Haves'. And though Italy acquired territory from the Austro-Hungarian Empire at the end of the War, she is nevertheless regarded as a 'Have-not' because she was expecting a greater share of the spoils of war. Italy was cajoled into joining the Allies in 1915 by the terms of the Secret Pact of London, wherein Britain and France promised her several things, including the Dalmatian Coast which later on was assigned by the Peace Conference to Yugoslavia (called in the Peace Treaty the kingdom of the Serbs, Croats and Slovenes).

Among 'Have-nots', Bulgaria is the quietest. She lost territory to all her neighbours (Roumania, Greece and Serbia—now Yugoslavia) as a result of the Balkan War of 1912 and the Great War as well. But she nurses her grievances in secret and sighs for better days, though she feels helpless within a ring of hostile powers. Hungary is more active, so far as propaganda goes. Her protagonists roam all over Europe and endeavour

[1] Published in *Modern Review*, September 1937, and reprinted in Subhas C. Bose, *Through Congress Eyes* (Kitabistan, Allahabad and London, 1938).

to canvass support among the Big Powers for revision of her frontiers. From the military point of view, Hungary is not an important factor today, having lost more than half of her former territory and population to Czechoslovakia, Jugoslavia (formerly Serbia) and Roumania.

Till recently, Soviet Russia would have been regarded as an explosive force of gigantic proportions, busy in stirring up revolution all over the World. But such is not the case today. After the death of Lenin and the elimination of Trotsky, Soviet Russia under the guidance of Stalin is interested only in building up Socialism within the Soviet frontiers. The sudden resurgence of Germany has helped to accentuate this tendency. Russia has therefore joined the League of Nations, which by the way is dominated by the capitalist powers, and under the slogan of 'Collective Security and Peace', is doing everything possible to prevent a disturbance of the status quo in Europe. The really explosive forces in Europe today are Fascist Italy and Nazi Germany. Ranged against them are Britain, France and Soviet Russia. On the complicated chess-board of Europe interminable moves are going on, and the scene is changing from day to day.

Before the Great War, the status quo was preserved by maintaining the 'Balance of Power'. The powers interested in preserving the status quo would have a secret alliance among themselves and would endeavour to play against one another the potentially hostile ones who refused to join them. The League of Nations which was constituted in 1919 was meant to put an end to secret diplomacy and to the division of the world into rival groups of powers, which served to keep up the bogey of war. In its place was introduced a new technique, whereby all nations were to be brought into the League and made jointly responsible for the maintenance of 'Collective Security and Peace'. Both the League of the Nations and its new technique seem to have failed in their objective, because there are powers that do not feel interested in preserving the status quo and among them Japan and Germany are no longer members of the League—while the most powerful factor in international politics, the U.S.A., has never been a member.

To understand the meaning and purpose behind the recent disturbances in Europe, one has to comprehend the aims of Fascist Italy and Nazi Germany. Since Mussolini came to power in 1922, Italy has been thinking aggressively of expansion—of a place in the sun—of a revival of the Roman Empire. But till January 1935, Italy did not herself know which direction her policy of expansion should follow. She had grievances against Jugoslavia, who had robbed her of the Dalmatian Coast.

She was snarling at France who had taken the Italian Districts of Savoy and Nice and was in possession of Tunisia, in North Africa, with a large Italian population, and of the Island of Corsica which belongs geographically to Italy. She was hostile to Imperialist Britain who was in control of Italian 'Malta' and had, with French acquiescence, converted the Mediterranean Sea into a British lake.

The tension between Italy and France was particularly acute, with the result that both sides of the Franco-Italian frontier were heavily fortified and guarded. Then in 1933, the Nazi Colossus suddenly appeared on the scene and changed the whole aspect of Europe. France rushed to England for support and alliance against the new danger. But Britain was noncommittal. Perhaps in her heart of hearts she relished the idea of checking French hegemony on the Continent. Perhaps she was simply following her traditional policy in international affairs. France, however, was nettled, and in annoyance she turned to Italy and Soviet Russia. France wanted to withdraw her troops from the Italian frontier and concentrate them against Germany, and she wanted, further, an ally on Germany's eastern flanks. Thus there came into existence the Laval-Mussolini Pact and the Franco-Soviet Pact.

The Laval-Mussolini Pact in January 1935, decided for Italy the direction of her future expansion. Italy squared up her differences with France and gave up territorial ambitions in Europe. In return, France agreed to give her a free hand in Africa. The result was the rape of Abyssinia.

After the conquest of Abyssinia, Mussolini made a speech in which he declared to the world that Italy had now become a 'satisfied' power. The annexation of Abyssinia had been regarded by Britain as an encroachment on her preserves in Africa and the speech appeared as a pointer in the direction of the renewal of Anglo-Italian friendship. That expectation was not fulfilled, however. Though Britain had at first challenged Italy over the Abyssinia question and then beaten a quick retreat before the bluff and swagger of Mussolini—she had not forgotten the humiliation. In order to repair the damage done to her prestige among the Mediterranean and Near Eastern nations—she set about strengthening her naval and aerial bases in the Mediterranean. The First Lord of the Admiralty, Sir Samuel Hoare, went on a tour of inspection in the Mediterranean and concluded it with a public declaration that Britain would not withdraw from that zone. Other Cabinet ministers like Anthony Eden, also made pronouncements to the effect that the Mediterranean was Britain's lifeline—that it was not merely a short cut, but a main arterial road.

It is this determination on the part of Britain to maintain her position in the Mediterranean and to strengthen it further which has irritated and antagonised Italy—for Italy is equally determined to increase her influence in the Mediterranean through the expansion of her Navy and Air Force and this could take place only at the expense of Britain. It should therefore be clear that the present Anglo-Italian tension is not a product of Il Duce's ill-humour, not is it a passing phase. It will continue until the question of the future hegemony over the Mediterranean is finally solved through the voluntary withdrawal or defeat of one of the two rival powers. Fraternising letters may pass between Neville Chamberlain and Signor Mussolini, Ambassadors and Foreign Ministers may shake hands—but a political conflict born of objective factors and forces will continue, so long as the causes remain.

Italy's reply to Britain's renewed interest in the Mediterranean is her intervention in the Spanish Civil War. It would be puerile to think or suggest that Italy has plumped for Franco because of her sympathy for the latter's Fascist aims or her hatred of Communism. Political sympathy she would have for Franco in any case, but she is pouring out her blood and money for Franco primarily for strategic reasons. The same is true of Germany and whoever does not realise this, understands nothing of the Spanish Civil War.

In spite of her progress in re-armament, Italy is no match for Britain. British re-armament throughout the world has made Italy's position weaker since the end of the Abyssinian War. In any case, Britain through her control of Gilbraltar and Suez can, in the event of a war with Italy, bottle up the Italian fleet and carry out an economic blockade which may prove disastrous to the latter. Italy has to import most of her raw materials like coal, iron, oil, wool, cotton, etc. and two-thirds of her seaborne trade comes from the Atlantic, while 80 per cent of her imports come over the Mediterranean. Her coastline is long and vulnerable and she can maintain contact with her African possessions, Libya, Eritrea and Abyssinia, only if she dominates the Mediterranean. For all these reasons, an economic blockade combined with an attack from British naval stations, like Malta and Cyprus, can create havoc for Italy and even strangle her. She may retaliate by attacking British possessions in the Mediterranean or British trade passing through that sea, but she can neither attack Britain nor touch Britain's sources of raw materials and food which lie outside the Mediterranean zone. Thus, matched against Britain in war, Italy is virtually helpless and can play a primarily defensive role.

And as long as Spain remains friendly to Britain, or even neutral, Italy's helplessness will remain unrelieved. Only with the help of Spain can Italy escape from her fatal strategic position. With Spain under her control, Italy could take the offensive against Britain. She could destroy Gibraltar and menace both the trade routes of Britain—the Mediterranean route and the cape route. What is more, she could get over the blockade by using the land routes over Spain in order to bring imports from the Atlantic side. As the advent of Air Force more than compensated Italy for the weakness of her navy, *vis-à-vis* Great Britain, during the Abyssinian campaign, so the control of Spain, or even a foothold in Spanish territory, would enable her to convert her present, fatally weak and defensive position into a strong, offensive one in the event of a future war.

Thus Italy is fighting Great Britain in Spain. She is helping Franco in order to get a foothold in Spanish territory.

After considering these strategic factors, one need not be surprised that Italy is so greatly interested in Franco's success. Rather, it is surprising that there should be people in England who sympathise with Franco and the rebels. As captain Liddell Hart, the well-known British strategist says in *Europe in Arms*:

'Strategically, the danger (to British interests) is so obvious that it is difficult to understand the eagerness with which some of the most avowedly patriotic sections of the British public have desired the rebels' success.'

This is probably a case of political prejudice (viz., hatred of the Socialists and communists) overriding the dictates of self-interest.

Notwithstanding all that I have just said, it has to be pointed out that Italy today is on the whole a satisfied power. She resents British supremacy in the Mediterranean and she thinks that as in days of yore, the Mediterranean should be a Roman lake. But she will not go to any extreme in her conflict with Great Britain. Intervention in the Spanish Civil War is all right for her, because she knows full well that none of the Big Powers is yet ready for an international war. Mussolini is far too shrewd a politician to stake his position or the position of his country in a risky adventure in the near or distant future. Therefore, we may rest assured that Italy will not take the offensive, in disturbing the peace of Europe—nor will she enter into a war unless she is pretty sure of victory.

শ্রীশ্রীদুর্গা
সহায়—

কটক
রবিবার

পরমপূজনীয়া
শ্রীমতী মাতাঠাকুরাণী—
শ্রীচরণকমলেষু—

মা,

ভারতবর্ষ ভগবানের বড় আদরের স্থান—এই মহাদেশে লোকশিক্ষার নিমিত্ত ভগবান যুগে ২ অবতাররূপে জন্মগ্রহণ করিয়া পাপপীড়িতা ধরণীকে পবিত্র করিয়াছেন এবং প্রত্যেক ভারতবাসীর হৃদয়ে ধর্ম্মের ও সত্যের বীজ রোপণ করিয়া গিয়াছেন। ভগবান মানবদেহ ধারণ করিয়া নিজের অংশাবতাররূপে অনেক দেশে জন্মগ্রহণ করিয়াছেন কিন্তু এতবার তিনি কোনও দেশে জন্মগ্রহণ করেন নাই — তাই বলি আমাদের জন্মভূমি ভারতমাতা ভগবানের বড় আদরের দেশ। দেখ, মা, ভারতে যা চাও সবই আছে — প্রচণ্ড গ্রীষ্ম, দারুণ শীত, ভীষণ বৃষ্টি, আবার মনোহর শরৎ ও বসন্ত কাল, সবই আছে। দাক্ষিণাত্যে দেখি — স্বচ্ছসলিলা, পুণ্যতোয়া গোদাবরী — দুই কূল ভরিয়া কল কল শব্দে নিরন্তর সাগরাভিমুখে চলিয়াছে — কি পবিত্র নদী! দেখিলে মাত্র বা ভাবিলেই মাত্র

1. A page from letter to mother Prabhabati, 1912.

FITZWILLIAM HALL CAMB.

~~Calcutta~~
Cambridge.
23. 2. 21.

My dear brother,

I did not hear from you by the last mail. You were too busy at the time – I presume.

I have already written to you more than once about my desire to resign the Civil Service and take up public service instead. I have submitted this desire of mine to a severe analysis and to a mature deliberation. I can assure you that I have not arrived at such a decision in a moment of mental excitement. The decision may be a regrettable one from a certain point of view but it is based on my whole outlook on life.

P.S.: Glad to receive your letter of the 2nd inst: and to learn that all of you are doing well. We are pretty well here. How are you all doing? Subhas

2. A page from letter to brother Sarat after resignation from ICS, February 1921.

I have remarked above that the essential principle in human life is love. This statement may be challenged when one can see so much in life that is opposed to love, but the paradox can be easily explained. The 'essential principle' is not fully manifest yet; it is unfolding itself in space and time. Love, like reality of which it is the essence, is dynamic.

What, now, is the nature of the process of unfolding? Firstly, is it a movement forward or not? Secondly, is there any law underlying this movement?

The unfolding process is progressive in character. This assertion is not quite dogmatic. Observation and study of nature point to the conclusion that everywhere there is progress. This progress may not be unilinear; there may be periodic set-backs — but on the whole, i.e. (considered) from a long period point of view, there is progress. Apart from this rational consideration, there is the intuitive experience that we are moving ahead with the lapse of time. And last but not least there is the necessity, both biological and moral, to have faith in progress.

As various attempts have been made to know reality and to describe it — so also have attempts been made.

3. A page from hand-written manuscript of 'My Faith Philosophical', 1937.

11

In this mortal world, everything perishes and will perish — but ideas, ideals and dreams do not. One individual may die for an idea — that idea will, after his death, incarnate itself a thousand lives. That is how the wheels of evolu-tion move on and the ideas, ideals and dreams one generation are bequeathed to the next. No idea has ever fulfilled itself in this world exce through an ordeal of suffering and sacrifice.

What greater solace can there be than the feeling that one has lived and died for a prin-ciple? What higher satisfaction can a man poss than the knowledge that his spirit will beget kindred spirits to carry on his unfinished task? What better reward can a soul desire than the certainty that his message will be wafted over hi and dales and over the broad plains to every corner of his land and across the seas to distant lands? What higher consummation can life attain than peaceful self-immolation at the altar of one's Cause?

Hence it is evident that nobody can lose through suffering and sacrifice. If he does lose anything of the earth earthy, he will gain much more in return by becoming the heir to

4. A page from letter to Bengal Government from Presidency Jail, Calcutta, 'My Political Testament', November 1940.

39

After the events of December, 1939, all that remained of the Left Consolidation Committee was the Forward Bloc and the Kishan Sabha. Their collaboration became closer and closer with the passage of time. It was owing to their cooperation and initiative that the All India Anti Compromise Conference ~~could be~~ was held at Ramgarh, in March, 1940, contemporaneously with the annual session of the Congress and proved to be such a remarkable success. // The question may very well be raised as to why the Forward Bloc was at all started and why the existing Leftist parties were not charged with the responsibility of bringing about Left-consolidation. This experiment was in fact tried but it failed and then th[illegible] arose a situation in

5. A page from hand-written manuscript of a political thesis written in Kabul, March 1941.

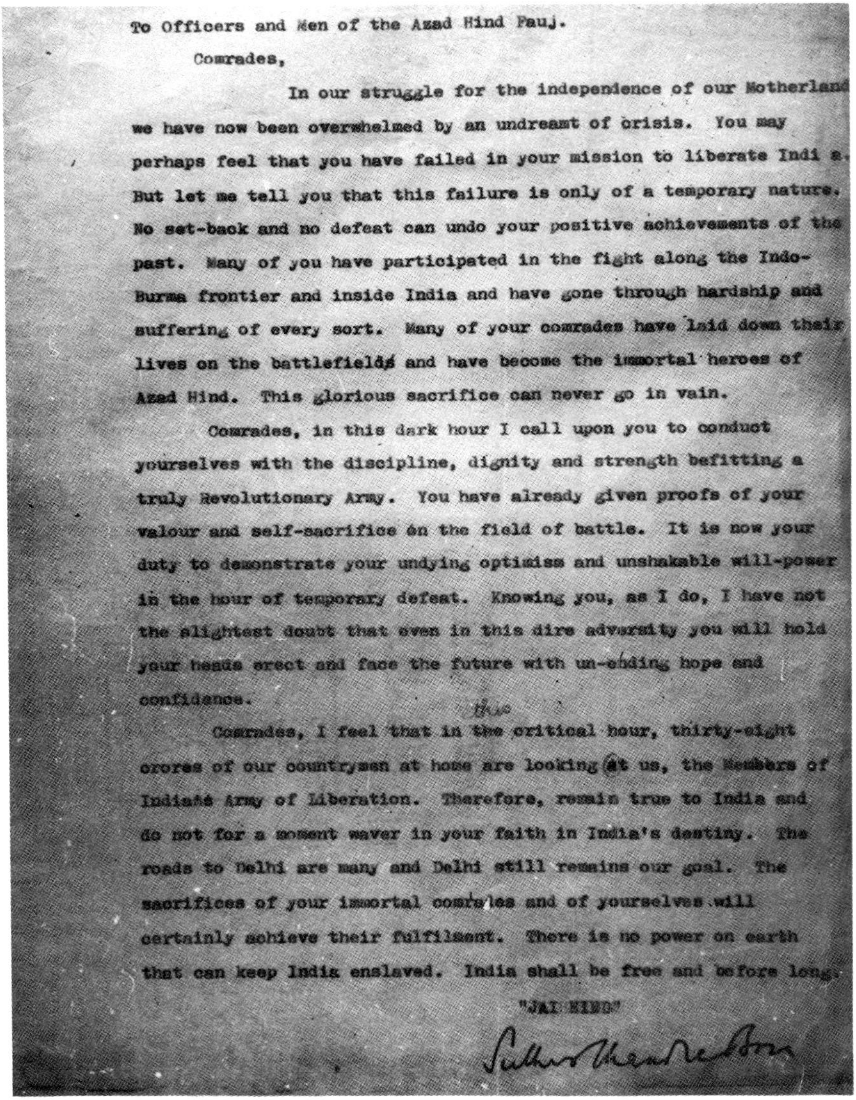

To Officers and Men of the Azad Hind Fauj.

Comrades,

In our struggle for the independence of our Motherland we have now been overwhelmed by an undreamt of crisis. You may perhaps feel that you have failed in your mission to liberate India. But let me tell you that this failure is only of a temporary nature. No set-back and no defeat can undo your positive achievements of the past. Many of you have participated in the fight along the Indo-Burma frontier and inside India and have gone through hardship and suffering of every sort. Many of your comrades have laid down their lives on the battlefields and have become the immortal heroes of Azad Hind. This glorious sacrifice can never go in vain.

Comrades, in this dark hour I call upon you to conduct yourselves with the discipline, dignity and strength befitting a truly Revolutionary Army. You have already given proofs of your valour and self-sacrifice on the field of battle. It is now your duty to demonstrate your undying optimism and unshakable will-power in the hour of temporary defeat. Knowing you, as I do, I have not the slightest doubt that even in this dire adversity you will hold your heads erect and face the future with un-ending hope and confidence.

Comrades, I feel that in this critical hour, thirty-eight crores of our countrymen at home are looking at us, the Members of India's Army of Liberation. Therefore, remain true to India and do not for a moment waver in your faith in India's destiny. The roads to Delhi are many and Delhi still remains our goal. The sacrifices of your immortal comrades and of yourselves will certainly achieve their fulfilment. There is no power on earth that can keep India enslaved. India shall be free and before long.

"JAI HIND"

Subhas Chandra Bose

6. Last Order of the Day to Indian National Army, 15 August 1945.

But the Germany under Hitler is an incalculable factor, despite the sober and cautious policy of the Reichswehr, the German Army. Nazi Germany has been dreaming dreams which can be fulfilled only through the arbitrament of war. Moreover, the economic crisis within Germany has been growing so acute, that many observers opine that the day is not far off when she may have to launch on a war abroad, in order to stave off discontent at home. To understand the future of Germany, we shall have to probe a little deeper.

Since the Great War there has been a French hegemony on the Continent. Not content with crushing Germany, France erected a diplomatic wall around Germany through alliances with Poland and with the Little Entente—the succession states, Czechoslovakia. Jugoslavia, and Roumania. She followed this up by establishing cordial relations with Turkey which was formerly within the German orbit of influence. Germany looked on helplessly while she was thus diplomatically isolated from the civilised world. Her only reply to this policy of encirclement was the Treaty of Rapallo with Soviet Russia.

French hegemony in post-War Europe has been anathema to Germany whose influence on the Continent had been paramount since the Franco-Prussian War of 1870, resulting in the ignominious defeat of France. Since then, Germany had been expanding in several directions. Outside Europe she went in for colonial expansion. In the sphere of trade she bid fair to be a rival to Great Britain and the U.S.A. She built a powerful navy which was looked upon with suspicion by Britain. She brought Austria, Bulgaria and Turkey within her sphere of influence and planned the Berlin-Baghdad Railway which was regarded as a thrust at Britain's Eastern possessions. But the War smashed all these achievements and aspirations and for a decade Germany lay in the slough of despair, while her thinkers began to philosophise about the decline of the West and Spengler wrote his *Untergand des Abend-Landes.* Then came the new awakening through the emergence of the National-Socialist or Nazi Party.

The political doctrine of the Nazi Party can be summed up in one phrase—'Drang Nach Osten'—or 'Drive to the East'. The doctrine was first propounded by Muller van den Bruck in his book, *Das dritte Reich* or 'the Third Empire'. He did not live to see the establishment of the third Reich under Hitler in 1933, for he committed suicide in 1925 in a fit of despair. His idea was, however, taken up by Hitler and amplified in his (Hitler's) book *Mein Kampf,* or 'My Struggle', which he wrote in prison in 1923. The essence of the above doctrine is that Germany should give up the idea of being a naval or colonial power. She should remain a continental power and her expansion should take place on the Continent—towards the East. It was pre-War Germany's greatest blunder to go in for colonial expansion and thereby come into conflict with Great Britain.

The new social philosophy of the Nazis, as expounded by Hitler, advocates the purification and strengthening of the German race through elimination of Jewish influence and a return to the soil. 'Blunt and Boden', or 'Blood and Soil', foreign policy, the Nazis advocate the unification of all German-speaking people and the acquisition eastward of more elbow-room for the prolific German race. In practical politics, the above objectives amount to the annexation 1) of Austria,[2] 2) of Memel which she has lost to Lithuania, 3) of Danzig which has been made a free city under the League of Nations, 4) of the German-speaking part of Czechoslovakia with a population of 3½ millions, 5) of the Polish Corridor and the Silesian coalfields which she has lost to Poland, 6) of the rich grain-producing lands of Soviet Ukraine and 7) possibly also of the German-speaking parts of Switzerland, Italian Tyrol and other adjoining countries.

Germany repudiated the military clauses of the Treaty of Versailles in March 1935, occupied the Rhineland in March 1936, and upset all calculations of European diplomats when she achieved the 'Anschluss' without firing a shot. Her continued rearmament under these circumstances can have but one meaning, viz., preparation for war. Her rearmament has driven the last nail in the coffin of international disarmament, and in sheer panic the whole of Europe is now engaged in rearming. When such frantic preparations for war are going on all round, the slightest incident may one day light an international conflagration.

It now remains for us to consider to what extremes Germany will go to realise her aims. At what stage will she go in for war and with whom?

Political prophecy is always a difficult job—but one thing is certain. Germany has not forgotten the lessons of her last defeat. Hers was not a military defeat, but an economic one. And it was the British Navy which was primarily responsible for starving her to submission. It is therefore certain that Germany will not enter into a war if she knows that Britain will be against her. In 1914, Germany foolishly enough did not believe till the last moment that Britain would take up the gauntlet on

[2] Since this was written the 'Anschluss' or union with Austria has already been achieved by the Nazis.

behalf of Belgium and France. It is now generally admitted by historians that if Britain had made her intentions known to Germany beforehand, the latter would probably have kept aloof from the Austro-Serbian conflict and thereby averted—or at least postponed—the World War.

Though in his book, *Mein Kampf*, Hitler asked for a final show-down with France, Germany's foreign policy has been modified since the Nazis assumed the reins of office. Germany no longer wants to get back Alsace-Lorraine from France or Eupen-Malmady from Belgium. In other words, Germany does not demand a revision of the frontiers in Western Europe. The reason for this is not far to seek. Germany knows quite well that an attack on France or Belgium or Holland will bring Britain into the arena at once and there would probably be a repetition of the last war. Germany has therefore been continually offering to sign a Western Pact which would guarantee the status quo in Western Europe. For a large number of British politicians this offer is a tempting one, because it removes once for all any possible threat to British interests. Germany while making this offer has been striving hard to drive a bargain at the international counter, her demand being that Britain and France should cease to interest themselves in Central and Eastern Europe so that Germany may have free hand in rearranging the map of that part of the world.

Germany is now preparing in these directions. Firstly, she is going in for an all-round re-armament. Secondly, she is trying to make herself self-sufficient as regards the supply of food and basic raw-materials. (This is a provision against a future economic blockade.) This work was started last year in accordance with Germany's Four-Year Plan. Thirdly, she is trying to persuade the Western Powers to agree to neutrality in the event of a war in Central or Eastern Europe. Until all these preparations are complete, it is extremely doubtful if Germany will voluntarily launch a war.

To win over Britain to an attitude of neutrality, Germany has launched a large-scale propaganda in that country and she has already attained a fair measure of success. In this effort, Germany has exploited the general hatred of Communism which can be found among the richer and middle class in Britain. The Franco-Soviet Pact has come handy and the Nazis continually emphasise that for Britain to be tied up with France means fighting a war in Eastern Europe on the side of Soviet Russia, though Britain has no interest in that zone. Alongside of this, the Nazis pledge themselves not to harm British interests in any quarter of the globe. As a result of this endeavour, there is an influential pro-Nazi group in Great Britain—with supporters in the House of Lords, in the City of London and generally among the ruling classes even among the Labourites, though they are attracted by different reasons. It is generally believed that Montagu Norman, Governor of the Bank of England, Premier Neville Chamberlain and Sir Robert Vansittart, formerly the strong man in the Foreign Office, are all pro-Nazi.

It is too early to say if Britain's foreign policy will ultimately follow a straight line or if it will continue to wobble, as it has often done in the past. At the present moment, British public opinion is terribly confused. Firstly, there is the pro-Nazi group, referred to above, who wants a Western Pact and no commitments in Central and Eastern Europe. Secondly, there is the anti-German Conservative Party represented by Winston Churchill who are distrustful of the Nazis and apprehend that when Germany is once supreme in Europe, she will challenge British interests abroad. They point out in this connection that Britain has nothing to fear from France and that outside Europe, British and French colonial interests are everywhere bound up together. Thirdly, there are the Socialists and Communists who on ideological grounds are anti-German and pro-French in their general attitude.

In the midst of this confusion, the British Foreign Office is following a definite policy, viz., to persuade France to give up her interest in Central and Eastern Europe. The aim of Vansittart's policy, now continued by Lord Halifax, is to force Germany to be and to remain a European Continental Power. That is why Britain has acquiesced in German rearmament, made the Naval Agreement with Germany in June 1935, advised France to ignore German Military occupation of Rhineland in March 1936, warned France not to help the Spanish Government though she was clearly entitled to do so under International Law. It is further alleged by those who are in a position to know diplomatic secrets that the British Foreign Office encouraged Poland in 1933 to come to terms with the Nazi Government. (The German-Polish non-Aggression Pact was adopted next year.) It also encouraged Belgium to break the alliance with France and return to neutrality and Jugoslavia to make friends with Italy and Germany, against the advice of France. It further encouraged the pro-Nazi Henlein Party in Czechoslovakia and intrigued for breaking or at least slackening, the bonds of the little Entente (Czechoslovakia, Jugoslavia and Roumania) and of the Balkan Entente (Jugoslavia, Roumania, Greece and Turkey) which are under French influence.

It would not be improper to conclude from the above facts that the

British Foreign Office has been secretly working contra France, at least in Europe, and that French hegemony on the Continent is distasteful to Whitehall. Perhaps because of this, French politicians of the Right were greatly annoyed with Great Britain and Laval proceeded to make alliances with Italy and Soviet Russia, independently of Britain. In fact, Laval's foreign policy might, from one point of view, be regarded as anti-British. But French politicians of the Left follow blindly the policy of the British Foreign office, believing that France and Britain should hold together through thick and thin.

At present the German Foreign Office is playing an aggressive role, while France is busy trying to counteract the former's moves and activities. Outside Britain, the Nazis have been remarkably successful in Belgium. A pro-Nazi Party (the Rexists) has come into existence in Belgium and Nazi propaganda is active among the Flemish-speaking people of Belgium. The Belgium Government has broken away from the alliance with France and will in future adopt an attitude of neutrality in the event of war in Central or Eastern Europe. The treaty of Rapallo with Soviet Russia has virtually lapsed since the Nazis came to power in 1933; but as if to compensate Germany for that, the Nazi Government entered into a non-Aggression Pact with Poland. This Pact served to undermine greatly French influence in Poland. Last year, France made gigantic efforts to recover her influence in Poland and a number of visits took place on both sides. But it seems probable that the Franco-Polish Alliance will never become a living force again and that in future Poland will follow an independent foreign policy—that is, a policy of neutrality in the event of a Franco-German or Russo-German conflict.

In addition to the above activities, Germany is now exceedingly busy in trying to weaken France by slackening the bonds of the Little Entente and Balkan Entente and by getting a foothold in Spanish territory. With the help of several alliances and friendly contacts, the position of France today is exceedingly strong and as long as this position continues, she will never agree to withdraw her interest in Central and Eastern Europe. She will continue to insist—as Litvinov, the Soviet Foreign Minister, also does—that peace is indivisible and that there should be one European Pact to guarantee collective security to all the states under the aegis of the League of Nations. Failing this, besides the Western Pact, there should be another Pact to guarantee peace in Central and Eastern Europe. To this, Germany does not agree and will not agree.

France has fortified herself with military alliances with Czechoslovakia and Soviet Russia. The two latter powers have also a military alliance between themselves. Consequently, these three powers will always be found together in the event of an international emergency. Czechoslovakia has an understanding with the other Little Entente powers, Jugoslavia and Roumania. And Jugoslavia and Roumania have an understanding with Greece and Turkey through the Balkan Entente. Germany hopes that by weaning away Jugoslavia and Roumania, she will isolate Czechoslovakia in Central Europe—for help from Russia can reach Czechoslovakia only through Roumania or through Poland. Poland is no longer a problem to Germany because of the non-aggression pact. Through Britain, she is trying to persuade France that as a military factor, Soviet Russia is not of much consequence and that France should give the go-by to the military clauses of the Franco-Soviet Pact. The recent execution of eight Army Generals in Russia has given a handle to the capitalist powers and they are carrying on a terrific propaganda to the effect that the Soviet military machine is racking with indiscipline and cannot be relied on in the event of war. Last but not least, Germany is trying her level best to obtain a foothold in Spanish territory, so that in the event of war with France she could stab her in the back by cutting off her communications with North Africa, from where France always obtains large supplies of men and materials when war breaks out in Europe. Germany hopes that by weakening France on all sides and by putting pressure on her through the British Foreign office, she will ultimately make her agree to a Western Pact, giving Germany a free hand in Central and Eastern Europe. If France does not agree to this and if she ultimately goes to war with Germany on the side of Soviet Russia, she will find herself considerably weakened compared to what she was in 1914.

But will France fall in with Germany's plans? Ostensibly not. For Britain it is immaterial who dominates the Continent—France or Germany—for Britain's interests lie outside Europe. But France cannot so easily give up the hegemony in Europe for, unlike Britain, she is a Continental Power, besides being a Colonial Power. Moreover, France is fighting not merely for power and prestige, but also for her national safety. She has not forgotten the tragic defeat of 1870. Her population is stationary and is about two-thirds of that of Germany, whose population is still growing. Consequently, France has a genuine horror of German invasion, while Britain has not, as long as the German Navy keeps to the prescribed limits of the Anglo-German Naval Agreement. To crown everything, there is in France, a deep distrust of German aims and aspirations which has been accentuated by violent denunciations of France in Hitler's book, *Mein Kampf*. As a writer has put it succinctly, in France the Right hates Germany, the Left hates Hitler. In these circumstances, it is extremely doubtful if France will ever give up her allies and alliances in Central and Eastern Europe as long as the violently nationalistic Nazi Party remains in power.

The issue of the Spanish Civil War is hanging in the balance and it is too early to say how far German diplomacy will succeed there. But in Central and Eastern Europe it has made considerable headway. In Roumania, the King and the Cabinet are, on the whole, pro-German and the Francophile ex-Foreign minister, Titulescu, lost considerable influence. There is an anti-Semitic pro-Nazi Party, the Iron Guard, led by Codreanu, which is behind the Government. In Jugoslavia, the Premier Stoyadinovitch is pro-Nazi, as also his Government, while the Royal Family is under British influence. In Greece, the Premier General Metaxas, who has made himself the Dictator, is undoubtedly under German influence. And Greece is important to Germany, because should the Russian Fleet in the Black Sea enter the Mediterranean through the Dardanelles, it could be attacked from a base in the Grecian Islands. Then Hungary and Bulgaria, being 'Have-not' powers, are expected to line up with Germany, if they see any chance of having their national grievances redressed thereby. Thus it appears that Germany has stolen a march over France throughout the Balkan Peninsula and she has been throwing out commercial baits in profusion.

But in international politics there is no finality. France is following on the heels of Germany everywhere. It is difficult to predict how long the Government of Metaxas in Greece or Stoyadinovitch in Jugoslavia will last. The pro-French party in Roumania, though out of power for the time being, is not negligible and the Balkan temperament is proverbially changeable. Moreover, Germany finds pitted against herself, one of the finest diplomats of modern Europe, President Eduard Benes of Czechoslovakia.

The scene is changing from day to day and political forecasts are anything but easy. One thing is certain. If war comes, it will come as the result of a German challenge to the status quo in Central and Eastern Europe. But will it come? The answer rests primarily with Britain. Germany will not repeat the errors of 1914 and will not go into a war, if she knows that Britain will be against her. She might be trapped into it as she was in 1914, thinking that Britain would keep out of it. If France and Britain agree to be neutral in a conflict in Central or Eastern Europe, war will break out in Europe, as sure as the sun rises in the East, the moment Germany is ready for it. Even if France lines up with Soviet Russia, with Britain remaining neutral, there may be a war, though the upshot of it will be doubtful.

If Franco wins, it will be a victory for Italy and Germany, and will mean the end of British hegemony in the Mediterranean and dark days ahead of France. But Russian Colossus has often proved to be an enigma. It baffled Napoleon—the conqueror of Europe. Will it baffle Hitler?

18

Japan's Role in the Far East*

19 September 1937

Every now and then we open our daily papers to read about some clash between China and Japan. Many pass over the columns as something happening too far away to interest us in India. Others go through the columns as a matter of routine. But I wonder how few of us understand the significance of the happenings reported.

The islands which form the homeland of the Japanese race are overpopulated. They have to support a population of about 70 millions, with the result that there is overcrowding and too much pressure on the land. But that is not the end of the trouble. The Japanese are exceedingly prolific, and their population has been growing by leaps and bounds. The number of people per square mile in China is 100. In Japan it is 313. Moreover, Japan's birth rate is twice that of Great Britain. Hence Japan wants more territory for her children to settle in—more raw materials for her growing industries and more markets for her finished goods. No one will make her a present of these three things—hence the resort to force. The only other solution for Japan is, to restrict her population, through birth-control, and live within her own resources—but that solution does not obviously appeal to her. This is, in short, the *raison d'être* of Japanese imperialist expansion.

Japanese expansion can take place only in the face of Chinese, Russian, British or American opposition. If she expands on the Asiatic mainland, she is bound to incur the wrath of China or Russia. If she expands southward—towards the Philippine Islands or Australia—she is bound to come into conflict with the United States of America or Great Britain. As far as one can judge, Japan seems to have decided in favour of the first course, notwithstanding the appeal made by Lt.-Commander

*Published in *Modern Review* in October 1937 and reprinted in Subhas C. Bose, *Through Congress Eyes* (Kitabistan, Allahabad and London, 1938).

Ishimaru in his book *Japan Must Fight England* to the effect, that she should make up with China, Russia and the U.S.A., and concentrate on fighting England. On the Asiatic mainland the territory on which Japan can cast her eyes belongs either to Russia or to China. To attack Russia would be folly for Japan, because under Soviet rule, Russia is fully reawakened. She has, moreover, a first-class military machine, both in Europe as well as in the Far East.

Therefore, the only alternative left to Japan for satisfying her imperialist ambitions is to expand at the expense of China. But though she may expand at the expense of China, that expansion can take place only in the teeth of Russian opposition, for reasons that will be explained below. So far as Britain is concerned, however much she may dislike the growth of Japanese power on the Asiatic continent, she will put up with the nuisance, knowing full well that the only alternative to it would be expansion to the south, bringing Japan into direct and unavoidable conflict with her; and in her present mood, the U.S.A. will certainly not go to war with Japan over her 'interests' in the Far East.

Being an Asiatic country and living in close proximity to a huge continent, it is but natural that Japan should look primarily to the mainland of Asia to fulfil her imperialist needs. There she finds a huge state—formerly the Celestial Empire, and now the Republic of China—ill-managed and disunited, and with more natural resources than she can herself develop. The vastness, the potential richness, and the internal weakness of China, constitute the greatest temptation for Japan.

The conflict between the two Asiatic countries is more than forty years old. It began towards the end of the last century. By that time, Japan had modernised her state-machinery, with the help of modern methods, and had modern weapons of warfare. She found that all the big European Powers had begun to exploit China and to enrich themselves at her expense. Why, then, should not Japan, an Asiatic Power living next-door, do the same and keep out the Western Powers from draining the Wealth of the East? This was the imperialist logic which started Japan on her race for expansion.

During the last forty years, Japan has not lost a single opportunity for wresting concessions from the Chinese Government, and during this period she has been undermining the influence of the Western exploiting powers, slowly and steadily. Her greatest rivals were Russia, Britain, the U.S.A. and Germany. During the Russo-Japanese War of 1904–1905, she was able to checkmate the Czarist Empire. During the Great War she was able to wipe out Germany from the map of China. But she has not been able to tackle Britain and the U.S.A. And in the meantime Russia, which was once beaten, has come back into the picture as a Soviet State, newly armed and considerably strengthened.

The disintegration of China began during the latter half of the nineteenth century. European powers like Britain, Russia, Germany, etc., and the U.S.A. put pressure on China, and obtained 'treaty-ports' like Hong Kong, Shanghai, etc., which virtually amounted to annexation of Chinese territory. Just before the end of the last century, Japan appeared on the scene and also adopted Western tactics in her dealings with China.

The island of Formosa lying to the south-east of China was acquired by Japan in the War of 1904–1905. About the same time Japan took over the Kwantung Railway, and the southern part of the Chinese Eastern Railway, running through Manchuria, thereby making South Manchuria a Japanese sphere of influence. Korea, formerly Chinese territory, was annexed by Japan openly in 1910, and it is interesting to note that Japan had professed to secure its independence, when she went to war with China in 1894. During the Great War, Japan declared war on Germany, and immediately proceeded to seize Tsingtao and other German possessions in the Shantung peninsula. In 1915, when she found all the Western Powers up to their neck in the war, Japan presented 21 demands to China, and extorted several concessions from her. After the war, Japan received as her share of the spoils, the mandate for the ex-German Pacific Islands, the strategic importance of which lies in their position athwart the direct sea-route from the United States to the Philippine Islands.

Then there was a lull in Japanese expansion for a period, since Japan wanted time to assimilate what she had annexed. The next period of feverish activity began in 1931 with the conquest of Manchukuo (Manchuria), when Manchukuo, formerly Chinese territory, was set up as a nominally independent state, just as Korea was in 1895. The present expansionist drive, which has been continuing since 1941, can be traced to the now famous, or rather notorious Tanaka Memorandum of 1928, in which plans for Japan's future expansion on the Asiatic mainland were clearly laid down. From this brief historical survey it should be clear that Japan's determination, to find more elbow-room for herself in this planet of ours, is unshakable. Outward circumstances can hardly thwart this imperious drive and can at best determine the direction and speed of her expansion.

A scientific examination of the internal economy of Japan will clearly explain Japan's military aggression since 1931. It is easy to understand her need for fresh territory, when her population is growing, and her existing territory is already too scanty for her present population. Looking to her industrial system, one finds that Japan has to import all her important raw materials, *viz.*, cotton, wool, pulp, iron, oil, etc., from a great distance. The expansion of her industrial system, like her need for territory, is necessitated by the growth of population. Therefore, to maintain her large population, Japan requires a safe and regular supply of raw materials. The expansion of industries, again, requires new markets.

Now, how are all these needs to be fulfilled? Will China, of her own accord, give up territory for colonization to Japan? Will she allow Japan to exploit her vast resources in raw materials, and her extensive market? Certainly not. Both national honour and self-interest will stand in the way. Further, the European Powers and the U.S.A. will not voluntarily permit Japan to monopolise China—her resources and her market. They will insist to the last on the 'Open Door' policy in China which permits all Powers to share the Chinese spoils. Hence Japan has to seize Chinese territory by force. She has been doing this by stages, biting off one slice at a time and taking time to digest it. Each attack is preceded by certain border incidents, which are carefully stage-managed, in order to serve as a pretext for Japanese aggression. The tactics are the same, whether one observes the north-western frontier of India, or Walwal in Abyssinia, or the Manchurian frontier in the Far East.

Japan's imperialist needs and demands in the Far East, can be fulfilled only if she can establish her political hegemony over China, to the exclusion of the white race, and by virtually scrapping the 'Open Door' policy. Time and again, her politicians have said as much in so many words. For instance, Japan's spokesmen have often said that she has special interests in the Far East, which cannot be compared to those of any other Western Power—that is, Japan's mission to umpire the Far East and maintain peace in that quarter, etc. No doubt, besides the purely economic motive, the Japanese are inspired by the desire to found an Empire, and the consciousness of being an unconquered race whets their imperialist appetite. Incidentally, the foundation of an empire abroad enables the fascist elements in Japanese society to get the upper hand.

If China could somehow persuade herself to accept the political and economic suzerainty, or patronage of Japan, the Sino-Japanese conflict would end in no time. This is what Hirota, Japan's foremost diplomat, has been trying to achieve for the last three years. His speeches have been extremely conciliatory on the surface, with a constant appeal for Sino-Japanese co-operation. Now, what is the objective of this co-operation? Obviously, the enrichment of Japan, and the virtual enslavement of China. But this naked truth cannot be blurted out—hence the slogan is 'Co-operation in a joint defence against Communism'. This slogan not only serves to cloak Japanese motives, but at the same time conciliates all anti-socialist elements whether in Japan, China, or elsewhere. Thus, the Indian papers of 7 August 1937, gave the following account of Hirota's foreign policy:

> Declaring that a major point in Japan's requests to China was co-operation in a joint defence against communism, M. Hirota in the House of Representatives said, he believed that Sino-Japanese co-operation was possible if the radical elements in China, particularly the communists, were effectively controlled. He added, the Japanese Government wished to settle the North China incident on the spot, and at the same time to effect a fundamental re-adjustment of Sino-Japanese relations.

And similar statements in similar language have been made ever since Hirota first became Japan's Foreign Minister a few years ago.

Can China submit to this demand even if it brings her peace? My own views is that left to himself, Marshal Chiang Kai-shek, the Dictator of the Nanking Central Government, would have done so. At heart he is violently anti-Communist and since the split in the Kuomintang (Chinese National Party) in 1927, when he managed to establish his supremacy, he has spared no pains to exterminate the Chinese Communists and their allies. But Marshal Chiang has encountered consistent opposition from two quarters. The Western provinces of China, known as the Chinese Soviet States, being practically independent of Nanking have kept up the fight against Japan and, on this point, have faithfully echoed the feelings of the Chinese masses. Secondly, the Western Powers with their vast interests in China, and with their prestige to maintain before the Eastern races, cannot easily persuade themselves to scuttle the foreign investments as in Latin America (Central and South America). Regarding British investments in China, the following extract from the *London Times* of 19 August 1937 is illuminating:

> British direct interests in China are worth about 250 million pounds, made up of 200 million pounds in business investments, and 50 million pounds in government obligations. Of the total sum, about 180 million pounds is tied up in Shanghai, and of this 180 million a high proportion is in the Settlement district, north of the Soochow Creek. This is the district now being most heavily

shelled and bombed. It is where most of the Public Utility offices and works, and where most of the large mercantile businesses, are established.

The *Times* writer goes on to point out with dismay, that whilst previously this district has been policed under British Superintendents, the police stations have been evacuated and occupied by the Japanese. The White Races are consequently alive to the fact, that Japanese hegemony over China will mean not only the subjugation of the latter, but their own exclusion from the Far East. Since the geography of a country often determines military strategy, it is necessary to note the salient features in the geography of China.

China's most important lines of communication are her three great rivers: the Hwang-ho (or Yellow River) in the North, the Yang-tse in the Centre, and the Si-Kiang in the South. The entrance to the Si-Kiang is controlled by the British port of Hongkong; to the Yang-tse by Shanghai, which is jointly held by the foreign powers with Britain and America predominating. The entrance to the Hwang-ho is dominated by Japan, entrenched first in Korea and now in Manchuria (Manchukuo) as well. The one practicable land route into China is that from the north. Along this route the Mongols and the Manchus entered China proper, and in the years preceding the Great War, both Russia and Japan had their eyes on it. Since 1931, Japan has been aiming at the possession of this route, and the country adjoining it, and since July 1937, fighting has been going on in this area. It should be remembered in this connection that high mountains separate China proper from the western part of the Republic (*viz.*, Sinkiang or Chinese Turkestan). The consequence of this is that the land route to China proper is from the north and we find that historically the power which has controlled Manchuria has always been in a strong position to dominate China.

In order to understand in their proper perspective the events in the Far East since 1931, it is necessary to understand the broad lines of Japanese strategy. Since Japanese hegemony in China through peaceful penetration was not possible, Japan laid down her plans for a military conquest of China, or at least for military pressure on her. To achieve this objective, Japanese strategy had to work along two lines; firstly, to break up Chinese unity and secondly, to make it impossible for any other power to come to the aid of China. This purpose could be served only if Japan could seize the entire northern part of the Republic, including Manchukuo, Mongolia and northern China proper. These territories taken together form a compact mass, cutting off Russian Siberia from China proper (the valleys of Hwang-ho, Yangtse and Si-kiang rivers). A reference to the map will show that if Japan holds this area, she can in the event of war with Russia, penetrate through outer Mongolia and cut the Trans-Siberian railway at Lake Baikal. And if Russia can be effectively isolated, no other country can come to China's rescue in an emergency. We shall see how Japan has progressed in the task of absorbing this area since 1931.

It is necessary to note at the outset that Japan never lays all her cards on the table and she proceeds with her aggression cautiously, taking care that she is not attacked by any other power when her own hands are full. Moreover, she always manages to stage some 'incident' in order to give her a pretext for seizing Chinese territory. The first 'incident' was staged on 18 September 1931, by Lieutenant Kawamoto of the Japanese Imperial Army, who was reconnoitring along the South Manchuria Railway track. This led to the seizure of Mukden the next day, and of the whole of Manchuria within a short period. At that time, the whole world was in the grip of an acute economic depression and Russia was feverishly pushing on her first Five-Year plan. Japan was, therefore, sure that there would be no effective challenge to her predatory moves. The Lytton Commission sent out by the League of Nations reported against Japan and following that, the League Assembly condemned the Japanese seizure of Manchuria. But Japan snapped her fingers at the League and walked out. This was followed by the sale of the Chinese Eastern Railway to Manchukuo by the Soviet Union in 1933, and in 1934 the Russo-Manchukuo Waterways Agreement was adopted. Though Manchukuo was not given *de jure* recognition by the other powers, she obtained *de facto* recognition from most of them.

Manchukuo is a huge territory with plenty of room for colonisation, though the climate is severe, and it is rich in several raw materials including coal. Moreover, it is exceedingly useful as a jumping-off ground for Japan in the event of war with Soviet Russia. Many people thought that it would take Japan years to develop Manchukuo and in the meantime, there would be peace in the Far East. But they were mistaken. Both on economic and on strategic grounds, Manchukuo cannot stand by itself. Only a part of the raw materials desired by Japan can be found there and the Manchukuan market is not big enough for Japan. Moreover, strategically Manchukuo is exceedingly weak, there being hostile territory on all sides. Consequently to satisfy her economic needs and to ensure the safety of the new state, Japan had to continue her aggression further.

In 1932, another 'incident' was staged in Shanghai and the Shanghai

War between China and Japan started. The upshot of it was that China was forced to demilitarise a certain area near Shanghai, and submit to a few other Japanese conditions. The strategic importance of Shanghai was not so clear in 1932, but the present war (1937) has brought it to light.

By 1933, the consolidation of Manchukuo under the puppet Emperor, Pu Yi, was complete and Japan was ready for further extension of her frontiers. Fighting took place in North China outside the frontiers of Manchukuo. The Japanese troops seized Jehol and a slice of Chahar and marched up to the gates of Peking (now called Peiping). Vanquished in battle, the Chinese had to bow to the inevitable and see another slice of their territory annexed by Japan. The war ended with the Tangku Truce in 1933.

The year 1934 was comparatively uneventful but hostilities broke out again in 1935. As always happens with Japan, a fresh act of aggression was preceded by conciliatory speeches and a show of moderation in foreign policy. On 23 January 1935, Hirota delivered an address, advocating a policy of non-aggression and the adoption of a 'good neighbour' policy with a view to effecting a rapprochement with China. This time, the slogan adopted by the Japanese was an autonomous North China (like an autonomous Manchukuo) and the Central Government of Nanking (new capital of China) was told not to interfere with Japanese activities and negotiations in North China. But Nanking could not wholly oblige Japan and the people of North China did not want to walk into the Japanese trap as blindly as the Manchurians had done in 1931. The result was that the Japanese plans did not succeed. Nevertheless, when the conflict was finally liquidated, it was found that China had virtually lost another portion of her territory.

In 1933, Jehol and a part of Chahar had been absorbed by Manchukuo. Now, a demilitarised zone was created in Hopei province with its capital at Tungchow, 12 miles east Peiping, called the East Hopei autonomous area. In charge of this area was a Chinese renegade, Yin-Ju-Keng, and the territory was under Japanese domination. (Later on, large-scale smuggling went on within this area, presumably with Japanese connivance, with a view to evading the Chinese Customs.) Further, the remaining part of Hopei (which contains Peiping and Tientsin) and a portion of Chahar were combined into a separate administrative unit under the Hopei-Chahar Political Council, headed by General Sung Cheh Yuan, the strongest leader outside Nanking. This council, while afraid to oppose Japan openly, did not sever its connections with Nanking. In February 1936, there was a military revolt in Tokyo and, for a time, the

Japanese Government had its hands full at home. Nevertheless, it was not altogether inactive. With a view to strengthening her position internationally, Japan entered into a Pact with Germany—the German-Japanese Anti-Comintern Pact. Towards the end of the year, in November 1936, an attempt was made to push into Inner Mongolia down the Peiping-Paotow Railway, but the Mongol-Manchukuo mercenaries of Japan were held at bay in the province of Suiyan by General Fu Tso I, with the aid of Nanking's troops.

It should be clear to any student of history that since 1931, Japan has been growing increasingly assertive not only in the Far East, but in world affairs in general. If she had not felt strong in the international sphere, she would never have ventured an aggression against China. We have already referred to her withdrawal from the League of Nations after the seizure of Manchuria. Prior to this she had allowed the Anglo-Japanese Alliance to lapse, probably because she felt that she was powerful enough to do without it.

In the Washington Naval Treaty, Japan had agreed to the ratio 5:5:3 in the matter of warships, etc., as between Britain, U.S.A. and herself. When this treaty lapsed in 1935, Japan insisted on parity and since this was not agreed to by the other Powers at the London Conference, she contemptuously walked out of it. When Britain wanted to bring about an economic understanding with Japan in the matter of world-markets, Japan refused to discuss any markets except those which were directly controlled by the former, and the London Conference of 1935 between the two powers broke up. From all these facts it will be clear that when 1937 dawned, Japan was morally and internationally prepared for a major conflict in the Far East.

But sometimes even the most well-informed are led astray. Between March and July 1937 Japan lulled the whole world into the belief that she was passing through an economic crisis, and was therefore unable to launch on any military aggression against China. Articles appeared in several American journals to show that while the rest of the world was enjoying an economic recovery, in Japan it was the reverse. Owing to this recovery, the price of raw materials had gone up considerably. Japan had to buy them at a high price and so her cost of production had gone up—making it virtually impossible for her to compete in the world-market successfully. (This statement is disproved by the remarkably low prices of Japanese textiles in India at the present time.) American Journalists took pains to argue that because of this economic crisis, Japan had decided to go slow with China and was therefore offering her the hand of friendship. It was further argued that owing to the same reason, extreme militarists were out of favour for the time being and moderate politicians were getting the upper hand in Japan.

It now appears that Japan's moderation was simply a cloak to hide her real intentions, in order to lull her enemies to a sense of security. Japan chose this particular moment for attacking China for obvious reasons. Neither the U.S.A. nor Britain nor Russia is yet ready to challenge Japan in war. All of them are preparing feverishly and are piling up armaments and two or three years later, the outlook for Japan may be gloomy. It was therefore a case of 'now or never' for Japan, and she struck. She carefully prepared for this attack by a period of sober talk and moderate action. And when everybody felt convinced that Japan was thinking in terms of peace, she launched her attack. Thus writing on 24 April 1937, the well-known journal of New York, *The Nation*, said: 'The prospects of peace in the Far East are greater than at any time since 1931.' Writing on 26 June, the same Journal remarked that there was a lull in Japan's offensive against China. But little did the writer know then that it was merely a lull before the storm.

Apart from Japan's general preparedness for another drive, certain factors precipitated the present crisis in the Far East. The Scian coup and the kidnapping of Marshal Chiang kai Shek in December 1936 prepared the ground for a 'United Front' policy of China. There seems to be little doubt now that before Chiang was released by his captors, an understanding had been arrived at between the Chinese Soviets and Nanking Government on the basis of a common resistance against Japan. This understanding meant the completion of the unification of China for the first time in recent history. The Chinese Soviets were to give up their Communism and Separatism and submit to the direction of Nanking. Chiang was to lead united China against Japanese aggression and the Communist leaders, Chow-En-lai and Chiang's own son were to fall in line with him. Japan come to know of this and attacked, before united China could proceed further with the work of consolidation.

The time is opportune for Japan in many ways. Though British, Russian and American re-armament is proceeding apace, as already stated, none of them is yet ready for a conflict. It will still take time for Britain to complete her Singapore base. The Neutrality Act adopted by the U.S.A. is a clear indication that she wants to keep out of every international conflict. The Russian Army, according to Fascist reports is seething with discontent and in any case is not as formidable as it appeared twelve months ago. The clash on the Soviet-Manchukuo border followed by he withdrawal on 4 July 1937, of the Soviet troops from the disputed islands which belong to Russia under the 1860 Agreement with China—was a further proof that the Soviet Government was not prepared for a war.

Three days after the withdrawal of the Soviet troops from the Amur River, a fresh 'incident' was staged near Peiping and the attack on North China was resumed on 8 July 1937.

Man is proverbially wiser after a calamity has befallen him. It is now reported by well-informed journalists that Japan had been preparing for this war for some time past. She is not satisfied with the occupation of Manchukuo. This country is too cold for Japanese immigrants. It has contributed only a small proportion of the raw materials needed by Japanese industry. It has, no doubt, brought some increase of trade to Japan, but this has been offset by the cost of administration and the losses incurred as a result for the competition of Manchurian products in the Japanese market. On the other hand, economically North China (*viz.*, the provinces of Shantung, Hopei, Chahar, Shansi and Suiyan) offers far more than Manchukuo. There are iron deposits in Chahar, Shansi and Southern Hopei. Shansi has also high-grade coal. Moreover, tin, copper, gold and oil are scattered throughout the five provinces. The Yellow river (Hwang-ho) valley is suitable for the cultivation of cotton, which is now imported into Japan from India and America to the value of 400 million yen annually. And the climate is more favourable to Japanese immigration than that of Manchukuo, as well as to cattle-breeding.

The Japanese drew up plans for the exploitation of this territory some time ago, but Japanese capital was loath to come in, as long as the area remained under Chinese sovereignty. Hence, militarism had to come to the aid of capitalism.

Apart from the economic urge behind the present aggression, there lurks the psychological factor. American journalists were partly right when they wrote during the earlier part of this year about the economic crisis in Japan, but their conclusions were wrong. Contrary to what they wrote, economic difficulties may instigate a 'totalitarian' government to launch on a war abroad in order to stave off discontent at home. (The same crisis may overtake Germany in the not distant future.) In the case of Japan, it may be averred that the economic difficulties which she encountered in the recent past as a result of her declining trade balance made a revival of war-psychology necessary.

Further, since the defeat of the Japanese directed expedition against Suiyan (a province in North China) in November 1936, it became apparent that the strategic area of Inner Mongolia could only be obtained if the whole of North China were brought into subjugation. Without controlling Chahar and Suiyan, in particular, it is impossible to push into Inner Mongolia from the direction of Manchukuo.

Why is Japan so keen about Inner Mongolia, a barren country of little economic value? The reason is strategic rather than economic. It has been remarked above that Japan has been aiming at a compact mass of territory comprising Manchukuo, North China and Mongolia. Now, in the meantime, Soviet diplomacy has not been idle and two big provinces of the Chinese Republic have passed under Russian influence—Sinkiang (or Chinese Turkestan) and Outer Mongolia (the upper portion of Mongolia adjoining Soviet Russia). Sinkiang is not of much strategic importance to Japan (though it is to Soviet Russia owing to its proximity to India)—but Outer Mongolia is. With Outer Mongolia under her control, Soviet Russia can easily descend into North China. The only way to prevent this and cut off Russia permanently from China proper is to seize Inner Mongolia (the Southern part of Mongolia) and North China, and thereby form a compact corridor from West to East, separating Russian Siberia and Outer Mongolia from China proper. To annex this territory is at present Japan's objective. Once she succeeds in this effort, her next endeavour would be to build a strategic railway through this newly acquired territory from East to West. If she is able to consolidate her position there, she may then think of moving into Outer Mongolia. What would then happen, it is difficult to predict. At present, Outer Mongolia is a Russian sphere of influence and the Soviet Government have declared very plainly that any move on the part of Japan within this territory would be tantamount to a *casus belli*.

But Japan has not given up all hope of uniting the Mongols under her suzerainty some time in future. Hence, Japanese agents often talk of 'Mengkukuo' as a worthy political ideal for all the Mongols. This plan, if it ever materialises, will be a counterpart of Manchukuo. It will give the Mongols their own state, with the Gilbertian facade of autonomy of course, but in reality under Japanese tutelage. There are approximately five million Mongols in the Far East. Two millions live in the Hsingan province of Manchukuo. A million live in Outer Mongolia—a territory half as large as the United States, but mostly desert. Another million live in Inner Mongolia, while about a million are scattered in Sinkiang (Chinese Turkestan), Tibet and Soviet Russia (Buriat Republic). The nucleus of the future Mongol State of 'Mengkukuo' has already come into existence with a Mongolian Political Council. Among the Mongol leaders who are under Japanese influence are Li Shouhsein and Prince Teh.

But while an 'autonomous' Mengkukuo may be a future project for Japan, an autonomous North China is her immediate objective.

Since the annexation of Manchukuo, Japanese influence in North China was steadily growing and this must have led them to hope that without a major conflict, another puppet state would be set up in the near future comprising the five provinces of North China. But the absorption of Canton province within Nanking's zone in the recent past, followed by the reported understanding of Marshal Chiang with the Chinese Communists in December last must have dashed Japanese hopes to the ground. A strong and united China was, at long last, rising before the world's eyes and that China would not give up her northern provinces without a fight.

Since January 1937, Nanking began to assert influence over North China officials. She interfered with the Japanese-protected smuggling through East Hopei. She dared to order the suspension of the new Tientsin-Tokyo airline, established by Japan without Chinese consent. In Northern Chahar there was a small-scale rebellion of Manchukuan and Mongolian Troops against Japanese domination. Anti-Japanese incidents, were thus occurring with increasing frequency and not settled by abject submission to Japan's demands . To crown all, there was the report of an understanding between Nanking and the Chinese Communists which would bring into the field against Japan, the 90,000 seasoned soldiers belonging to the latter.

On 3 July 1937, the Japanese Ambassador, Shigeru Kawagoe, started negotiations with Nanking. Japan trimmed her sails and proposed the relinquishment of Japanese political control in North China, provided Nanking would recognize Manchukuo *de jure* and undertake 'economic co-operation' with Japan. Nanking is reported to have rejected this proposal and her counter-proposals fell short of Japanese requirements. No further proof was needed that a new China had come into existence which would soon exercise its full authority over the northern provinces. Therefore, Japan struck without delay and an 'incident' was staged at Lukouchaio, about 18 miles west of Peiping (Peking) when Japanese troops engaged in night-manoeuvres clashed with units of the Chinese Twenty-Ninth Army stationed in that area.

Looking at this incident legally, there can be no doubt that the Japanese were in the wrong. Though the Boxer protocol of 1901 entitled them to station troops in the Peiping Legation quarter and at certain points in the Peiping-Tientsin railroad, they sent their troops outside the specified areas and obstructed, rather than maintained, communications with the sea—the purpose for which the protocol was designed. Soon after the clash however, the Japanese Government made the following demands:

1) Withdrawal of the Twenty-Ninth Army from its present lines west of Peiping.
2) Punishment of the Chinese responsible for the conflict.
3) Adequate control of all anti-Japanese activities in North China; and
4) Enforcement of measures against communism.

It is reported that the Hopei-Chahar Political Council submitted to these demands on 19 July, and the terms of the settlement were published in Tokyo, on 23 July. The expectation on the Chinese side was that both the Chinese and Japanese fighting forces would withdraw from the zone and it is extremely probable that Nanking would have reluctantly endorsed the above settlement. But when the Japanese troops did not leave the area, the subordinate officers and the rank and file of the Chinese troops refused to withdraw. On 26 July, the Japanese military commanders issued an ultimatum that the Chinese troops must withdraw by noon, 28 July. The latter refused to budge and the Japanese thereupon proceeded to evict them by force. Thus the war started.

Though Marshal Chiang, the Nanking Dictator, is not ready for a war, he has stood up to Japan and it is not likely that he will give in without a fight.

Japan is preparing for a long fight and the Japanese Diet has already voted large sums for the campaign. It is reported that she will spend up to £11,76,50,000 in order to carry on the war till the end of January 1938.

The latest development in the Far Eastern War is the extension of the fight to the Shanghai area. On the 9 August a fresh 'incident' took place at the Hungjao aerodrome near Shanghai. Two Japanese naval officers were shot dead while attempting to enter the aerodrome. Thereupon, Japanese naval forces took drastic action to avenge the shooting and the Japanese Admiral demanded, among other things, that all Chinese troops should be withdrawn to a distance not less than 30 miles from Shanghai, and that all the defences prepared within the area should be immediately dismantled. The Chinese response to the demand was the movement into the Shanghai area of the 88th Division from Nanking in order to reinforce the local troops. The Japanese regarded this as a flagrant breach of the 1932 Agreement—but the Chinese retorted by saying that the Japanese themselves, by posting troops in Chinese territory and provocatively bringing a large fleet to the scene, had absolved China from any obligation to observe the terms of that Agreement.

Thus the war is going on along two fronts—Peiping and Shanghai. A moot point in this connection is as to which party desired the extension of the war to the Shanghai front. In all probability the Japanese.

The Japanese, being blocked on land, as they were when Nanking troops moved into Hopei province, turned to the sea. The semi-circle of armies which Marshal Chiang threw round Peiping (under Japanese occupation) based on a well-prepared line efforts, was a bold and important strategic move. The left flank of the Government Army is at Nankow, the famous pass, where the Peiping-Paotow railway cuts through the hills. The centre of the semicircle descends on Paotingfu, 100 miles south of Peiping on the Hankow Railway. The right flank sweeps round to within 30 miles of Tientsin, also under Japanese occupation. The task of forcing this semicircle—'Hindenburg' line—is a formidable one. Hence, the decision from a strategic point of view to undermine Chinese resistance by attacking Shanghai.

If China has a heart, it is the financial and commercial centre at the mouth of the Yangtse. Japan is attacking this heart in order to disorganize the foreign-controlled industrial, commercial and financial centre of China with a view to imperilling the economic basis of the Central Government, demoralizing national feeling and terrifying the Chinese bourgeoisie. Shanghai is virtually at the mercy of the Japanese navy and an attack on this prosperous and ever-growing city is the obvious way to bring the war to a rapid conclusion. But the effectiveness of this thrust will depend on the extent of the dislocation of trade and of the material damage accruing from the war.

The war will go on for some time. Japan will try 'to paralyse the heart of China in order to amputate the limbs. China must stand or fall, therefore, by the war in Shanghai'—as an eminent strategist has declared. Will China be able to survive this bloodbath? If Canton remains open for supplies of armaments and the loss in revenue due to the fighting in Shanghai is not too serious—China may, perhaps, keep going sufficiently long to be able to endanger the social and economic stability of Japan. As against this consideration is the fact that the Japanese Navy is attempting a blockade of the Chinese ports and further, that there is a war fever among the Japanese people, and there does not seem to be any difference between the aims of the military and the civilians in the Island Empire.

China has appealed once again to the League of Nations, as she did in 1931. But what is the value of this moribund League in such an emergency? World-opinion is, of course, on the side of China—but world-opinion is not of much value when pitted against machine-guns. The outlook for China is gloomy indeed. The mellow view that time is on China's side is not correct any longer. Today, China is fighting against time. God grant that she may succeed.

Japan has done great things for herself and for Asia. Her reawakening at the dawn of the present century sent a thrill throughout our Continent. Japan has shattered the white man's prestige in the Far East and has put all the Western imperialist powers on the defensive—not only in the military but also in the economic sphere. She is extremely sensitive—and rightly so—about her self-respect as an Asiatic race. She is determined to drive out the Western Powers from the Far East. But could not all this have been achieved without Imperialism, without dismembering the Chinese Republic, without humiliating another proud, cultured and ancient race? No, with all our admiration for Japan, where such admiration is due, our whole heart goes to China in her hour of trial. China must still live—for her own sake and for humanity. Out of the ashes of this conflict she will once again rise phoenix-like as she has so often done in the past.

Let us learn the lessons of this Far Eastern Conflict. Standing at the threshold of a new era, let India resolve to aspire after national self-fulfillment in every direction—but not at the expense of other nations and not through the bloody path of self-aggrandisement and imperialism.

19
My Faith (Philosophical)*

In 1917 I became very friendly with a Jesuit father. We used to have long talks on matters of common interest. In the Jesuit order founded by Ignatius Loyala I then found much that appealed to me, for instance, their triple vow of poverty, chastity, and obedience.[1] Unlike many Jesuits, this father was not dogmatic and he was well versed in Hindu philosophy. In our discussions he naturally took his stand on Christian theology as interpreted by his church, while I took my stand on the Vedanta as interpreted by Shankaracharya. I did not of course comprehend the Shankarite Doctrine of Maya[2] in all its abstruseness, but I grasped the essential principles of it—or at least I thought I did. One day the Jesuit father turned round to me and said—'I admit that Shankara's position is logically the soundest—but to those who cannot live up to it, we offer the next best.'

There was a time when I believed that Absolute Truth was within the reach of human mind and that the Doctrine of Maya represented the quintessence of knowledge. Today I would hesitate to subscribe to that position. I have ceased to be an absolutist (if I may use that word in my own sense) and am much more of a pragmatist. What I cannot live up to—what is not workable—I feel inclined to discard. Shankara's Doctrine of Maya intrigued me for a long time, but ultimately I found that I could not accept it because I could not live it. So I had to turn to a different philosophy. But that did not oblige me to go to Christian theology. There are several schools of Indian philosophy which regard the world, creation, as a reality and not as an illusion. There is, for example,

*The final chapter in his unfinished autobiography, *An Indian Pilgrim*, 1937.

[1] There is some anology to the triple prayer of the Buddhists which has to be repeated daily—'I take refuge in Buddha: I take refuge in Dharma (Truth): I take refuge in the Sangha (Order)'.

[2] In brief, this theory implies that the world as we perceive it through our senses is an illusion. It is a case of the rope being mistaken for a snake, the snake being the world of the senses.

the theory of Qualified Monism according to which the ultimate reality is One and the world is a manifestation of it. Ramakrishna's view is similar, that both the One (God) and the Many (Creation) are true. Several theories have been advanced to explain the nature of creation. According to some the universe is the manifestation of Ananda or Divine Bliss. Others hold that it is the manifestation of Divine Play or 'Leela'. Several attempts have also been made to describe the One—the Absolute—God—in human language and imagery. To some, like the Vaishnavas, God is Love, to some like the Shaktas, He is Power; to others He is Knowledge; to still others He is Bliss. Then there is the traditional conception of the Absolute in Hindu philosophy as 'Sat-Chit-Ananda', which may be translated as 'Existence-Consciousness (or Knowledge)-Bliss'. The more consistent philosophers say that the Absolute is indescribable or inexpressible (anirvachaneeya). And it is reported of Buddha that whenever he was questioned about the Absolute he remained silent.

It is impossible to comprehend the Absolute through our human intellect with all its limitations. We cannot perceive reality as it is objectively—as it is in itself—we have to do so through our own spectacles, whether these spectacles be Bacon's 'Idola' or Kant's 'forms of the understanding' or something else. The Hindu philosopher will probably say that as long as the duality of Subject (Jnata) and Object (Jneya) remains, knowledge is bound to be imperfect. Perfect knowledge can be attained only when Subject and Object merge into oneness. This is not possible on the mental plane—the plane of ordinary consciousness. It is possible only in the supra-mental plane—in the region of super-consciousness. But the conception of the supramental, of the super-conscious, is peculiar to Hindu philosophy and is repudiated by Western philosophers. According to the former, perfect knowledge is attainable only when we reach the level of the super-conscious through Yogic perception, i.e., intuition of some sort. Intuition as an instrument of knowledge has, of course been admitted in Western philosophy since the time of Henri Bergson, though it may still be ridiculed in certain quarters. But Western philosophy has yet to admit the existence of the supra-mental and the possibility of our comprehending it through Yogic perception.

Assuming for a moment for argument's sake that we can comprehend the Absolute through Yogic perception, the difficulty about describing it will still remain. When we attempt to describe it, we fall back into the plane of normal consciousness and we are handicapped by all the limitations of the normal human mind. Our descriptions of the Absolute God are consequently anthropomorphic. And what is anthropomorphic cannot be regarded as Absolute Truth.

Now can we comprehend the Absolute through Yogic perception? Is there a supra-mental plane which the individual can reach and where the Subject and the Object merge into oneness? My attitude to this question is one of benevolent agnosticism—if I may coin this expression. On the one hand, I am not prepared to take anything on trust. I must have first-hand experience, but this sort of experience in the matter of the Absolute, I am unable to get. On the other hand, I cannot just rule out as sheer moonshine what so many individuals claim to have experienced in the past. To repudiate all that would be to repudiate much, which I am not prepared to do. I have, therefore, to leave the question of the supra-mental open, until such time as I am able to experience it myself. Meanwhile I take up the position of a relativist. I mean thereby, that Truth as known to us is not absolute but relative. It is relative to our common mental meanwhile I take our distinctive characteristics as individuals—and to changes in the same individual during the process of time.

Once we admit that our notions of the Absolute are relative to our human mind, we should be relieved of a great deal of philosophical controversy. It would follow that when such notions differ, they may all be equally true—the divergence being accounted for by the distinctive individuality of the subject. It would follow, further, that the notions of the same individual with regard to the Absolute may vary with time along with his mental development. But none of these notions need be regarded as false. As Vivekananda used to say, 'Man proceeds not from error to truth but from truth to higher truth'. There should accordingly be scope for the widest toleration.

The question now arises: Granting that reality as known to me is relative and not absolute, what is its nature? In the first place, it has an objective existence and is not an illusion. I come to this conclusion not from *a priori* considerations but mainly from the pragmatic point of view. The Doctrine of Maya does not work. My life is incompatible with it, though I tried long and hard to make my life fit in with it. I have, therefore, to discard it. On the other hand, if the world be real (not, of course, in an absolute but in a relative sense) then life becomes interesting and acquires meaning and purpose.

Secondly, this reality is not static, but dynamic—it is ever changing. Has this change any direction? Yes, it has; it is moving towards a better state of existence. Actual experience demonstrates that the changes imply progress—and not meaningless motion.

Further, this reality is, for me, Spirit working with a conscious purpose through time and space. This conception does not, of course, represent the Absolute Truth which is beyond description for all time and which for me is also beyond comprehension at the present moment. It is therefore a relative truth and is liable to change along with the changes in my mind.[3] Nevertheless, it is a conception which represents my utmost effort to comprehend reality and which offers a basis on which to build my life.

Why do I believe in Spirit? Because it is a pragmatic necessity. My nature demands it. I see purpose and design in nature; I discern an 'increasing purpose' in my own life. I feel that I am not a mere conglomeration of atoms. I perceive, too, that reality is not a fortuitous combination of molecules. Moreover, no other theory can explain reality (as I understand it) so well. This theory is in short an intellectual and moral necessity, a necessity of my very life, so far as I am concerned.

The world is a manifestation of Spirit and just as Spirit is eternal so also is the world of creation. Creation does not and cannot end at any point of time. This view is similar to the Vaishnavic conception of Eternal Play (Nitya Leela). Creation is not the offspring of sin; nor is it the result of 'avidya' or 'ignorance' as the Shankarites would say. It reflects the eternal play of eternal forces—the Divine Play, if you will.

I may very well be asked why I am bothering about the ultimate nature of reality and similar problems and am not contenting myself with experience as I find it. The answer to that is simple. The moment we analyse experience, we have to posit the self—the mind which receives—and the non-self—the source of all impressions, which form the stuff of our experience. The non-self—reality apart from the self—is there and we cannot ignore its existence by shutting our eyes to it. This reality underlies all our experience and on our conception of it depends much that is of theoretical and practical value to us.

No, we cannot ignore reality. We must endeavour to know its nature—though, as I have already indicated, that knowledge can at best be relative and cannot be dignified with the name of Absolute Truth. This relative truth must form the basis of our life—even if what is relative is liable to change.

What then is the nature of this Spirit which is reality? One is reminded of the parable of Ramakrishna about a number of blind men trying to describe an elephant—each giving a description in accordance with the organ he touched and therefore violently disagreeing with the rest. My own view is that most of the conceptions of reality are true, though

[3] There is nothing wrong in this—for as Emerson said, a foolish consistency is the hobgoblin of little minds. Moreover, what is progress if it does not involve change?

partially, and the main question is which conception represents the maximum truth. For me, the essential nature of reality is LOVE. LOVE is the essence of the Universe and is the essential principle in human life. I admit that this conception also is imperfect—for I do not know today what reality is in itself and I cannot lay claim to knowing the Absolute today—even if it be within the ultimate reach of human knowledge or experience. Nevertheless, with all its imperfection, for me this theory represents the maximum truth and is the nearest approach to Absolute Truth.

I may be asked how I come to the conclusion that the essential nature of reality is LOVE. I am afraid my epistemology is not quite orthodox. I have come to this conclusion partly from a rational study of life in all aspects—partly from intuition and partly from pragmatic considerations. I see all around me the play of love; I perceive within me the same instinct; I feel that I must love in order to fulfil myself and I need love as the basic principle on which to reconstruct life. A plurality of considerations drives me to one and the same conclusion.

I have remarked above that the essential principle in human life is love. This statement may be challenged when one can see so much in life that is opposed to love; but the paradox can be easily explained. The 'essential principle is not fully manifest yet; it is unfolding itself in space and time. Love, like reality of which it is the essence, is dynamic.

What, now, is the nature of the process of unfolding? Firstly, is it a movement forward or not? Secondly, is there any law underlying this movement?

The unfolding process is progressive in character. This assertion is not quite dogmatic. Observation and study of nature point to the conclusion that everywhere there is progress. This progress may not be unilinear; there may be periodic setbacks—but on the whole, i.e., considered from a long period point of view, there is progress. Apart from this rational consideration there is the intuitive experience that we are moving ahead with the lapse of time. And last but not least, there is the necessity, both biological and moral, to have faith in progress.

As various attempts have been made to know reality and to describe it—so also have attempts been made to comprehend the law of progress. None of these efforts is futile; each gives us a glimpse of the truth. The Sankhya Philosophy of the Hindus was probably the oldest endeavour to describe the evolutionary process in nature. That solution will not satisfy the modern mind. In more recent times ,we have various theories, or perhaps descriptions, of evolution. Some like Spencer would have us believe that evolution consists in a development from the simple to the complex. Others like von Hartmann would assert that the world is a manifestation of blind will—from which one could conclude that it is futile to look for an underlying idea. Bergson would maintain his own theory of creative evolution; evolution should imply a new creation or departure at every stage, which cannot be calculated in advance by the human intellect. Hegel, on the contrary, would dogmatise that the nature of the evolutionary process, whether in the thought world or in reality outside, is dialectic. We progress through conflicts and their solutions. Every thesis provokes an antithesis. This conflict is solved by a synthesis, which in its turn, provokes new antithesis—and so on.

All these theories have undoubtedly an element of truth. Each of the above thinkers has endeavoured to reveal the truth as he has perceived it. But undoubtedly Hegel's theory is the nearest approximation to truth. It explains the facts more satisfactorily than any other theory. At the same time it cannot be regarded as the whole truth since all the facts as we know them do not accord with it. Reality is, after all, too big for our frail understanding to fully comprehend. Nevertheless, we have to build our life on the theory which contains the maximum truth. We cannot sit still because we cannot, or do not, know the Absolute Truth.

Reality, therefore, is Spirit, the essence of which is Love, gradually unfolding itself in an eternal play of conflicting forces and their solutions.

20
The Haripura Address

Presidential Address at the 51st Session of the Indian National Congress Held at Haripura in February 1938

Mr Chairman and Friends,

I am deeply sensible of the honour you have done me by electing me as the President of the Indian national Congress for the coming year. I am not so presumptuous as to think for one moment that I am in any way worthy of that great honour. I regard it as a mark of your generosity and as a tribute to the youths of our country, but for whose cumulative contribution to our national struggle, we would not be where we are today. It is with a sense of fear and trepidation that I mount the tribune which has hitherto been graced by the most illustrious sons and daughters of our motherland. Conscious as I am of my numerous limitations, I can only hope and pray that with your sympathy and support I may be able in some small measure to do justice to the high office which you have called upon me to fill.

At the outset, may I voice you feelings in placing on record our profound grief at the death of Shrimati Swaruprani Nehru, Acharya Jagadish Chandra Bose and Dr Sarat Chandra Chatterji? Shrimati Swaruprani Nehru was to us not merely the worthy consort of Pandit Motilal and the revered mother of Pandit Jawaharlal Nehru. Her suffering, sacrifice and service in the cause of India's freedom were such as any individual could feel proud of. As compatriots we mourn her death and our hearts go out in sympathy to Pandit Nehru and other members of the bereaved family.

To Acharya Jagadish Chandra Bose India will always remain beholden for being the first to secure for her an honoured place in the modern scientific world. A nationalist to the core of his heart, Acharya Jagadish gave his life not merely to science, but to India as well. India knows it and is grateful for it. We convey our heartfelt sympathy to Lady Bose.

Through the untimely death of Dr Sarat Chandra Chatterji, India has lost one of the brightest stars in her literary firmament. His name, for years a household word in Bengal, was not less known in the literary world of India. But if Sarat Babu was great as a litterateur, he was perhaps greater as a patriot. The Congress in Bengal is distinctly poorer today because of his death. We send our sincerest condolence to the members of his family.

Before I proceed further I should like to bow my head in homage to the memory of those who have laid down their lives in the service of the country since the Congress met last year at Faizpur. I should mention especially those who died in prison or in internment or soon after release from internment. I should refer in particular to Sjt. Harendra Munshi, a political prisoner in the Dacca Central Jail, who laid down his life the other day as a result of hunger-strike. My feelings are still too lacerated to permit me to say much on this subject. I shall only ask you if there is not 'something rotten in the state of Denmark' that such bright and promising souls as Jatin Das, Sardar Mahabir Singh, Ramkrishna Namadas, Mohit Mohan Maitra, Harendra Munshi and others should feel the urge not to live life but to end it.

When we take a bird's-eye view of the entire panorama of human history, the first thing that strikes us is the rise and fall of empires. In the East as well as in the West, empires have invariably gone through a process of expansion and after reaching the zenith of prosperity, have gradually shrunk into insignificance and sometimes death. The Roman empire of the ancient times and the Turkish and Austro-Hungarian empires of the modern period are striking examples of this law. The empires in India—the Maurya, the Gupta and the Mogul empires—are no exceptions to this rule. In the face of these objective facts of history, can anyone be so bold as to maintain that there is in store a different fate for the British empire? That empire stands today at one of the crossroads of history. It will either go the way of other empires or it must transform itself into a federation of free nations. Either course is open to it. The Czarist empire collapsed in 1917 but of its debris sprang the Union of Soviet Socialist Republics. There is still time for Great Britain to take a leaf out of Russian history. Will she do so?

The British empire is a hybrid phenomenon in politics. It is a peculiar combination of self-governing countries, partially self-governing dependencies and autocratically-governed colonies. Constitutional device and human ingenuity may bolster up this combination for a while, but not for ever. If the internal incongruities are not removed in good time, then quite apart from external pressure, the empire is sure to break down under its own strain. But can the British empire transform itself into a federation of free nations with one bold sweep? It is for the British people to answer this question. One thing, however, is certain. This transformation will be possible only if the British people become free in their own homes—only if Great Britain becomes a socialist state. There is an inseparable connection between the capitalist ruling classes in Great Britain and the colonies abroad. As Lenin pointed out long ago, 'reaction in Great Britain is strengthened and fed by the enslavement of a number of nations'. The British aristocracy and bourgeoisie exist primarily because there are colonies and overseas depedencies to exploit. The emancipation of the latter will undoubtedly strike at the very existence of the capitalist ruling classes in Great Britain and precipitate the establishment of a socialist regime in that country. It should, therefore, be clear that a socialist order in Great Britain is impossible of achievement without the liquidation of colonialism and that we who are fighting for the political freedom of India and other enslaved countries of the British empire are incidentally fighting for the economic emancipation of the British people as well.

It is a well-known truism that every empire is based on the policy of divide and rule. But I doubt if any empire in the world has practised this policy so skilfully, systematically and ruthlessly as Great Britain. In accordance with the policy, before power was handed over to the British people, Ulster was separated from the rest of Ireland. Similarly, before any power is handed over to the Palestinians, the Jews will be separated from the Arabs. An internal partition is necessary in order to neutralise the transference of power. The same principle of partition appears in a different form in the new Indian Constitution. Here we find an attempt to separate the different communities and put them into water-tight compartments. And in the Federal Scheme there is juxtaposition of autocratic princes and democratically elected representatives from British India. If the new Constitution is finally rejected, whether owing to the opposition of British India or owing to the refusal of the princes to joining it, I have no doubt that British ingenuity will seek some other constitutional device for partitioning India and thereby neutralising the transference of power to the Indian people. Therefore, any Constitution for India which emanates from Whitehall must be examined with the utmost care and caution.

The policy of divide and rule, though it has its obvious advantages, is by no means an unmixed blessing for the ruling power. As a matter of fact, it creates new problems and new embarrassments. Great Britain seems to be caught in the meshes of her own political dualism resulting from her policy of divide and rule. Will she please the Muslim or the Hindu in India? Will she favour the Arab or the Jew in Palestine—the Arab or the Kurd in Iraq? Will she side with the King or the Wafd in Egypt? The same dualism is visible outside the empire. In the case of Spain, British politicians are torn between such alternatives as Franco and the lawful government—and in the wider field of European politics, between France and Germany. The contradictions and inconsistencies in Britain's foreign policy are the direct outcome of the heterogeneous composition of her empire. The British Cabinet has to please the Jews because she cannot ignore Jewish high finance. On the other hand, the India office and Foreign Office have to placate the Arabs because of imperial interests in the Near East and India. The only means whereby Great Britain can free herself from such contradictions and inconsistencies is by transforming the empire into a federation of free nations. If she could do that, she would be performing a miracle in history. But if she fails, she must reconcile herself to the gradual dismemberment of a vast empire where the sun is supposed not to set. Let the lesson of the Austro-Hungarian empire be not lost on the British people.

The British empire at the present moment is suffering from strain at a number of points. Within the empire, in the extreme West, there is Ireland and in the extreme East, India. In the middle lies Palestine with the adjoining countries of Egypt and Iraq. Outside the empire, there is the pressure exerted by Italy in the Mediterranean and Japan in the Far East, both of these countries being militant, aggressive and imperialist. Against this background of unrest stands Soviet Russia, whose very existence strikes terror into the heart of the ruling classes in every imperialist state. How long can the British empire withstand the cumulative effect of this pressure and strain?

Today, Britain can hardly call herself 'the Mistress of the Seas'. Her phenomenal rise in the eighteenth and nineteenth centuries was the result of her sea power. Her decline as an empire in the twentieth century will be the outcome of the emergence of a new factor in world history—Air Force. It was due to this new factor, Air Force, that an impudent Italy could successfully challenge a fully mobilised British Navy in the Mediterranean. Britain can rearm on land, sea and air up to the utmost limit. Battleships may still stand up to bombing from the air, but air force as a powerful element in modern warfare has come to stay. Distances have been obliterated and despite all anti-aircraft defences, London lies at the mercy of any bombing squadron from a continental centre. In short, air force has revolutionised modern warfare, destroyed the insularity of Great Britain and rudely disturbed the balance of power in world politics. The clay feet of a gigantic empire now stand exposed as these have never been before.

Amid this interplay of world forces India emerges much stronger than she has ever been before. Ours is a vast country with a population of 350 millions. Our vastness in area and in population has hitherto been a source of weakness. It is today a source of strength if we can only stand united and boldly face our rulers. From the standpoint of Indian unity the first thing to remember is that the division between British India and the Indian states is an entirely artificial one. India is one and the hopes and aspirations of the people of British India and of the Indian states are identical. Our goal is that of an Independent India and in my view that goal can be attained only through a federal republic in which the provinces and the states will be willing partners. The Congress has, time and again, offered its sympathy and moral support to the movement carried on by the states' subjects for the establishment of democratic government in what is known as Indian India. It may be that at this moment our hands are so full that the Congress is not in a position to do more for our compatriots in the states. But even today there is nothing to prevent individual Congressmen from actively espousing the cause of the states' subjects and participating in their struggle. There are people in the Congress like myself who would like to see the Congress participating more actively in the movement of the states' subjects. I personally hope that in the near future it will be possible for the Indian National Congress to take a forward step and offer a helping hand to our fellow-fighters in the states. Let us not forget that they need our sympathy and our help.

Talking of Indian unity the next thing that strikes us is the problem of the minorities. The Congress has, from time to time, declared its policy on this question. The latest authoritative pronouncement made by the All-India Congress Committee at its meeting in Calcutta in October 1937, runs thus:

> The Congress has solemnly and repeatedly declared its policy in regard to the rights of the minorities in India and has stated that it considers it its duty to protect these rights and ensure the widest possible scope for the development of these minorities and their participation in the fullest measure in the political, economic and cultural life of the nation. The objective of the Congress is an independent and united India where no class or group or majority or minority may exploit another to its own advantage, and where all the elements in the

nation may co-operate in a common good and the advancement of the people of India. The objective of unity and mutual co-operation in a common freedom does not mean the suppression in any way of the rich variety and cultural diversity of Indian life, which have to be preserved in order to give freedom and opportunity to the individual as well as to each group to develop unhindered according to its capacity and inclination.

In view, however, of attempts having been made to misinterpret the Congress policy in this regard, the All-India Congress Committee desire to reiterate this policy. The Congress has included in its resolution on Fundamental Rights that:

(i) Every citizen of India has the right of free expression of opinion, the right of free association and combination, and the right to assemble peacefully and without arms, for a purpose not opposed to law or morality;
(ii) Every citizen shall enjoy freedom of conscience and the right freely to profess and practise his religion, subject to the public order and morality;
(iii) The culture, language and script of the minorities and of the different linguistic areas shall be protected;
(iv) All citizens are equal before the law, irrespective of religion, caste, creed or sex;
(v) No disability attaches to any citizen by reason of his or her religion, caste, creed or sex, in regard to public employment, office of power or honour, and in the exercise of any trade or calling;
(vi) All citizens have equal rights and duties in regard to wells, tanks, roads, schools and places of public resort, maintained out of state, or local funds, or dedicated by private persons for the use of the general public;
(vii) The state shall observe neutrality in regard to all religions;
(viii) The franchise shall be on the basis of universal adult suffrage;
(ix) Every citizen is free to move throughout India and to stay and settle in any part thereof, to acquire property and to follow any trade or calling, and to be treated equally with regard to legal prosecution or protection in all parts of India.

These clauses of the Fundamental Rights resolution make it clear that there should be no interference in matter of conscience, religion, or culture, and a minority is entitled to keep its personal law without any change in this respect being imposed by the majority.

The position of the Congress in regard to the communal decision has been repeatedly made clear in Congress resolutions and finally in the Election manifesto issued last year. The Congress is opposed to this decision as it is anti-national, anti-democratic and is a barrier to Indian freedom and the development of Indian unity. Nevertheless, the Congress has declared that a change in or suppression of the Communal Decision should only be brought about by the mutual agreement of the parties concerned. The Congress has always welcomed and is prepared to take advantage of any opportunity to bring about such a change by mutual agreement.

In all matters affecting the minorities in India, the Congress wishes to proceed by their co-operation and though their goodwill in a common undertaking and for the realization of a common aim which is the freedom and betterment of all the people of India.

The time is opportune for renewing our efforts for the final solution of this problem. I believe I am voicing the feelings of all Congressmen when I say that we are eager to do our very best to arrive at an agreed solution, consistent with the fundamental principles of nationalism. It is not necessary for me to go into details as to the lines on which a solution should take place. Much useful ground has already been covered in past conferences and conversations. I shall merely add that only by emphasising our common interests, economic and political, can we cut across communal divisions and dissensions. A policy of live and let live in matters religious and an understanding in matters economic and political should be our objective. Though the Muslim problem looms large whenever we think of the question of the minorities and though we are anxious to settle this problem finally, I must say that the Congress is equally desirous of doing justice to other minorities and especially the so-called depressed classes whose number is a very large one. I would put it to the members of the minority communities in India to consider dispassionately if they have anything to fear when the Congress programme is put into operation. The Congress stands for the political and economic rights of the Indian people as a whole. If it succeeds in executing its programme, the minority communities would be benefited as much as any other section of the Indian population. Moreover, if after the capture of political power, national reconstruction takes place on socialistic lines—as I have no doubt it will—it is the 'have-nots' who will benefit at the expense of the 'haves' and the Indian masses have to be classified among the 'have-nots'. There remains but one question which may be a source of anxiety to the minorities, viz., religion and that aspect of culture that is based on religion. On this question the Congress policy is one of live and let live—a policy of complete non-interference in matters of conscience, religion and culture as well as of cultural autonomy for the different linguistic areas. The Muslims have, therefore, nothing to fear in the event of India winning her freedom—on the contrary, they have everything to gain. So far as the religious and social disabilities of the so-called depressed classes are concerned, it is well known that during the last seventeen years the Congress has left no stone unturned in the effort to remove them, and

I have no doubt that the day is not far off when such disabilities will be things of the past.

I shall now proceed to consider the method which the Congress should pursue in the years to come as well as its role in the national struggle. I believe more than ever that the method should be Satyagraha or non-violent non-co-operation in the widest sense of the term, including civil disobedience. It would not be correct to call our method passive resistance. Satyagraha, as I understand it, is not merely passive resistance but active resistance as well though that activity must be of a non-violent character. It is necessary to remind our countrymen that Satyagraha or non-violent non-co-operation may have to be resorted to again. The acceptance of office in the provinces as an experimental measure should not lead us to think that our future activity is to be confined within the limits of strict constitutionalism. There is every possibility that a determined opposition to the forcible inauguration of Federation may land us in another big campaign of civil disobedience.

In our struggle for independence we may adopt either of two alternatives. We may continue our fight until we have our full freedom and in the meantime decline to use any power that we may capture while on the march. We may, on the other hand, go on consolidating our position while we continue our struggle for Purna Swaraj or complete independence. From the point of view of principle, both the alternatives are equally acceptable and *a priori* considerations need not worry us. But we should consider. very carefully at every stage as to which alternative would be more conducive to our national advancement. In either case, the ultimate stage in our progress will be the severance of the British connection. When that severance takes place and there is no trace left of British domination, we shall be in a position to determine our future relations with Great Britain through a treaty or alliance voluntarily entered into by both parties. What out future relations with Great Britain will or should be, it is too early to say. That will depend to a large extent on the attitude of the British people themselves. On this point I have been greatly impressed by the attitude of President de Valera. Like the President of Eire, I should also say that we have no enmity towards the British people. We are fighting Great Britain and we want the fullest liberty to determine our future relations with her. But once we have real self-determination, there is no reason why we should not enter into the most cordial relations with the British people.

I am afraid there is a lack of clarity in the minds of many Congressmen as to the role of the Congress in the history of our national struggle. I know that there are friends who think that after freedom is won, the Congress Party having achieved its objective, should wither away. Such a conception is entirely erroneous. The party that wins freedom for India should be also the party that will put into effect the entire programme of post-war reconstruction. Only those who have won power can handle it properly. If other people are pitchforked into seats of power which they were not responsible for capturing, they will lack that strength, confidence and idealism which is indispensable for revolutionary reconstruction. It is this which accounts for the difference in the record of the Congress and non-Congress ministries in the very narrow sphere of Provincial Autonomy.

No, there can be no question of the Congress Party withering away after political freedom has been won. On the contrary, the Party will have to take over power, assume responsibility for administration and put through its programme of reconstruction. Only then will it fulfil its role. If it were forcibly to liquidate itself, chaos would follow. Looking at post-war Europe we find that only in those countries has there been orderly and continuous progress where the party which seized power undertook the work of reconstruction.

I know that it will be argued that the continuance of a party in such circumstances, standing behind the state, will convert that state into a totalitarian one; but I cannot admit the charge. The state will possibly become a totalitarian one, if there be only one party as in countries like Russia, Germany and Italy. But there is no reason why other parties should be banned. Moreover, the party itself will have a democratic basis, unlike, for instance, the Nazi Party which is based on the 'leader principle'. The existence of more than one party and the democratic basis of the Congress Party will prevent the future Indian state becoming a totalitarian one. Further, the democratic basis of the party will ensure that leaders are not thrust upon the people from above, but are elected from below.

Though it may be somewhat premature to give a detailed plan of reconstruction, we might as well consider some of the principles according to which our future social reconstruction should take place. I have no doubt in my mind that our chief national problems relating to the eradication of poverty, illiteracy and disease and to scientific production and distribution can be effectively tackled only along socialistic lines. The very first thing which our future national government will have to do would be to set up a commission for drawing up a comprehensive plan of reconstruction. This plan will have two parts—an immediate programme and a long-period programme. In drawing up the first part, the immediate objectives which will have to be kept in view will be threefold—first, to prepare the country for self-sacrifice; secondly, to unify India; and thirdly, to give scope for local and cultural autonomy. The second and third objectives may appear to be contradictory, but they are not really so. Whatever political talent or genius we may possess as a people, will have to be used in reconciling these two objectives. We shall have to unify the country so that we may be able to hold India against any foreign invasion. While unifying the country through a strong central government, we shall have to put all the minority communities as well as the provinces at their ease, by allowing them a large measure of autonomy in cultural as well as governmental affairs. Special efforts will be needed to keep our people together when the load of foreign domination is removed, because alien rule has demoralised and disorganised us to a degree. To promote national unity we shall have to develop our lingua franca and a common script. Further, with the help of such modern scientific contrivances as aeroplanes, telephone, radio, films, television, etc., we shall have to bring the different parts of India closer to one another and through a common educational policy we shall have to foster a common spirit among the entire population. So far as our lingua franca is concerned, I am inclined to think that the distinction between Hindi and Urdu is an artificial one. The most natural lingua franca would be a mixture of the two, such as is spoken in daily life in large portions of the country and this common language may be written in either of the two scripts. Nagari or Urdu. I am aware that there are people in India who strongly favour either of the two scripts to the exclusion of the other. Our policy, however, should not be one of exclusion. We should allow the fullest latitude to use either script. At the same time, I am inclined to think that the ultimate solution, and the best solution would be the adoption of a script that would bring us into line with the rest of the world. Perhaps, some of our countrymen will gape with horror when they hear of the adoption of the Roman script, but I would beg them to consider this problem from the scientific and historical point of view. If we do that, we shall realise at once that there is nothing sacrosanct in a script. The Nagari script, as we know it today, has passed through several phases of evolution. Besides, most of the major provinces of India have their own script and there is the Urdu script which is used largely by the Urdu-speaking public in India and by both Muslims and Hindus in provinces like the Punjab and Sind. In view of such diversity, the choice of a uniform script for the whole of India should be made in a thoroughly scientific and impartial spirit, free from bias of every kind. I confess that there was a time when I felt that it would be anti-national to adopt a foreign script. But my visit to Turkey in 1934 was responsible for converting me. I then realised for the first time what a great advantage it was to have the same script as the rest of the world. So far as our masses are concerned, since more than 90 per cent are illiterate and are not familiar with any script, it will not matter to them which script we introduce when they are educated. The Roman script will, moreover, facilitate their learning a European language. I am quite aware how unpopular the immediate adoption of the Roman script would be in our country. Nevertheless, I would beg my countrymen to consider what would be the wisest solution in the long run.

With regard to the long-period programme for a Free India, the first problem to tackle is that of our increasing population. I do not desire to go into the theoretical question as to whether India is over-populated or not. I simply want to point out that where poverty, starvation and disease are stalking the land, we cannot afford to have our population mounting up by thirty million during a single decade. If the population goes up by leaps and bounds, as it has done in the recent past, our plans are likely to fall through. It will, therefore, be desirable to restrict our population until we are able to feed, clothe and educate those who already exist. It is not necessary at this stage to prescribe the methods that should be adopted to prevent a further increase in population, but I would urge that public attention be drawn to this question.

Regarding reconstruction, our principal problem will be how to eradicate poverty from our country. That will require a radical reform of our land system, including the abolition of landlordism. Agricultural indebtedness will have to be liquidated and provision made for cheap credit for the rural population. An extension of the co-operative movement will be necessary for the benefit of both producers and consumers. Agriculture will have to be put on a scientific basis with a view to increasing the yield from the land.

To solve the economic problem agricultural improvement will not be enough. A comprehensive scheme of industrial development under state-ownerships and state-control will be indispensable. A new industrial system will have to be built up in place of the old one which has collapsed as a result of mass production abroad and alien rule at home. The planning commission will have to carefully consider and decide which of the home industries could be revived despite the competition of modern factories and in which sphere large scale production should be encouraged. However much we may dislike modern industrialism and condemn the evils which follow in its train, we cannot go back to the pre-industrial era, even if we desire to do so. It is well, therefore, that we should reconcile ourselves to industrialisation and devise means to minimise its evils and at the same time explore the possibilities of reviving cottage industries where there is a possibility of their surviving the inevitable competition of factories. In a country like India, there will be plenty of room for cottage industries, especially in the case of industries including hand-spinning and hand-weaving allied to agriculture.

Last but not the least, the state on the advice of a planning commission will have to adopt a comprehensive scheme for gradually socialising our entire agricultural and industrial system in the spheres of both production and appropriation. Extra capital will have to be procured for this, whether through internal or external loans or through inflation.

Opposing or resisting the provincial part of the Constitution will be hardly possible now, since the Congress Party has accepted office in seven out of eleven provinces. All that could be done would be to strengthen and consolidate the Congress as a result of it. I am one of those who were not in favour of taking office—not because there was something inherently wrong in doing so, not because no good could come out of that policy, but because it was apprehended that the evil effects of office acceptance would out-weigh the good. Today I can only hope that my forebodings were unfounded.

How can we strengthen and consolidate the Congress while our ministers are in office? The first thing to do is to change the composition and character of the bureaucracy. If this not done, the Congress Party may come to grief. In every country, the ministers come and go, but the steel frame of the permanent services remains. If that is not altered in composition and character, the governmental party and its cabinet are likely to prove ineffective in putting their principles into practice. This is what happened in the case of the Social Democratic Party in post-war Germany and perhaps in the case of the Labour Party in Great Britain in 1924 and 1929. It is the permanent services who really rule in every country. In India they have been created by the British and in the higher ranks they are largely British in composition. Their outlook and mentality are in most cases neither Indian nor national and a national policy cannot be executed until the permanent services become national in outlook and mentality. The difficulty, of course, will be that the higher ranks of the permanent services being, under the Statute, directly under the Secretary of State for India and not under the Provincial Government, it will not be easy to alter their composition.

Secondly, the Congress ministers in the different provinces should, while they are in office, introduce schemes of reconstruction in the spheres of education, health, prohibition, prison reforms, irrigation, industry, land reform, workers' welfare etc. In this matter, attempts should be made to have as far as possible, a uniform policy for the whole of India. This uniformity could be brought about in either of two ways. The Congress ministers in the different provinces could themselves come together—as the Labour Ministers did in October 1937, in Calcutta—and draw up a uniform programme. Over and above this, the Congress Working Committee, which is the supreme executive of the Congress could lend a helping hand by giving directions to the different departments of the Congress-controlled provincial governments in the light of such advice as it may get from its own experts. This will mean that the members of the Congress Working Committee should be conversant with the problems that come within the purview of the Congress governments in the provinces. It is not intended that they should go into the details of administration. All that is needed is that they should have a general understanding of the different problems so that they could lay down the broad lines of policy. In this respect, the Congress Working Committee could do much more than it has hitherto done and unless it does so, I do not see how that body can keep an effective control over the different Congress ministries.

At this stage I should like to say something more about the role of the Congress Working Committee. This Committee, in my judgement, is not merely the directing brain of the national army of fighters for freedom. It is also the Shadow Cabinet of Independent India and it should function accordingly. This is not an invention of my own. It is the role which has been assigned to similar bodies in other countries that have fought for their national emancipation. I am one of those who think in terms of a Free India—who visualise a national government in this country within the brief span of our own life. It is consequently natural for us to urge that the Working Committee should feel and function as the Shadow Cabinet of a Free India. This is what President de Valera's Republican Government did when it was fighting the British Government and was on the run. And this is what the Executive of the Wafd Party in Egypt did before it got into office. The members of the Working Committee while carrying on their day to day work should accordingly study the problems they will have to tackle in the event of their capturing political power.

More important than the question of the proper working of the Congress Governments is the immediate problem of how to oppose the inauguration of the federal part of the Constitution. The Congress attitude towards the proposed Federal Scheme has been clearly stated in the resolution adopted by the Working Committee at Wardha on 4 February 1938, which will be placed before this Congress after the Subjects Committee has considered it. That resolution says:

> The Congress has rejected the new Constitution and declared that a Constitution for India which can be accepted by the people must be based on Independence and can only be framed by the people themselves by means of a Constituent Assembly without the interference by any foreign authority. Adhering to this policy of rejection, the Congress has, however, permitted the formation in provinces of Congress Ministries with a view to strengthening the nation in its struggle for Independence. In regard to the proposed Federation, no such consideration applies even provisionally, or for a period, and the imposition of this Federation, will do grave injuries to India and tighten the bonds which hold her under the subjection of an imperialist domination. This scheme of Federation excludes from the sphere of responsibility the vital function of a government.
>
> The Congress is not opposed to the idea of Federation but a real Federation must, even apart from the question of responsibility, consist of free units, enjoying more or less the same measure of freedom and civil liberty and representation by a democratic process of election. Indian states participating in the Federation should approximate to the provinces in the establishment of representative institutions, responsible government, civil liberties and the method of election to the Federal House. Otherwise Federation as it is now contemplated will, instead of building Indian unity, encourage separatist tendencies and involve the states in internal and external conflict.
>
> The Congress, therefore, reiterates its condemnation of the proposed scheme and calls upon Provincial and Local Congress Committees and the people generally as well as Provincial Governments and Ministries to prevent its inauguration.
>
> In the event of an attempt being made to impose it, despite the declared will of the people, such an attempt must be combated in every way and the Provincial Government and Ministries must refuse to co-operate with it.
>
> In case such a contingency arises, the A.I.C.C. is authorised and directed to determine the line of action to be pursued in this regard.

I should like to add some more arguments to explain our attitude of uncompromising hostility towards the proposed Federation. One of the most objectionable features of the Federal Scheme relates to the commercial and financial safeguards in the new Constitution. Not only will the people continue to be deprived of any power over defence or foreign policy, but the major portion of the expenditure will also the entirely out of popular control. According to the budget of the Central Government for the year 1937–38, the army expenditure comes to 44.61 crores of rupees (£33.46 million) out of a total expenditure of 77.90 crores of rupees (£58.42 million)—that is, roughly 57 per cent of the total expenditure of the Central Government. It appears that the reserved side of Federal Government which will be controlled by the Governor-General will handle about 80 per cent of the Federal expenditure. Moreover, bodies like the Reserve Bank and the Federal Railways Authority are already created or will be created which will work as *imperium in imperio* uncontrolled by a Federal Legislature. The Legislature will be deprived of the powers it possesses at present to direct and influence railway policy, and it will not have any voice in determining the currency and exchange policy of the country which has a vital bearing on its economic development.

That fact that external affairs will be a reserved subject under the Federal Government will prejudically affect the freedom of the Indian Legislature to conclude trade agreements and will seriously restrict, in effect, fiscal autonomy. The Federal Government will not be under any constitutional obligation to place such trade agreements before the Legislature for their ratification, even as they decline at present to give an undertaking to place the Indo-British Trade Agreement before the Indian Legislative Assembly. The so-called fiscal autonomy convention will have no meaning unless it is stipulated that no trade agreement on behalf of India shall be signed by any party without its ratification by the Indian Legislature. In this connection, I should like to state that I am definitely of opinion that India should enter into bilateral trade agreements with countries like Germany, Czechoslovakia, Italy and the United States of America with whom she had close trade relations in the past. But under the new Constitution, it will not be within the power of the Federal Legislature to force the Federal Government to enter into such bilateral trade agreements.

The iniquitous and inequitable commercial safeguards embodied in the Act will make it impossible for any effective measure to be adopted in order to protect and promote Indian national industries especially where they might, as they often do, conflict with British commercial or industrial interests. In addition to the Governor-General's special responsibility to see that provisions with regard to discrimination, as laid down in the Act, are duly carried out, it is also his duty to prevent any action which would subject British goods imported into India to any kind of discriminatory or penal treatment. A careful study of these stringent and wide provisions will show that India can adopt no measures against British competition which the Governor-General cannot, in effect, stultify or veto, whether in the legislative or in the administrative sphere. It is, of course, preposterous to permit foreigners in this country to compete with the nationals on equal terms and there can be no genuine Swaraj if India is to be denied the power to devise and adopt a national economic policy including the right, if her interests so require, of differentiating between nationals and non-nationals. In a famous article in *Young India*, under the caption 'The Giant and the Dwarf' written soon after the conclusion of the Gandhi-Irwin Pact in 1931, Mahatma Gandhi declared plainly that 'to talk of no discrimination between Indian interests and English or European, is to perpetuate Indian helotage. What is equality of rights between a giant and a dwarf?' Even the meagre powers enjoyed by the Central Legislature at present to enact a measure like the reservation of the Indian coastal trade for Indian-owned and Indian-managed vessels has been taken away under the so-called reformed Constitution. Shipping is a vital industry which is essential for defensive as well as for economic purposes, but all the accepted and legitimate methods of developing this key industry including those adopted even by several British Dominions are henceforth rendered impossible for India. To justify such limitations on our sovereignty on the ground of 'reciprocity' and 'partnership' is literally to add insult to injury. The right of the future Indian Parliament to differentiate or discriminate between nationals and non-nationals, whenever Indian interests require it, should remain intact and this right we cannot sacrifice on any account. I would like in this connection to cite the Irish parallel. The Irish Nationality and Citizenship Act of 1935 provides for a distinct Irish citizenship in connection with the electoral system, entry into public life, merchant shipping law, aircraft, as also in connection with special privileges which it thought proper to reserve for Irish nationals, such as those conferred through measures for assisting Irish industry. Irish citizenship, in other words, is distinct from British, which cannot claim equal rights in the State of Eire (or Ireland) on the basis of British citizenship, which is not recognised there. I feel that India must similarly seek to develop her own distinct nationality and establish a citizenship of her own.

While on the question of fiscal autonomy and commercial safeguards, I might refer briefly to the need of an active foreign trade policy for India. India's foreign trade should be viewed not in a haphazard or piecemeal manner as is often done in order to provide some immediate or temporary benefit to British industry, but in a comprehensive manner so as to co-ordinate India's economic development with its export trade on the one hand and its external obligation on the other. The very nature of India's export trade makes it essential that it should not have any restrictive agreement with England such as would jeopardise its trade with the various non-empire countries which have been in several respects its best customers, or such as would tend to weaken India's bargaining power *vis-à-vis* other countries. It is unfortunate that the protected negotiations for an Indo-British Trade Agreement are still proceeding, while the Ottawa Agreement, even after the expiry of its notice-period and despite the decision of the Legislative Assembly to terminate it, still continues, and along with the differential duties on British steel and textiles, the said Ottawa Agreement secures the prevailing advantages for British industries. There is no doubt that under the existing political conditions, any trade agreement between England and India is bound to be of an unequal character because our present political relationship would weigh the scales heavily in favour of England. There is also no doubt that the British preferential system is political in origin and before we permit non-Indian vested interests to be established or consolidated in this country under the shelter of a trade agreement, we should be careful as to its political repercussions and economic consequences. I trust that the present Indo-British Trade negotiations will not be allowed to impede the conclusion of bilateral trade agreements with other countries whenever possible and that no such trade agreement will be signed by the Government of India unless it is ratified by the Indian Legislature.

From the above, it will be quite clear that there is no analogy between the powers of the Provincial Ministries and those of the proposed Federal Ministry. Moreover, the composition of the Federal Legislature is reactionary to a degree. The total population of the Indian states is roughly 24 per cent of that of the whole of India. Nevertheless, the Rulers of the States, not their subjects, have been given 33 per cent of the seats in the Lower House and 40 per cent in the Upper House of the Federal legislature. In these circumstances, there is no possibility, in my opinion, of the Congress altering its attitude towards the Federal Scheme at any time. On our success in resisting the imposition of Federation by the British Government will depend our immediate political future. We have to fight Federation by all legitimate and peaceful means—not merely along constitutional lines—and in the last resort, we may have to resort to mass civil disobedience which is the ultimate sanction we have in our hands. There can be little doubt that in the event of such a campaign being started in the future, the movement will not be confined to British India but will spread among the states' subjects.

To put up an effective fight in the near future, it is necessary to put our own house in order. The awakening among our masses during the last few years has been so tremendous that new problems have arisen concerning our party organisation. Meetings attended by fifty thousand men and women are a usual occurrence nowadays. It is sometimes found that to control such meetings and demonstrations, our machinery is not adequate. Apart from these passing demonstrations, there is the bigger problem of mobilising this phenomenal mass energy and enthusiasm and directing them along proper lines. But have we got a well-disciplined Volunteer Corps for this purpose? Have we got a cadre of officers for our national service? Do we provide any training for our budding leaders, for our promising young workers? The answers to these questions are too patent to need elaboration. We have not yet provided all these requirements of a modern political party, but it is high time that we did. A disciplined Volunteer Corps manned by trained officers is exceedingly necessary. Moreover, education and training should be provided for our political workers so that we may produce a better type of leaders in future. This sort of training is provided by political parties in Britain through Summer Schools and other institutions—and is a speciality in totalitarian states. With all respect to our workers who have played a glorious part in our struggle, I must confess that there is room for more talent in our party. This defect can be made up partly by recruiting promising young men for the Congress and partly by providing education and training for those whom we already have. Everybody must have observed how some European countries have been dealing with this problem. Though our ideals and methods of training are quite different from theirs, it will be admitted on all hands that a thorough scientific training is a requisite for our workers. Further, an institution like the Labour Service Corps of the Nazis deserves careful study and, with suitable modification may prove beneficial to India.

While dealing with the question of enforcing discipline within our own party, we have to consider a problem which has been causing worry and embarrassment to many of us. I am referring to organisations like the Trade Union Congress and the Kisan Sabhas and their relations with the Indian National Congress. There are two opposing schools of thought on this question—those who condemn any organisations that are outside the Congress and those who advocate them. My own view is that we cannot abolish such organisations by ignoring or condemning them. They exist as objective facts and since they have come into existence and show no signs of liquidating themselves, it should be manifest that there is a historical necessity behind them. Moreover, such organisations are to be found in other countries. I am afraid that whether we like it or not, we have to reconcile ourselves to their existence. The only question is how the Congress should treat them. Obviously, such organisations should not appear as a challenge to the National Congress which is the organ of mass struggle for capturing political power. They should, therefore, be inspired by Congress ideals and methods and work in close co-operation with the Congress. To ensure this, Congress workers should in large numbers participate in trade union and peasant organisations. From my own experience of trade union work I feel that this could easily be done without landing oneself in conflict or inconsistency. Co-operation between the Congress and the other two organisations could be facilitated if the latter deal primarily with the economic grievances of the workers and peasants and treat the Congress as a common platform for all those who strive for the political emancipation of their country.

This brings us to the vexed problem of the collective affiliation of workers' and peasants' organisations of the Congress. Personally, I hold the view that the day will come when we shall have to grant this affiliation in order to bring all progressive and anti-imperialist organisations under the influence and control of the Congress. There will, of course, be difference of opinion as to the manner and the extent to which this affiliation should be given and the character and stability of such organisations will have to be examined before affiliation could be agreed to. In Russia, the united front of the Soviets of workers, peasants and soldiers played a dominant part in the October Revolution—but, on the contrary, in Great Britain we find that the British Trade Union Congress exerts a moderating influence on the National Executive of the Labour Party. In India, we shall have to consider carefully what sort of influence organisations like the Trade Union Congress and the Kisan Sabhas will exert on the Indian National Congress in the event of affiliation being granted and we should not forget that there is the possibility that the former may not have a radical outlook if their immediate economic grievances are not involved. In any case, quite apart from the question of collective affiliation, there should be the closest co-operation between the National Congress and other anti-imperialist organisations and this object would be facilitated by the latter adopting the principles and methods of the former.

There has been a great deal of controversy over the question of forming a party, like the Congress Socialist Party, within the Congress. I hold no brief for the Congress Socialist Party and I am not a member of it. Nevertheless, I must say that I have been in agreement with its general principles and policy from the very beginning. In the first place, it is desirable for the leftist elements to be consolidated into one party. Secondly, a leftist bloc can have a *raison d'être* only if it is socialist in character. There are friends who object to such a block being called a party, but to my mind it is quite immaterial whether you call that bloc a group, league or party. Within the limits prescribed by the Constitution of the Indian National Congress, it is quite possible for a leftist bloc to have a socialist programme, in which case it can be very well called a group, league or party. But the role of the Congress Socialist Party, or any other party of the same sort, should be that of a left-wing group. Socialism is not an immediate problem for us—nevertheless, socialist propaganda is necessary to prepare the country for socialism when political freedom has been won. And that propaganda can be conducted only by a party like the Congress Socialist Party, which stands for and believes in socialism.

There is one problem in which I have been taking a deep personal interest for some years and in connection with which I should like to make my submission—I mean the question of a foreign policy for India and of developing international contacts. I attach great importance to this work because I believe that in the years to come, international developments will favour our struggle in India. But we must have a correct appreciation of the world situation at every stage and should know how to take advantage of it. The lesson of Egypt stands before us as an example. Egypt won her Treaty of Alliance with Great Britain without firing a shot, simply because she knew how to take advantage of the Anglo-Italian tension in the Mediterranean.

In connection with our foreign policy, the first suggestion that I have to make is that we should not be influenced by the internal politics of any country or the form of its state. We shall find in every country men and women who will sympathise with Indian freedom, no matter what their own political views may be. In this matter we should take a leaf out of Soviet diplomacy. Though Soviet Russia is a communist state, her diplomats have not hesitated to make alliances with non-socialist states and have not declined sympathy or support coming from any quarter. We should, therefore, aim at developing a nucleus of men and women in every country who feel sympathetic towards India. To create and develop such a nucleus, propaganda through the foreign press, through Indian-made films and through art exhibitions would be helpful. The Chinese, for example, have made themselves exceedingly popular in Europe through their art exhibitions. Above all, personal contacts are necessary. Without such personal contacts it would be difficult to make India popular in other countries. Indian students abroad could also help in this work, provided we in India look to their needs and requirements. There should be closer contact between Indian students abroad and the Indian National Congress at home. If we could send out cultural and educational films made in India, I am sure that India and her culture would become known and appreciated by people abroad. Such films would prove exceedingly useful to Indian students and Indian residents in other countries, who at present are like our non-official ambassadors.

I do not like the word propaganda—there is an air of falsity about it. But I insist that we should make India and her culture known to the world. I say this because I am aware that such efforts will be welcomed in every country in Europe and America. If we go ahead with this work, we shall be preparing the basis for our future embassies and legations in different lands. We should not neglect Great Britain either. We have even in that country a small but influential group of men and women who are genuinely sympathetic towards Indian aspirations. Among the rising generation and students, in particular, interest in and sympathy for India is rapidly on the increase. One has only to visit the universities of Great Britain to realise that.

To carry on this work effectively, the Indian National Congress should have its trusted agents in Europe, Asia, Africa and in North, Central and South America where there is profound interest in India. The Congress should be assisted in this work of developing international contact by cultural organisations in India, working in the field of international culture and by the Indian Chambers of Commerce working in the sphere of international commerce. Further, Indians should make it a point to attend every international congress or conference; participation in such conferences is a very useful and healthy form of propaganda for India.

While talking of international contacts, I should remove a misgiving which may be present in some minds. Developing international contacts does not mean intriguing against the British Government. We need not go in for such intrigues and all our methods should be aboveboard. The propaganda that goes on against India all over the world is to the effect that India is an uncivilised country and it is inferred therefrom that the

British are needed in order to civilise us. As a reply, we have only to let the world know what we are and what our culture is like. If we can do that, we shall create such a volume of international sympathy in our favour that India's case will become irresistible before the bar of world opinion.

I should not forget to refer to the problems, the difficulties and the trials which face our countrymen in different parts of Asia and Africa—notably in Zanzibar, Kenya, South Africa, Malaya and Ceylon. The Congress has always taken the keenest interest in their affairs and will continue to do so in future. If we have not been able to do more for them it is only because we are still slaves at home. A free India will be a healthy and potent factor in world politics and will be able to look after the interests of its nationals abroad.

I must in this connection stress the desirability and necessity of developing closer cultural relations with our neighbours, viz., Persia, Afghanistan, Nepal, China, Burma, Siam, Malay States, East Indies and Ceylon. It would be good for both parties if they knew more of us and we knew more of them. With Burma and Ceylon, in particular, we should have the most intimate cultural intercourse, in view of our agelong contacts.

Friends, I am sorry I have taken more of your time than I had intended at first, but I am now nearing the end of my address. There is one important matter—the burning topic of the day—to which I should now draw your attention—the question of the release of detenues and political prisoners. The recent hunger-strikes have brought this question to the forefront and have focussed public attention on it. I believe that I am voicing the feelings of at least the rank and file of the Congress when I say that everything humanly possible should be done to expedite release. So far as the Congress ministries are concerned, it would be well to note that the record of some of them has not come up to public expectation. The sooner they satisfy the public demand, the better it will be for the Congress and for the people who are suffering in provinces ruled by non-Congress ministries. It is not necessary for me to labour this point and I fervently hope that in the immediate future, the public will have nothing to complain of so far as the record of the Congress ministries on this point is concerned.

It is not only the detenues and political prisoners in jail and detention who have their tale of woe. The lot of those who have been released is sometimes no better. They often return home in shattered health, victims of fell diseases like tuberculosis. Grim starvation stares them in the face and they are greeted, not with the smiles but with the tears of near and dear ones. Have we no duty to those who have given of their best in the service of their country and have received nothing but poverty and sorrow in return? Let us, therefore, send our heart-felt sympathy to all those who have suffered for the crime of loving their country and let us all contribute our humble mite towards the alleviation of their misery.

Friends, one word more and I have done. We are faced with a serious situation today. Inside the Congress there are differences between the right and the left which it would be futile to ignore. Outside, there is the challenge of British Imperialism which we are called upon to face. What shall we do in this crisis? Need I say that we have to stand foursquare against all the storms that may beset out path and be impervious to all the designs that our rulers may employ? The Congress today is the one supreme organ of mass struggle. It may have its right bloc and its left—but it is the common platform for all anti-imperialist organisations striving for Indian emancipation. Let us, therefore, rally the whole country under the banner of the Indian National Congress. I would appeal specially to the leftist groups in the country to pool all their strength and their resources for democratising the Congress and reorganising it on the broadest anti-imperialist basis. In making this appeal, I am greatly encouraged by the attitude of the leaders of the British Communist Party whose general policy with regard to India seems to me to be in keeping with that of the Indian National Congress.

In conclusion, I shall voice your feelings by saying that all India fervently hopes and prays that Mahatma Gandhi may be spared to our nation for many many years to come. India cannot afford to lose him and certainly not at this hour. We need him to keep our people united. We need him to keep our struggle free from bitterness and hatred. We need him for the cause of Indian Independence. What is more—we need him for the cause of humanity. Ours is a struggle not only against British Imperialism but against world Imperialism as well, of which the former is the keystone. We are, therefore, fighting not for the cause of India alone but of humanity as well. India freed means humanity saved.

'Bande Mataram'

21

Sadhana*

Subhas Chandra Bose's Extempore Reply to Rabindra Nath Tagore's Address of Welcome at Santiniketan, 21 January 1939

Gurudev,

My visit here this time has a new meaning. I have been here in the past several times. Probably twice. But my coming here today has new significance. Principally I have two reasons for this visit. The first is that you have called me. The other reason is that I felt a desire and inspiration from within to come.

It is unfair to expect that ordinary people or ordinary Indians will realise, in the least easily realise, your comprehensive *Sadhana*. I am also one among such ordinary people. Therefore, that I will grasp the greatness and glory of your *Sadhana* is a forlorn hope, that realisation when it comes does not come in a day. The realisation is gradual and takes a lifetime. However I believe if we go on and on in the pursuit the realisation will spread.

There is a sense of pain and remorse inside you—it is probably there—that your countrymen failed to know you, they did not understand your *Sadhana*. But should you for that reason blame your countrymen? If they could understand you so easily, they would be your equals. The truth that reveals itself to the creator, it is as difficult, as time-consuming to comprehend for the ordinary person. We can only claim that we are on our way, trying to go forward. We are trying wholeheartedly to realise the truth of the Creator. We are trying to understand your *Sadhana* to the best of our ability. In that case you cannot accuse your countrymen. It has been seen in all countries and in all people—ordinary people do not appreciate the worth and greatness of those who strike out a new road, those who try to make people realise truth. On the contrary they try to persecute the seekers after truth and their *Sadhana*. Therefore

*Translated from the original Bengali—eds.

the characteristic you have discovered in your own countrymen is not merely the way of life of our countrymen but that of all humanity. However poor the human mind may be, those of us who are optimists feel that behind all the poverty, meanness and filth there is hidden divinity and that the true *Sadhana* that our countrymen cannot understand today they will understand some day, will try to comprehend.

From time to time the point is made and is discussed amongst us, perhaps this has occurred to you also—as to the future of your *Sadhana* when you are no longer present. The other day I tried to respond to this question in Calcutta. I should like to say that nothing or no *Sadhana* can die so long as it has real worth. So long as your countrymen will not understand and learn what you have been trying to teach them and make them understand, your visible and practical *Sadhana* cannot die. When one day the truth and *Sadhana* represented in your life is established in the heart of every man or woman of India, it will matter little whether Santiniketan lives or dies. So long as that truth and *Sadhana* is not established in the national mind, the usefulness and need of your Santiniketan and Sriniketan will by all means remain. Not only that, this *Sadhana* will be accepted in all places and corners of India.

Those of us who spend most of our time in the political life of the country feel very deeply about the poverty of the inner life. We want the inspiration of the treasure that enriches the mind without which no man or nation can rise to great heights. Because we know if we can get a taste of that inspiration and truth, our *Sadhana* for the fulfilment and success of our working life and outer life can be achieved. We seek that inspiration from you.

We are today no doubt working tirelessly to attain national freedom, but our ideal is greater. We want complete fulfilment in personal and national life. We desire that every man and woman of the country and the entire nation may in every respect realise Truth. In this quest, in this *Sadhana*, political freedom is only a means. The ideal that is in front of us, the dream that has taken possession of us completely is very great. I do not know how far we shall be able to translate that dream and ideal into reality. We do not know ourselves how much strength we have for this purpose. Whatever strength and competence may be there, we are trying to go ahead in pursuit of a great ideal. At the same time, regardless of whatever strength and competence we may personally have, the path we have chosen is the path of truth. Those who will follow us will be stronger, more powerful and more competent than us. We are working in the belief that they will be able to rectify our lapses and mistakes. You have shown to the nation—why only the nation, the whole humanity—the road to an ideal, you have not merely indicated the path, you have been to trying to guide people along that road. Thus your efforts were not limited to letters and literature, your *Sadhana* was not limited to worship of the Divine, you have striven to transform your inner ideal into external reality. We only wish to submit to you in all humility—that that ideal is also our life's ideal because it is our national ideal. Whether or not we are able to attain that ideal in our lifetime we have accepted it inside us, in our external existence and we are trying to follow that ideal and shall continue to do so in the future.

Those of us who are trying to work in a small way feel immensely gratified to have boundless affection, encouragement and inspiration from you. What is more, when we have had to face all kinds of hardship and danger, when we suffered the rigours of imprisonment, when we became frustrated and mentally weak, to recall the boundless affection and inspiration we received from our countrymen, the great leaders of the country and the torch-bearers of freedom, we feel our lives are thrice blessed and that temporary dangers and difficulties do not matter at all.

We are apt to interpret sacrifice wrongly. It looks as if there is in it pain and suffering. In genuine sacrifice there is no pain. Man cannot sacrifice when he has the feeling of pain. The immense happiness in sacrifice has manifested in a big way in your life. Let that happiness inspire and encourage us is our earnest prayer. We seek blessings from you every moment of our lives. Because we know so long as we have your blessings we shall know that we are on the right path. We all feel that your blessings are the greatest asset in our journey.

22
The Tripuri Address

Presidential Address at the 52nd Session of the Indian National Congress Held at Tripuri in March 1939

Comrade Chairman, Sister and Brother Delegates,

I thank you from the bottom of my heart for the great honour you have done me by re-electing me to the Presidential chair of the Indian National Congress and also for the warm and cordial welcome you have given me here at Tripuri. It is true that at my request you have had to dispense with some of the pomp that is usual on such occasions—but I feel that enforced step has not taken away one iota of the warmth and cordiality of your reception and I hope that nobody will regret the curtailment of it on this occasion.

Friends, before I proceed any further, I shall voice your feelings by expressing our joy at the success of Mahatma Gandhi's mission to Rajkot and the termination of his fast in consequence thereof. The whole country now feels happy and tremendously relieved.

Friends, this year promises to be an abnormal or extraordinary one in many ways. The Presidential election this time was not of the humdrum type. The election was followed by sensational developments culminating in the resignation of twelve out of fifteen members of the Working Committee, headed by Sardar Vallavbhai Patel, Maulana Abul Kalam Azad and Dr Rajendra Prasad. Another distinguished and eminent member of the Working Committee, Pandit Jawaharlal Nehru, though he did not formally resign, issued a statement which led everybody to believe that he had also resigned. On the eve of the Tripuri Congress, events at Rajkot forced Mahatma Gandhi to undertake a vow of fast unto death. And then the President arrived at Tripuri a sick man. It will, therefore, be in the fitness of things if the Presidential address this year can claim to be a departure from precedent in the matter of its length.

Friends, you are aware that the Wafdist Delegation from Egypt have arrived in our midst as guests of the Indian National Congress. You will join me in according a most hearty welcome to all of them. We are extremely happy that they found it possible to accept our invitation and make the voyage to India. We are only sorry that political exigencies in Egypt did not permit the President of the Wafd, Mustapha El Nahas Pasha, to personally lead this Delegation. Having had the privilege of knowing the President and leading members of the Wafdist Party, my joy today is all the greater. Once again, I offer them on behalf of our countrymen a most hearty and cordial welcome.

Since we met at Haripura in February 1938, several significant events have taken place in the international sphere. The most important of these is the Munich Pact of September 1939, which implied an abject surrender to Nazi Germany on the part of the Western Powers, France and Great Britain. As a result of this, France ceased to be the dominant power in Europe and the hegemony passed into the hands of Germany without a shot being fired. In more recent times, the gradual collapse of the Republican Government in Spain seems to have added to the strength and prestige of Fascist Italy and Nazi Germany. The so-called democratic powers, France and Great Britain, have joined Italy and Germany in conspiring to eliminate Soviet Russia from European politics, for the time being. But how long will that be possible? There is no doubt that as a result of recent international developments, in Europe as well as in Asia, British and French Imperialism have received a considerable setback in the matter of strength and prestige.

Coming to home politics, in view of my ill-health, I shall content myself with referring to only a few important problems. In the first place, I must give clear and unequivocal expression to what I have been feeling for some time past, namely, that the time has come for us to raise the issue of Swaraj and submit our national demand to the British Government in the form of an ultimatum. The time is long past when we could have adopted a passive attitude and waited for the Federal scheme to be imposed on us. The problem no longer is as to when the Federal scheme will be forced down our throats. The problem is as to what we should do if the Federal scheme is conveniently shelved for a few years till peace is stabilized in Europe. There is no doubt that once there is stable peace in Europe, whether through a Four-Power Pact or through some other means, Great Britain will adopt a strong-Empire policy. The fact that she is now showing some signs of trying to conciliate the Arabs as against the Jews in Palestine is because she is feeling herself weak in the international sphere. In my opinion, therefore, we should submit our national demand to the British Government in the form of an ultimatum and give a certain time-limit within which a reply is to be expected. If no reply is received within this period or if an unsatisfactory reply is received, we should resort to such sanctions as we possess in order to enforce our national demand. The sanctions that we possess today are mass civil disobedience or Satyagraha. And the British Government today are not in a position to face a major conflict like an All-India Satyagraha for a long period.

It grieves me to find that there are people in the Congress who are so pessimistic as to think that the time is not ripe for a major assault on British Imperialism. But looking at the situation in a thoroughly realistic manner, I do not see the slightest ground for pessimism. With Congress in power in eight provinces, the strength and prestige of our national organization have gone up. The mass movement has made considerable headway throughout British India. And last but not the least, there is an unprecedented awakening in the Indian States. What more opportune moment could we find in our national history for a final advance in the direction of Swaraj, particularly when the international situation is favourable to us? Speaking as a cold-blooded realist, I may say that all the facts of the present-day situation are so much to our advantage that one should entertain the highest degree of optimism. If only we sink our differences, pool all our resources and pull our full weight in the national struggle, we can make our attack on British Imperialism irresistible. Shall we have the political foresight to make the most of our present favourable position or shall we miss this opportunity, which is a rare opportunity in the life-time of a nation?

I have already referred to the awakening in the Indian States. I am definitely of the view that we should revise our attitude towards the States as defined by the Haripura Congress resolution. The resolution, as you are aware, put a ban on certain forms of activity in the States being conducted in the name of the Congress. Under that resolution, neither parliamentary work nor struggle against the State should be carried on in the name of the Congress. But since Haripura much has happened. Today we find that the Paramount Power is in league with the State authorities in most places. In such circumstances, should we of the Congress not draw closer to the people of the States? I have no doubt in my own mind as to what our duty is today.

Besides lifting the above ban, the work of guiding the popular movements in the States for Civil Liberty and Responsible Government should be conducted by the Working Committee on a comprehensive and systematic basis. The work so far done has been of a piecemeal nature and there has hardly been any system or plan behind it. But the time has come when the Working Committee should assume this responsibility and discharge it in a comprehensive and systematic way and, if necessary, appoint a special subcommittee for the purpose. The fullest use should be made of the guidance and co-operation of Mahatma Gandhi and of the co-operation of the All-India States' Peoples Conference.

I have referred earlier to the advisability of our making a final advance in the direction of Swaraj. That will need adequate preparation. In the first place, we shall have to take steps to ruthlessly remove whatever corruption or weakness has entered our ranks largely due to the lure of power. Next, we shall have to work in close co-operation with all anti-imperialist organisations in the country particularly the Kisan movement and the Trade Union movement. All the radical elements in the country must work in close harmony and co-operation and the efforts of all anti-imperialist organisations must converge in the direction of a final assault on British Imperialism.

Friends, today the atmosphere within the Congress is clouded and dissensions have appeared. Many of our friends are consequently feeling depressed and dispirited. The cloud that you see today is a passing one. I have faith in the patriotism of my countrymen, and I am sure that before long we shall be able to tide over the present difficulties and restore unity within our ranks. A somewhat similar situation had arisen at the time of the Gaya Congress in 1922 and thereafter, when Deshbandhu Das and Pandit Motilal Nehru, of hallowed memory, started the Swarajya Party. May the spirit of my late Guru, of revered Motilalji and of other great sons of India inspire us in the present crisis and may Mahatma Gandhi, who is still with us to guide and assist our nation, help the Congress out of the present tangle is my earnest prayer.

MY STRANGE ILLNESS

Full text of an article in the *Modern Review*, April 1939

The 15 February 1939. After meeting Mahatma Gandhi at Shegaon and having a long talk with him, I returned to Wardha at about 6 p.m. At night, some friends came to see me and in the absence of anything urgent or important to do, we were having a chat. I had begun to feel unwell, so I took my temperature in their presence. It was 99.4. I did not take it seriously however.

The next morning, 16 February, I was to leave Wardha for Calcutta.

In the morning, instead of feeling fresh, I felt out of sorts. I thought that that was due to disturbed sleep the night before. At Wardha and Nagpur stations, a large number of friends had come to see me and I had no time to think of myself. Only after the train steamed out of Nagpur station did I realise that I was extremely unwell. When I took my temperature this time, it was 101. So I went straight to bed.

After a couple of hours or so, an Anglo-Indian gentleman came into my compartment. I did not welcome his presence, particularly when I gathered that he would be travelling all the way to Calcutta—because I wanted to be left quite alone with my fever. But there was no help; he had as much right to be there as I had. After a while he looked intently at me and in a kindly tone, asked, 'What is wrong with you? You look completely washed out.' I replied that I was not feeling well and that I had a temperature. Then he continued, 'You are perspiring I see. You must have got influenza.'

The whole day and night I lay on my berth, perspiring all the time. Again and again I pondered over his words, 'you look completely washed out'. How could I look so bad as that? My facial expression always was such that even after a prolonged illness I rarely 'looked' really bad. Besides, how could a day's illness make me look pulled down to such a degree? I was puzzled.

The next morning I got up with a determination to look fit. I went into the bathroom, had a good wash and shave and came out looking somewhat better than the day before. My fellow-passenger sympathetically asked me how I was feeling and after hearing my reply, remarked, 'Yes, you are looking better this morning. Yesterday you were looking completely washed out.'

From the station I went home only to find that some friends were waiting to see me. With some exertion I managed to carry on a conversation with them, but by 11 a.m. I felt to tired that I took leave of them and retired. I had to go to bed—the bed I was destined to stick to for several weeks.

The doctor came in and after a thorough examination shook his head and took a serious view of the case. The pathologist was then sent for and he took specimens of blood, etc., for the usual tests. Later, other doctors were brought in, including the First Physician to the Calcutta Medical College, Sir Nilratan Sircar, etc.

While the doctors were feeling worried about the disease and were taxing their brains as to how best they could combat it, I was concerned more with my public engagements. On 18 and 19 February, I had public engagements at Hajipur and Muzaffarpur in Bihar and on 22 February, the Working Committee of the Congress was to meet at Wardha. I reached Calcutta on 17 February from Wardha and I was due to leave the same evening for Patna. Telegrams and telephone-calls came in from Bihar enquiring if my previous programme was O.K., and I would adhere to it. I replied in the affirmative, adding that though I was unwell, I would come at any cost. I only wanted that they should cancel all processions and make my programme as light as possible. To my people at home I said that I would leave by the night train from Patna, *en route* to Hajipur, the same evening (17 February) notwithstanding what the doctors were saying, as I was determined to fulfil my engagements on 18 and 19 February. On being pressed to listen to medical advice I retorted that I would start even if I had a temperature of 105. Thereafter I gave instruction for my ticket to be purchased and berth reserved.

But as the hours rolled by, my temperature began to mount up and up. What was worse—a splitting headache got hold of me. And when the time came for me to start, though everything was ready, I could not lift my head. To my great sorrow I had to humble myself and give up my determination. Telegrams had to be sent regretfully that it was impossible for me to start that night, but that I would make every possible effort to start the following night. The next day my condition was no better, in fact it was worse. Moreover, all arrangements had been upset by my not leaving on the 17th. So the Muzaffarpur tour had to be abandoned altogether. Nothing can describe my deep regret over this unexpected development.

Though Muzaffarpur was out of my programme after 18 February, my mind was not at ease. I began to plan for the Wardha meeting of the Working Committee. Doctors began to give me repeated warnings that it was impossible to go to Wardha. If I gave up all thought of the Working Committee and concentrated my mind on getting well, I might be able to go to the Tripuri Congress—otherwise, even Tripuri might have to be dropped. But all these warnings were like speaking to a deaf person. My preparations went on despite medical advice, and, thanks to friends, I had an aeroplane ready to take me to Nagpur on or about the 22 February.

On the 21st, I slowly began to realise that the doctors were right and that it was quite impossible to go to Wardha either by train or by plane. I informed Mahatma Gandhi and Sardar Patel by wire to that effect and suggested postponement of the Working Committee meeting till the Tripuri Congress. At that time I had not the faintest idea that twelve (of thirteen) members of the Working Committee would resign almost immediately.

Much fuss has been made by interested parties over the above two telegrams and it has been alleged that I did not permit the Working Committee to transact even routine business. Such an allegation is altogether unfounded. In the first place, there was nothing in the telegrams to indicate that I did not want the Working Committee to go through routine business. My concern was over the draft resolutions for the Congress, which are usually framed by the Working Committee on the eve of its annual plenary session. In the second place, in my telegram to Sardar Patel, after giving my view regarding postponement, I requested him to ascertain the views of other members and wire same to me. The reply to my telegrams was the resignation of twelve members of the Working Committee. If these members had desired to frame the resolutions for the Tripuri Congress in my absence, I would certainly not have stood in their way. Regarding the transaction of business, if the other members of the Working Committee did not agree with me regarding postponement of if they were in doubt as to what my real intentions were, they could very easily have put through a trunk-call or telegraphed to me. To the transaction of routine business there was not the slightest objection on my part. And as to other and more important business they would have found, if only they had enquired, that there would have been no obstruction from my side if they had desired to carry on in my absence. My only anxiety was to have such draft resolutions for the Congress prepared by the Working Committee as all the members would agree to—otherwise there was this danger that when the 'official' draft resolutions came up before the Subjects Committee, members of the Working Committee would be found arrayed on different sides. To obtain this unanimity, my presence was necessary when the draft resolutions were being prepared by the Working Committee. Hence I had suggested the postponement of the Working Committee meeting till the Tripuri Congress. My proposal would have worked very well indeed if twelve (of thirteen) members had not responded by throwing the bombshell of resignation.

The following telegram was sent by me to Sardar Patel on 21 February:

KINDLY SEE MY TELEGRAM TO MAHATMAJI. REGRETFULLY FEEL WORKING COMMITTEE MUST BE POSTPONED TILL CONGRESS. PLEASE CONSULT COLLEAGUES AND WIRE OPINION—SUBHAS.

But I am sorry that I have digressed. This is not a 'political' article and when I began scribbling, I wanted to write about 'My Strange Illness' and to explain why I called my illness 'Strange'. I shall now continue my story.

Till the evening of 21 February, I was hoping against hope that I would be able to attend the Wardha meeting of the Working Committee or at least fly there on the 22nd. But the doctors had no such worry. For them, Wardha was out of the question—their eyes were on Tripuri. Their one effort was to pull me up to such a condition during the next few days that I could at least undertake the journey to the Tripuri Congress. Sir Nilratan Sircar's bulletin had banned even the Tripuri Congress, but I pleaded and argued with my doctors and ultimately told them plainly that so long as I was alive, I could not keep away from the Tripuri Congress during such a crisis in our history. I gratefully confess that they did all that was humanly possible for them to enable me to attend the Congress.

As I look back on my five week's illness, I must make one confession. From the beginning, I did not take my illness as seriously as the doctors did—in fact I thought that they were unduly alarmist—and I did not co-operate with them as much as I should have. On the other hand, I have a legitimate excuse to offer. It was quite impossible for me to take complete physical and mental rest. I fell ill at a most critical period. The resignation of the members of the Working Committee aggravated the crisis. Statement after statement was being issued attacking me. The 'unkindest' cuts came from a quarter where they were least expected. The General Secretary of the Congress having resigned, I had perforce to attend to urgent business sent in by the office of the All-India Congress Committee. Regarding interviews, while I could decline to see local friends and visitors, I could not very well refuse to see Congressmen coming to see the Congress President on Congress business from far-off places. Owing to these and other factors, even with the best will in the world, I could not have complied with the advice of my doctors regarding physical and mental rest. I shall give one relevant instance here. When statement after statement was being issued against me, my silence was being misconstrued and friends in different, and even remote provinces began to urge me to issue some sort of a reply in order to meet at least some of the unfounded charges levelled against me. After a great deal of procrastination due to my ill-health, I made up my mind one afternoon to write my statement that day—come what may. It was not an easy affair, however. I had first to wade through some of the statements that had appeared so far, in order to understand what the charges were. Only after that could I commence dictating my statement. By the time I finished glancing through the typed copy and gave orders for issuing it to the Press, it was mid-night. Then the temperature was taken and it was 103. Prior to that there was an improvement in my general condition and the evening temperature was not rising beyond 101 for the last two days. The doctors, therefore, deplored the set-back caused by my voluntarily undertaking mental work prematurely, but I could not help it, circumstanced as I was.

I must now come to the crux of my difficulties, because only that will explain much of what has happened. When I was lying ill in Calcutta after my return from Wardha on 17 February, it was widely propagated by interested people that my illness was a 'fake' and that my 'political' fever was being utilised for avoiding the meeting of the Congress Working Committee on 22 February. This news was communicated to me by friends from a number of provinces and I cannot doubt its authenticity. Even the bulletin issued by Sir Nilratan Sircar made no impression at all on the people who were consciously and maliciously carrying on the above false propaganda. The same propaganda was carried on at Jubbulpore and Tripuri. When I reached Jubbulpore on 6 March at about 4 p.m., my temperature was 101. When I reached my camp at Tripuri after an ambulance-ride, it shot up to 103. On my arrival at Tripuri the Reception Committee Doctors took charge of me. After examining me, one of them looked significantly at the other and this struck me at once as strange. After a couple of days I learnt the whole story. Everybody in Tripuri had been told that I was not really ill and this propaganda had affected the doctors as well. When they examined me after my arrival and discovered that I was seriously ill, they were surprised and they then felt indignant about the false and malicious propaganda that had been carried on. What increased their indignation was that even their bulletins were not believed by interested people in Tripuri. For instance, an important ex-member of the Working Commitee one day asked one of the Reception Commitee Doctors if I really had a temperature of 102 and if he (the doctor) had taken the temperature himself. Reports came to me from several independent sources that even in the highest circles, my illness was not believed in. One day out of sheer exasperation, the Reception Committee Doctors sent for a medical Board consisting of the Inspector-General of Civil Hospitals, C.P. and Berar, and the Civil Surgeon of Jubbulpore. After their joint statement was issued, there was a change in the atmosphere. But the result of bringing in these big officials was that my attending the open session of the Congress was definitely banned. I could have somehow coaxed and cajoled the Reception Committee Doctors into allowing me to attend the plenary session of the Congress. But this was not possible with the officials. Before issuing their report, they were clever enough to ask me if I would trust their opinion and accept their advice. Naturally, I had to reply in the affirmative and I was, as it were, trapped—for I was then told that I could not attend the open session of the Congress. The arrangements made by the Reception Committee for myself were quite satisfactory and, from the physical point of view, I had nothing to complain of. But owing to the above and other reasons, the moral atmosphere of Tripuri was sickening to a degree. I have not experienced anything like it at any previous session of the Congress.

The letters, telegrams, etc., I have been receiving since 17 February, not only make interesting reading but when piled up make a regular volume. Everyday they pour in—and not only do letters and telegrams come, but parcels and packets containing medicine of all kinds and amulets of every description. I was trying to analyse the above writers and senders according to their religious faith and I found that every religious denomination was represented. And not only every religious denomination, but every system of medicine (all the 'pathies', if I may use that word) and both the sexes! Hindus, Muslims, Christians, Parsis, etc.—Allopaths, Homeopaths, Vaids, Hakims, Naturopaths, Astrologers, etc.—men and women—all have been writing to me, giving me their advice and sometimes also samples of medicine and amulets. Naturally, it is quite impossible for me now to write and thank them for their kindness. Sometimes they write more than once when they do not get a reply from me. Now what am I to do with all these prescriptions? The first thing I do is to hand them over to my doctors, who can best judge how to utilise them. But in most cases, the doctors are reluctant to make any use of the prescriptions or the medicine sent. Is it ungracious on their part or on my part? I wonder.

Besides prescriptions and medicine, I have been receiving numbers of letters and parcels of a different sort. Astrologers and *Sadhus* send me amulets and blessings. And unknown well-wishes and sympathisers send me *ashirvàdi* flowers, etc. after offering prayers for my health and welfare at some temple or place of worship. According to prevailing custom these *ashirvàdi* flowers, leaves, sacrificial ashes, etc. (or *nirmalya*) have to be received with reverence and placed on the head or against the forehead for a while. But the fairer sex go even further. They are reluctant to throw them away after this operation is over, with the result that any number of these packets and amulets can be found underneath my pillow. And they are daily growing in number. Personally, I am of an exceedingly rationalistic frame of mind, but I respect the feelings and sentiments of others even where I do not agree with them.

So I go on pondering within me as to the real value of these prescriptions, medicine, amulets, flowers, sacrificial ashes, etc. It moved me profoundly to find that they came from every section of the vast Indian community and from every corner of India—from Kashmir to Cape Comorin. It brought tears of gratitude to my eyes when I found that I had such a large circle of well-wishers and sympathisers. I had never imagined it even in my dreams. It may be that a few of the writers wanted some sort of advertisement for themselves—but there is no doubt that the vast majority were actuated solely by a genuine feeling of sympathy for me in my suffering. The prescriptions or medicine or amulets may have no objective value, but behind them all there was a genuine feeling of sympathy and affection which had for me unbounded value and deep significance. I have no doubt that these good wishes will help me greatly in my recovery—much more than earthly medicine or astrological amulets. Even where I cannot make use of medical advice or medicine or amulets, I gratefully accept the good-wishes that move the hearts of the senders.

Owing to the morally sickening atmosphere of Tripuri, I left that place with such a loathing and disgust for Politics as I have never felt before during the last nineteen years. As I tossed in my bed at Jamadoba, by day and by night, I began to ask myself again and again what would become of our public life when there was so much of pettiness and vindictiveness even in the highest circles. My thoughts naturally turned towards what was my first love in life—the eternal call of the Himalayas. If such was the consumation of our Politics—I asked myself—why did I stray from what Aurobindo Ghose would describe as 'the life divine'. Had the time now come for me to tear the veil of *Maya* and go back to the fountain-head of all love? I spent days and nights of moral doubt and uncertainty. At times the call of the Himalayas became insistent. I prayed for light in my dark mind. Then slowly a new vision dawned on me and I began to recover my mental balance—as well as my faith in man and in my countrymen. After all, Tripuri was not India. There was another India revealed by these letters, prescriptions, medicine, amulets, flowers, etc. What grievance could I have against that India—which was perhaps the real India? Then again, it struck me that at Tripuri there were two worlds. The pettiness and vindictiveness that I had experienced, referred only to a part of Tripuri. What about the other part? What grievance could I have against that part? Further, in spite of what I had experienced at Tripuri, how could I lose my fundamental faith in man? To distrust man was to distrust the divinity in him—to distrust one's very existence. So, gradually all my doubts were dispelled till I once again recovered my normal robust optimism. In this effort to regain my normal self, these prescriptions, medicine, amulets, flowers, etc., were a great help.

I have suffered a lot physically and have had experience of a large number of diseases. Sometimes I think that I have exhausted the whole gamut described in text-books of pathology. I have fallen ill at home and abroad as well as in prison. In fact, I often wonder that I am still alive and kicking. But in all my life I have not experienced such acute and concentrated physical suffering continuously for a month, as I have since 17 February 1939. True, I have suffered much in prison. But that suffering was spread out over comparatively long periods. What has happened to me this time? I looked comparatively hale and hearty during the first part of last month. Why and how did I suddenly fall so seriously ill? Perhaps, doctors alone should attempt the answer, but cannot a layman—the patient himself—also try?

Doctors have before them heaps of pathological test-reports. They have, moreover, examined me repeatedly. Though they are not communicative to the patient as to the exact disease he has been suffering from, I gather that my present malady is some kind of pneumonia with perhaps liver and intestinal complications. Blood-pressure—they add—is abnormally low. Moreover, power of resistance as revealed by sedimentation tests, etc., is also very low and weakness is excessive. The system lacks sufficient strength to combat infection and recover normality. Is this explanation sufficient and adequate? I don't know.

Beyond the explanation that my vitality, for some reason or other, is exceedingly low at present—I wonder if all the clinical and other forms of examination have revealed the real causes of this prolonged illness and this acute physical suffering. A few days after I fell ill, I began to receive letters and telegrams from different places suggesting the nature of my malady. Among them were some telegrams suggesting that I had been poisoned. My doctors were amused at first. Then they gave thought to the matter but could not find any clinical data to support this theory. So they put it aside.

A few days later I was visited by a Professor of the Calcutta University, an erudite scholar in Sanskrit Literature and a man of exemplary character, for whom our family has high regard and esteem. He had been commissioned to deliver a message to us. A number of Pundits and astrologers including himself had met the day before to discuss my illness. They had come to the conclusion that ordinary causes could not account for my strange and acute illness. They were of the view that somebody in some part of the country had been practising what is known in the Tantra-Shastra as *Marana-Kriya*—that is, attempt to kill by tantric process or will-power. Everybody was intrigued and amused as well. Without disbelieving the possibility of exerting abnormal will-power in accordance with tantric mental exercises—was it possible in the year of grace, 1939, for such mental phenomena as *Maran, Uchchatan, Basheekaran*, etc., to take place? Our visitor was definite that, though such phenomena were rare now, they did take place nevertheless. And he cited instances. He added that, though *Marana-Kriya* had taken place, owing to my strength, it would not have any fatal result, but would only damage my health. And he concluded by offering some advice as to how I should be careful in protecting my health.

I confess that all this talk did not convince me in the least, but it nevertheless left an uncanny feeling within me. At the back of my mind there was the faint impression of a question mark. Any other man talking in the above manner would have been dismissed with scant courtesy—but this gentleman of undoubted integrity, unimpeachable character and profound scholarship—who had nothing to do with Politics and had no axe to grind—had to be listened to even if he was not to be taken seriously.

About this time—that is a few days before I left for Tripuri—a number of friends began to press me to wear amulets in order to help me in recouping my health. My rationalistic mind revolted against this at first, but in a moment of weakness, I yielded. I accepted a couple of rings and four amulets. I accepted only those from friends whom I knew and who were not actuated by any professional motive. Amulets from people whom I did not know personally I did not wear and there were any number of them. To wear all of them would be tantamount to converting myself into an amulet-exhibition. I was to anxious to be well during the Tripuri Congress that I argued within myself that even if there was mere 5 per cent chance of my getting well by using amulets, why should I miss it? So I compromised with my innate rationalism—but as soon as the Tripuri Congress was over, I relieved myself of the two rings and four amulets. And now my rationalism is safe and I can trust to nature and my luck!

There are certain things about my illness which I at least as a lay-man cannot account for. There is no regularity or periodicity. For some days the temperature would begin to rise at noon, reach its maximum at about 6 p.m. and then slowly decline. Next morning it would be normal. Rise of temperature would be accompanied by unbearable headache which would subside only after four or five hours' continuous application of ice. Remission would be accompanied by heavy perspiration and complete prostration. Then suddenly this order would change. Fever would persist day and night without any remission on the one side and high increase on the other. Sometimes the symptoms would point to malignant malaria, sometimes to enteric fever and sometimes to something else.

But every time the pathological test would be negative. If one day the fever shot up to 104 degrees, the next day it would come down to normal and people would expect a permanent remission. But the third day it would mount up again. The arbitrariness of the fever and the variety of symptoms would baffle both doctors and lay-men. And the excessive weakness and exhaustion which have got hold of me remain a mystery. Even today I do not think I look half as bad as I really am.

During the last five weeks or more, though I have been cut off from the outside world to a large extent—in another sense I have been in close touch with it. People who have no connection whatsoever with Politics, whom I do not personally know at all, people in remote corners of the country—even orthodox Pundits have shown such solicitude and sympathy for me in my illness that I could never imagine. I have often asked myself—'What is the bond that binds us? Why do they feel for me? What have I done to merit such affection?' The answer to these questions can be given by them alone.

One thing I know. This is the India for which one toils and suffers. This is the India for which one can even lay down his life. This is the real India in which one can have undying faith, no matter what Tripuri says or does.

Jamadoba
Jealgora P.O.,
District Manbhum

23

Riding Two Horses

To Jawaharlal Nehru

Jealgora P.O.
Dt Manbhum, Bihar,
28 March 1939

My dear Jawahar,

I find that for some time past you have developed tremendous dislike for me. I say this because I find that you take up enthusiastically every possible point against me; what could be said in my favour you ignore. What my political opponents urge against me you concede, while you are almost blind to what could be said against them. In the course of what follows I shall try to illustrate the above.

Why you should have developed this strong dislike for me remains a mystery to me. On my side, ever since I came out of internment in 1937, I have been treating you with the utmost regard and consideration, in private life and in public. I have looked upon you as politically an elder brother and leader and have often sought your advice. When you came back from Europe last year, I went to Allahabad to ask you what lead you would give us. Usually, when I approached you in this way, your replies have been vague and non-committal. For instance, last year when you returned from Europe, you put me off by saying that you would consult Gandhiji and then let me know. When we met at Wardha after you had seen Gandhiji, you did not tell me anything definite. Later on, you produced some resolutions before the Working Committee in which there was nothing new and there was no lead to the country.

The last Presidential election was followed by an acrimonious controversy in which many things were said—some for and some against me. In your utterances and statements every point was stretched against me. At a speech in Delhi you were reported to have said that you disliked that canvassing should have been done by or for me. I do not know what exactly was in your mind, but you were blissfully oblivious of the fact that my election appeal was made after Dr Pattabhi's appeared in the Press. As for canvassing, you were, consciously or unconsciously, oblivious of the fact that there was much more canvassing on the other side and the fullest use was made of the machinery of the Congress Ministries in order to secure votes for Dr Pattabhi. The other side had a regular organisation (Gandhi Seva Sangh, Congress Ministries and perhaps also the Charkha Sangh and A.I.V.I.A.) which was immediately set in motion. Moreover, they had all the big guns and yourself against me, as well as the full weight of Mahatma Gandhi's name and prestige—and the majority of the Provincial Congress Committees was also in their hands. As against them, what did I have—a solitary individual? Do you know—as I know from personal knowledge—that in many places canvassing was done not for Dr Pattabhi, but for Gandhiji and Gandhism—though many people refused to be taken in by such disingenuous propaganda. Still, standing in a public meeting, you tried to run me down on what appear to be absolutely false grounds.

Then let me come to the resignations. Twelve members resigned. They wrote a straightforward letter—a decent letter—in which they made their position unequivocally clear. Considering my illness, they did not say one unkind word about me, though they could have criticised me adversely if they had wanted to. But your statement—how shall I describe it? I shall refrain from using strong language and simply say that it was unworthy of you. (I am told that you wanted your statement to be substantially embodied in the general letter of resignation, but that this was not agreed to.) Then your statement gave one the impression that you had resigned, as the other twelve members had done—but up till now, to the general public, your position remains a mystery. When a crisis comes, you often do not succeed in making up your mind one way or the other—with the result that to the public you appear as if you are riding two horses.

To come back to your statement of 22 February. You have an idea that you are extremely logical and consistent in what you say or do. But other people are often puzzled and perplexed at the stand you take on different occasions. Take a few instances. In your statement of the 22 February you said that you were against my re-election and you gave certain reasons you mentioned in your statement of the 26 January, issued from Almora. You clearly shifted your ground. Then again I was told by some Bombay friends that you had told them previously that you had no objection to my standing, provided I stood as a candidate for the Left.

In your Almora statement you concluded by saying that we should forget persons and remember only principles and our cause. It never struck you that you want us to forget persons, only when certain persons are concerned. When it is a case of Subhas Bose standing for re-election, you run down personalities and lionize principles etc. When it is a case of Maulana Azad standing for re-election, you do not hesitate to write a long panegyric. When it is a case of Subhas Bose versus Sardar Patel and others, then—Subhas Bose must first of all clear up the personal issue. When Sarat Bose complains of certain things at Tripuri (viz. of the attitude and conduct of those who call themselves orthodox followers of Mahatma Gandhi)—he is, according to you, coming down to personal questions, when he should be confining himself to principles and programmes. I confess that my poor brain is unable to follow your consistency.

Let me now came to the personal question which in my case becomes so very important in your eyes. You alleged that in my statements I had wronged my colleagues. Evidently, you were not among them—and if I had made any allegation, it was against the others, so you were not speaking on your behalf, but as an advocate for the others. An advocate is usually more eloquent than his client. It will therefore surprise you to know that when I talked to Sardar Patel (and Rajen Babu and Maulana) at Tripuri over this question he gave me the surprising news that this main grievance or allegation against me referred to the period prior to the Bardoli meeting of the Working Committee in January last. When I retorted that the general impression among the public was that the main grievance or allegation against me was in connection with my 'election statements', he said that that was an additional allegation. So, after all, your clients did not attach as much importance to the 'aspersion affair' as you did as their advocate. At Tripuri, since Sardar Patel and the others left for the A.I.C.C. meeting and did not return after the meeting though they had promised to do so, I could not pursue the matter further, with a view to finding out what exactly were the incidents prior to the Bardoli meeting of the Working Committee which they had referred to. But my brother Sarat had a talk with Sardar Patel on the subject and the latter told him that his main grievance was about my attitude at the Delhi meeting of the A.I.C.C. in September 1938 when there was a walk-out of the Socialists. The allegation came as an utter surprise to both my brother and myself, but incidentally it showed that in the minds of Sardar Patel and others, the 'aspersion affair' did not have the importance which you lent it. As a matter of fact, when I was at Tripuri, several delegates (not my supporters, I may tell you) told me that the 'aspersion affair' had been practically forgotten, until your statements and utterances raised the controversy once again. And in this connection I may tell you that since the Presidential election, you have done more to lower me in the estimation of the public than all the twelve ex-members of the Working Committee put together. Of course if I am such a villain, it is not only your right but also your duty to expose me before the public. But perhaps it will strike you that the devil who has been re-elected President in spite of the opposition of the biggest leaders including yourself, of Mahatma Gandhi and of seven or eight provincial governments, must have some saving grace. He must have rendered some service to the cause of the country during his year of Presidentship to be able to draw so many votes without any organisation behind him and in spite of tremendous odds.

In your statement of the 22 February you said further, 'I suggested to the Congress President that this was the first and most essential point to be considered, but no attempt has so far been made to deal with it'. Before you penned these lines did it not strike you for once that in order to clear up this misunderstanding, it was necessary for me to meet Sardar Patel and the other members and that the time for doing so was the meeting of the Working Committee on 22 February? Or did you think that I avoided the meeting of the Working Committee? It is true that I did not discuss the 'aspersion affair' with Mahatma Gandhi on 15 February, though he mentioned it once. But then I was following your own dictum of attaching more importance to principles and programmes than to personal issues. Nevertheless, I may tell you that when Mahatma Gandhi told me that Sardar Patel and the others would not cooperate with me on the same Committee, I told him that I would talk over matters with them when we met on 22 February and try to secure their cooperation. You will, perhaps, agree that the aspersions, if any, referred not to Mahatma Gandhi but to the members of the Working Committee and the matter had to be talked over with the latter.

In the above statement you wanted me to define exactly in writing what I meant by the words Left and Right. I should have thought that you were the last person to ask such a question. Have you forgotten the reports submitted by Acharya Kripalani and yourself to the All India Congress Committee at Haripura? Did you not in your report say that the Right had been trying to suppress the Left? If it is permissible for you to use the words Left and Right when necessary, is it not equally permissible for other people?

You have charged me further with not clarifying my policy in national and international affairs. I think I have a policy, whether that policy be right or wrong. In my short presidential speech at Tripuri I gave an indication of it in the most unequivocal terms. In my humble opinion, considering the situation in India and abroad, the one problem—the one duty—before us is to force the issue of Swaraj with the British Government. Along with this, we need a comprehensive plan for guiding the States' people's movement simultaneously throughout the country. I think I gave you a clear indication of my ideas even before Tripuri, when we met at Santiniketan and later at Anand Bhawan. What I have just written is at least a definite policy. May I now ask you what your policy is? In a recent letter, you have referred to the resolution on National Demand passed by the Tripuri Congress and you seem to think much of it. I am sorry that such a beautifully vague resolution, containing pious platitudes, does not appeal to me. It leads us nowhere. If we mean to fight the British Government for our Swaraj, and if we feel that that the time is opportune, let us say so clearly and go ahead with our task. You have told me more than once that the idea of an ultimatum does not appeal to you. During the last twenty years Mahatma Gandhi has been repeatedly giving ultimata to the British Government. It is only through such ultimata and simultaneous preparation to fight if necessary that he has been able to get so much out of the British Government. If you really believe that the time has come for us to enforce our National Demand, how else can you proceed, except through an ultimatum? The other day Mahatma Gandhi delivered an ultimatum over the Rajkot issue. Do you object to the ideas of an ultimatum because I have been suggesting it? If so, why not say it clearly and without ambiguity.

To sum up, I fail to understand what policy you have with regard to our internal politics. I remember to have read in one of your statements that in your view, Rajkot and Jaipur would overshadow every other political issue. I was astounded to read such a remark from such an eminent leader as yourself. How any other issue could eclipse the main issue of Swaraj passes my comprehension. Rajkot is one tiny spot in this vast country. Jaipur has a somewhat bigger area than Rajkot, but even the Jaipur issue is a flea-bite when compared with our main struggle with the British Government. Moreover, we cannot forget that there are six hundred and odd states in India. If we follow the present piecemeal, tinkering and nibbling policy, suspending the popular struggle in every other state, it will take us 250 years to obtain civil liberty and responsible government in the states. And after that we shall think of our Swaraj!

In international affairs, your policy is perhaps even more nebulous. I was astounded when you produced a resolution before the Working

Committee some time ago seeking to make India an asylum for the Jews. You were mortified when the Working Committee (with probably Mahatma Gandhi's approval) turned it down. Foreign policy is a realistic affair to be determined largely from the point of view of a nation's self-interest. Take Soviet Russia, for instance. With all her communism in her internal politics, she never allows sentiment to dominate her foreign policy. That is why she did not hesitate to enter into a pact with French Imperialism when it suited her purpose. The Franco-Soviet Pact and the Czechoslovak-Soviet Pact are instances in point. Even today, Soviet Russia is anxious to enter into a pact with British Imperialism. Now, what is your foreign policy, pray? Frothy sentiments and pious platitudes do not make foreign policy. It is no use championing lost causes all the time and it is no use condemning countries like Germany and Italy on the one hand and on the other, giving a certificate of good conduct to British and French Imperialism.

For some time past I have been urging on everybody concerned, including Mahatma Gandhi and yourself, that we must utilise the international situation to India's advantage and, to that end, present the British Government with our National Demand in the form of an ultimatum; but I could make no impression on you or on Mahatmaji, though a large section of the Indian public approved of my stand and the Indian students in Great Britain sent me a largely-signed document approving of my policy. Today when you must find fault with me for not appointing the Working Committee forthwith, despite the shackles of the Tripuri resolution, the international situation suddenly assumes exaggerated importance in your eyes. What has happened today in Europe may I ask which is unexpected? Did not every student of international politics know that there would be a crisis in Europe in Spring? Did I not refer to it again and again when I pressed for an ultimatum to the British Government.

Let me now take another portion of your statement. You say, 'This Working Committee has for the time being ceased to be and the President, as he probably wishes, has a free hand to frame and put forward his proposals before the Congress. In accordance with his desire, no meeting was held here even to transact routine business'. I wonder how you could be guilty of such half-truths or shall I say untruths? Twelve members of the Working Committee suddenly and unexpectedly throw their resignation at my face and still you blame me and not them on the supposed ground that I probably wished to have a free hand in framing the resolutions. Then again, when did I prevent you from transacting routine business? Even with regard to the main task of framing resolutions for the

Congress, though I suggested postponement of the Working Committee till the Tripuri Congress, did I not ask Sardar Patel, nevertheless, in my telegram, to consult the other members and wire their opinion to me? If you have any doubt on this point, please have a look at my telegram to the Sardar. My telegram was:

'KINDLY SEE MY TELEGRAM TO MAHATMAJI. REGRETFULLY FEEL WORKING COMMITTEE MUST BE POSTPONED TILL CONGRESS. PLEASE CONSULT COLLEAGUES AND WIRE OPINION—SUBHAS'.

Seven days after the Tripuri Congress was over you sent me a telegram to the effect that I was responsible for causing a stalemate in the affairs of the Congress. With all your sense of fairness, it never struck you that the Tripuri Congress when passing Pandit Pant's resolution knew full well that I was seriously ill, that Mahatma Gandhi had not come to Tripuri and that it would be difficult for us to meet in the immediate future. It never struck you that the Congress itself was responsible for the stalemate by taking out of my hands in an unconstitutional and ultra vires manner the power of appointing the Working Committee. If the constitution had not been wantonly violated by Pandit Pant's resolution than I would have appointed the Working Committee on 13 March 1939. You commenced a public agitation against me only seven days after the Congress was over, though you knew quite well the condition of my health and your telegram to me appeared in the press even before it reached my hands. When for a full fortnight there was a stalemate in the affairs of the Congress prior to Tripuri, caused by the resignation of twelve members of the Working Committee, did you utter one word in protest? Did you offer me one word of sympathy? You say in one of your recent letters that you speak and act for yourself alone and should not be taken as representing anybody else. Unfortunately for us, it never strikes you that you appear to others in the role of an apologist for the Rightists. Take your last letter, dated 26 March, for instance. You say therein, 'I have today read your statement in the press, I fear that such argumentative statements will not help much'.

At a time when I am being unfairly attacked from several quarters—being hit below the belt, as they say—you do not utter one word of protest—you do not offer me one word of sympathy. But when I say something in self-defence, your reaction is—'Such argumentative statements do not help much'. Have you said the same thing of argumentative statements written by my political opponents? Perhaps you gloat over them.

Again, in your statement of 22 February you said, 'There is a tendency also for local Congress disputes to be dealt with not in the usual routine way, but directly from the top, with the result that particular groups and parties are favoured and confusion increased and Congress work suffers . . . It pains me to see that in the very heart of our organisation new methods are being introduced which can only lead to local conflicts spreading to higher planes'.

I was painfully surprised to read such an indictment when you had not cared to ascertain all the facts. The least that you could have done was to have asked me for the facts as I knew them. I do not know what exactly you had in mind when you wrote this. A friend suggested that you were thinking of the affairs of the Delhi Provincial Congress Committee. If so, let me tell you quite plainly that what I did with regard to Delhi was the only right thing for me to do.

In this connection, let me tell you that in the habit of interfering from the top, no Congress President can beat you. Perhaps you have forgotten all that you did as Congress President or perhaps it is difficult to look at oneself objectively. On 22 February you charged me with interfering from the top. Did you forget that on 4 February you had written me a letter in which you had charged me with being a non-assertive, passive President. You wrote, 'In effect you have functioned more as a speaker than as a directing President'. Most objectionable was your charge that I was acting in a partisan manner and was favouring a particular party or group. Did you not owe it to the official head of the Congress organisation (if not to me personally) to make a proper enquiry before hurling such a serious allegation at him in the public press?

If one takes the election controversy as a whole, one would have thought that after the contest was over, the whole episode would be forgotten, the hatchet would be buried and, as happens after a boxing-bout, the boxers would smilingly shake hands. But in spite of truth and non-violence, this did not happen. The result was not taken in a sporting spirit, a grievance was nursed against me and the spirit of vendetta set to work. You took up cudgels on behalf of other members of the Working Committee and you had every right to do so. But did it never strike you that something could also be said on my behalf? Was there nothing wrong in the other members of the Working Committee meeting in my absence and behind my back and deciding to set up Dr Pattabhi for the Presidentship? Was there nothing wrong in Sardar Patel and the others appealing to the Congress delegates, as members of the Working Committee, to support the candidature of Dr Pattabhi? Was there nothing wrong in Sardar Patel making full use of the name and authority of

Mahatma Gandhi for electioneering purposes? Was there nothing wrong in Sardar Patel stating that my re-election would be harmful to the country's cause? Was there nothing wrong in making use of the Congress Ministries in different provinces for canvassing votes?

With regard to the so-called 'aspersions', I have already said what I have to say, both in the press statement as well as in the remarks which I made before the Subjects Committee at Tripuri. But I would like to ask you one question. Have you forgotten that when Lord Lothian was touring India, he remarked publicly that all the Congress leaders did not agree with Pandit Nehru in their attitude towards the Federal Scheme? What is the implication and significance of this remark?

You have complained of an atmosphere of mutual suspicion and lack of faith at the top in your statement of 22 February. May I tell you that till the Presidential election, there was far less suspicion and lack of faith among the members of Working Committee in my regime than in yours? We never came to the point of resignation in consequence thereof as according to yourself, you did more than once. The trouble, so far as I am aware, started with my success at the election contest. If I had been defeated, then in all probability the public would not have heard of the 'aspersion' affair.

You are in the habit of proclaiming that you stand by yourself and represent nobody else and that you are not attached to any party. Occasionally you say this in a manner as if you are either proud or happy because of it. At the same time, you call yourself a Socialist—sometimes, a full-blooded Socialist. How a Socialist can be an individualist as you regard yourself, beats me. The one is the anti-thesis of the other. How Socialism can ever come into existence through individualism of your type is also an engima to me. By bearing a non-party label one can be popular with all parties, but what is the value of it? If one believes in certain ideas or principles, one should strive to translate them into reality and that could be done only through a party or an organisation. I have not heard of Socialism being established in any country or progressing in that direction, except through a party. Even Mahatma Gandhi has his party.

There is another idea on which you often harp, regarding which I would like to say something—I mean the idea of national unity. I am all for it as, I believe, the whole country is. But there is an obvious limitation. The unity that we strive for or maintain must be the unity of action and not the unity of inaction. Splits are not an evil under all circumstances. There are occasions when splits are necessary in the interests of progress. When the Social Democrat Party of Russia broke up into Bolsheviks and Mensheviks in 1903, Lenin heaved a sigh of relief. He was relieved of the dead-weight of the Mensheviks and felt that the path to speedy progress was after all thrown open. When in India the 'Moderates' isolated themselves from the Congress, nobody of a progressive frame of mind regretted the split. Subsequently, when a large section of Congressmen withdrew from the Congress in 1920, the rest did not mourn their secession. Such splits were really aids to progress. Latterly, we have been making a fetish of unity. There is a potential danger in this. It may be used as a cover for weakness, or as an excuse for effecting compromises which are inherently anti-progressive. Take your own case. You were against the Gandhi–Irwin Pact—but you submitted to it on the plea of unity. Again, you were against the acceptance of office in the provinces—but when office acceptance was decided upon, you submitted to it perhaps on the same plea. Supposing for argument's sake that somehow the majority in the Congress agreed to work the Federal Scheme, then the anti-federationists, in spite of their strong principles, may be tempted by the selfsame plea of unity to accept the Federal Scheme against the dictates of their political conscience. Unity in a revolutionary movement is not an end in itself but only a means. It is desirable only so long as it furthers progress. The moment it tends to hamper progress it becomes an evil. What would you do, may I ask, if the Congress by a majority resolved to accept the Federal Scheme? Would you abide by that decision or revolt against it?

Your letter of 4 February from Allahabad is interesting as showing that you had not then hardened against me as you subsequently did. For instance, you said in that letter, 'As I told you, your contested election has done some good and some harm'. Later on, you came to hold the view that my re-election was an unmixed evil. Then again, you wrote, 'This future we have to view from the larger viewpoint and not in terms of personalities. Obviously it is not good enough for any one of us to get into a huff because matters have not shaped as one wished them to. We have to give our best to the cause whatever happens'. It is clear that you had not come to attach the importance to the 'aspersion' affair which you did thereafter. Not only that; as I have already said, the agitation over the 'aspersion' affair that was fomented subsequently was largely of your own making. In this connection, you may perhaps remember that when we met at Santiniketan, I suggested to you that if in spite of our endeavour we failed to retain the cooperation of the other members of the Working

Committee, we should not shirk the responsibility of running the Congress. You then agreed with me. Later on, owing to reasons which I cannot comprehend, you went over, bodily as it were, to the other side. Of course, you have every right to do so, but then what about your Socialism and Leftism?

In the letter of 4 February you have alleged more than once that vital questions like Federation were not discussed during my presidentship. It is a curious charge to make when you yourself were out of the country for nearly six months. Do you know that when there was a storm over Shri Bhulabhai Desai's supposed speech in London, I suggested to the Working Committee that we should reiterate our resolution against Federation and also carry on an anti-Federation propaganda in the country and that my proposal was regarded as unnecessary? Do you know that when the Working Commitee met subsequently in September at Delhi, it was at last considered necessary to have a resolution condemning Federation and that this resolution was adopted by the All India Congress Committee?

Another accusation you made in that letter was that I adopted an entirely passive attitude in the Working Committee and that in effect I functioned more as a Speaker than as a directing President. That was a rather unkind statement to make. Would it be wrong to say that usually you monopolised most of the time of the Working Committee? If the Working Committee had another member as talkative as yourself, I do not think that we would ever have come to the end of our business. Besides your manners were such that you would almost usurp the functions of the President. I could, of course, have dealt with the situation by pulling you up, but that would have led to an open breach between us. To be brutally frank, you sometimes behaved in the Working Committee as a spoilt child and often lost your temper. Now, in spite of all of your 'nerviness' and jumpiness, what results did you achieve? You would generally hold forth for hours together and then succumb at the end. Sardar Patel and the others had a clever technique for dealing with you. They would let you talk and talk and they would ultimately finish up by asking you to draft their resolution. Once you were allowed to draft the resolution, you would feel happy, no matter whose resolution it was. Rarely have I found you sticking to your point till the last.

Another strange charge against me is that the A.I.C.C. office has deteriorated greatly during the past year. I do not know what you consider to be the functions of a President. In my view, he is much more than a glorified clerk or even a glorified Secretary. As President you were in the habit of usurping the functions of the Secretary, but that is no reason why other Presidents should do the same thing. Apart from this, my chief difficulty was that the A.I.C.C. office was situated at a distance and that the General Secretary was not a man of my choice. It would be no exaggeration to say that the General Secretary was not loyal to me in the sense that a Secretary ought to be loyal to his President (I am purposely putting the case very mildly). As a matter of fact, Kripalaniji was thrust on me against my will. You may perhaps remember that I tried my best to have a part of the A.I.C.C. office transferred to Calcutta so that I would be able to supervise its work properly. All of you set your face against it and now you turn round and blame me for the defects of the A.I.C.C. office! If the A.I.C.C. office has really deteriorated as you allege, it is the General Secretary who is responsible for it and not myself. All that you can charge me with is that during my presidentship there was less interference with the work of the General Secretary and that the latter, in actual practice, enjoyed larger powers than before. Consequently, if the A.I.C.C. office has really deteriorated, it is the General Secretary who is responsible for it and not myself.

I am surprised that without knowing the facts you have alleged that I did not do my best to prevent the enactment of the Bombay Trades Disputes Bill in its present form. In fact, you have latterly developed the art of making accusations, sometimes publicly, without even caring to ascertain facts, where I am concerned. If you desire to know what I did in this connection the best thing would be to ask Sardar Patel himself. The only thing that I did not do was to break with him on this issue. If that be an offence, I plead guilty to the charge. By the way, do you know that the Bombay C.S.P. lent its support to the Bill in its present form? And now, coming to yourself, may I ask what you did to prevent the enactment of this Bill? When you returned to Bombay, there was still time for you to act and I believe you were approached by a number of Trade Unionists to whom you gave some hopes. You were in a much better position than myself, because you can always influence Gandhiji much more than I can. If you had exerted yourself, you might have succeeded where I had failed. Did you do so?

There is one matter regarding which you often have a fling at me—the idea of a Coalition Ministry. As a doctrinaire politician you have decided once for all that a Coalition Ministry is a Rightist move. Will you kindly do one thing before expressing a final verdict on this question? Will you tour the province of Assam for a fortnight and then come and tell me if the present Coalition Ministry has been a progressive or a reactionary institution? What is the use of your sitting in Allahabad and uttering words of wisdom which have no relation to reality? When I went to Assam after the fall of the Saadullah Ministry, I did not find one single Congressman who did not insist that there should be a Congress Coalition Ministry. The fact is that the province had been groaning under a reactionary Ministry. Things were going from bad to worse and corruption was daily on the increase. The entire Congress-minded public of Assam heaved a sigh of relief and recovered confidence and hope when the new Ministry came into office. If you scrap the policy of office acceptance for the whole country, I shall welcome it, along with Congressmen in provinces like Assam and Bengal. But if the Congress Party accepts office in seven provinces, it is imperative that there should be coalition ministries in the rest. If only you knew the improvement that has taken place in Assam, in spite of all the various obstacles and handicaps, since the Coalition Ministry came into office, you would change your opinion completely.

Regarding Bengal, I am afraid you know practically nothing. During two years of your presidentship you never cared to tour the province, though that province needed your attention much more than any other, in view of the terrible repression it had been through. Have you ever cared to know what has happened to the province ever since the Huq Ministry came into office? If you did, then you would not talk like a doctrinaire politician. You would then agree with me that if the province is to be saved, the Huq Ministry must go and we should have the best government under the present circumstances, namely, a Coalition Ministry. But while I say all this I must add that the proposal of a Coalition Ministry arises because the active struggle for Purna Swaraj has been suspended. Resume this struggle tomorrow and all talk of a Coalition Ministry will vanish into thin air.

I shall now refer to your telegram of 20 March from Delhi. You said therein, 'In view international situation and critical national problems formation Working Committee Office arrangements urgently necessary' etc. Anyone can appreciate the necessity of the early formation of the Working Committee—but what struck me in your telegram was the utter lack of sympathy for my difficulties. You knew full well that if Pant's resolution had not been moved and passed, the Working Committee would have been announced on 13 March. When that resolution was passed, the Congress knew full well that I was seriously ill—that Mahatma Gandhi had not come to Tripuri and that it would be difficult for us to meet in the immediate future. I can understand that if a month had elapsed without the Working Committee being appointed, people would naturally feel restless. But the agitation was started exactly one week after the Tripuri Congress was over and once again—as in the case of the 'aspersion' affair—it was you who started the campaign against me. Was it easy to form the Working Committee without meeting Mahatma Gandhi? How could I possibly meet Mahatmaji? And did you forget that last year the Working Committee met about six weeks after the Haripura Congress? Do you think that the agitation started by a certain section of the public and the press against me, after your telegram appeared in the press, was an altogether bona fide one? Was I consciously causing a stalemate in the affairs of the Congress by deliberately refraining from appointing the Working Committee? If the agitation against me was not altogether fair, did you not, as a public leader, feel called upon to put in a word on my behalf at a time when I was laid up in bed?

I have already referred to your accusation that the A.I.C.C. has deteriorated under my Presidentship. I shall add a word in that connection. Did it not strike you that besides damning the General Secretary, you were, while trying to damn me, damning the entire staff as well?

In your telegram, you have referred to 'critical national problems' for which you want the Working Committee to be formed at once—though, as you say, you do not desire to be on that Committee. What are these 'critical national problems' pray? In a previous letter, you said that the most critical problem was the situation in Rajkot and Jaipur. Since Mahatmaji has been handling these matters, they are in a way outside the jurisdiction of the Working Committee and the A.I.C.C.

Then again, in your telegram, you have referred to the international situation. I noticed in the press that after you mentioned this, several persons who have no international sense at all, who have no desire to understand international affairs and who have no intention of using the international situation to India's advantage—suddenly became concerned over the fate of Bohemia and Slovakia. Obviously it was a convenient stick to beat me with. Nothing has happened in Europe during the last two months which was not to be expected. What has happened in Czechoslovakia recently is but a sequel to the Munich Pact. As a matter of fact, I have been telling Congress friends during the last six months, on the basis of information which I had been getting from Europe, that there would be a crisis in Europe in Spring which would last till Summer. I have, therefore, been pressing for a dynamic move from our side—for an ultimatum to the British Government demanding

Purna Swaraj. I remember that when I once spoke to you about the international situation recently (at Santiniketan or at Allahabad) and used it as an argument for submitting our National Demand to the British Government, your cold reply was that the international tension would continue for some years. Suddenly you seem to have grown enthusiastic about the international situation! But let me tell you that there is no sign of any intention on your part or on the part of the Gandhian group to utilise the international situation for our benefit. Your telegram also says that the international crisis demands an early meeting of the A.I.C.C. To what end? To pass a long-worded resolution of no practical consequence? Or will you change your mind and tell the A.I.C.C. that we should now push on towards Purna Swaraj and present the British Government with our National Demand in the form of an ultimatum? No, I feel that either we should take international politics seriously and utilise the international situation for our benefit—or not talk about it at all. It is no use making a show, if we do not mean business.

I am told that when you were at Delhi you carried a message to Mahatmaji to the effect that he should pay a visit to Allahabad to meet Maulana Azad. This information may be quite wrong. But if it is not—did you also suggest to him that he could pay a visit to Dhanbad as well? When my Secretary telephoned to you on 24 March to contradict the press report that Mahatmaji could not come to Dhanbad because of Doctor's prohibition, you did not show any desire that he should visit Dhanbad, though you were awfully anxious that I should announce the formation of the Working Commitee in accordance with Gandhiji's wishes. Over the telephone you said that Dhanbad was not on his programme. Was it so terribly difficult for you to persuade Mahatmaji to come to Dhanbad? Did you try? You may say that he had to go back to Delhi for the Rajkot affair. But he had already finished his interview with the Viceroy. And so far as interviewing Sir Maurice Gwyer was concerned, that was for Sardar Patel and not for Mahatmaji.

Apropos of the Rajkot affair, I want to say a few words. You thought a lot of the terms of settlement which terminated Mahatmaji's fast. There is no Indian who did not feel happy and relieved that Mahatmaji's life was saved. But when one analysed the terms of settlement with the cold eye of logic, what did one find? In the first place, Sir Maurice Gwyer, who is a part and parcel of the Federal Scheme , was recognised as the umpire or arbitrator. Did that not amount to a tacit recognition of that Scheme (Federal) itself? Secondly, Sir Maurice is neither our man nor an independent agent. He is a Government man—pure and simple. In any conflict with the British Government, if we accept a High Court Judge or a Sessions Judge as umpire or arbitrator, the British Government will very gladly agree to it. For instance, in the matter of State prisoners detained without trial, the Government always boasts that the relevant papers are placed before 2 High Court or Sessions Judges. But we never accept that as a satisfactory settlement. Why then has there been a departure in the case of Rajkot?

There is another point in this connection which I cannot understand and on which you will be able to enlighten me. Mahatma Gandhi went to see the Viceroy and the interview took place duly. Why is he still waiting there? It is Sardar Patel who has to wait, in case Sir Maurice Gwyer wants him. Does it not indirectly enhance the prestige of the British Government, if Mahatmaji lingers on in Delhi after his interview with the Viceroy? You said in your letter of 24 March that Mahatmaji was completely fixed in Delhi for several days and could not leave at all. I should have thought that there are more important things for Gandhiji to do now than wait in Delhi. The drift, stalemate etc. of which you complain so much could be brought to an end in no time, if Mahatmaji exerted himself a bit. But on that point you are silent and all the blame is reserved for me.

In your letter of 23 March you said, 'I found later some vague talk among other people that a meeting of the A.I.C.C. should be held. I do not know exactly who were thinking on these lines and what their objective was in holding the meeting, except in so far as it might be a further clarification of the situation'. News travels fast and far and I got the information that some M.L.A.'s (Central) were trying to get a requisition signed by members of the A.I.C.C. for an early meeting of that body (A.I.C.C.)—as if I was avoiding calling a meeting of the A.I.C.C. and was deliberately causing a deadlock in the affairs of the Congress. Did you not hear anything of this sort—either at Delhi or elsewhere? If so, do you think that such a move was fair and honourable?

In the same letter (of 23 March) you refer to the National Demand resolution and Sarat's opposing it. As for Sarat's attitude, he will probably be writing to you about it. But it is not correct to say that apart from his opposition, the resolution was passed unanimously. I have heard from several people that they opposed the resolution—not because there was anything inherently wrong in it—but because it contained nothing of practical significance. It was like one of those innocuous resolutions which towards the end of every Congress are moved and seconded and passed either unanimously or *nem. con.* Really, I fail to understand how you can enthuse so much over this resolution. What practical lead does it give?

In this connection I cannot help remarking that in recent years Congress resolutions are often too verbose and long-worded. One should call them 'theses' or 'essays' rather than 'resolutions'. Formerly, our resolutions used to be brief, pertinent and practical. I am afraid that you have had a hand in giving this new shape and form to our resolutions. So far as I am concerned, I would rather have practical resolutions than lengthy theses.

More than once you have referred in your letters to the 'adventurist tendencies' in the Congress of today. What exactly do you mean? It strikes me that you have in view certain individuals. Are you against new men and women coming into the Congress and getting prominence? Do you desire that the top leadership in the Congress should be the close preserve of a few individuals? If my memory does not betray me, the Council of the U.P. Provincial Congress Committee once adopted a rule to the effect that in certain Congress organisations, the same individual should not continue as an office-bearer for more than three years. Evidently this rule was to apply to subordinate organisations and in the higher bodies, the same individuals could continue in the same post for decades. Whatever you might say, we are, in a sense, all adventurers, for life is one long adventure. I should have thought that those who regard themselves as progressive would welcome fresh blood in all ranks of the Congress organisation.

There is no reason for you to think (here I am referring to your letter of 24 March) that Sarat's letter was written on my behalf. He has a personality of his own. He got Gandhiji's telegram asking him to write, after he returned to Calcutta from here. If Gandhiji had not telegraphed in that way, I doubt if he would have written at all. I must say, however, that there are certain things in his letter to Mahatmaji which echo my feelings.

Regarding your letter to Sarat, I have a few observations to make. I must infer from your letter that what he wrote about the atmosphere etc. at Tripuri came as a surprise to you. This surprises me. Though I could not move about freely, I had sufficient reports from independent sources about the morally sickening atmosphere of the place. How you could have moved about the place without sensing it and hearing about it—beats me.

Secondly, you have remarked that at Tripuri personal issues coloured the consideration of other issues. You are right. Only, you did not add that though you did not speak on the subject either in the Subjects Committee or in the open session of the Congress—you did more than any other individual to accentuate these personal issues and make them prominent in the public eye.

You have said in your letter to Sarat, 'It was absurd for anyone to say that Subhas's illness was a fake and none of my colleagues hinted at this to my knowledge'. You must be completely jaundiced to be able to make such a remark when before and at Tripuri, a systematic campaign to that effect was carried on everywhere by my political opponents. This is an additional proof that for some time past you have become completely biased against me (see the beginning of this letter). I do not think that what Sarat has said about the atmosphere etc. at Tripuri is any exaggeration at all.

You have referred to some unsavoury reports which you heard at Tripuri. It is somewhat strange and unbecoming on your part that only such reports impress you as go against us. Let me give you a few examples. Do you know that Bengal is not the only province against which complaints were made regarding the issue of delegates' tickets? Do you know that a similar complaint was made against Andhra province? But you mention only Bengal. Again, do you know that when duplicate receipts were issued by the Bengal P.C.C. office on the ground that the originals were lost, the B.P.C.C. office warned the A.I.C.C. office about the matter and asked the latter to be careful while issuing delegates' tickets? Do you care to enquire as to who was responsible for the error—the B.P.C.C. office or the A.I.C.C. office?

Further, you have referred to large sums being spent in bringing delegates. Don't you know on which side are to be found the capitalists and moneyed people? Have you heard of lorry-loads of Punjab delegates being brought from Lahore? At whose instance were they brought? Perhaps Dr Kitchlew could throw light on this. A reputed lady Congress worker from the Punjab who saw me here 5 days ago, said that they had been brought under Sardar Patel's instructions. I do not know. But surely, you should have some sense of impartiality.

Regarding the role of the Congress Ministers at Tripuri, I have two remarks to make. I had requests from a large number of A.I.C.C. members to the effect that voting should be by ballot. On my asking why, they said that if they openly voted against the Congress Ministers they would get into trouble. What is the meaning of this? Secondly, I am against the idea of Ministers canvassing in this partisan way. No doubt they have the constitutional right to do so—but the effect of it will be that in every province there will be splits in the Congress Parliamentary Party. How can the Ministers carry on if they do not have the undivided support of all Congress M.L.A.'s and M.L.C.'s in their respective provinces?

Don't you agree that at the Tripuri Congress (including the Subjects Committee), the Old Guard played a passive role in the eyes of the public and that the Ministers dominated the scene? Was Sarat wrong when he made this remark?

It is adding insult to injury—as they say—for you to remark in your letter to Sarat that 'The Tripuri resolution envisaged cooperation between the Congress President and Gandhiji'.

You claim in the above letter that you laboured to bring about cooperation among Congressmen at Tripuri and before. May I tell you the unpleasant fact that other people hold a different view? In their view, you cannot be absolved of the responsibility for the gulf that the Tripuri Congress created between Congressman and Congressman.

I should now invite you to clarify your policy and programme—not in vague generalities but in the realistic details. I should also like to know what you are—Socialist or leftist or Centrist or Rightist or Gandhist or something else?

There are two admirable sentences in your letter to Sarat, 'What pains me most is the overshadowing of all political issues by the personal equation. If there is to be conflict among Congressmen, I earnestly hope that it will be kept on a higher level and will be confined to matters of policy and principle'. If only you had adhered to your dictum, what a difference it would have made to our Congress Politics!

When you say that you do not understand what obstruction there was at Tripuri, I cannot help admiring your 'naivete'. The Tripuri Congress, in reality, passed only one resolution, viz. Pant's resolution, and that resolution was charged with the spirit of pettiness and vindictiveness. The protagonists of truth and non-violence had told the world after the Presidential election that they would not obstruct the majority party and out of a spirit of non-obstruction they resigned their membership of the Working Committee. At Tripuri they did nothing but obstruct. They had every right to do so—but why did they make professions which they belied in practice?

I shall refer to a few other things before I finish this unusually long letter.

You referred to the trouble about issue of tickets to Bengal delegates at Tripuri. The other day I read in the papers that at a public meeting in Calcutta, it was stated by a member of the A.I.C.C. that he had heard from some U.P. delegates that similar trouble had taken place with regard to U.P. also.

Don't you think that the fundamental motive behind Pant's resolution was to pit Mahatmaji against me? Do you consider such a move to be an honest one, when no breach had taken place between Mahatmaji and myself, at least from my side? If the Old Guard wanted to fight me, why did they not do so in a straightforward manner? Why did they bring Mahatma Gandhi between us? It was a clever artifice no doubt, but the point is if such a move accords with Truth and Non-violence.

I have already asked you if you consider it fair on the part of Sardar Patel to declare that my re-election would be harmful to the country's cause. You never said a word that he should withdraw such a remark—thereby indirectly supporting his allegation. Now I would like to ask you what you think of Mahatmaji's remark to the effect that after all, I am not an enemy of the country. Do you think that such a remark was justified? If not, then did you put in a word on my behalf to Mahatmaji?

What do you think of the trick indulged in by some people by publishing in the daily press, while we were at Tripuri, that Pant's resolution had the full support of Mahatmaji?

And now, what do you think of Pant's resolution? There was a rumour at Tripuri that you were one of the authors of it. Is that a fact? Do you approve of this resolution, though you remained neutral at the time of voting? What is your interpretation of it? Was it, in your view, a motion of no-confidence?

I am sorry that my letter has become so long. It will no doubt tire your patience. But I could not avoid it—there were so many things to say.

Possibly, I shall have to write to you again or issue a press statement. There is an unconfirmed report that in some articles you have been adversely criticising my presidentship. When I see your articles I shall be in a position to say something on the subject and to compare our work—particularly how far you have advanced the cause of Leftism in two years and I in one year.

If I have used harsh language or hurt your feelings at any place, kindly pardon me. You yourself say that there is nothing like frankness and I have tried to be frank—perhaps brutally frank.

I am progressing steadily though slowly. Hope you are all right.

Yours affectionately
SUBHAS

24
The Ramgarh Address

Presidential Address at the
All-India Anti-Compromise Conference,
Ramgarh, Bihar, 19 March 1940

Comrades,

You have done me a very great honour by inviting me to preside over the deliberations of the All-India Anti-Compromise Conference at Ramgarh today. At the same time the responsibility you have thrown on my shoulders is onerous to a degree. This Conference is intended to focus all the anti-imperialist forces in the country that are now determined to resist a compromise with Imperialism. To preside over such a Conference is by no means an easy task. This task becomes all the more serious and arduous when the Chairman of the Reception Committee is no less a person than Swami Sahajanand Saraswati. It is in response to Swamiji's clarion call that we have assembled here today.

Comrades, I shall fail in my duty if before proceeding to discuss the problem of the day, I do not pay a tribute to those who are responsible for organising this Conference. I happen to know something of the obstacles and the difficulties that had to be overcome before this Conference could meet and I can, therefore, speak with a certain amount of authority. These obstacles and difficulties were of a twofold character. In the first place, there were physical and material obstacles and difficulties to be overcome at Ramgarh before adequate arrangements for the Conference could be made. In the second place, persistent hostile propaganda all over the country had to be faced and counteracted by the organisers of the Conference. The most surprising and painful of this propaganda was the determined endeavour of a section of Leftists (or shall I say pseudo-Leftists) to make the Conference impossible by openly condemning it and also by trying to sabotage it. As a matter of fact, during the last few months it has become more and more evident that a number of Leftists have begun to play the role of apologists of the Rightists—but such a phenomenon is not new in history. Man lives to learn and the longer he lives, the more does he realise the aptness of the oft-repeated truism that history repeats itself.

It has been argued by the apologists of the Congress Working Committee that the Congress is itself the biggest Anti-Compromise Conference and that such a Conference is, therefore, unnecessary. The resolution of the last meeting of the Congress Working Committee which met at Patna is held up before our eyes in order to demonstrate that the Congress has adopted an uncompromising policy. One cannot but admire the naivete of such an argument, but is it meet and proper for politicians and political workers to be so very naive?

One has only to go through the whole of the Patna resolution and particularly through the latter portion of it in order to realise that there are loopholes which detract from the intrinsic value of that resolution. No sooner was this resolution passed than Mahatma Gandhi came forward with the statement that the door had not been banged on future negotiations for a settlement. Mahatmaji's subsequent lengthy remarks on Civil Disobedience do not assure us by any means that the period of struggle has commenced. In fact, what has distressed and bewildered us during the last year and a half is the fact that while on the one hand red-hot resolutions are passed and statements issued by members of the Congress Working Committee, simultaneously other remarks are made and statements issued either by Mahatma Gandhi or by other Rightist leaders which create a totally different impression on the average mind. Then there is the moot question as to whether the Patna resolution would have been passed at all, but for the pressure exerted by the Left during the last six months.

The country eagerly awaits a clear and unequivocal declaration from the Congress Working Committee that the door has finally been banged on all talks of a compromise with Imperialism. But will this declaration be forthcoming? If so, when?

Comrades, those who aver that the Congress is the biggest Anti-Compromise Conference perhaps suffer from shortness of memory and their brains consequently need refreshing. Have they forgotten that as soon as the War began, Mahatama Gandhi proceeded to Simla without caring to consult the Congress Working Committee and informed His Excellency the Viceroy that he was in favour of rendering unconditional help to Great Britain in the prosecution of the War? Do they not realise that Mahatma Gandhi being the sole dictator of the Congress, his personal views necessarily have a far-reaching implication? Have they forgotten that since the outbreak of War, the Congress Working Committee has side-tracked the main issue—namely, our demand for Purna Swaraj—by putting forward a demand for a fake Constituent Assembly? Have they forgotten that some prominent Rightist leaders, including members of the Congress Working Committee, have been continuously whittling down the implications of a Constituent Assembly and that they have gone so far as to accept separate electorate and the existing franchise for the Legislative Assembly as the basis for electing the Constituent Assembly of their dreams? Have they forgotten that after the resignation of Congress ministries, several Congress Ministers have been showing an inordinate desire to get back to office? Have they forgotten the consistent attitude which Mahatma Gandhi has adopted during the last six months in the matter of a compromise with the British Government? And do they not know that behind the smoke-screen of hot phrases, negotiations for a compromise have been going on apace?

Unfortunately for us, the British Government have ceased to take the Congress seriously and have formed the impression that however much Congressmen may talk, they will not ultimately show fight. Since September 1939, there has not been any dearth of resolutions and statements. Some members of the Congress Working Committee opine that these resolutions have impressed the world. But whether they have impressed the world or not, they have certainly not impressed the British, who are essentially a realistic race. During the last six months we have offered them only words and words and we have received the timeworn reply that so long as the Hindu-Muslim problem remains unsolved, Purna Swaraj is unthinkable.

Since September last India has been passing through a rare crisis when men's minds have fallen prey to doubt and vacillation. The first to fall were the leaders themselves and the demoralisation that seized them has been spreading as a contagion throughout the land. A determined and widespread effort is needed if we are to stem the rot. To make this effort really effective, our activities should be focused at an all-India conference of all those who are determined to have no truck with Imperialism.

The crisis that has overtaken us may be rare in Indian history, but it is nothing new in the history of the world. Such crises generally appear in periods of transition. In India we are now ringing down the curtain on an age that is passing away, while we are at the same time ushering in the dawn of a new era. The age of Imperialism is drawing to a close and the era of freedom, democracy and Socialism looms ahead of us. India, therefore, stands today at one of the crossroads of history. It is for us to share, if we so will, the heritage that awaits the world.

It is not to be wondered at that men's minds should be bewildered when the old structure is crashing under its own weight and the new is yet to rise out of the ashes of the old. But let us not lose faith in ourselves, or in our countrymen or in humanity in this hour of uncertainty. To lose faith would be a calamity of the first magnitude.

Such crises constitute the supreme test of a nation's leadership. The present crisis has put our own leadership to the test and the latter has been unfortunately found wanting. It is only by analysing and exposing the causes of its failure that we can learn the lesson of history and lay the foundation of our future effort and achievement. But such analysis and exposure will necessarily be painful to all concerned, though there is means of avoiding it.

I may digress at this stage and draw an analogy with similar crises in other climes and ages. When the October Revolution broke out in Russia in 1917, nobody had a clear conception as to how the revolution should be directed. Most of the Bolsheviks were then thinking in terms of coalition with other parties. It was left to Lenin to denounce all coalitions and give out the slogan—'All Power to the Soviet. Who knows what turn Russian history would have taken but for this timely lead of Lenin's during a period of doubt and vacillation? Lenin's unerring instinct (or intuition) which ultimately proved to be prophetic, saved Russia from disaster and from a tragedy similar to that which overtook Spain the other day.

Let us now take a contrary case. Italy in 1922 was to all intents and purposes ripe for socialism. All that she needed was an Italian Lenin. But the man of the hour did not arrive and the opportunity slipped out of Socialist hands. It was immediately seized by the Fascist leader, Benito Mussolini. By his march to Rome and his seizure of power Italian history took an altogether different turn and Italy ultimately went Fascist instead of going socialist. Doubt and vacillation had seized the Italian leaders and so they failed. Mussolini had one supreme virtue which not only saved him but brought him the laurels of victory. He knew his mind and he was not afraid to act. That constituted the essence of leadership.

Today our leaders are wobbling and their vacillation has demoralised a section of Leftists as well. 'Unity', 'National Front', 'Discipline'—those have become cheap slogans which have no relation to reality. Befogged by such attractive slogans, they seem to have forgotten that the supreme need of the hour is a bold, uncompromising policy leading us on to a national struggle. Whatever strengthens us for this purpose is to be welcomed. Whatever weakens us is to be esehewed. Unity which ties us to the apron strings of Rightist politicians is by no means a blessing. We might as well induce the Congress to effect unity with the Liberal Federation—if unity is to be desired under all conditions and circumstances.

In the present crisis, the most distressing phenomenon is the disruption within the ranks of those who were hitherto regarded as Leftists. The immediate future will prove to be the acid test of Leftism in India. Those who will be found wanting will be soon exposed as pseudo-Leftists. The members of the Forward Bloc, too, will have to demonstrate by their work and conduct that they are really forward and dynamic. It may be that in the ordeal that is ahead of us, some of those who are branded as Rightists today, will prove to be genuine Leftists—Leftists in action, I mean.

A word is necessary here in order to explain what we mean by Leftism. The present age is the anti-imperialist phase of our movement. Our main task in this age is to end Imperialism and win national Independence for the Indian people. When freedom comes, the age of national reconstruction will commence and that will be the socialist phase of our movement. In the present phase of our movement, Leftists will be those who will wage an uncompromising fight with Imperialism. Those who waver and vacillate in their struggle against Imperialism—those who tend towards a compromise with it—cannot by any means be Leftists. In the next phase of our movement, Leftism will be synonymous with socialism—but in the present phase, the words 'Leftist' and 'Anti-imperialist' would be interchangeable.

The problem of the hour is—'Will India still remain under the thumb of the Rightists or will she swing to the Left, once for all?' The answer to this can be furnished only by the Leftists themselves. If they adopt a bold, uncompromising policy in their struggle with Imperialism, regardless of all dangers, difficulties and obstacles, then the Leftists will make history and India will go Left.

To those who may still be thinking of a compromise, the recent history of Ireland and the sequel to the Anglo-Irish Treaty should prove highly instructive and edifying.

A compromise with Imperialism will mean that an anti-imperialist national struggle will soon be converted into a civil war among the people themselves. Would this be desirable from any point of view?

In the event of a compromise being effected with Imperialism in this country, Indian Leftists will in future have to fight not only Imperialism, but its new-fangled Indian allies as well. This will necessarily mean that the national struggle with Imperialism will be converted into a civil war among the Indians themselves.

Let us take time by the forelock and let us act while it is not too late. Swami Sahajanand Saraswati has sounded the clarion call. Let us respond to it with all the strength and courage that we possess. From this Conference let us send out a warning to both Imperialism and its Indian allies. The success of this Conference should mean the death-knell of compromise with Imperialism.

Before we part, let us also set up a permanent machinery for implementing the resolutions of this Conference and for waging an uncompromising war with Imperialism. Everybody now realises that if the Working Committee of the Congress does not give the call for launching a national struggle, others will have to do so. It would, therefore, be in the fitness of things for this Conference to set up a permanent machinery for undertaking this responsibility—should the Working Committee fail us in this crisis. I hope and trust that the deliberations of this Conference will be a prelude to work and struggle on a nation-wide scale and on an All-India front.

'Inquilab Zindabad'

25
My Political Testament

To H.E. the Governor of Bengal,
The Hon. Chief Minister and
The Council of Ministers

26 November 1940

Your Excellency and Gentlemen!

I am writing this in connection with my letter of 30 October 1940, addressed to the Hon. Home Minister (copy of which was forwarded to the Hon. Chief Minister) and my confidential letters to the Superintendent, Presidency Jail, dated 30 October and 14 November, which were forwarded to Government in due course. Herein I shall recapitulate what I have to say regarding my own case and shall also put down in black and white the considerations that are impelling me to take the most fateful step in my life.

I have no longer any hope that I shall obtain redress at your hands. I shall, therefore, make but two requests, the second of which will be at the end of this letter. My first request is that this letter be carefully preserved in the archives of the Government, so that it may be available to those of my countrymen who will succeed you in office in future. It contains a message for my countrymen and is therefore my political testament.

I was arrested without any official explanation or justification on 2 July 1940, as per orders of the Government of Bengal, under Section 129 of the Defence of India Rules. The first explanation subsequently emanating from official sources came from the Rt. Hon. Mr Amery, Secretary of State for India, who stated in the House of Commons quite categorically that the arrest was in connection with the movement for the demolition of the Holwell Monument in Calcutta.

The Hon. Chief Minister virtually confirmed this pronouncement at a sitting of the Bengal Legislative Assembly and stated that it was the Holwell Monument Satyagraha which stood in the way of my release.

When the Government decided to remove the Monument, all those who had been detained without trial in connection therewith were set free, with the exception of Mr Narendra Narayan Chakravarti, M.L.A. and myself. These releases took place towards the end of August 1940 and almost simultaneously an order for my permanent detention was served under Section 26 of the Defence of India Rules, in lieu of the original order under Section 129, which provided for temporary detention.

Strangely enough, with the new order under Section 26, came the news that prosecution was being launched against me under Section 38 of the D.I. Rules before two Magistrates—for three of my speeches and for a contributed article in the weekly journal of *Forward Bloc*, of which I had been the Editor. Two of these speeches had been delivered in February 1940, and the third one early in April. Thus the Government created a unique and unprecedented situation towards the end of August last by detaining me permanently without trial under one Section of the Defence of India Rules and simultaneously prosecuting me before judicial tribunals under another Section of the same Rules. I had not seen a similar combination of executive flat and judicial procedure before this occurrence took place. Such a policy is manifestly illegal and unjust and smacks of vindictiveness, pure and simple.

One cannot fail to notice that the prosecution was launched long after the alleged offences had taken place. Nor can it be overlooked that for the relevant article in *Forward Bloc*, the paper had already been penalised through forfeiture of the security of Rs 500 and deposit of a further security of Rs 2,000. Moreover, the attack on the paper was made all of a sudden, after a long period during which no warning had been given to the paper in accordance with the practice of Government.

The attitude of the Bengal Government was further exposed when applications for my release on bail were made before the two trying Magistrates. Both these applications were stoutly opposed by the Government spokesmen. On the last occasion, one of the Magistrates. Mr Wail-ul-Islam granted the bail application, but was constrained to remark that this order would remain infructuous till the Government withdrew their order for my detention without trial under Section 26 of the D.I. Rules. It is thus as clear as daylight that the Government have been pursuing a policy which fetters the discretion of judicial tribunals and interferes with the administration of law. The action of the local Government appears all the more objectionable when it is remembered that they have given the go-by to the instructions of the Government of India with regard to such cases.

Another interesting feature of the Government's policy is my simultaneous prosecution before two Magistrates. If the intention was to place more than one speech of mine before a court of law, that could very well have been fulfilled without resorting to two Magistrates, for I have delivered any number of speeches during the last twelve months within the limits of Calcutta proper. The man in the street is, therefore, forced to think that Government are so keen on seeing me convicted that they have provided for a second string to the legal bow.

Last but not least. Government's action appears to an impartial man to be altogether mala fide, because proceedings were instituted so long after the alleged prejudicial acts had been committed. If the acts in question were in fact prejudicial, then action should have been taken by Government long ago, i.e. at the time that the alleged offences were committed.

May I request you to compare for one moment your attitude towards people like myself and towards Muslims arrested and imprisoned under the Defence of India Rules? How many cases have occurred up till now in which Muslims apprehended under the D.I. Rules have been suddenly released without rhyme or reason? The latest example of the Maulvi of Murapara is too fresh in the public mind to need recounting. Are we to understand that under your rule there is one law for the Muslim and another law for the Hindu and that the D.I. Rules have a different meaning when a Muslim is involved? If so, the Government might as well make a pronouncement to that effect.

Lest it be argued or suggested for one moment that for my incarceration, the Government of India and not the Local Government are responsible, I may remind you that in connection with an adjournment motion concerning myself, tabled by Pandit L.K. Maitra before the Indian Legislative Assembly only the other day, it was stated on behalf of the Government of India that the matter should not come before the Central Assembly, since I had been incarcerated by the Bengal Government. I believe a similar admission was made in the Bengal Legislative Assembly on behalf of the Ministry.

And we cannot forget that here in Bengal we live under the benign protection of a 'popular' ministry.

My recent election to the Indian Legislative Assembly has raised another issue—that of 'immunity' from imprisonment for members of the legislature, while the legislature is in session. This is a right inherent in every constitution, no matter whether it is explicitly provided in the statute or not and this right has been established after a protracted struggle. Quite recently, the Burma Government allowed a convicted prisoner to attend the sittings of the Burma Legislative Assembly, but though I am not a convicted prisoner, I have been denied that right by our 'popular' ministry.

If apologists attempt to invoke the precedent of Captain Ramsay, M.P. in support of the Government, I may point out that Capt. Ramsay's case stands on a different footing altogether. Serious charges have been preferred against him, but all the facts not being known to us, it is difficult to argue either way. One may, however, urge that if Capt. Ramsay has been unjustly imprisoned and no redress will be ultimately forthcoming, it would lend substance to what Mr Kennedy (American Ambassador to Great Britain) and others are reported to have said—namely, that democracy is dead in England. In any case, Capt. Ramsay has had the opportunity of getting his case examined by a Committee of the House of Commons.

In dealing with my case generally, two broad issues have now to be considered. Firstly, have the Defence of India Rules any sanction—ethical or popular? Secondly, have the rules, as they stand, been properly applied in my case? The answers to both the questions are in the negative.

The D.I. Rules have no ethical sanction behind them because they constitute an infringement of the elementary rights and liberties of the people. Moreover, they are essentially a war-measure and, as is known to everybody, India was declared a belligerent power and was dragged into the war, without the consent of the Indian people or the Indian Legislature. Further, these Rules militate against the claim so vociferously made in Britain that she is fighting the cause of freedom and democracy. And lastly, the Congress Party in the Central Assembly was not a party to the adoption of the Defence of India Act or the Defence of India Rules. In these circumstances, it would not be improper to ask whether the Defence of India Rules should not more appropriately be called the Suppression of India Rules or the Defence of Injustice Rules.

It may be urged on behalf of this Government that the Defence of India Act being an Act of the Central Legislature, all provincial Governments are obliged to administer the Rules framed thereunder. But enough has already been said above to justify the charge that the Rules, even as they stand, have not been properly applied in my case. There has been manifest illegality and injustice. Only one explanation can, to my mind, account for such a strange conduct, viz. that Government have been pursuing a frankly vindictive policy towards me for reasons that are quite inexplicable.

For more than two months, the question has been knocking at the door of my conscience over and over again as to what I should do in such a predicament. Should I submit to the pressure of circumstances and accept whatever comes my way—or should I protest against what to me is unfair, unjust and illegal? After the most mature deliberation I have come to the conclusion that surrender to circumstances is out of the question .It is a more heinous crime to submit to a wrong inflicted than to perpetrate that wrong. So, protest I must.

But all these days, protest has been going on and the ordinary methods of protest have all been exhausted. Agitation in the press and on the platform, representations to Government, demand in the Assembly, exploration of legal channels—have not all of these been already tried and found ineffective? Only one method remains—the last weapon in the hands of a prisoner, i.e. hunger-strike or fast.

In the cold light of logic I have examined the pros and cons of this step and have carefully weighed the loss and gain that will accrue from it. I have no illusions in the matter and I am fully conscious that the immediate tangible gain will be nil, for I am sufficiently conversant with the behaviour of Governments and bureaucracies in such crises. The classic and immortal examples of Terence Macsweeney and Jatin Das are floating before my mind's eye at the moment. A system has no heart that could be moved, though it has a false sense of prestige to which it always clings.

Life under existing conditions is intolerable for me. To purchase one's continued existence by compromising with illegality and injustice goes against my very grain. I would throw up life itself, rather than pay this price. Government are determined to hold me in prison by brute force. I say in reply: 'Release me or shall I refuse to live—and it is for me to decide whether I choose to live or to die.'

Though there may be no immediate, tangible gain—no suffering, no sacrifice is ever futile. It is through suffering and sacrifice alone that a cause can flourish and prosper and in every age and clime, the eternal law prevails—'the blood of the martyr is the seed of the church.'

In this mortal world, everything perishes and will perish—but ideas, ideals and dreams do not. One individual may die for an idea but that idea will, after his death, incarnate itself in a thousand lives. That is how the wheels of evolution move on and the ideas, ideals and dreams of one generation are bequeathed to the next. No idea has ever fulfilled itself in this world except through an ordeal of suffering and sacrifice.

What greater solace can there be than the feeling that one has lived and died for a principle? What higher satisfaction can a man possess than the knowledge that his spirit will beget kindred spirits to carry on his unfinished task? What better reward can a soul desire than the certainty that his message will be wafted over hills and dales and over the broad plains to every corner of his land and across the seas to distant lands? What higher consummation can life attain than peaceful self-immolation at the altar of one's cause?

Hence it is evident that nobody can lose through suffering and sacrifice. If he does lose anything of the earth earthy, he will gain much more in return by becoming the heir to a life immortal.

This is the technique of the soul. The individual must die, so that the nation may live. Today I must die, so that India may live and may win freedom and glory.

To my countrymen I say, 'Forget not that the greatest curse for a man is to remain a slave. Forget not that the grossest crime is to compromise with injustice and wrong. Remember the eternal law: You must give life, if you want to get it. And remember that the highest virtue is to battle against iniquity, no matter what the cost may be.'

To the Government of the day I say, 'Cry halt to your mad drive along the path of communalism and injustice. There is yet time to retrace your steps. Do not use a boomerang which will soon recoil on you. And do not make another Sindh of Bengal.'

I have finished. My second and last request to you is that you should not interfere forcibly with my fast, but should permit me to approach my end peacefully. In the case of Terence Macsweeney, of Jatin Das, of Mahatma Gandhi and in our own case in 1926 Government did decide not to interfere with the fast. I hope they will do the same this time—otherwise any attempt to feed me by force will be resisted with all my strength, though the consequences thereof may be even more drastic and disastrous than otherwise.

I shall commence my fast on 29 November 1940.

Presidency Jail
26 November 1940

Yours faithfully
SUBHAS CHANDRA BOSE

26
Forward Bloc—Its Justification

This thesis was written in Kabul in February–March 1941
during his secret sojourn there
en route to Europe—eds

The evolution of a Movement in analogous to that of a tree. It grows from within and at every stage it throws out new branches, so that there may be ever increasing progress. When no fresh branches sprout forth, the Movement may be presumed to be in a process of decay or death.

While every Movement draws its sustenance from the soil from which it springs, it also assimilates nourishment coming from outside—from the atmosphere, environment, etc. Internal sustenance and external nourishment are both necessary for a living Movement.

When the main stream of a Movement begins to stagnate, but there is still vitality in the Movement as a whole—a Left Wing invariably appears. The main function of the Left Wing is to stimulate progress when there is danger of it being arrested. The appearance of a Left Wing is followed by a conflict between it and the main stream, which now becomes the Right Wing. This conflict is a temporary phase and through it a higher stage is reached, when the conflict is resolved. The solution of the conflict takes place through some sort of agreement or adjustment, whereby the Left Wing begins to dominate the Movement as a whole. Thus the Left Wing becomes, in time, the main stream of the Movement.

One may describe this process of evolution in philosophical language by saying that the 'Thesis' throws up its 'Antithesis', and the conflict between the two is resolved in a 'Synthesis'. This 'Synthesis', in its turn, becomes the 'thesis' of the next stage of evolution.

This process of evolution—called the 'dialectical process'—if properly comprehended, can give a new meaning and significance to the developments that have taken place within the Indian National Congress during the last few decades. We shall herein study the Gandhi Movement from the dialectical point of view.

We may observe at this stage that it would be an error to suppose that conflicts inside a Movement are unhealthy or undesirable under all circumstances. It would indeed be more correct to say that conflicts which arise from the logic of history are essential to progress, whether in the sphere of thought or in the sphere of action.

There is no fixed rule as to when a Movement or a particular phase of it should lose its dynamism and begin to stagnate. So long as it can assimilate from outside and go on creating something new, decay cannot set in.

To come now to a study of the Gandhi Movement. By 1919, after the close of the World War, a new situation arose in India and with it, new problems. The official Indian National Congress could not face this situation as it had lost its dynamism altogether, and a Left Wing was clearly necessary if the entire Congress was not to stagnate and die. At this juncture a Left Wing appeared in the form of the Gandhi Movement. Conflict ensued for a time and the old leaders were driven out of the Congress or voluntarily withdrew. Ultimately, a 'Synthesis' took place. The Congress accepted the tenets of Mahatma Gandhi and the Left Wing then became the official Congress.

In 1920, Gandhiism took possession of the Indian National Congress and for two decades it has maintained its hold. This has been possible, not merely because of Mahatma Gandhi's personality but also because of his capacity to assimilate other ideas and policies. But for the latter factor, Gandhiism would have ceased to dominate the Congress long ago. During its twenty years' domination of the Congress, whenever revolts appeared, the Gandhi Movement took the wind out of their sails by accepting many of their ideas and policies—and only recently has it shown signs of failing to adapt itself to the changing environment. For instance, when the Swarajya Party arose in 1923, the conflict that followed continued only for a time. At the Cawnpore Congress in 1925, the Swarajist policy of carrying non-co-operation inside the Legislatures was accepted by the Gandhiites and was thereupon adopted by the Congress as a whole.

Again in December 1928, at the Calcutta Congress there was a revolt against Gandhiism sponsored by the Independence League on the issue of Independence. Mahatma Gandhi then advocated Dominion Status and he fought and defeated our resolution on Independence. But a year later, at the Lahore Congress, he himself moved their solution declaring that henceforth Independence was to be the goal of the Indian National Congress.

By this process of assimilation, the Gandhi Movement was able to maintain its progressive character and prevent the emergence of any big Left Wing movement. There was a temporary setback after the Gandhi–Irwin Pact in March 1931, but Gandhiji recovered lost ground when he launched Satyagraha or Civil Disobedience in January 1932.

The failure of this Civil Disobedience Movement and its abandonment in May 1933, created a new situation which gave birth to a fresh revolt—this time from the Right. Disappointed at the failure of the Movement, a large section of Gandhiites urged the revival of the parliamentary programme which had been scrapped by them at the Lahore Congress in December 1929, before the launching of Satyagraha by Mahatma Gandhi in 1930. Gandhiji surrendered to this demand in 1934, ostensibly because he had no alternative plan for the Congress. This incident was an indication that stagnation in the Gandhi Movement had set in and this was confirmed when a big Left Wing revolt arose through the medium of the Congress Socialist Party which was inaugurated in 1934, almost contemporaneously with the swing towards parliamentarianism.

The Gandhi Movement did not lose its elasticity and adaptability in a day and the attitude of the Gandhiites towards the Congress Socialists and other Leftists remained benevolent on the whole in 1934 and after. As a matter of fact, the Congress Socialists were offered seats on the Congress Working Committee in 1936, 1937, and 1938. (They did not accept the offer in 1938.) In January 1938, the Gandhiites, at the instance of Mahatma Gandhi himself, supported my candidature for the Congress Presidentship. And at the Haripura Congress in February 1938, when I was to nominate the Working Committee for the year, Gandhiji was clearly of opinion that there could be no objection to having Socialists on the Working Committee.

A distinct—and what has still remained inexplicable—change in Mahatma Gandhi's attitude came in September 1938, after a meeting of the All-India Congress Committee at Delhi, at which there was a walkout of the Left Wingers over a controversial issue. It was then that one heard Gandhiji saying that there could be no compromise with the Leftists in conducting the affairs of the Congress. A few months later, in January 1939, he gave proof of the same mentality by opposing my re-election as Congress President.

Since September 1938, Gandhiism has tended to become increasingly static and hide-bound. At the Haripura Congress in February of the same year, the two most important resolutions passed were on the questions of Federation and the coming War. Though the resolution on Federation was one of uncompromising opposition, throughout that year the air was thick with rumours that negotiations for a compromise between the Gandhiites and the British Government were going on behind the scenes. My attitude of uncompromising hostility towards Federation was the first item in the Gandhian charge-sheet against my Presidentship. The second item was what the Gandhiites regarded as my unduly friendly attitude towards the Leftists. The third item in the charge-sheet was my sponsoring and subsequent inauguration of the National Planning Committee which, in the view of the Gandhiites, would give a fillip to large-scale production at the sacrifice of village industries, the revival of which was a very important item in the Gandhian constructive programme. The next charge against me was that I advocated an early resumption of the national struggle for Independence, to be preceded by an ultimatum to the British Government.

By September 1938, any intelligent person could have foreseen that in future the relations between the Gandhiites and the Leftists would cease to be cordial. As already indicated above, Gandhiji himself gave a frank expression to the change in his mentality. Furthermore, it became clear to esoteric circles in the Congress at the time of the Munich Pact that in the event of a War-crisis overtaking India in the future—an open rupture between the Gandhiites and the Leftists would become unavoidable. It is true that from 1927 (Madras Congress) to 1938—the War-policy of the Congress was clearly enunciated in successive annual sessions of the Congress and one would not under ordinary circumstances have expected any divergence of opinion, not to speak of a rupture, among Congressmen on the war issue. Nevertheless, discussions among important Congress leaders during the international crisis preceding the Munich Pact left no room for doubt that the Gandhiites cherished no enthusiasm for the war-resolutions passed by preceding sessions of the Congress and they would not hesitate to circumvent them should they find it necessary or convenient to do so. Now the two questions on which the Leftists were tremendously keen and on which they would not countenance any compromise were those of Federation and the coming War. Consequently, the vacillating and compromising attitude of the Gandhiites on these two issues presaged a breach between them and the Leftists in the days to come.

Though the Munich Pact staved off the war in Europe for the time being, students of International Politics could not but feel that the War was nevertheless unavoidable and imminent. The conviction began thereafter to grow within me that in view of the international situation, the British Government would give up the idea of forcing Federation down the throats of the Indian people. Federation being no longer a live issue for the Indians, it was necessary for them to decide about their future political plans. Since the much-expected battle royal on the Federation issue was off, how were they to continue the fight for Independence?

In November 1938, when I began my North India tour, I put forward a solution of this problem. I urged that it was no use waiting for the Government to take the initiative against the Indian people. Federation being dead, at least for the time being, and war being ahead of us in the not-distant future, it was time for Congress to take the initiative. The proper method for doing so would be to send an ultimatum to the British Government demanding Independence within a certain period and start preparing the country for a national struggle. This idea was widely propagated by us from November onwards and it came before the Tripuri Congress in March, 1939, in the form of a resolution—but it was defeated at the instance of the Gandhiites. The resolution stated, inter alia, that after the ultimatum was sent to the British Government, a period of six months would be given within which a definite reply was called for. Six months after the Tripuri Congress when war broke out in Europe, the political wisdom underlying our resolution was admitted even by the Gandhiites who were so much against us at Tripuri.

Soon after War was declared in Europe, Mahatma Gandhi who was then the unofficial Dictator of the Congress, issued a public statement advocating unconditional co-operation with Great Britain in the prosecution of the War. The resolutions repeatedly passed by the Congress during a period of eleven years were conveniently forgotten. (Federation was officially postponed by the Government after the War broke out.)

Since 1938, the issues on which we Leftists have found ourselves at loggerheads with the Gandhiites and on which no compromise has been possible—are the resumption of the national struggle for Independence and the correct war-policy of the Indian people. It is to be noted that till November 1940, Mahatma Gandhi consistently declared in private and in public, that any Satyagraha or Civil Disobedience was out of the question and that anybody who launched such a movement would be doing harm to his country. It is true that in November 1940, Individual Satyagraha was started under his auspices. But as Gandhiji himself has declared and as we all know very well, it is not a mass struggle for the attainment of Independence. As responsible British officials in India and in England have already declared, this movement has not embarrassed the British Government to any appreciable degree. In conformity with his desire that Great Britain should win the War, Mahatma Gandhi has refrained from creating an embarrassing situation for the Government which a mass struggle for winning Independence would naturally have done.

In September 1939, Mahatma Gandhi advocated unconditional co-operation with Great Britain in the prosecution of the War, but in November 1940, he demanded liberty to carry on anti-war propaganda. Since 1938, he consistently denounced all attempts to resume the national struggle for Independence, but in November 1940, he modified that stand so far as to actually launch the Individual Civil Disobedience Movement. Would it not be a moot-question to ask as to what could explain this change however small? And would it be wrong to say that this change has been due entirely to the pressure from the left?

That Gandhiji could, even at his present age, alter a position consistently and tenaciously advocated and upheld by him for a fairly long period—though this change may be due to pressure and be only partial—is evidence of his adaptability and mobility. Nevertheless it is not adequate for the needs of the times. We are now living in the 'Blitzkrieg' period of history and if we do not move with the times, we shall have to go under. So far, Gandhiji has been unable to prove by his action that he can keep abreast of the times and lead his nation—and this accords with our belief which we have already stated that the Gandhi Movement is becoming static and hide-bound.

The uncompromising attitude towards heterodox thought which the Gandhiites have been evincing since September 1938, and their increasing desire and endeavour to expel dynamic and radical elements from the Congress—not only prove that they are losing their adaptability and mobility but will, like a vicious circle, make them more and more static. The various non-political organizations which Gandhiji has started for the Gandhiites (e.g., the All-India Spinners Association, the Gandhi Seva Sangh, the Harijan Sevak Sangh, the All-India Village Industries Association, the Hindi Prachar Samity, etc.) will also undermine the political dynamism of the Gandhi Movement in future by creating non-political vested interests, as it has already been doing. And more than anything else, peaceful parliamentary life and ministerial office has been, and will be, the political grave of Gandhism.

Whatever revolutionary fervour the Gandhi Movement had, was sapped more by the acceptance of ministerial office than by any other factor. It would be no exaggeration to say that under the influence of this factor, a large number of Congressmen have definitely turned from the thorny path of Revolution to the rosy path of Constitutionalism. Congress Ministries in the provinces were formed in 1937 and neo-Constitutionalism reared its head in a menacing from within the Congress in 1938. Ever since then, the main task of Leftism has been to fight this 'Frankenstein' created by the Congress itself. How to stem this drift towards Constitutionalism, how to create afresh a revolutionary mentality among the people in place of the neo-constitutionalist mentality, how to face the war-crisis in a bold and adequate manner, how to bring the Congress back to the path of uncompromising National Struggle and how ultimately to establish Leftist ascendancy in the Congress—these have been the main problems for the Leftists since 1938.

The Gandhi Movement today has become a victim of not only Constitutionalism but also of Authoritarianism. A certain amount of Authoritarianism is permissible and natural in a militant organization. But the excessive Authoritarianism that one finds today is traceable to the same cause as Constitutionalism. Since the acceptance of Ministerial office, the Gandhiites have had a taste of power and they are anxious to monopolise it for themselves in future. What has been going on within the Congress of late, is 'power politics', though of a sham kind. The fountainhead of this 'power politics' is Wardha. It is the aim of this 'power-politics' to beat down all opposition within the Congress so that the Gandhiites may comfortably rule the roost for all time. But this game will not succeed. Real power has yet to come and it will never come if we travel along the safe path of Constitutionalism. It is certainly possible for the Gandhiites to expel all discordant elements from the Congress and make it a close preserve. But that does not mean that they will be able to win liberty for India. And without real power, there cannot be real 'power-politics'. What we see therefore today is sham 'power-politics'.

Personally I would have no objection to the Gandhiites trying to monopolise power for themselves or acting in an authoritarian manner, if they had been a revolutionary force. But unfortunately, Gandhism has ceased to be revolutionary. There is no hope. that it will succeed in carrying the nation towards its goal of national independence. Consequently, the more our Gandhiite friends try to consolidate their power, position and influence, the more stagnation they will bring into the Congress. Liberal does of disciplinary action against non-conformists may make the Congress a more homogeneous body than at present, but that process will only create more enemies outside and in the end will strike at the 'mass-basis' of the Congress and undermine the hold which the Congress has over the country at large.

The efforts of the Gandhiites to consolidate themselves is nothing else than 'Right-consolidation' within the Congress. This had gone on slowly for a long time and unnoticed, till it was accentuated with the acceptance of ministerial office. When the danger was detected and the Leftists began to organise in self-defence, a furore arose in Gandhian circles. For the latter, self-consolidation, i.e., Right-consolidation, was right and natural; but Left-consolidation was a crime.

Ever since Gandhiism has begun to stagnate and a big Left Wing has emerged in opposition to it, the Gandhiites have become Rightists and Gandhian-consolidation has come to mean Right-consolidation.

Philosophically speaking, Right-consolidation is the 'thesis' which demands its 'anti-thesis' in Left-consolidation. Without this 'anti-thesis' and the conflict following in its wake, no further progress is possible. All those who believe in progress and desire it, should therefore actively assist in this task of Left-consolidation and should be prepared for the conflict resulting therefrom. For bringing about Left-consolidation, the Forward Bloc was born in May 1939, soon after a momentous Session of the All-India Congress Committee in Calcutta, at which I tendered my resignation of the office of President.

Left-consolidation could have been achieved in either of the following ways:

(i) By forming one party and rallying all the Leftist elements therein. This, however, was not possible because several parties claiming to be Leftists, already existed, and they were not prepared to liquidate themselves in favour of one Party.

(ii) By organizing a new Bloc which all Leftists and existing Leftist parties would join, while retaining the separate identity of their respective parties, if they so desired.

This was the first aim and endeavour of the Forward Bloc when it was launched. It did not want to start rivalry with the existing Leftist parties, nor did it want to undermine any of them. If the Bloc's proposal had been accepted and all Leftist parties had joined the Forward Bloc, while retaining their separate identity—Left-consolidation would have been easily and promptly achieved and the Rightists would have been faced with a formidable force. But unfortunately for the Leftist cause, this also was not possible, because some of the existing Leftist parties prohibited their members from joining the newly formed Forward Bloc. What accounted for this inexplicable attitude on the part of these parties, need not be discussed here.

(iii) In the above circumstances, a fresh attempt at Left-consolidation was made in the following manner. The existing Leftist parties and the Forward Bloc agreed among themselves to form a new Committee to be called the Left-consolidation Committee. This Committee was to function as the organ of the entire Left—but it would act only when there was unanimity among the component elements of the Left-consolidation Committee.

The Left-consolidation Committee was formed in Bombay in June 1939, and the effect was immediate and striking. For the first time, the entire Left presented a united and organised front at the meeting of the All-India Congress Committee which was being held at the time. Though numerically in a minority, the Leftists were thereby able to prevent several changes being enacted in the Congress constitution, on which the Rightists were known to be very keen. That meeting of the All-India Congress Committee was a moral victory for the Leftists and on the surface, it seemed to augur well for the Leftist Cause.

But on 9 July 1939, the first blow at the Left-consolidation Committee was struck and by Mr M.N. Roy. The Committee had decided to observe 9 July as an All-India Day for protesting against two resolutions of an anti-Left character which had been passed by the All-India Congress Committee at its Bombay meeting in June in the teeth of Leftist opposition. The Congress President, Babu Rajendra Prasad, issued a statement in July calling upon Leftists to abandon the All-India Day on pain of disciplinary action. As a result of this threat, Mr M.N. Roy made an announcement at the eleventh hour to the effect that his Party, the Radical League, would not participate in the observance of the All-India Day. He also telegraphed to Pandit Jawaharlal Nehru requesting him to use his influence with the Congress Socialist Party and dissuade them from participating in the All-India Day. Since Mr M.N. Roy was then looked upon as a Leftist leader and his Radical League was one of the component units of the Left-consolidation Committee, his action amounted to a betrayal of the Leftist cause and was warmly acclaimed by the Rightists.

Though handicapped by the defection of the Radical League, the other members of the Committee carried on as usual, and their determination to hold together increased when the War situation overtook the country in September 1939. But in October, a new crisis appeared when the leader of the Congress Socialist Party announced in Lucknow that in future their Party would act on its own and would not follow the direction of the Left-consolidation Committee. Nevertheless, consultations between them and other members of the Committee continued for a time.

The next blow struck at the Left-consolidation Committee was in December 1939, when a breach between the Forward Bloc and the National Front took place. The relations between the two had hitherto remained close and cordial. For instance, when the Anti-Imperialist Conference was held at Nagpur in October, on the eve of the meeting of the Congress Working Committee at Wardha, the National Front enthusiastically participated in it, along with the Forward Bloc, Kishan Sabha and others, though the Congress Socialists from other provinces outside C.P. and Berar did not. And after the Congress Socialists withdrew from the L.C.C. later in October at Lucknow the Forward Bloc and National Front continued to collaborate. It was, however, brought to the notice of the Forward Bloc that the National Front had been carrying on propaganda against the former, while outwardly collaborating on the Left-consolidation Committee. What is more, it appeared that in an official journal of the National Front, an official article had appeared painting the Forward Bloc as a counter-revolutionary organization and adversely criticising it in many ways. This matter was brought up at a meeting of the leaders of the Bloc and of the National Front held in Calcutta in December 1939. The latter refused to disown the above article or to withdraw it. Thereupon they were told by the Forward Bloc leaders that a 'counter-revolutionary' organization could not collaborate with the National Front on the Left-consolidation Committee.

The attitude of the National Front leaders showed that they wanted to use the platform of the L.C.C. for popularising their organization, while carrying on reprehensible propaganda, both secret and open, against the component unit of the Committee.

When the breach took place at Calcutta in December 1939, the National Front openly informed the Forward Bloc that if a national struggle was launched by the latter independently of the Congress, the former would openly denounce it and resist it.

This breach was further accentuated by a conflict between the Bengal Branch of the Forward Bloc and of the National Front over some other issues.

Even before the Left Consolidation Committee was started, there was in operation something like a L.C.C. in Bengal. As a result, the Leftists were in an overwhelming majority in the Bengal Provincial Congress Committee, the dominant partner in the Leftist Combination being those who later on joined the Forward Bloc when it was formed. The Leftist Combination naturally became stronger when the Left Consolidation Committee was started on an All-India basis.

After 9 July 1939, Disciplinary action was taken against the President of the Bengal Provincial Congress Committee (i.e., myself) by the Congress Working Committee for participating in the All-India Day. This was resented by all the Leftists in the B.P.C.C. including the National Front and a united protest was made by them. It soon became apparent that the above action of the Working Committee was but the beginning of a long chain of unwarranted interference and persecution on the part of that Committee. All the Leftists in the B.P.C.C. then resolved not to submit meekly to the Working Committee but to continue their protest. After a few months, it became evident that the Working Committee was determined to go to any length, including the suspension of the valid B.P.C.C. and the setting up of an Ad Hoc Committee instead. At this stage the National Frontiers in the B.P.C.C. began to show signs of weakness as well as reluctance to continue their attitude of protest against the high-handed action of the Working Committee. This was regarded by other Leftists as something like an act of betrayal in the midst of a grim fight and it looked as if the National Frontiers were frightened at the prospect of disciplinary action. But the National Frontiers wanted to cloak their real motive and they tried to side-track the issue by saying that instead of engaging in an organizational conflict with the Working Committee, the B.P.C.C. as a Leftist body should launch a struggle against the Government on the issue of Civil Liberty. The other Leftists were quite prepared to do this, but they wanted to continue their organizational protest against the Working Committee simultaneously. Ultimately, after a period of tension, an agreement was arrived at between the National Frontiers and all the other Leftists in January 1940, whereby the B.P.C.C. was to launch a struggle on the issue of Civil Liberty and the National Frontiers were to join the other Leftists in continuing the protest against the Working Committee. Towards the end of January 1940, the B.P.C.C. launched the movement as agreed upon and public meetings began to be held in defiance of the official ban. But after some time it was noticed that when the National Frontiers held any public meeting, they did so after obtaining the permission of the authorities. In July 1940, when the B.P.C.C. launched the Holwell Monument Satyagraha, not only did the National Frontiers not join it—but some of them

actually opposed it. Furthermore, after the All-India Anti-Compromis
Conference at Ramgarh in March 1940, when the Forward Bloc ar
nounced the launching of a nation-wide struggle, the National Frontie
did their best to resist that move as well.

So much about participating in a struggle. With regard also to joinin
in the protest against the Congress High Command, the National Fror
tiers did not fulfil their part of the agreement and they began to drop of
When the Working Committee in an unwarranted and illegal manne
suspended the valid B.P.C.C. which had been dominated by the Leftis
and set up an Ad Hoc Committee instead, the National Frontiers quietl
parted company with the other Leftists. The latter decided to ignore th
fiat of the High Command and the valid B.P.C.C. continued to func
tion. The National Frontiers at first made a show of neutrality by declar
ing that they would not join either side. A little later, however, the
began to apply to the Ad Hoc Committee for the recognition of thei
membership. Today they have cast off all sense of shame and openl
declare that they cannot sever their connection with the Congress Work
ing Committee.

The behaviour of the National Frontiers in Bengal towards the For
ward Blocers and other Leftists there had repercussion in the All-Indi
field and served to widen the breach between the two organization
which took place at Calcutta in December 1939, on All-India issues.

After the events of December 1939, all that remained of the Lef
Consolidation Committee was the Forward Bloc and the Kishan Sabha
Their collaboration became closer and closer with the passage of time. I
was owing to their co-operation and initiative that the All-India Anti
Compromise Conference was held at Ramgarh, in March 1940, contem
poraneously with the annual session of the Congress and proved to b
such a remarkable success.

The question may very well be raised as to why the Forward Bloc wa
at all started and why the existing Leftist parties were not charged witl
the responsibility of bringing about Left-consolidation. The experimen
was in fact tried but it failed and then there arose a situation in which i
became imperative to start the Forward Bloc, if the Leftists were to b
rallied under one banner and the menace of Right-consolidation was t
be countered.

With the formation of the Congress Socialist party, Radical Leagu
and similar organizations in 1934 and after, and the decision of th
National Front to join the Congress—the Leftists in the Congress bega
to gain appreciably in influence and in numbers. This continued til

1937 but in 1938 the process suffered a check and it was quite noticeable at the Haripura Congress in February 1938. After Haripura, Leftists belonging to different parties began to put their heads together with a view to devising ways and means for increasing the Leftist strength. These efforts continued from February 1938 to April 1939. The proposal then was to form a Left Bloc and the Congress Socialist Party and the National Front were requested to take the lead in organising it. I took an active part in these efforts and many individuals like myself who had not till then joined any of the existing parties—pledged their support to the Leftist Bloc. Both the C.S.P. and the National Front at first took the idea of the Left Bloc with great enthusiasm, but they ultimately gave it up. Why they did so, remains a mystery to me up to the present day. Perhaps they thought that if the Left Bloc was organised and if it began to flourish—the importance of their respective parties would wane. Be that as it may, there is no doubt that if the Left Bloc had been launched in time, it would have taken the place of the Forward Bloc. The failure to start the Left Bloc belonged primarily to the C.S.P. and the N.F.

Now why did the existing parties fail to serve the Leftist cause adequately and why was a new organization necessary? The answer evidently is that for some reason or other they failed to rally all those who should and could have been brought into the Leftist fold. Perhaps they were too keen on propagating Socialism—a thing of the future—whereas the immediate task was the widening and strengthening of the anti-imperialist front and an intensification of the anti-imperialist struggle. There was a large number of Congressmen who viewed with dismay the growth of Right-consolidation and the consequent drift towards Constitutionalism, following the acceptance of ministerial office in the provinces. They were naturally more interested in widening and strengthening the anti-imperialist front than in anything else. It was with the help of these men that we could hope to resist the onslaught from the Right and establish Leftist ascendancy in the Congress. It had therefore been decided that the programme of the Left Bloc would be a minimum anti-imperialist programme, on the basis of which we could hope to rally all genuine anti-imperialists under one banner and give battle to the Rightists.

This was also our idea at the time we launched the Forward Bloc. Our immediate task was to fight the increasing drift towards Constitutionalism, reconvert the Congress into a revolutionary organization and bring it back to the path of national struggle and prepare the country for the coming War crisis.

Since its birth, the Forward Bloc has developed greatly, along with changes in the Indian political scene. But it has failed to bring other parties together on one platform, as originally intended. Does that mean that there is no hope of Left-consolidation? No. It only means that Left-consolidation will be achieved by some other means.

A word is necessary here as to what exactly is meant by Leftism. When different individuals and organizations claim to be Leftists, how are we to decide who are—and who are not genuine Leftists?

In the present political phase of Indian life, Leftism means anti-imperialism. A genuine anti-imperialist is one who believes in undiluted independence (not Mahatma Gandhi's substance of independence) as the political objective and in uncompromising national struggle as the means for attaining it. After the attainment of political independence Leftism will mean Socialism and the task before the people will then be the reconstruction of national life on a Socialist basis. Socialism or Socialist reconstruction before achieving our political emancipation is altogether premature.

Genuine anti-imperialists i.e. Leftists have always to fight on two fronts. So also in India, they have to fight on one side, foreign Imperialism and its Indian allies, and on the other, our milk-and-water nationalists, the Rightists, who are prepared for a deal with Imperialism. Genuine anti-imperialists should therefore anticipate persecution not only at the hands of the known agents of alien Imperialism but also at the hands of their Rightist friends—and at times it may be difficult to say which persecution is more severe and trying. In the case of present-day India, the Rightists will stoop to any degree of ruthlessness in their persecution of the Leftists, because they have had a taste of power and are determined to monopolise it for themselves in future by rooting out all opposition.

To carry on a struggle on two fronts simultaneously and to face the above two-fold persecution is not an easy affair. There are people who may stand up to one type of persecution at a time, but not to both. There are others who can stomach persecution at the hands of an alien Government, but who quail when it comes to a question of fighting their Rightist friends. But if we are genuine anti-imperialists and want to function as such, we must muster courage to fight on a double-front and face all the persecution that may come our way.

In India we often come across people who pose as Leftists and talk big things, including Socialism—but who manage to shirk a struggle when they are confronted with it and spin out ingenious arguments for buttressing themselves. Thus we see pseudo-Leftists who through sheer cowardice avoid a conflict with Imperialism and argue in self-defence that Mr Winston Churchill (who we know to be the arch-Imperialist) is the greatest revolutionary going. It has become a fashion with these pseudo-Leftists to call the British Government a revolutionary force because it is fighting the Nazis and Fascists. But they conveniently forget the imperialist character of Britain's war and also the fact that the greatest revolutionary force in the world, the Soviet Union, has entered into a solemn pact with the Nazi Government.

Those who are prepared to face Imperialism but shrink from a clash with the Rightists, take shelter under a different argument. They hide their weakness under the plea of unity. But this is a specious plea which often results in self-deception. One should always distinguish between unity and unity—between the unity of action and the unity of inaction. And one should never forget that to talk of unity between those who are genuine anti-imperialists and those who are not—is mere moonshine. If unity under all circumstances is an end in itself, then why not establish unity between Congressmen and those who are outside the Congress or are against it? The argument of unity should not be carried beyond a certain point. Unity is certainly desirable, but only when there is agreement in principle and in policy. Unity at the sacrifice of one's principles or convictions is worthless and leads to inaction, while real unity is always a source of strength and stimulates activity. To avoid a clash with the Rightists by putting forward the plea of unity is nothing but weakness and cowardice.

In the light of these observations it should be easy to decide who are, and who are not, genuine Leftists and as to whether the Forward Bloc has proved by its action and conduct to be a genuine Leftist organisation.

The question now is as to how Left-consolidation will ultimately be brought about. We have seen that three possible methods for achieving Left-consolidation have all failed. We also know that different individuals and parties have claimed to be Leftist. How then will the Left Movement develop in future?

The answer to this question is that the logic of history will determine who are the genuine Leftists. History will separate the chaff from the grain—the pseudo-Leftists from the genuine Leftists. When this elimination takes place, all the genuine Leftists will come together and fusion will take place. By this natural or historical process, Left-consolidation will be achieved. For this purpose, the acid-test of a fight on a double front is essential. Those who pass the test will be the genuine Leftists and they will all coalesce in time.

Since the Indians are a living nation, their political movement cannot die. And since stagnation has overtaken the Rightists, the logic of history demands a big Left Movement so that progress may continue. Conflict is bound to follow, but only for a time. Ultimately, Leftism will establish its supremacy over the entire political Movement of the land.

Since its inception, the Forward Bloc has been functioning as the spearhead of the Left Movement in India. Through its instrumentality, the Left forces have been gaining ground everyday and along with its ally, the Kishan Sabha, it will be largely responsible for bringing about Left-consolidation in future. By waging a fearless fight on a double-front and by welcoming simultaneous persecution at the hands of alien Imperialism and of the Indian Rightists it has established its claim to be a genuine Leftist organization. It has therefore succeeded where other parties have failed.

The Forward Bloc is to the Left Movement what the Gandhiites are to the Right Movement. Philosophically speaking, the former may be regarded as the 'anti-thesis' of the latter. Though the Forward Bloc has always desired to work in close co-operation with the Gandhiites on the anti-imperialist front, the differences between the two are deep and fundamental. Gandhiism envisages an ultimate compromise with Imperialism for Gandhian Satyagraha (or Civil Disobedience) must end in a compromise. But Forward Bloc will have no truck with Imperialism. Socially, Gandhiism is intimately linked up with the 'haves'—the vested interests. As the 'have-nots' are becoming class-conscious, as is inevitable, the breach between them and the Gandhiites is widening. One therefore finds that unlike what was the position twenty years ago, today Gandhiism does not appeal to large masses of the peasantry and factory workers, nor does it appeal to middle class youths and students, the vast majority of whom sympathise with the poverty-stricken masses. With regard to the future Gandhian ideas of post-struggle reconstruction which are partly medieval and partly anti-socialist are contrary to those of the Forward Bloc which has a thoroughly modern outlook and stands for Socialist Reconstruction.

Since its inauguration in May 1939, the Forward Bloc has developed in its ideology and programme—and naturally too—but there has been no change in fundamentals, except that at the Second All-India Conference held at Nagpur in June 1940, it was declared to be a party. Today as it did yesterday, it stands for uncompromising national struggle for the attainment of Independence, and for the post struggle period, it stands for socialist reconstruction.

It would not be irrelevant to ask as to what the Forward Bloc has achieved so far and what potentiality it has for the future. Without indulging in exaggeration or in self-praise, we may make the following claim:

(1) It has saved the Congress from stagnation and death at the hands of the Rightists by building up a Leftist force. It has thereby fulfilled its historical role to a large extent.
(2) It has served to stem the drift towards Constitutionalism, to create a new revolutionary mentality among the people and to bring the Congress back to the path of struggle, however inadequately. Today nobody will gainsay the fact that but for the Anti-compromise Conference held at Ramgarh in March 1940, the Forward Bloc propaganda preceding it and the activities of the Bloc following it—Mahatma Gandhi would not have felt obliged to start the campaign of individual Civil Disobedience.
(3) The analysis and the forecast of the War made by the Forward Bloc have been proved to be correct.
(4) The propaganda and activities of the Forward Bloc have been responsible for inducing the Congress and Mahatma Gandhi to give the go-by to the original stand of the latter in September 1939, with reference to the War and to return to the war-policy advocated by the Congress from 1927 to 1938.
(5) In building up the Left Movement, the Forward Bloc has clarified the issues which separate the Left from the Right and has stimulated the intellectual and ideological progress of the Congress.
(6) The Forward Bloc has been functioning as a watchdog for warning the Congress and the country against any back-sliding on the part of any individual or party—particularly with reference to the major issues of the war-crisis and national struggle.

With reference to the future it may be confidently asserted:

(1) That the Forward Bloc will in the fullness of time succeed in establishing Leftist ascendency in the Congress so that the future progress of the latter may continue unhampered.
(2) It will prove to be the party of the future—the party that will give the proper lead in bringing the national movement to its fruition and will thereafter undertake the task of national reconstruction. Having sprung from the soil of India as a product of historical necessity and having at the same time the capacity to assimilate what is healthy and beneficial in the environment and in the world outside, it will be able to fulfil the dual role of conducting

the National Struggle to its cherished goal and of building up new India on the principles of liberty, equality and social justice.

(3) It will, by fulfilling its proper role, restore India to her proper and legitimate place in the comity of free nations.

(4) It will thereby enable India to play her historical role so that human progress may be taken a few stages beyond the point it has so far reached.

The ideas that are now uppermost in the minds of the members of the Forward Bloc at the present time may be summarised as follows:

The Forward Bloc stands for:

(1) Complete National Independence and uncompromising anti-imperialist struggle for attaining it.
(2) A thoroughly modern and Socialist State.
(3) Scientific large-scale production for the economic regeneration of the country.
(4) Social ownership and control of both production and distribution.
(5) Freedom for the individual in the matter of religious worship.
(6) Equal rights for every individual.
(7) Linguistic and cultural autonomy for all sections on the Indian Community.
(8) Application of the principles of equality and social justice in building up the New Order in Free India.

The Forward Bloc is a revolutionary and dynamic organization. As such it does not swear by copy-book maxims or by text-books of Politics or Economics. It is anxious to assimilate all the knowledge that the outside world can give and to profit by the experience of other progressive nations. It regards progress or evolution as an eternal process to which India also has a contribution to make.

Regarding the future career of the Forward Bloc we may confidently say that if it is the product of historical necessity, it will not die. If it has a philosophical justification, it will surely endure. And if it serves the cause of India, of humanity and of human progress, it will live and grow and no power on earth will every destroy it.

Forward, therefore, and ever forward, my countrymen!

SUBHAS CHANDRA BOSE

27

Free India and its Problems[1]

THE NEW AWAKENING

The British occupation of India began in 1757 when one province—namely Bengal—first passed into the hands of the British. The occupation was extended by stages and was finally completed in 1858, after the failure of the great revolution of 1857. This revolution is described by the English historians as 'Sepoy Mutiny', but is regarded by the Indian people as the 'First War of Independence'. In the early stages the revolution was very successful, but it failed at the end, owing to certain defects in strategy and in diplomacy, on the part of the Indian leaders. On the British side, both strategy and diplomacy were superior. Nevertheless the British could win only with the greatest difficulty. After the failure of the revolution there was a reign of terror throughout the country. The Indian people were thoroughly disarmed and they continue disarmed up to the present day. They now realise that they committed the greatest blunder in their history by submitting to disarmament in 1858, because disarmament weakened and emasculated the nation to a large extent. After the failure of the great revolution of 1857, the Indian people were depressed for a time. Then, in 1885, with the birth of the Indian National Congress began the political awakening—which was stimulated by revolutions in other parts of the world. With the beginning of the present century, the nationalist movement developed two methods, economic boycott of British goods and secret insurrection. In 1920, after the last world war, Gandhi introduced the new method of 'mass civil disobedience', or passive resistance, the object of which was the overthrow of the foreign administration even without arms. All these developments have now brought India to a stage when it is possible for the Indian people to throw out the British from India.

[1] This article by Subhas Chandra Bose was first published in the German Periodical, *Wille und Macht*, in August 1942 and reprinted in *Azad Hind*, the official publication of the Free India Centre in Berlin.

THE SITUATION TODAY

The situation in India today is such that the British are hated by everybody. But while the vast majority of the people wants to utilise the present international crisis for overthrowing the British yoke, a section of the population does not feel strong enough to do so and therefore wants to come to a compromise with the British Government, with a view to getting what is possible out of them. There is no Indian who co-operates with the British out of moral conviction. Hence British rule does not rest on the goodwill of the Indian people but only on British bayonets. Many people cannot understand how the British can dominate such a big country like India with a comparatively small army. The secret, however, is that with a small but modern army, it is possible to suppress a vast but unarmed population. So long as this modern army of occupation is not involved in a war with another power, it can put down by sheer brute-force any internal upheaval organised by the people. But now that the British are engaged in a war with other powers and have been considerably weakened thereby, it has become possible for the Indian people to work up a revolution which will end British rule once for all. But it is necessary for the Indian people to take up arms in their struggle and to cooperate with those powers that are fighting Britain today. This task, Gandhi will not accomplish—hence India now needs a new leadership.

WHEN INDIA IS FREE

A question which many people ask is as to what will happen when the British are forced to leave India. British propaganda has made many people think that without the British there will be anarchy and chaos in India. These people conveniently forget that British occupation began only in 1757 and was not complete till 1857—while India is a land whose history is measured by thousands of years. If culture, civilisation, administration and economic prosperity were possible in India before British rule—they will also be possible after British rule. In fact, under British rule, the culture and civilisation of India has been suppressed, the administration has been denationalised and a land that was formerly rich and prosperous has become one of the poorest in the world.

A NEW CIVIL ADMINISTRATION

When the British are expelled from India, the first task will be to set up a new Government and establish order and public security. A new

Government will necessarily imply the reorganisation of the civil administration and the creation of a national army. Reorganising the civil administration will be a comparatively easy task. In the past, the civil administration has always been run by the Indians and only at the top, have there been Britishers. But during the last twenty years, Indians have been gradually replacing Britishers in the highest positions. In the Central Government, the members of the Viceroy's Cabinet have been partly Indians. In the provincial Governments, since 1937, the Ministers have been all Indians and English officials have worked under them. In the highest positions wherever Indians have replaced Britishers, they have proved more capable than the latter. Indian Ministers and Indian officials know the country much better and are more interested in its welfare than Britishers. It is, therefore, natural that they should work more efficiently than Britishers have done in the past. In short, we have such a trained and experienced body of Indian officials today, that reorganising the civil administration will not be at all difficult. The new Government of Free India will only have to lay down a new policy and a new programme and furnish a new leadership at the top, for the civil administration.

A NATIONAL ARMY

Building up a national army will be more difficult task. India has, of course, a large number of trained and experienced soldiers and their number has been augmented as a result of the present war. But till quite recently, the Indian Army was officered largely by Britishers, and in the higher ranks, the officers were exclusively Britishers. Owing to war-conditions, the British have now been forced to appoint a large number of Indian officers and the higher ranks have also been opened to a few Indians. Modern weapons, like tanks, aeroplanes, heavy artillery, etc. which were formerly reserved for Britishers, have, under the pressure of circumstances, also been handed over to Indians. Nevertheless, the death of Indian officers of high rank remains and will present some difficulty in building up a national army. In this connection, India's chief problem will be to train up a large number of officers of all ranks within a short period—say ten years—and thereby complete the formation of National Army. Along with the Army, a Navy and Air Force will also have to be built up and all this work will have to be speeded up as much as possible. If India can enjoy peace for some time and the assistance of some friendly powers be forthcoming, then the problem of organising national defence can be satisfactorily solved.

THE NEW STATE

It would be wrong to dogmatise from now about the exact form of the future Indian state. One can only indicate the principles which will underlie that state and determine its form. India has had experience of several Empires in the past and this experience will furnish the background on which we shall have to build in future. Then we shall have to consider the causes which led to our political downfall and prevent their recurrence in future. Further, we shall have to remember that the intelligentsia of India today is quite familiar with modern political institutions and is greatly interested in them. We shall also have to consider the political experiments made in different parts of Europe in the post-Versailles period. And lastly, we shall have to consider the requirements of the Indian situation.

One thing, however, is clear. There will be a strong Central Government. Without such a Government, order and public security cannot be safeguarded. Behind this Government will stand a well-organised, disciplined all-India party, which will be the chief instrument for maintaining national unity.

The state will guarantee complete religious and cultural freedom for individuals and groups and there will be no state-religion. In the matter of political and economic rights there will be perfect equality among the whole population. When every individual has employment, food and education and has freedom in religious and cultural matters, there will be no more any minorities problem in India.

When the new regime is stabilised and the state-machinery begins to function smoothly, power will be decentralised and the provincial governments will be given more responsibility.

NATIONAL UNITY

The state will have to do everything possible to unify the whole nation and all methods of propaganda—press, radio, cinema, theatre, etc.—will have to be utilised for this purpose. All anti-national and disruptive elements will have to be firmly suppressed—along with such secret British agents as may still exist in the country. An adequate police force will have to be organised for this purpose and the law will have to be amended, so that offences against national unity may be punished heavily. Hindustani, which is already understood in most parts of the country, will be adopted as the common language for India. Special emphasis will have to be laid on the proper education of boys and girls and of students in the schools and in the universities, so that they may imbibe the spirit of national unity at an early age.

British propaganda has deliberately created the impression that the Indian Mohammedans are against the Independence movement. But this is altogether false. The fact is that in the nationalist movement, there is a large percentage of Mohammedans. The President of the Indian National Congress today is Azad—a Mohammedan. The vast majority of the Indian Mohammedans are anti-British and want to see India free. There are no doubt pro-British parties among both Mohammedans and Hindus which are organised as religious parties. But they should not be regarded as representing the people.

The great revolution of 1857 was a grand example of national unity. The war was fought under the flag of Bahadur Shah, a Mohammedan, and all sections of the people joined in it. Since then, Indian Mohammedans have continued to work for national freedom. Indian Mohammedans are as much children of the soil as the rest of the Indian population and their interests are identical. The Mohammedan (or Muslim) problem in India today is an artificial creation of the British similar to the Ulster-Problem in Ireland and the Jewish problem in Palestine. It will disappear when British rule is swept away.

SOCIAL PROBLEMS

When the new regime is established, India will be able to concentrate her whole attention on the solution of the social problems. The most important social problem is that of poverty and unemployment. India's poverty under British rule has been due principally to two causes—systematic destruction of Indian industries by the British Government and lack of scientific agriculture. In pre-British days, India produced all her requirements in food and industry and she exported her surplus industrial products to Europe e.g. textile goods. The advent of the industrial revolution and political domination by Britain destroyed the old industrial structure of India and she was not allowed to build up a new one. Britain purposely kept India in the position of a supplier of raw materials for British industries. The result was that millions of Indians who formerly lived on industry, were thrown out of employment. Foreign rule has impoverished the peasantry and has prevented the introduction of modern scientific agriculture. The result of this has been that the once rich soil of India has a very poor yield and can no longer feed the present population. About 70 per cent of the peasantry have no work for about six months in the year. India will therefore need industrialisation and scientific agriculture through state aid, if she has to solve the problem of poverty and unemployment.

Under foreign rule, the Britisher was not only the ruler, but also the employer of labour. Hence labour has been kept in a wretched condition. The Free Indian State will have to look after the welfare of the labourer, providing him with a living wage, sickness insurance, compensation for accident etc. Similarly, the peasant will have to be given relief from excessive taxation and also from his appalling indebtedness. In this connection, institutions for the welfare of labour, like 'Arbeitsdienst', 'Winterhilfe', 'Kraft durch Freude', etc. will be of great interest to India. Next in importance is the problem of public health. This has also remained unsolved under British rule. Fortunately India now has a large number of qualified doctors who are even superior to the English doctors available in India and who are well acquainted with questions of public health. Given state-support and sufficient financial help, they can launch a gigantic effort for eradication of disease. India's ancient systems of medicine, Ayurveda and Unani, can also be helpful in this connection.

Then we have the terrific problem of illiteracy, the percentage of which is about 90 per cent in many parts of the country. But this problem is not at all difficult to tackle, if the state can provide the necessary funds. We have now a large number of educated men and women, who are without employment. Under Free India, all these men and women could be sent to work at once all over the country in order to erect Schools, Colleges and Universities. Side by side with this work, experiments will have to be made for evolving a national system of education in accordance with the needs of the Indian people. Fortunately, experiments are already being made in several places in this connection, e.g. at Tagore's school, Santiniketan, at the Gurukul institution at Hardvar, at the Hindu University at Benares, at Jamia-Milia (National Muslim) University at Delhi, at Gandhi's school near Wardha etc. Moreover, there are the educational institutions which have been handed down to us from pre-British days which are also interesting.

Regarding the future script for India, my own view is that without forcibly abolishing the scripts now prevalent in the country, the Free India Government should encourage and popularise the Latin script.

FINANCE

The problem as to how Free India will get the money required for her big schemes is an important one. Britain has robbed India of her gold and silver and what little still remains, will certainly be removed, before the British leave the country. India's national economy will, naturally, have to discard the Gold Standard and accept the doctrine that national wealth depends on Labour and production and not on gold. Foreign trade will have to be brought under state control and organised on the principle of barter (exchange of goods) as Germany has done since 1933.

PLANNING COMMITTEE

While dealing with the problems of reconstruction, it would be interesting to know that in December 1938 when I was the President of the Indian National Congress, I inaugurated a National Planning Committee, for drawing up plans for reconstruction in every department of life. This Committee has already done valuable work and its reports will be helpful for our future activity.

THE PRINCES

The Indian Princes and their States are an anachronism which must soon be abolished. They would have disappeared long ago, if the British had not preserved them in order to hamper the unification of the country. Most of the Princes are active supporters of the British Government and there is not a single Prince who is likely to play a role, similar to that which Piedmont played in the Risorgimento movement in Italy. Among the people of the States who are one-fourth of the total Indian population, there is a popular movement which is closely connected with the Congress movement in British India. The Princes will naturally disappear along with the British rule, since most of them are very unpopular with their own people. But they cannot present any difficulty to the Free India Government as the British Government has not allowed any prince to have a modern Army. Contrary to expectation, if the Princes were to join the revolution, one would naturally come to a settlement with them.

INTERNATIONAL RELATIONS

In the past, one of the causes of India's downfall has been her isolation from the outside world. In future, India must, therefore, remain in intimate contact with other nations. Geographically, India has a position between the East and the West, which will probably conform to her cultural, economic and political role. It is but natural that in future India should have the closest relations with the Tripartite Powers who are now fighting India's enemy.

India will need help from abroad for her speedy industrialisation as well as for the organisation of her Army, Navy and Air Force. She will, therefore, require machinery of all kinds, scientific and technical knowledge and equipment, and scientific and technical experts. She will also require military experts and military equipment for building up her national defence. In these matters, the Tripartite Powers can render valuable assistance. In Free India, the standard of living will rise rapidly and, in consequence thereof, consumption will increase by leaps and bounds. Free India will thereby become one of the biggest markets for manufactured goods. This should be of interest to all industrially advanced countries.

In return, India could contribute something to the common culture and civilisation of humanity. In religion and philosophy, in architecture, in painting, dancing and music and in other arts and handicrafts, India could offer something unique to the world. And judging from the progress made, despite the handicaps of foreign rule, I feel sure that very soon India will be able to achieve much in scientific research and industrial development.

Young India has a gigantic task to fulfil. There are tremendous difficulties to overcome, no doubt, but there is also the joy and glory of struggle and ultimate victory.

28
Azad Hind

SPECIAL ORDER OF THE DAY ON THE OCCASION OF TAKING OVER DIRECT COMMAND OF THE ARMY

In the interests of the Indian Independence Movement and of the Azad Hind Fauj I have taken over the direct command of our army from this day.

This is for me a matter of joy and pride—because for an Indian, there can be no greater honour than to be a Commander of India's Army of Liberation. But I am conscious of the magnitude of the task that I have undertaken and I feel weighed down with a sense of responsibility. I pray that God may give me the necessary strength to fulfil my duty to India under all circumstances, however difficult or trying they may be.

I regard myself as the servant of thirty-eight crores of my countrymen who profess different religious faiths. I am determined to discharge my duties in such a manner that the interests of these thirty-eight crores may be safe in my hands, and that every single Indian will have reason to put complete trust in me. It is only on the basis of undiluted nationalism and of perfect justice and impartiality that India's Army of Liberation can be built up.

In the coming struggle for the emancipation of our Motherland, for the establishment of a Government of Free India, based on the goodwill of thirty-eight crores of Indians and for the creation of a permanent army which will guarantee Indian independence for all time, the Azad Hind Fauj has a vital role to play. To fulfil this role, we must weld ourselves into an army that will have only one goal—namely, the freedom of India—and only one will—namely to do or die in the cause of India's freedom. When we stand, the Azad Hind Fauj has to be like a wall of granite; when we march, the Azad Hind Fauj has to be like a steam-roller.

Our task is not an easy one: the war will be long and hard, but I have complete faith in the justice and the invincibility of our cause. Thirty-eight crores of human beings, who form about one-fifth of the human race, have a right to be free and they are now prepared to pay the price of freedom. There is consequently no power on earth that can deprive us of our birthright of liberty any longer.

Comrades, Officers and men! With your unstinted support and unflinching loyalty, the Azad Hind Fauj will become the instrument of India's liberation. Ultimate victory will certainly be ours, I assure you.

Our work has already begun. With the slogan 'Onward to Delhi!' on our lips, let us continue to labour and fight till our National Flag flies over the Viceroy's House in New Delhi, and the Azad Hind Fauj holds its victory parade inside the ancient Red Fortress of India's metropolis.

25 August 1943

SUBHAS CHANDRA BOSE
Supreme Commander

PROCLAMATION OF THE PROVISIONAL GOVERNMENT OF AZAD HIND

After their first defeat at the hands of the British in 1757 in Bengal, the Indian people fought an uninterrupted series of hard and bitter battles over a stretch of one hundred years. The history of this period teems with examples of unparalleled heroism and self-sacrifice. And, in the pages of that history, the names of Sirajuddoula and Mohanlal of Bengal, Haider Ali, Tippu Sultan and Velu Tampi of South India, Appa Sahib Bhonsle and Peshwa Baji Rao of Maharashtra, the Begums of Oudh, Sardar Shyam Singh Atariwala of Punjab and last, but not least, Rani Laxmibai of Jhansi, Tantia Topi, Maharaja Kunwar Singh of Dumraon and Nana Sahib—among others—the names of all these warriors are for ever engraved in letters of gold. Unfortunately for us, our forefathers did not at first realise that the British constituted a grave threat to the whole of India, and they did not therefore put up a united front against the enemy. Ultimately, when the Indian people were roused to the reality of the situation, they made a concerted move—and under the flag of Bahadur Shah, in 1857, they fought their last war as free men. In spite of a series of brilliant victories in the early stages of this war, ill-luck and faulty leadership gradually brought about their final collapse and subjugation. Nevertheless, such heroes as the Rani of Jhansi, Tantia Topi, Kunwar Singh and Nana Sahib live like eternal stars in the nation's memory to inspire us to greater deeds of sacrifice and valour.

Forcibly disarmed by the British after 1857 and subjected to terror and brutality, the Indian people lay prostrate for a while—but with the birth of the Indian National Congress in 1885, there came a new awakening. From 1885 until the end of the last World War, the Indian people, in their endeavour to recover their lost liberty, tried all possible methods—namely agitation and propaganda, boycott of British goods, terrorism and sabotage—and finally armed revolution. But all these efforts failed for a time. Ultimately in 1920, when the Indian people, haunted by a sense of failure, were groping for a new method, Mahatma Gandhi came forward with the new weapon of non-cooperation and civil disobedience.

For two decades thereafter, the Indian people went through a phase of intense patriotic activity. The message of freedom was carried to every Indian home. Through personal example, people were taught to suffer, to sacrifice and to die in the cause of freedom. From the centre to the remotest villages, the people were knit together into one political organisation. Thus, the Indian people not only recovered their political consciousness but became a political entity once again. They could now speak with one voice and strive with one will for one common goal. From 1937 to 1939, through the work of the Congress Ministries in eight provinces, they gave proof of their readiness and their capacity to administer their own affairs.

Thus, on the eve of the present World War, the stage was set for the final struggle for India's liberation. During the course of this war, Germany, with the help of her allies has dealt shattering blows to our enemy in Europe—while Nippon, with the help of her allies, has inflicted a knockout blow to our enemy in East Asia. Favoured by a most happy combination of circumstances, the Indian people today have a wonderful opportunity for achieving their national emancipation.

For the first time in recent history, Indians abroad have also been politically roused and united in one organisation. They are not only thinking and feeling in tune with their countrymen at home, but are also marching in step with them, along the path to freedom. In East Asia, in particular, over two million Indians are now organised as one solid phalanx, inspired by the slogan of 'Total Mobilisation'. And in front of them stand the serried ranks of India's Army of Liberation, with the slogan 'Onward to Delhi', on their lips.

Having goaded Indians to desperation by its hypocrisy and having driven them to starvation and death by plunder and loot, British rule in India has forfeited the goodwill of the Indian people altogether and is now living a precarious existence. It needs but a flame to destroy the last vestige of that unhappy rule. To light that flame is the task of India's

Army of Liberation. Assured of the enthusiastic support of the civil population at home and also of a large section of Britain's Indian Army, and backed by gallant and invincible allies abroad—but relying in the first instance on its own strength, India's Army of Liberation is confident of fulfilling its historic role.

Now that the dawn of freedom is at hand, it is the duty of the Indian people to set up a provisional Government of their own, and launch the last struggle under the banner of that Government. But with all the Indian leaders in prison and the people at home totally disarmed—it is not possible to set up a Provisional Government within India or to launch an armed struggle under the aegis of that government. It is, therefore, the duty of the Indian Independence League in East Asia, supported by all patriotic Indians at home and abroad, to undertake this task—the task of setting up a provisional Government of Azad Hind (Free India) and of conducting the last fight for freedom, with the help of the Army of Liberation (that is, the Azad Hind Fauj or the Indian National Army) organised by the League.

Having been constituted as the provisional Government of Azad Hind by the Indian Independence League in East Asia, we enter upon our duties with a full sense of the responsibility that has devolved on us. We pray that providence may bless our work and our struggle for the emancipation of our motherland. And we hereby pledge our lives and the lives of our comrades in arms to the cause of her freedom, of her welfare, and her exaltation among the nations of the world.

It will be the task of the provisional Government to launch and to conduct the struggle that will bring about the expulsion of the British and their allies from the soil of India. It will then be the task of the Provisional Government to bring about the establishment of a permanent National Government of Azad Hind constituted in accordance with the will of the Indian people and enjoying their confidence. After the British and their allies are overthrown and until a permanent national Government of Azad Hind is set up on Indian soil, the provisional Government will administer the affairs of the country in trust for the Indian people.

The provisional Government is entitled to, and hereby claims, the allegiance of every Indian. It guarantees religious liberty, as well as equal rights and equal opportunities to all its citizens. It declares its firm resolve to pursue the happiness and prosperity of the whole nation and of all its parts, cherishing all the children of the nation equally and transcending all the differences cunningly fostered by an alien government in the past.

In the name of God, in the name of bygone generations who have welded the Indian people into one nation, and in the name of the dead heroes who have bequeathed to us a tradition of heroism and self-sacrifice—we call upon the Indian people to rally round our banner and strike for India's freedom. We call upon them to launch the final struggle against the British and all their allies in India and to prosecute that struggle with valour and perseverance and full faith in final victory—until the enemy is expelled from Indian soil and the Indian people are once again a Free Nation.

SIGNED ON BEHALF OF THE PROVISIONAL GOVERNMENT OF AZAD HIND.

Subhas Chandra Bose
(Head of the State, Prime Minister and Minister for War and Foreign Affairs)

Captain Mrs Lakshmi (Women's Organisation)

S.A. Ayer (Publicity and Propaganda)

Lt.-Col. A.C. Chatterji (Finance)

Lt.-Col. Aziz, Lt.-Col. N.S. Bhagat, Lt. Col. J.K. Bhonsle, Lt.-Col. Gulzara Singh, Lt.-Col. M.Z. Kiani, Lt.-Col. A.D. Loganadhan, Lt.-Col. Ehsan Qadir, Lt. Col. Shah Nawaz (Representatives of the Armed Forces)

A.M. Sahay (Secretary)

Rash Behari Bose (Supreme Adviser)

Karim Ghani, Debnath Dass, D.M. Khan, A. Yellappa, J. Thivy, Sardar Ishar Singh (Advisers)

A.N. Sarkar (Legal Adviser)

Syonan, 21 October 1943

29

Father of Our Nation

(Address to Mahatma Gandhi over the Rangoon Radio on 6 July 1944)

Mahatmaji,

Now that your health has somewhat improved, and you are able to attend to public business to some extent, I am taking the liberty of addressing a few words to you with a view to acquainting you with the plans and the activities of patriotic Indians outside India.

Before I do so I would like to inform you of the feelings of deep anxiety which Indians throughout the world had for several days after your sudden release from custody on grounds of ill-health. After the sad demise of Shrimati Kasturbaiji in British custody it was but natural for your countrymen to be alarmed over the state of your health. It has, however, pleased Providence to restore you to comparative health, so that three hundred and eighty-eight millions of your countrymen may still have the benefit of your guidance and advice.

I should like to say something about the attitude of your countrymen outside India towards yourself. What I shall say in this connection is the bare truth and nothing but the truth.

There are Indians outside India, as also at home, who are convinced that Indian Independence will be won only through the historic method of struggle. These men and women honestly feel that the British Government will never surrender to persuasion or moral pressure or non-violent resistance. Nevertheless, for Indians outside India, differences in method are like domestic differences.

Ever since you sponsored the Independence Resolution at the Lahore Congress in December 1929, all members of the Indian National Congress have had one common goal before them. For Indians outside India, you are the creator of the present awakening in our country. In all their propaganda before the world, they give you that position and the respect due to that position. For the world-public, we Indian nationalists are all one—having but one goal, one desire and one endeavour in life.

In all the countries free from British influence that I have visited since I left India in 1941, you are held in the highest esteem, as no other Indian political leader has been, during the last century.

Each nation has its own internal politics and its own attitude towards political problems. But that cannot affect a nation's appreciation of a man who has served his people so well and has bravely fought a first-class modern power all his life. In fact, your worth and your achievements are appreciated a thousand times more in those countries that are opposed to the British Empire than in those countries that pretend to be the friends of Freedom and Democracy. The high esteem in which you are held by patriotic Indians outside India and by foreign friends of India's freedom, was increased a hundredfold when you bravely sponsored the 'Quit India' Resolution in August 1942.

From my experience of the British Government while I was inside India—from the secret information that I have gathered about Britain's policy while outside India—and from what I have seen regarding Britain's aims and intentions throughout the world, I am honestly convinced that the British Government will never recognise India's demand for Independence. Britain's one effort today is to exploit India to the fullest degree, in her endeavour to win this war. During the course of this war, Britain has lost one part of her territory to her enemies and another part to her friends. Even if the Allies could somehow win the war, it will be United States of America, and not Britain that will be top dog in future and it will mean that Britain will become a protege of the U.S.A.

In such a situation the British will try to make good their present losses by exploiting India more ruthlessly than ever before. In order to do that, plans have been already hatched in London for crushing the nationalist movement in India once for all. It is because I know of these plans from secret but reliable sources that I feel it my duty to bring it to your notice.

It would be a fatal mistake on our part to make a distinction between the British Government and the British people. No doubt there is a small group of idealists in Britain as in the U.S.A. who would like to see India free.

These idealists who are treated by their own people as cranks form a microscopic minority. So far as India is concerned, for all practical purposes the British Government and the British people mean one and the same thing.

Regarding the war aims of the U.S.A. I may say that the ruling clique at Washington is now dreaming of world domination. This ruling clique and its intellectual exponents talk openly of the 'American Century', that is, that in the present century the U.S.A. will dominate the world. In this ruling clique there are extremists who go so far as to call Britain the forty-ninth State of the U.S.A.

There is no Indian, whether at home or abroad, who would not be happy if India's freedom could be won through the method that you have advocated all your life and without shedding human blood. But things being what they are I am convinced that if we do desire freedom we must be prepared to wade through blood.

If circumstances had made it possible for us to organise an armed struggle inside India through our own efforts and resources that would have been the best course for us. But Mahatmaji, you know Indian conditions perhaps better than anybody else. So far as I am concerned, after twenty years' experience of public service in India, I came to the conclusion that it was impossible to organise an armed resistance in the country without some help from outside—help from our countrymen abroad, as well as from some foreign power or powers.

Prior to the outbreak of the present war, it was exceedingly difficult to get help from a foreign power, or even from Indians abroad. But the outbreak of the present war threw open the possibility of obtaining aid—both political and military—from the enemies of the British Empire. Before I could expect any help from them however I had first to find out what their attitude was towards India's demand for freedom. British propagandists, for a number of years, had been telling the world that the Axis Powers were the enemies of freedom and, therefore, of India's freedom. Was that a fact? I asked myself. Consequently, I had to leave India in order to find out the truth myself and as to whether the Axis Powers would be prepared to give us help and assistance in our fight for freedom.

Before I finally made up my mind to leave home and homeland, I had to decide whether it was right for me to take help from abroad. I had previously studied the history of revolutions all over the world, in order to discover the methods which had enabled other nations to obtain freedom. But I had not found a single instance in which an enslaved people had won freedom without foreign help of some sort. In 1940 I read my history once again, and once again, I came to the conclusion that history did not furnish a single instance where freedom had been won without help of some sort from abroad. As for the moral question whether it was right to take help, I told myself that in public, as in private life, one can always take help as a loan and repay that loan later on. Moreover, if a powerful Empire like the British Empire, could go round the world with the begging bowl what objection could there be to an enslaved, disarmed people like ourselves taking help as a loan from abroad?

I can assure you, Mahatmaji, that before I finally decided to set out on a hazardous mission, I spent days, weeks and months in carefully considering the pros and cons of the case. After having served my people so long to the best of my ability, I could have no desire to be a traitor, or to give anyone a justification for calling me a traitor.

It was the easiest thing for me to remain at home and go on working as I had worked so long. It was also an easy thing for me to remain in an Indian prison while the war lasted. Personally, I had nothing to lose by doing so. Thanks to the generosity and to the affection of my countrymen, I had obtained the hightest honour which it was possible for any public worker in India to achieve. I had also built up a party consisting of staunch and loyal colleagues who had implicit confidence in me.

By going abroad on a perilous quest, I was risking—not only my life and my whole future career—but what was more, the future of my party. If I had the slightest hope that without action from abroad we would win freedom, I would never have left India during a crisis. If I had any hope that within our life-time we would get another chance—another golden opportunity for winning freedom as during the present war, I doubt if I would have set out from home. But I was convinced of two things: firstly that such a golden opportunity would not come within another century—and secondly, that without action from abroad we would not be able to win freedom, merely through our own efforts of home. That is why I resolved to take the plunge.

Providence has been kind to me. In spite of manifold difficulties, all my plans have succeeded so far. After I got out of India, my first endeavour was in organise my countrymen, wherever I had happened to meet them. I am glad to say that everywhere I found them to be wide awake and anxious to do everything possible for winning freedom for India. I then approached the Governments that were at war with our enemy, in order to find out what their attitude was towards India. I found out that contrary to what British propaganda had been telling us for a number of years—the Axis Powers were now openly the friends of India's freedom. I also discovered that they were prepared to give such help as we desired, and as was within their own power.

I know the propaganda that our enemy has been carrying on against me. But I am sure that my countrymen, who know me so well will never be taken in. One who has stood for national self-respect and honour all his life and has suffered considerably in vindicating it, would be the last person in this world to give in to any other foreign power. Moreover, I have nothing to gain personally at the hands of a foreign power. Having received the highest honour possible for an Indian at the hands of my own countrymen, what is there for me to receive from a foreign power? Only that man can be a puppet who has either no sense of honour and self-respect or desires to build up a position for himself through the influence of others.

Not even my worst enemy can dare to say that I am capable of selling national honour and self-respect. And not even my worst enemy can dare to assert that I was a nobody in my own country and that I needed foreign help to secure a position for myself. In leaving India, I had to risk everything that I had, including my life. But I had to take that risk because only by doing so could I help the achievement of India's freedom.

There remains but one question for me to answer with regard to the Axis Powers. Can it be possible that I have been deceived by them?

I believe it will be universally admitted that the cleverest and the most cunning politicians are to be found amongst Britishers. One who has worked with and fought British politicians all his life, cannot be deceived by any other politicians in the world. If British politicians have failed to coax or coerce me, no other politician can succeed in doing so. And if the British Government, at whose hands I have suffered long imprisonment, persecution and physical assault, has been unable to demoralise me, no other power can hope to do so.

Moreover as you personally are aware, I have been a close student of international affairs. I have had personal contacts with international figures before the outbreak of this war. I am therefore no novice who could be duped by a shrewd and cunning politician. Last but not least, before forming an opinion about the attitude of the Axis Powers I established close personal contact with important leaders and personalities in the Axis countries who are responsible for their national affairs.

Consequently, I make bold to say that my countrymen can have the fullest confidence in my judgment of international affairs. My countrymen abroad will testify to the fact that since I left India, I have never done anything which could compromise in the least, either the honour or the self-respect or the interests of my country. On the contrary, whatever I have done has been for the benefit of my nation, for enhancing India's prestige before the world and for advancing the cause of India's freedom.

Mahatmaji, since the beginning of the war in East Asia our enemies have been carrying on a raging and tearing campaign against Japan. I shall, therefore, say something about Japan—particularly because at the present moment I am working in the closest cooperation with the Government, army and people of Japan.

There was a time when Japan had an alliance with our enemy. I did not come to Japan so long as there was an Anglo-Japanese alliance. I did not come to Japan, so long as normal diplomatic relations obtained between the two countries. It was only after Japan took what I consider to be the most momentous step in her history—namely, declaration of war on Britain and America—that I decided to visit Japan of my own free will.

Like so many of my countrymen I had read anti-Japanese propaganda material for a number of years. Like so many of my countrymen, I did not understand why Japan went to war with China in 1937. And like so many of my countrymen, my sympathies in 1937 and 1938 were with Chungking. You may remember that as President of the Congress. I was responsible for sending out a medical mission to Chungking in December 1938. But what I realised after my visit to Japan and what many people at home do not yet realise, is that since the outbreak of the war in East Asia, Japan's attitude towards the world in general, and towards Asiatic nations in particular has been completely revolutionised.

It is a change that has overtaken not merely the Government, but also the people of Japan. A new consciousness—what I may best describe as an Asiatic consciousness—has seized the souls of the people of Japan. That change explains Japan's present attitude towards the Philippines, Burma, and India. That is what explains Japan's new policy in China.

After my visit to japan and after establishing close contact with the present-day leaders of that country I was fully satisfied that Japan's present policy towards Asia was no bluff but was rooted in sincerity.

This is not the first instance in history when an entire nation has been seized with a new consciousness. We have seen instances of it before in France during the French revolution and in Russia during the Bolshevik revolution. After my second visit to Japan in November 1943. I visited the Philippines, and met Filipino leaders there and saw things for myself. I have also been in Burma for a fairly long time and I have been able to see things with my own eyes after the declaration of its independence. And I have been to China to find out if Japan's new policy was real or if it was a fake. The latest agreement between Japan and the National Government of China has given the Chinese people practically all that they had been demanding. Japan, under that agreement, has even agreed to withdraw her troops from China on the termination of hostilities.

What then is Chungking-China fighting for? Can one believe that

Britain and America are helping Chungking-China out of purely altruistic motives? Will not Britain and America demand their pound of flesh in return for the help that they are now giving to Chungking to make her continue the fight against Japan? I clearly see that Chungking is being mortgaged to Britain and America because of past hatred and antagonism towards Japan.

So long as Japan did not initiate her present policy towards China, there might have been some justification or excuse for the Chinese to seek British and American aid for fighting Japan. But now that an entirely new chapter in Sino-Japanese relations has begun, there is not the slightest excuse for Chungking to continue her meaningless struggle against Japan. That is not good for the Chinese people; it is certainly not good for Asia.

In April 1942, you said that if you were free to do so you would work for an understanding between China and Japan. That was an utterance of rare statesmanship. It is India's slavery that is at the bottom responsible for the chaos in China. It is because of the British hold over India that Anglo-Americans could bluff Chungking into hoping that sufficient help could be brought to Chungking to enable Chungking to continue the war against Japan. You were absolutely right in thinking, Mahatmaji, that free India would work for peace between Japan and China. I go so far as to say that the freedom of India will automatically bring about an honourable understanding between Chungking and Japan, by opening the eyes of Chungking to the folly that she is now committing.

Since I came to East Asia and visited China. I have been able to study the Chinese question more deeply. I find that there is a dictatorship ruling in Chungking. I have no objection personally to dictatorship, if it is for a righteous cause. But the dictatorship that rules at Chungking is clearly under foreign American influence. Unfortunately, the Anglo-Americans have been able to deceive the ruling clique at Chungking into thinking that if Japan could be somehow defeated, then China would become the dominant power in Asia. The fact, however, is that if Japan were defeated by any chance, then China would certainly pass under American influence and control. That would be a tragedy for China and for the whole of Asia.

It is through this false hope of becoming the dominant power in Asia, if Japan could be somehow defeated, that the ruling clique at Chungking has entered into an unholy alliance with the ruling clique at White House and at Whitehall. I know something of the propagandist activities of the

Chungking Government in India and of its efforts to play upon the emotions of the Indian people and win their sympathy. But I can honestly say that Chungking which has been mortgaged to Wall Street and Lombard Street, does not deserve the sympathy of the Indian people any longer especially after Japan has initiated her new policy towards China.

Mahatmaji, you know better than anybody else how deeply suspicious the Indian people are of mere promises. I would be the last man to be influenced by Japan if her declarations of policy had been mere promises. But I have seen with my own eyes how in the midst of a world war Japan has put through revolutionary changes in countries like the Philippines, Burma and National China. Japan is true to her word and her actions are in full conformity with her declarations.

Coming to India, I must say that Japan has proved her sincerity by her deeds. There was a time when people used to say that Japan had selfish intentions regarding India. If she had them, why should she recognise the Provisional Government of Free India? Why should she decide to hand over the Andaman and Nicobar Islands to the Provisional Government of Free India? Why should there now be an Indian Chief Commissioner of the Andaman and Nicobar Islands stationed at Port Blair? Last but not least, why should Japan unconditionally help the Indian people in East Asia in their struggle for their independence?

There are Indians all over East Asia and they have every opportunity of seeing Japan at close quarters. Why should three million Indians distributed all over East Asia adopt a policy of the closest cooperation with Japan if they had not been convinced of her *bona fides* and of her sincerity? You can coerce one man or coax him into doing what you want him to do. But no one can coerce three million Indians distributed all over East Asia.

If Indians in East Asia had taken help from Japan without putting forward their own efforts and without making the maximum sacrifice, they would have been guilty of wrong-doing. But, as an Indian, I am happy and proud to be able to say that my countrymen in East Asia are putting forward the maximum efforts to mobilise men, money and materials for the struggle for India's freedom.

I have had experience at home in collecting funds and materials and in recruiting men for national service for a period of twenty years. In the light of this experience, I can properly assess the worth and value of the sacrifice that our countrymen in East Asia are now making. Their effort is magnificent. It is because they are putting forward a magnificent effort themselves and are prepared to make the maximum sacrifice that I see no objection to taking help from Japan for such necessary articles as arms, ammunition, etc. that we ourselves cannot produce.

Mahatmaji, I should now like to say something about the Provisional Government that we have set up here. The Provisional Government of Azad Hind (or Free India) has been recognised by Japan, Germany and seven other friendly powers and this has given Indians a new status and a new prestige in the eyes of the whole world. The Provisional Government has as its one objective, the liberation of India from the British yoke, through an armed struggle. Once our enemies are expelled from India and order is established ,the mission of the Provisional Government will be over. It will then be for the Indian people themselves to determine the form of Government that they choose and also to decide as to who should take charge of that Government.

I can assure you, Mahatmaji, that I and all those who are working with me, regard themselves as the servants of the Indian people. The only reward that we desire for our efforts, for our suffering and for our sacrifice is the freedom of our motherland. There are many among us who would like to retire from the political field once India is free. The remainder will be content to take up any position in Free India, however humble it may be. The spirit that animates all of us today is that it is more honourable to be even a sweeper in Free India than to have the highest position under British rule. We all know that there are hundreds of thousands of able men and women at home to whom India's destiny could be entrusted once freedom is achieved.

How much help we shall need from Japan till the last Britisher is expelled from the soil of India, will depend on the amount of cooperation that we shall receive from inside India. Japan herself does not desire to thrust her assistance upon us. Japan would be happy if the Indian people could liberate themselves through their own exertions. It is we who have asked for assistance from Japan after declaring war on Britain and America, because our enemy has been seeking help from other powers. However, I have every hope that the help we shall receive from our countrymen at home will be so great that we shall need the minimum help from Japan.

Nobody would be more happy than ourselves if by any chance our countrymen at home should succeed in liberating themselves through their own efforts or if by any chance the British Government accepts your 'Quit India' Resolution and gives effect to it. We are, however, proceeding on the assumption that neither of the above is possible and that an armed struggle is inevitable.

Mahatmaji, there is one other matter to which I shall refer before I close and that is about the ultimate outcome of this war. I know very well the kind of propaganda that our enemies have been carrying on in order to create the impression that they are confident of victory. But I hope that my countrymen will not be duped thereby and will not think of compromising with Britain on the issue of independence under the mistaken notion that the Anglo-Americans will win the war.

Having travelled round the world under wartime conditions with my eyes open, having seen the internal weakness of the enemy on the Indo-Burma frontier and inside India and having taken stock of our own strength and resources I am absolutely confident of our final victory.

I am not so foolish as to minimise in the least the strength of the enemy. I know that we have a long and hard struggle in front of us. I am aware that on the soil of India Britain will fight bravely and fight hard in a desperate attempt to save her Empire. But I know also that however long and hard the struggle may be it can have but one outcome—namely, our victory.

India's last war of independence has begun. Troops of the Azad Hind Fouj are now fighting bravely on the soil of India and in spite of all difficulty and hardship they are pushing forward, slowly but steadily. This armed struggle will go on until the last Britisher is thrown out of India and until our Tricolour National Flag proudly floats over the Viceroy's House in New Delhi.

Father of our nation! In this holy war for India's liberation we ask for your blessings and good wishes. Jai Hind.

30
The Fundamental Problems of India[1]

I do not propose to speak to such a distinguished gathering on the commonplace things that you hear or read about India. I think it would be far better if I speak to you on the more fundamental problems of India. Having been a student of philosophy myself, I am naturally more interested in fundamental problems. I hope you will also agree with me that I should rather speak to you today on some of the fundamental problems that face my country, both in the present as well as in the future.

In my travels abroad, I have often found that people generally have a wrong and sometimes a rather funny idea about my country. For instance, among the people in Europe, the general idea about India is that it is a land in which three things can be found: snakes, fakirs and maharajas. Among those who have been influenced by British propaganda, the general idea about India is that it is a country where people are always fighting among themselves, and where the strong hand of Britain is required in order to maintain peace and order among the people.

If you approach the Orientalists in Europe, that is, the experts in Indology, you will find that they look upon India as a land of mystics and philosophers, a land which at one time produced a very rich philosophy, but which is today as dead as the ancient civilisations of Egypt and Babylon are dead today.

Now the question is, what is India in reality? No doubt we have a very ancient civilisation, but unlike other ancient civilisations, such as Egypt or Babylon, Phoenicia or even Greece, the ancient culture and civilisation of India is not dead. It still lives in the present. And we Indians of today think the same thoughts, fundamentally the same thoughts, and have the same feelings, the same ideals of life, as our forefathers who lived 2,000 or 3,000 years ago. In other words, there is a continuity, historical and

[1] An address to faculty and students of Tokyo University, November 1944.

cultural continuity, extending from the ancient times till the present day—which is in some ways a very remarkable thing in history. Now, in order to understand India, this fundamental fact should first be understood, namely, that the India of the past is not dead. India of the past lives in the present, and will live on in the future.

Against this background, this ancient background, we see changes in our national life from age to age. During the last 3,000 years, people have come into India from outside with new ideas, sometimes with new cultures. All these new influences, ideas and cultures have been gradually absorbed into the national life of India, so that in spite of the fact that, fundamentally we have the same culture and civilisation as we had several thousand years ago, we have nevertheless changed and moved with the times. Today, in spite of our ancient background, we are able to live in a modern world and adapt ourselves to that world.

Those who have been influenced, whether consciously or unconsciously by British propaganda, have the impression that India was very easily conquered by the British and also that after the British conquest of India our country was for the first time politically unified. Both these notions are entirely wrong and without foundation.

In the first place, it is not true that India was easily conquered by the British. It took the British 100 years, from 1757 to 1857, to finally subjugate India. Secondly, it is also an entirely wrong notion to think that India was politically unified by the British. The fact is that India was for the first time politically unified nearly 2,500 years ago under the Buddhist Emperor, Asoka. In reality, the India of the time of Asoka the Great was even larger than the India of today. Asoka's India included not only modern India, but also Afghanistan and a part of Persia.

After the time of Asoka, India has gone through many ups and downs in her national life. There have been periods of decay, followed by periods of progress and national upheaval. But throughout these ups and downs in our national life, we have been able, in the long run, to keep up our progress. About one thousand yeas after Asoka, India again reached the zenith of progress under the Gupta Emperors. This was followed by another glorious epoch in Indian history about nine hundred years later under the Mogul Emperors. Therefore, it is worth remembering that the British notion that we have been unified politically under British rule is entirely wrong. All that the British have tried to do during their regime in India is to divide the Indian people and to weaken, disarm and emasculate them.

I shall now present before you a problem which will interest scientists, and in particular, students of sociology. The question is whether the Indian people have any right to live as a free nation. In other words, have they the strength and the vitality left in them to live and to develop themselves as a free nation? I personally hold the opinion that if a nation once loses its vitality, its inner vitality, then it has no right to exist. And even if it does continue to exist after losing its vitality, that existence will have hardly any worth or value for mankind. The only reason why I stand for India's freedom and believe that as a free nation we shall have a glorious future is that I believe that we have sufficient vitality left in us to live as free men and to develop as a nation.

Now, if I have to answer this question as to whether sufficient vitality is left in us, I shall have to answer two questions: firstly, has our nation any creative faculty and secondly, is it prepared to fight and to die in order to preserve its existence? These two tests have to be applied to India.

With regard to the first question, we have seen that in spite of the British in India, in spite of the innumerable restrictions and disadvantages which follow from foreign rule, we have been able during the century to give numerous proofs that in different departments of our national life we still have creative power.

The number of philosophers and thinkers produced in India under British rule, the number of writers and poets that enslaved India has produced, the artistic revival in India in spite of British rule, the scientific progress made by the Indian people in spite of so many difficulties in the way of their education, the standard already attained by our leading scientists as compared with scientists in different parts of the world, the industrial progress made by India as the result of her own effort and initiative and, last but not least, the distinction which we have attained in the field of sport, all these go to show that in spite of being politically subjugated the vitality of the nation has remained intact.

If under foreign rule and in spite of the obstacles and restrictions that follow from foreign rule, we could give so much proof of our creative faculty, then it stands to reason that when India is free and when the masses of the Indian people are afforded educational facilities, they will be able to give much better proof of their intellectual calibre and creative faculty in different walks of life.

I have just referred to the first test of a nation's vitality, namely, creative faculty. I shall now consider the second test, namely, as to whether the Indian people are able to fight and to die for the sake of freedom. On this point I should like to say, first of all, that, since the last great fight that they had with the British in 1857, the Indian people have not given up the struggle against the enemy, even for one day.

Unfortunately, owing to what I would call the folly of our forefathers, after our final defeat in 1857, the leaders in those days had allowed themselves to be disarmed. Whatever difficulty we have subsequently experienced in winning back our freedom has been due largely to our having been disarmed. But though owing to the mistake of the leaders the people were disarmed, nevertheless they continued to fight for their freedom in other ways.

I shall not take up your time unnecessarily by giving a description of all the methods that have been used in India against the British. I will only say this, that all the methods that have been tried by revolutionaries in different parts of the world for the achievement of their own independence have been tried in India.

At the beginning of this century, particularly after the victory of Japan over Russia in 1904 and 1905, the Freedom movement in India got a new impetus and since then, during the last 40 years, our revolutionaries have been studying very closely the methods of revolutionaries in other countries and they have tried to adopt as many of their methods as possible.

They have tried also to manufacture secretly arms and explosives inside the country and to use those arms and explosives for the achievement of independence. As a development of this struggle for freedom, India tried a new experiment—Civil Disobedience or Passive Resistance—of which the best exponent was Mahatma Gandhi. Though personally I believe that this method will not succeed in bringing us complete independence, there is no doubt that it has greatly helped to rouse and unify the Indian people and also to keep up a movement of resistance against the foreign government. I should, therefore, say that the fact that in spite of all the difficulties that result from foreign rule, a nation can produce a new method and practice that method with a large measure of success is also a proof of that nation's vitality. It shows that, that nation does not accept enslavement as a settled fact and is determined to struggle against it and to work out new methods for achieving independence.

I have, as a revolutionary, made a very close study of the revolutionary movements in other countries, and I can say without any exaggeration that since 1857 we have used every possible method of revolutionary struggle. In the course of this struggle, tremendous sacrifices have been made and many have given their lives. There was, however, one method that still remained for us to take up and that was the organisation of a real modern national army.

That work we had not done up till recently because it was impossible to do that inside India under the eyes of the British army and the British police. But the moment this war gave the Indian people an opportunity of organising a modern Indian national army outside India they at once seized it. As a result of that effort, and with the help of the Japanese Government and the armed forces of Japan, they have been able to build up this army.

So my point is that throughout our revolutionary struggle against the British Government and their armed forces we have shown sufficient initiative, creative power and vitality and have made tremendous sacrifices. We now hope that under the conditions, and with the advantages that this war has given us, we shall be able, after all, to fulfil our national aspirations and win freedom for India.

Having replied to the question regarding the vitality of the Indian people and their right to live as a free nation, I shall now attempt a sociological analysis of modern India. If your are to understand modern India, you have to take note of three important factors. The first factor is the ancient background, that is, the ancient culture and civilisation of India, of which the Indian people of today are conscious, and of which they feel proud. The second factor is the struggle which has gone on without any break or interruption since we were finally overpowered by the British. And the third factor consists of certain influences which have come into India from outside.

Modern India is composed of this ancient background, the unbroken national struggle against Britain, and the impact of influences from abroad.

I shall now deal, in some detail, with the influences which have reacted on India from outside and which have been responsible, to some extent, in making modern India what it is today. Among these outside influences, the first factor is the influence of Western thought which was crystallised in Liberalism, Constitutionalism and Democracy.

In other words, since 1857, modern liberal and democratic thought has been influencing the intellectuals of India to a large extent.

From the beginning of the present century, a new factor came into operation. After the victory of Japan over Russia in 1904–1905, the eyes of the Indian people were opened to a new movement in Asia, the movement for the revival, not merely of Japan—but along with Japan—of other Asiatic countries. Since then, Indian thought has been greatly interested in Asiatic revival. During the last 40 years we have been thinking not merely of what was happening inside India, but also of what was happening in other parts of Asia.

Another important factor which had influence on our mind consisted of the revolutionary struggles that have gone on in different parts of the world. Indian revolutionaries studied the Risorgimento Movement in Italy under the leadership of Mazzini and Garibaldi and the struggle of the Irish people against their British oppressors. In Russia, before the last World War, there was, as you know, a movement against the Czar called the Nihilist movement That also was studied. And nearer India the new awakening in China under the leadership of Dr Sun Yat-sen was also studied very closely and with great interest by Indian revolutionaries.

Thus, Indian revolutionaries have been exceedingly receptive to the influences exerted by revolutionary struggles abroad. Then during the last World War, when the revolution broke out in Russia and, as a result of it, a new government—the Soviet Government—came into existence, the work of that Government was studied with great interest in our country.

People in India have not been interested so much in the Communist movement as in the work of reconstruction in Soviet Russia—in the rapid industrialisation of that country and also in the way in which the Soviet Government solved the problem of minorities. It is this constructive achievement of the Soviet Government which was studied with great interest by people in our country. As a matter of fact, intellectuals like our poet Tagore, who had no interest in Communism as such, were profoundly impressed when they visited Russia by the work of educational reconstruction in that country. Then there is another influence which came to India from outside in more recent times—I mean, the new movement in Europe headed by Italy and Germany called Fascism or National Socialism. This movement was also studied by our revolutionaries.

I have just dealt with some of the influences that have reached India from different parts of the world, from England, France, Japan, China, Russia, Germany and so on. I will now take up another question viz., as to how we have reacted to these influences—how much we have accepted and how much we have rejected out of these outside influences.

In dealing with this question of our reaction to these outside influences, I must first point out that there is a big gulf between our generation and the last generation. As typical exponents of the last generation, I would like to mention Tagore and Gandhi. They represent for us the last generation, and between their thoughts and ideas and the thoughts and ideas of our generation there is a big gulf.

If you study the works of Tagore and Gandhi, you will find that all along there is a conflict in their minds as to what their reaction to Western influence should be. So far as Mahatma Gandhi is concerned, he has never given us any clear solution of this problem. He has left people in doubt as to what his attitude is toward the acceptance of Western ideas. Generally speaking his attitude is one of antagonism. But in actual practice he has not always acted in accordance with his own ideas, the reason being that the rest of his countrymen do not share that inner hostility or antagonism which Mahatma Gandhi personally has towards Western ideas and conceptions.

You all know about Mahatma Gandhi's attitude on the question of violence or physical force. He does not advocate the use of arms, or the shedding of the blood of the enemy for gaining one's freedom. This attitude toward violence or physical force is closely related to his general attitude toward foreign influence, particularly Western influence.

Our generation has followed Mahatma Gandhi as the leader of a political struggle, but has not accepted his ideas on all these questions. Therefore, it would be a mistake to take Mahatma Gandhi as the exponent of the thoughts and ideas of the present generation in India.

Gandhi is in some ways a complex personality, and I would like to analyse his personality, so that you may understand him better. In Gandhi, there are two aspects—Gandhi as a political leader and Gandhi as a philosopher. We have been following him in his capacity as a political leader, but we have not accepted his philosophy.

Now the question arises as to how we can separate the two aspects. Why, if we do not accept his philosophy, are we following him? Though Gandhi has his own philosophy of life, he is a practical politician and therefore, he does not force his own philosophy on the people. Consequently though we are following him in our political struggle, we are free to follow our own philosophy. If Gandhi had tried to thrust his philosophy on us, we would not have accepted him as a leader. But he has kept his philosophy separate from his political struggle.

I have mentioned as representatives and exponents of the last generation Tagore and Gandhi. Now let us compare their philosophies. There are some points on which they agree, but on some other points they do not. The points on which they agree are firstly, that they would like to see the national struggle being conducted without the use of arms. In other words, on the question of physical force, they have the same views. On the question of the industrialisation of the country, they also have the same views. Both Tagore and Gandhi are against modern industrial civilisation. But in the realm of culture, their views are not the same. So far as thought, art and culture are concerned, Tagore is prepared to accept foreign influence. He believes that in the realm of culture there should be full cooperation between India and the rest of the world and there should be reciprocity. We should not be hostile or antagonistic to the culture or art or ideas of any other nation. In the realm of culture, while Tagore advocates full cooperation between India and the rest of the world, Gandhi's general attitude is antagonistic to foreign influence. We must however, remember that Mahatma Gandhi has nowhere given a very clear exposition of his views. I am only referring to his general attitude on this question.

I have previously remarked that there is a big gulf between the fundamental thoughts and ideas of the last generation and of our generation. I will now explain what I meant thereby. As I have just said, this problem as to what our reaction should be toward foreign influence and toward industrial civilisation troubled the leaders of the old generation all their lives and we see proofs of it in their actions. But this problem does not exist for us. It does not exist for us, because our starting-point is that we want a modern India based of course on the past. We do not believe that India can achieve freedom without the use of arms. Now once you take up this attitude, that for winning freedom we have to fight and to use arms, it follows that we must have modern industries to manufacture the arms. So we take our stand on modernism. We have to fight the enemy with modern methods and with modern arms—so we must have modern industries. What constituted the biggest problem for the old leaders constitutes our starting-point. The problem for modern India is not our attitude toward modernism or foreign influence or industrialisation, but how we are to solve our present-day problems.

I believe that modern Japan will understand our generation much better than modern Japan understood the last generation in India. Our stand is virtually the same. We want to build up a new and modern nation on the basis of our old culture and civilisation. For that we need modern industries, a modern army and all those things necessary to preserve our existence and our freedom under modern conditions.

Having dealt with this fundamental standpoint of my generation, I will go on to discuss some of the detailed problems. For the present, of course, the biggest problem is how to fight and win this war. But that is a problem of which you are aware from what you have read in the papers or heard over the radio. I will now consider some of the problems of Free India. The moment India is free, the most important problem will be the organising of our national defence in order to safeguard our freedom in the future. For that we shall have to build up modern war industries, so that we may produce the arms that we shall need for self-defence. This will mean a very big programme of industrialisation.

After satisfying the needs of our nation in the matter of self-defence, the next problem in the degree of importance will be that of poverty and unemployment. India today is one of the poorest countries in the world, but India was not poor before we came under British rule. In fact, it was the wealth of India which attracted the European nations to India. One cannot say that in the matter of national wealth or resources India is poor. We are rich in natural resources, but, owing to British and foreign exploitation, the country has been impoverished. So our second most important problem will be how to give employment to the millions of unemployed in India and how to relieve the appalling poverty which now exists among the masses of the Indian people.

The third problem in Free India will be the problem of education. At present, under British rule, about 90 per cent of the people are illiterate. Our problem will be to give at least an elementary education to the Indian masses as soon as possible, and along with that to give more facilities to the intellectual classes in the matter of higher education.

Connected with the question of education is another problem which is important for India and that is the question of script. In India there are principally two scripts in vogue. One is the script known as the Sanskrit (or Nagri) script and the other is the Arabic (or Persian) script. Up till today, in all national affairs and conferences we have been using both these scripts. I must add that in some provinces, there are scripts in vogue which are modifications of the Sanskrit script. But fundamentally there are two scripts, and in all national affairs and conferences we have to use both these two scripts.

There is now a movement to solve this problem of scripts by using the Latin script. I personally am an advocate of the Latin script. Since we have to live in a modern world, we have to be in touch with other countries and, whether we like it or not, we have to learn the Latin script. If we could make the Latin script the medium of writing throughout the country, that would solve our problem. Anyway that is my own view and the view of my closest friends and collaborators.

I have referred to three important problems in Free India: national defence, how to remove poverty, and how to give education to the people. If we are to solve these three important problems, how are we going to do it? Shall we leave it to private agency and private initiative or will the State take up the responsibility of solving these problems?

Well, at present, public opinion in India is that we cannot leave it to private initiative to solve these national problems, especially the economic problem. If we leave it to private initiative to solve the problem of poverty and unemployment, for instance, it will probably take centuries. Therefore, public opinion in India is in favour of some sort of socialist system, in which the initiative will not be left to private individuals, but the State will take over the responsibility for solving economic questions. Whether it is a question of industrialising the country or modernising agriculture, we want the State to step in and take over the responsibility and put through reforms within a short period, so that the Indian people could be put on their legs at a very early date.

But in solving this problem, we want to work in our own way. We will, naturally, study experiments made in other countries—but, after all, we have to solve our problems in an Indian way and under Indian conditions. Therefore, the system that we shall ultimately set up will be an Indian system to suit the needs of the Indian people.

Now if we do not tackle the economic question from the point of view of the masses, the majority of whom are poor, if we do not do that in India, we shall produce the same confusion or the same difficulties in our country, as we see in China today. You see in China today a split between the Kuomintang and the Chinese Communist Party. Personally I do not see why this should have occurred or why, if the Kuomintang Party has the interests of the Chinese masses at heart, there should be any need to have a separate party like the Communist Party under foreign influence.

Having learnt from experience, we do not want to repeat the mistake that China has made. We actually find today that because the nationalist movement in our generation has identified itself with the interests of the masses, that is, of the workers and the peasants who form more than 90 per cent of the people, because we have their interests at heart, there is no *raison d'etre* for a separate party like the Communist Party. If the nationalists in India did not have the interests of the masses at heart, then you would have seen the same phenomenon as you see in China today.

Now we come to another question—namely, the political system or the Government. If we are to have an economic structure of a socialistic character, then it follows that the political system must be such as to be able to carry out that economic programme in the best possible way. You cannot have a so-called democratic system, if that system has to put through economic reforms on a socialistic basis. Therefore, we must have a political system—a State—of an authoritarian character.

We have had some experience of democratic institutions in India and we have also studied the working of democratic institutions in countries like France, England and United States of America. And we have come to the conclusion that with a democratic system we cannot solve the problems of Free India. Therefore, modern progressive thought in India is in favour of a State of an authoritarian character, which will work as an organ, or as the servant of the masses, and not of a clique or of a few rich individuals.

That is our idea with regard to the political institutions in Free India. We must have a government that will function as the servant of the people and will have full powers to put through new reforms concerning industry, education, defence, etc., in Free India.

Before I pass on to the next problem, I should like to mention another point, namely, the attitude of Free India toward religion and caste. This is a question that is frequently asked. India has several religions. Consequently, the Government of Free India must have an absolutely neutral and impartial attitude toward all religions and leave it to the choice of every individual to profess or follow a particular religious faith.

With regard to caste, that is now no problem for us, because caste, as it existed in the old times, does not exist today. Now, what is the caste system? The caste system means that a community is divided into certain groups on a professional or vocational basis and marriage takes place within each group.

In modern India there is no such caste distinction. A member of one caste is free to take up any other profession. So, caste in that sense does not exist today. Then there remains the question of marriage. In the old times, it was the custom to marry within each caste. Nowadays, intermarriage between the different castes takes place freely. Hence caste is fast disappearing. As a matter of fact, in the nationalist movement we never inquire as to what caste a man belongs to and we do not even know the caste of some of our closest collaborators, which shows that in our generation we do not think at all about caste. For Free India, therefore, caste is no problem at all.

In this connection, I should like to tell you that it was the British who created the impression throughout the world that we are a people quarrelling among ourselves, especially over religion. But that is an absolutely wrong picture of India. It may be that there are certain differences among the Indian people, but such differences you will find in every other country. If we take the so-called progressive countries of the world e.g., France before the outbreak of the present war, or Germany before Hitler and his Party came to power, you will find that there were acute differences among the people in these countries. Spain had even a first-class civil war.

But nobody ever says that, because the people in these countries had disputes and differences, they are not fit to rule themselves. It is only in the case of India that the British say that, because there are certain differences among the Indian people therefore they are not fit to be free. Again, the fact is that whatever differences there are among the Indian people are largely the creation of the British Government. There are hundreds of examples to show you that throughout the history of British rule, the British have tried by every possible means to divide the Indian people. After having done so much to artificially create differences among the Indian people, the British turn around and say that we are not fit to be free.

I should also point out that if you take a modern Power like Soviet Russia and see how heterogeneous the composition of the Soviet Union is, you will realise that if, in spite of this heterogeneous character, so many different races professing so many different religions could be unified in one political system and become such a strong Power, there is absolutely no reason why India which has much more homogeneity than the Soviet Union, should not be united as one nation. As a matter of fact, you will find that outside India, where there is no British influence, there are no differences among the Indian people. In the Indian Independence Movement in East Asia and in the Indian National Army there is no question of religion or caste or class. It is just in India where the British have influence and control that you will find these differences.

On the question of national unity, I should like to give you a friendly warning that British propaganda tries to give the world the impression that the Muslims of India do not support the independence movement. This is wrong. Very often you read in the papers about certain organisations like the Muslim League or the Hindu Mahasabha. The British boost these organisations, because they are in their policy pro-British and are against the Indian National Congress, and they try to make out that the Muslim League represents the Muslims of India. But that is British propaganda. The fact is that the Muslim League and its leader, Mr Jinnah, represent only a minority of the Indian Muslims. The majority of the Indian Muslims are nationalists and they support the independence movement, as much as anyone else. The President of the Indian National Congress is a Muslim, and so are many other members of the Congress, many of whom are in prison today.

These facts are not known to the outside world and the outside world gets the impression that Mr Jinnah represents all the Muslims of India, and that they are not supporting the nationalist movement. I would like to give out this warning about British propaganda.

I have already told you about the kind of economic and political system that we would like to have in Free India. Out of this, arises the problem as to what our political philosophy is. On this question, I gave my own views in a book I wrote about ten years ago called 'The Indian Struggle.' In that book I said that it would be our task in India to evolve a system that would be a synthesis of the systems in vogue in different parts of the world. For instance, if you take the conflict between Fascism (or what you might call National Socialism) on the one side and Communism on the other, I see no reason why we cannot work out a synthesis of the two systems that will embody the good points of both. It would be foolish for any one to say that any one system represents the last stage in human progress. As students of philosophy, you will admit the human progress can never stop and out of the past experience of the world we have to produce a new system. Therefore, we in India will try to work out a synthesis of the rival systems and try to embody the good points of both.

Now I would like to compare some of the good points of National Socialism and Communism. You will find some things common to both. Both are called anti-democratic or totalitarian. Both are anti-capitalistic. Nevertheless, in spite of these common points, they differ on other points. When we see National Socialism in Europe today, what do we find? National Socialism has been able to create national unity and solidarity and to improve the condition of the messes. But it has not been able to radically reform the prevailing economic system which was built up on a capitalistic basis.

On the other side, let us examine the Soviet experiment based on Communism. You will find one great achievement and that is planned economy. Where Communism is deficient is that it does not appreciate the value of national sentiment. What we in India would like to have is a progressive system which will fulfil the social needs of the whole people and will be based on national sentiment. In other words, it will be a synthesis of Nationalism and Socialism. This is something which has not been achieved by the National Socialists in Germany today.

There are a few points in which India does not follow Soviet Russia.

Firstly, class conflict is something that is quite unnecessary in India. If the Government of Free India begins to work as the organ of the masses, then there is no need for class conflict. We can solve our problems by making the State the servant of the masses.

There is another point which has been overemphasised by Soviet Russia and that is the problem of the working classes. India being predominantly a country of peasants, the problem of the peasants will be more important than the problem of the working classes.

Another point on which we do not fully agree is that, according to Marxism, too much importance is given to the economic factor in human life. We fully appreciate the importance of the economic factor which was formerly ignored, but it is not necessary to overemphasise it.

To repeat once again, our political philosophy should be a synthesis between National Socialism and Communism. The conflict between thesis and antithesis has to be resolved in a higher synthesis. This is what the Law of Dialectic demands. If this is not done, then human progress will come to an end. India will, therefore, try to move to the next stage of political and social evolution. I will now pass on to the last point in my address, and that is our conception of an international order. On this point I have already spoken several times in Tokyo. I full support the steps that have been taken through the Joint Declaration to create a new order in East Asia on the right basis of freedom, justice and reciprocity. I have been personally greatly interested in international problems, having tried to work in several countries in order to get support for our movement and, in that connection, I also had the opportunity of studying the work of the League of Nations.

The experiment of the League of Nations has failed, and it is desirable and profitable for us to investigate as to why it failed. If I were to answer that I would say that it failed because the sponsor-nations were too selfish and short-sighted. The sponsor-nations were England, France and America. America dropped out of the League, so the Powers that controlled the League were England and France. Now these two leading Powers, instead of setting an example of unselfishness, tried to use the League of Nations for their selfish interests and for their own benefit. The only basis on which we can set up an international order is freedom, justice and reciprocity. Therefore, the work in East Asia has commenced on the right lines and on the right basis. The only task that remains for us is to see that in actual work the principles embodied in the Joint Declaration are put into effect. If they are so put into effect, then the experiment will be a success. If not, then it will again prove to be a failure.

You must have seen in my speeches and press statements that I have been very enthusiastic about this Joint Declaration. There are several reasons. Firstly, it is on the right basis and on the right lines that the work has begun. Secondly, if you want to set up an international order, it has to have a beginning in a particular region. If we make it a success in one region, it can gradually be expanded all over the world.

It is very difficult to set up a world order suddenly out of nothing and make it a success. But if you begin in one region where friendship and reciprocity between the nations can be developed, and if in that region you meet with success, then that example will be emulated by other nations in other parts of the world. So the method of setting up a regional order is the only way in which a world order can gradually be built up.

The third reason is that I have found that this idea or plan finds support among the mass of the people of this country, and especially among the youths. If I had found that this new order was being sponsored by a few politicians or leaders and that the rest of the nation was apathetic or indifferent, I should certainly not be optimistic. But it is because I have found that the people as a whole, and especially the youths are vitally interested in it and support it enthusiastically, that I believe that through the cooperation of the leaders and the people and the youths, it can be made a success.

I should like to repeat that this undertaking is for the Government and the people of this country a very great responsibility. As you know, your Government was responsible for sponsoring this idea, so you are the sponsor-nation. The success of this experiment will depend on the example set by the sponsor-nation. The League of Nations failed, because the sponsor-nations were selfish and short-sighted. This time if the nations that have joined together, and particularly the sponsor-nation, avoid a selfish and short-sighted policy and work on a moral basis, then I see no reason why the experiment should not be a success.

I should like to emphasise again the tremendous responsibility which Japan has undertaken by becoming the sponsor-nation in this task. And when I talk of the responsibility of the nation, I want also to stress the responsibility of the youths. The youths of today will be the nation and the leaders of tomorrow. An idea that is welcomed and supported by the youths will one day be supported by the whole nation. But an idea which does not find support among the youths will die a natural death. Therefore, the responsibility for making this new order a success devolves, in the last analysis, on the youths of this country. I hope and pray and trust that the youths and the students who are the future representatives of the nation will realise the tremendous moral responsibility which Japan has undertaken in initiating this new order.

There may be people who doubt whether a nation can rise to a high moral level, whether a nation can be farsighted and unselfish and undertake the work of establishing a new order. I have every faith in mankind. If it is possible for one individual to be unselfish, to live one's life at a high moral level, I see no reason why an entire nation cannot also rise to that level. In the history of the world we have seen examples in which a revolution has changed the mentality of a whole nation and made it rise to a high level of morality. Therefore, if anybody has any doubt whether an entire nation can rise to that level, then I do not share that doubt.

I repeat, in conclusion, that the sponsor-nation should realise the tremendous responsibility that it has undertaken. This is a task not only for the leaders and the politicians, but for the whole nation and especially for those who are the hopes of the nation—the youths and the students.

31
The Roads to Delhi are Many

Comrades,

In our struggle for the independence of our Motherland, we have now been overwhelmed by an undreamt of crisis. You may perhaps feel that you have failed in your mission to liberate India. But let me tell you that this failure is only of a temporary nature. No setback and no defeat can undo your positive achievements of the past. Many of you have participated in the fight along the Indo-Burma frontier and also inside India and have gone through hardship and suffering of every sort. Many of your comrades have laid down their lives on the battlefield and have become the immortal heroes of Azad Hind. This glorious sacrifice can never go in vain.

Comrades, in this dark hour I call upon you to conduct yourselves with the discipline, dignity and strength befitting a truly Revolutionary Army. You have already given proofs of your valour and self-sacrifice on the field of battle. It is now your duty to demonstrate your undying optimism and unshakable will-power in the hour of temporary defeat. Knowing you as I do, I have not the slightest doubt that even in this dire adversity you will hold your heads erect and face the future with unending hope and confidence.

Comrades, I feel that in this critical hour, thirty-eight crores of our countrymen at home are looking to us, the members of India's Army of Liberation. Therefore, remain true to India and do not for a moment waver in your faith in India's destiny. The roads to Delhi are many and Delhi still remains our goal. The sacrifices of your immortal comrades and of yourselves will certainly achieve their fulfilment. There is no power on earth that can keep India enslaved. India shall be free and before long. Jai Hind.

SUBHAS CHANDRA BOSE

32
India Shall be Free

Sisters and Brothers,

A glorious chapter in the history of India's struggle for Freedom has just come to a close and, in that chapter, the sons and daughters of India in East Asia will have an undying place.

You set a shining example of patriotism and self-sacrifice by pouring out men, money and materials into the struggle for India's Independence. I shall never forget the spontaneity and enthusiasm with which you responded to my call for 'Total Mobilisation'. You sent an unending stream of your sons and daughters to the camps to be trained as soldiers of the Azad Hind Fouj and of the Rani of Jhansi Regiment. Money and materials you poured lavishly into the war chest of the Provisional Government of Azad Hind. In short, you did your duty as true sons and daughters of India. I regret more than you do, that your sufferings and sacrifices have not borne immediate fruit. But they have not gone in vain, because they have ensured the emancipation of our Motherland and will serve as an undying inspiration to Indians all over the world. Posterity will bless your name, and will talk with pride about your offerings at the altar of India's Freedom and about your positive achievement as well.

In this unprecedented crisis in our history, I have only one word to say. Do not be depressed at our temporary failure. Be of good cheer and keep up your spirits. Above all, never for a moment falter in your faith in India's destiny. There is no power on earth that can keep India enslaved. India shall be free and before long. Jai Hind.

SUBHAS CHANDRA BOSE

Index